Educating China

In this major study, Peter Zarrow examines how textbooks published for the Chinese school system played a major role in shaping new social, cultural, and political trends, the ways in which schools conveyed traditional and "new style" knowledge and how they sought to socialize students in a rapidly changing society in the first decades of the twentieth century. Focusing on language, morality and civics, history, and geography, Zarrow shows that textbooks were quick to reflect the changing views of Chinese elites during this period. Officials and educators wanted children to understand the physical and human worlds, including the evolution of society, the institutions of the economy, and the foundations of the nation-state. Through textbooks, Chinese elites sought ways to link these abstractions to the concrete lives of children, conveying a variety of interpretations of enlightenment, citizenship, and nationalism that would shape a generation as modern citizens of a new China.

PETER ZARROW is professor in the Department of History at the University of Connecticut, where he focuses on the intellectual and cultural history of modern China, and adjunct research fellow at the Institute of Modern History, Academia Sinica. He is the author of *After Empire: The Conceptual Transformation of the Chinese State, 1885–1924* (2012).

Educating China
*Knowledge, Society, and Textbooks
in a Modernizing World, 1902–1937*

Peter Zarrow
University of Connecticut

CAMBRIDGE
UNIVERSITY PRESS

CAMBRIDGE
UNIVERSITY PRESS

University Printing House, Cambridge CB2 8BS, United Kingdom

Cambridge University Press is part of the University of Cambridge.

It furthers the University's mission by disseminating knowledge in the pursuit of education, learning and research at the highest international levels of excellence.

www.cambridge.org
Information on this title: www.cambridge.org/9781107115477

© Peter Zarrow 2015

This publication is in copyright. Subject to statutory exception and to the provisions of relevant collective licensing agreements, no reproduction of any part may take place without the written permission of Cambridge University Press.

First published 2015

Printed in the United Kingdom by Clays, St Ives plc

A catalogue record for this publication is available from the British Library

ISBN 978-1-107-11547-7 Hardback
ISBN 978-1-107-53575-6 Paperback

Cambridge University Press has no responsibility for the persistence or accuracy of URLs for external or third-party internet websites referred to in this publication, and does not guarantee that any content on such websites is, or will remain, accurate or appropriate.

Contents

List of figures		*page* vi
Acknowledgments		ix
	Introduction	1
1	The construction of the state school system	11
2	Reading modern China	41
3	Textbook morality, self-cultivation, and civics	77
4	Good citizens	113
5	The national subject in time	147
6	A usable past	184
7	The importance of space	214
	Conclusion	246
Glossary		253
Bibliography		261
Index		279

Figures

1. Students receiving their new books at the beginning of the semester. Their hairstyle and gowns indicate that they are boys in the late Qing period. The lesson this woodblock illustrates is called "The School." Zhuang Weiqiao and Zhuang Yu, *(Zhonghuaminguo/chudeng xiaoxueyong) Zuixin guowen jiaokeshu* (Shanghai: Shangwu, 1912), 2: 1. *page* 4
2. "Recognizing characters and learning characters; from the simple to the complex" – a late Qing Chinese class. Zhu Shizhai, *Gailiang huitu sizishu* (Guangzhou, 1903), 3: 6b. 43
3. Huang Xiang fans and warms his father's bed. Zhuang Yu, *Guoyu jiaokeshu* (Shanghai: Shangwu, 1917), 1: 59. 50
4. Good parenting is the root of filial piety. *Mengxue duben quanshu sanbian* (no publishing information; in possession of the Shanghai Library), 3: 13a. 51
5. The world's races by skin color: White, Yellow, Red, Black, and Brown. Jiang Weiqiao and Zhuang Yu, *Zuixin guowen jiaokeshu* (Shanghai: Shangwu, 1904–1911), 9: 51a. 55
6. "How to be a guest" – China Bookstore publishing company advertisement. Shen Yi et al., *Zhonghua (guomin xiaoxue) guowen jiaokeshu* (Shanghai: Zhonghua shuju, 1920 [1913]) vol. 1, front matter. 62
7. (a) Chinese clothes are comfortable. (b) Western clothes are convenient. Zhuang Yu, *Guoyu jiaokeshu* (Shanghai: Shangwu, 1917), 2: 9–10. 65
8. At work in the fields. Ye Shengtao, *Guoyu duben* (Kaiming, 1932), 1: 108. 70
9. With unity, even lions can be defeated. Ye Shengtao, *Guoyu duben* (Kaiming, 1932), 2: 22. 72
10. Kong Rong takes the smallest pear because he is the smallest child. In this particular telling of the story, yielding and harmony are not the only virtues: the equality of all siblings, girls and boys, was also emphasized. Zhu Shizhai, *Gailiang huitu sizishu* (Guangzhou, 1903), 3: 5b. 74

List of figures vii

11 In 2012, students in Shanghai were quizzed on the Kong Rong story. One boy's answer was marked wrong: "If you were Kong Rong, would you give up [the pear]?" "I would not." Li Zheng, "Xiaoxuesheng yuwen shiti da'an yin gefan zhenglun," *Dongfangwang* (18 April 2012), http://sh.eastday.com/m/20120418/ula6497074.html, accessed 27 September 2012. 75
12 Play drill with bamboo swords and wooden rifles. Jiang Weiqiao and Zhang Yu, *Zuixin guowen jiaokeshu* (Shanghai: Shangwu, 1904–1911), 2: 34b–35a. 85
13 From right to left: nestlings and fledglings illustrate the meaning of filial piety. Qin Tongpei, *Xin xiushen jiaoshoufa (Guomin xuexiao / gongheguo jiaokeshu)* (Shanghai: Shangwu, 1912–18), 6b–7a. 97
14 The military arts. Qin Tongpei, *Xin xiushen (gongheguo jiaokeshu)* (Shanghai, Shangwu, 1912–1918), 2: 11b. 99
15 Building the nest together. Qin Tongpei, *Xin xiushen (gongheguo jiaokeshu)* (Shanghai, Shangwu, 1912–1918), 3: 11b. 100
16 Bowing to the national flag at the beginning of the school day. Dong Wen, *(Xinzhuyi jiaokeshu jiaoyuan yongshu/gaoji xiaoxue) Dili keben jiaoxuefa* (Shanghai: Shijie, 1932), 3: 2b–3a. 103
17 "National Day Has Arrived." Ma Jingwu and Wang Zhicheng, eds., *(Chuxiao) Fuxing shehui jiaokeshu* (Shanghai: Shangwu, 1934), pp. 12–13. 122
18 Local self-government: "Municipal election assembly." Wei Bingxin and Dai Weiqing, *(Pingmin jiaoyu yongshu) Qianzi keben* (Shanghai: Shijie, 1925), 1: 25. 131
19 "Rail system planning chart." Lu Shaochang, *Xin Zhonghua sanmin zhuyi keben Xin Zhonghua sanmin zhuyi keben (xiaoxuexiao gaojiyong)* (Shanghai: Xin'guomin tushushe/Zhonghua, 1932), 4: 18–19. 135
20 "I don't believe in ghosts and spirits." Lü Jinlu et al., eds., *Fuxing gongmin jiaokeshu (Gaoxiao)* (Shanghai: Shangwu, 1941), 5: 30. 141
21 Eastern and Western hemispheres: China in the world. Hu Chaoyang, *Diyi jianming lishi qimeng* (Shanghai: Xinxue huishe, 1923), p. 2a. 156
22 The Yellow Emperor. Fan Zuoguai and Han Feimu, *(Xiuzheng kecheng biaozhun shiyong) Gaoxiao lishi keben jiaoxuefa* (Shanghai: Zhonghua, 1937), p. 17. 158
23 The Yellow Emperor, Conqueror of the Tribes. Ding Baoshu, *Mengxue Zhongguo lishi jiaokeshu* (Shanghai: Wenming shuju, n.d.), p. 1b. 159

viii List of figures

24 The Yellow Emperor. Hu Chaoyang, *Diyi jianming lishi qimeng* (Shanghai: Xinxue huishe, 1923), p. 5a. 160
25 Qin Shihuang. Fan Zuoguan and Han Feimu, *(Xiuzheng kecheng biaozhun shiyong) Gaoxiao lishi keben jiaoxuefa* (Shanghai: Zhonghua, 1937), p. 79. 173
26 Qin Shihuang. *(Chudeng xiaoxue) Zhongguo lishi jiaokeshu* (n.p.: Nanyangguan shuju, 1906?), p. 14. 174
27 Map of the Ming dynasty. Zhao Zhengduo, *Gaodeng xiaoxue lishi keben* (n.p.: Zhongguo tushu gongsi, 1907–10), 2: 9b. 176
28 Map of the Qing dynasty at its greatest extent. Zhao Yusen and Jiang Weiqiao, *Benguoshi (zhongxuexiao yong / gongheguo jiaokeshu)* (Shanghai: Shangwu, 1926), 2: 34/35. 180
29 The Nine Districts of Yu the Great. Zhao Yusen, *Xinlishi jiaoshoufa (gongheguo jiaokeshu/gaodeng xiaoxuexiao)* (Shanghai: Shangwu, 1913–14), 5: 5. 182
30 Map of the Republic of China. Zhao Yusen and Jiang Weiqiao, *Benguoshi (zhongxuexiao yong / gongheguo jiaokeshu)* (Shanghai: Shangwu, 1926), 2: 108/109. 185
31 "The early Qing conquest of Mongolia, Turkestan, and Tibet." Jin Zhaozi, *(Chuji zhongxueyong) Xin Zhonghua benguoshi jiaokeshu* (n.p.: Xin guomin tushushe, 1934), 2: 74–75. 193
32 "Borders of the Qing at its greatest extent" [contrasted with contemporary borders]. Fan Zuoguai and Han Feimu, *(Xiuzheng kecheng biaozhun shiyong) Gaoxiao lishi keben jiaoxuefa* (Shanghai: Zhonghua, 1937), 3: 49. 195
33 Chart of territories lost to imperialist powers. Zhao Tizhen and Ma Pengnian, *Xiaoxue shehui keben jiaoxuefa (xin kecheng biaojun shiyong)* (Shanghai: Zhonghua, 1933–1934), 7: 56. 202
34 "General Map of the Dynasty." Shangwu yinshugan bianyisuo, comp., *(Gaodeng xiaoxue tang yong) Zhongguo ditu* (Shanghai: Shangwu, 1908), no pagination. 215
35 Transportation: trains, Tianjin. Guan Qi, *Zhongguo dili xin jiaokeshu* (Shanghai: Shanghai lequn tushu bianyiju, 1906), 1: 3a. 220
36 The world's major races. Wang Bangqu, *(Chudeng) Zhongguo dili jiaokeshu* (n.p.: Nanyangguan shuju, 1907), 1: 6a. 228
37 The Republic of China as a begonia leaf, a common mnemonic. Tan Lian and Tan Yunhua, *(Xin xuezhi xiaoxuexiao gaoji yong) Xinzhuan dili jiaoshoushu* (Shanghai: Shangwu, 1926), 1: 2. 233
38 National Humiliation Map. Ge Suicheng, *(Xinkecheng biaozhun shiyong) Chuzhong benguo dili* (Shanghai: Zhonghua, 1933), 3: endpaper. 242

Acknowledgments

My two research assistants, Hong Jingyi (Jodie) and Yeh I-chun, have supplied invaluable help to this project over the too-many years. I relied on numerous libraries and their staffs – above all, the Shanghai Municipal Library for textbooks from the late Qing and early Republic, and the Textbook Materials Center, National Bureau of Compilation and Translation (Taiwan; now the National Academy for Educational Research) for textbooks from the early Republic and especially the 1930s. In addition, I am grateful to the staffs of the Yung Sze-chiu Collection, Hong Kong Public Library; Cishu chubanshe Library, Shanghai; Renmin jiaoyu chubanshe, Beijing; National Library, Beijing; Cubberley Library, Stanford University; Cotsen Collection, Princeton University; Academia Sinica libraries; Harvard-Yenching Library; Beijing Normal University Library; and finally to Teachers College Library, Columbia University, for digitalizing and throwing online at least a few volumes of their otherwise inaccessible collection. Special thanks for sharing materials to Wang Youping of Cishu chubanshe; Joan Judge of York University; and Hosen Chan of Leiden University.

This work would not have been possible without generous grants from the National Science Council of Taiwan (grants 93–2411-H-001–059; 94–2411-H-001–047). Numerous scholars and students have given me helpful advice, some of which I actually took, at various forums where I presented preliminary versions of this study. I want to particularly thank Eugenia Lean, Joan Judge (again), Shen Guowei, and especially Robert Culp. I thank audiences at Academia Sinica, University of California – Santa Cruz, Cambridge University, Chinese University of Hong Kong, Columbia University, East China Normal University, Fudan University, University of Göttingen, Harvard University, University of Hong Kong, Leiden University, Princeton University, Hong Kong Shue Yan University, and Yangzhou University, as well as the meetings of the Association of Asian Studies and the International Conference of Asian Studies. It is at moments like this one realizes that there is no such thing as original, individually produced research.

Finally, the three readers for Cambridge University Press were trenchant and offered many useful criticisms, and I have accepted many though not all of their suggestions.

Portions of Chapters 3 and 4 have been published in Sha Peide 沙培德, "Lunli jiaokeshu: minchu xuexiao jiaoyuli de xiushen yu gongmin daode" 伦理教科书: 民初学校教育里的修身与公民道德 (Textbook morality: Self-cultivation and civics and early Republican schools), pp. 214–242 in Xu Jilin 许纪霖 and Liu Qing 刘擎, eds., *Duowei shiye Zhongguo de geren, guojia yu tianxia rentong* 多维视野中国的个人、国家与天下认同 *(Chinese individual, national, and world identities in multidimensional perspectives)*, (Shanghai: Huadong shifan daxue chubanshe, 2013). Portions of Chapters 5 and 6 have been published in Sha Peide, "Qimeng 'xinshixue' – zhuanxingqi zhong de Zhonguo lishi jiaokeshu" 啟蒙『新史學』——轉型期中的中國歷史教科書 (Enlightenment "New History": Chinese history textbooks in the transitional period), pp. 51–80 in Wang Fansen 王汎森, ed., *Zhongguo jindai sixiang de zhuangxing shidai: Zhang Hao yuanshi qizhi zhushou lunwenji* 中國近代思想史的轉型時代: 張灝院士七秩祝壽論文集》(*The transitional period in modern Chinese intellectual history: Essays in honor of Hao Chang's seventieth birthday*), (Taibei: Lianjing Press, 2007); Peter Zarrow, "The New Schools and National Identity: Chinese History Textbooks in the Late Qing," pp. 21–54 in Tze-ki Hon and Robert J. Culp, eds., *The Politics of Historical Production in Late Qing and Republican China* (Leiden: Brill, 2007); and Peter Zarrow "Discipline and Narrative: Chinese History Textbooks in the Early Twentieth Century," pp. 169–207 in Brian Moloughney and Peter Zarrow, eds., *Transforming History: The Making of a Modern Academic Discipline in Twentieth-Century China* (Hong Kong: Chinese University Press, 2011).

Introduction

Let us imagine a 7-year-old Chinese boy entering the first grade in 1904. He (no girls have been admitted to the official schools yet) will have a long day. He devotes at least two hours every day to incomprehensible Confucian classics. Short passages of these he memorizes and recites. His Chinese language readers are simpler, but still assume he had already learned at least a few hundred basic characters at home. The stories in them deal with simple events surrounding school and family. On alternate days, he studies self-cultivation, history, and geography. His self-cultivation textbooks have little stories about good boys, and his teacher spells out the moral demands of filial piety, respect for elders, and patriotism. Many of these lessons correspond with the stories in his readers – not in a one-to-one fashion, but still with an echoing effect. His history and geography textbooks are more objective and focus on recounting facts. In his first year or two, he learns about his local history and geography, and at the more advanced grades moves on to China and the world.

Most students did not go on to upper primary school, but let us say this student did. In upper primary school – let us say he is 13 years old and in grade 7 and the year is 1910 – he is beginning to have a real understanding of the classics. His readers are introducing him to excerpts from the great prose and poetry of past masters. And in addition to the officially prescribed Confucian classics, his school uses a modern self-cultivation textbook. Here he learns some simple definitions of the state and patriotism as well as stories of filiality and neighborliness. He begins to study a foreign language, and chooses Japanese, along with a study of mathematics and science in greater depth. Once a day he lines up with his classmates, and they go outside to practice drills. His Chinese history textbook, over a sequence of four semesters, describes the origins of Chinese civilization, the rise and fall of dynasties, and the triumphs and sorrows of his own Qing dynasty. It teaches him to hope in constitutional reform, for with a constitution the Qing will revive and China will become strong and prosperous again. His geography textbooks teach him about the races and religions of the world, and also a good deal of practical information about the human and physical geography of China. His home province, say, is famous and important for its coal and iron works.

It is quite likely he is reading revolutionary pamphlets and battered copies of smuggled revolutionary newspapers that his classmates are passing around. That is a subject for another book, however. Assuming he rides out the revolution, as most did, and then goes on to middle school, our student might be in grade 12 in 1915, aged 18 and thinking about graduating soon. He reads only excerpts of the Confucian classics in his Chinese classes, which take up the plurality of the school day. He takes classes in ethics ("self-cultivation"), but most of the lessons are about China's political structure and the nature of republicanism, and there is less about filial piety. His history classes say a little less about the glories of old China and more about the coming of the Republic. His geography textbook laments the loss of Chinese territory such as Hong Kong and Macau to foreigners and urges the Chinese people to unite to defend their territory. After graduation from his middle school, there is a possibility he could go on to university – in which case we might imagine him four years later in May of 1919 marching in protest against the Beijing government and the Versailles Treaty, which ignored Chinese interests in spite of the contribution of Chinese laborers to the Allied war effort. The May Fourth movement, as it became known, reshaped Chinese politics. (I believe it resulted in part from the ideas and behaviors instilled in the schools.) Or he may have gone to work as a teacher, a major source of employment for school graduates as the educational system continued to expand.

Let us now imagine a 7-year-old entering lower primary school a few years after the first boy graduated from middle school. In 1920, in first grade, she encounters no Confucian classics. She attends classes with boys, causing her parents some anxiety. She learns how to read simple stories about families, schools like hers, and the flag of the Republic and patriotism. Her language readers also introduce her to the names of tools and clothing, plants and animals, even the flags of different nations. In the introductory self-cultivation class she learns of the importance of respect for elders, generosity, and love of school. Like her readers, her self-cultivation textbook starts with pictures but soon moves on to simple stories. Some of these are about taking care of parents and respecting teachers, and some are about the morality of the Chinese people and the relationship between family and state. Her history book introduces the great sage heroes who first formed China, offers simple stories about the many dynasties, and concludes triumphantly with the 1911 Revolution and the founding of the Republic. Her geography textbook discusses how large is the Chinese territory and how numerous its people.

In 1926, aged 13, she enrolls in her first year of a girls' lower middle school (grade 7). The establishment of this school followed the reorganization of the educational system in 1923 – under the old system, she would have been in higher primary school. Her textbooks are mostly written in the vernacular, not classical Chinese. It is easier to read the vernacular, but the teacher insists on a strange northern pronunciation of many characters. Maths and sciences take more class time, and she decides to learn English as her foreign language. Her Chinese readers have lots of stories about Chinese heroes of the past; there is some fiction and poetry, but also many lessons about the contemporary world, Woodrow Wilson, Thomas Edison, and other heroes of the modern world. Her Chinese readers also introduce her to the classical Chinese grammar and excerpts from the ancient classics and original literary works. She does not take separate courses in civics (which has replaced self-cultivation), history, and geography, but rather a big class on the study of society. However, her readings still deal with these topics separately. So in civics units there are many discussions of how to conduct school assemblies, and many details about the institutions of the Republic, even though these are not fully functional. Nonetheless, she learns that by understanding the role of the citizens, she and her classmates will be able to revive China. In history she is introduced to both Western history and more detailed accounts of China's long history. And her Chinese geography lessons talk as much about foreign relations and territorial issues as about China's rivers and mountains. She also learns some sports and takes special classes in home management and needlework.

At age 18, she is in her final year of senior middle school (grade 12). The year is 1931, and the threat from Japan consumes her classmates, her teachers, and even her parents. Nonetheless, they agree that it is important to continue with classes in order to help China. In this, her senior year, she is taking both Chinese and English classes every day, as well as both world history and world geography. These classes stress China's vulnerable position in a world of great powers. She is also studying the Three People's Principles, first thought up by the great revolutionary founder of the Republic, Sun Yat-sen. She learns that the Chinese people need racial unity to oppose the threats of imperialism and Communism (as she knew already). She also learns that the Three People's Principles are based on traditional Confucian morality: not a break with tradition but a culmination. She concludes that Sun's formula is the basis for building a new Chinese nation, but she is not quite sure that Nationalist government is strong enough or dedicated enough to do this. It will require all the people's participation, but the government wants to limit the actions students can take.

After graduation, she too might just possibly go on to university. Constantly dismayed by the failure of the Nanjing government to resist Japanese incursions, in 1935 she joins the mass student protest known to history as the December 9th Movement to Resist Japan and Save the Nation, which she vaguely understands was secretly organized by the Communists in Beijing but which spread to other cities on its own momentum. Or instead of university she may have taken a job as a teacher and helped to promote the New Life movement, the campaign for moral revitalization (and anti-communism) promoted

Figure 1 Students receiving their new books at the beginning of the semester. Their hairstyle and gowns indicate that they are boys in the late Qing period. The lesson this woodblock illustrates is called "The School."

by the Nationalist government. Few educated Chinese avoided some sort of civic involvement and political commitment.

This book is written with two types of readers in mind: first, students of modern Chinese history who want to know how textbooks fit into the broader cultural changes of the period; and second, students of education who want to know something about Chinese textbooks, one of many national cases of this peculiar artifact of modernity.

Textbooks are interesting. This counterintuitive notion does not mean that they are all fun to read. Many make the eyelids heavy. But they are an important feature of modern culture. No modern society does without them. A century ago, they were one of the very few widely available sources of knowledge. Today, when moderns are surrounded by a cacophony of sources of knowledge, they are one of the few books many people read cover to cover.

This book is a study of Chinese primary and secondary school textbooks from the beginning of the state school system at the turn of the twentieth century to the demise of the central "Nanjing government" following Japan's invasion of China in 1937. It is a book about what certain people were thinking and writing in a certain textual genre, or more specifically, about what textbook authors, schoolteachers, commercial publishers, and educational officials thought students should learn. By and large these people were themselves members of an educated elite that placed great hopes in education for the future of China. Some of them envisioned a coming era of mass schooling, but places in China's classrooms remained limited. Most peasant and worker families could not afford school fees, or even the lost labor of their children. Thus schooling was largely limited to the children of elites and designed to produce the next generation of leaders.

This book focuses on how Chinese schools conveyed traditional and "new style" knowledge and sought to socialize students to a rapidly changing society in the first decades of the twentieth century. The categories of knowledge covered in textbooks were broad. In fact, textbooks did much to establish those categories in the minds of students: categories such as "geography" and "physics" and the like. School subjects also included language and literature and the Chinese classics. Brought together, these various forms of knowledge promised to teach students not merely how to behave but how the world worked. They explained the operations of the physical and human worlds, not least the evolution of society, the institutions of the economy, and the foundations of the nation-state. Through textbooks among other means, educators sought ways to link these abstractions to the concrete lives of children. Thus this book is also about the effort to spread enlightenment, which is to say true understanding of the world. As this was a world in which modern China was struggling to be born, nationalism was a major feature of the enlightenment project (but not its only feature) and played a prominent role in textbooks.

Themes such as enlightenment, nationalism, and citizenship are familiar in many studies of modern China, and they shape much of this book as well. Yet whereas histories of modern China emphasize crisis and even collapse, textbooks highlight a story of rebuilding. If, broadly speaking, the textbooks I examine in the following pages reflected the intellectual zeitgeist, they also reveal a multiplicity of voices and even dissent. Perhaps more importantly, they reveal the ever-changing boundaries of what counted as basic and necessary knowledge. Not incidentally, the production and "consumption" of textbooks in China were part of global currents of technology, capital, and ideas. By studying Chinese textbooks in the late Qing period (1902–1911), the early republican period (1912–1927), and the Nanjing Decade (1928–1937), we can trace the major questions of each era as its debates were reformulated for the consumption of children. Who is Chinese, and what does it mean to be Chinese? What are the rights and duties of citizens? What is the correct attitude toward the past? How can social problems such as poverty be ameliorated? How can imperialist pressures be resisted? How much of traditional Chinese culture should be continued or modified? This last debate informed the changing content of "moral education," where norms, skills, and knowledge meshed confusingly together.[1] All these debates remain living questions today.

We can read textbooks through the lenses of the histories of pedagogy, of consumption and reading, and of textual and cultural production. My study largely focuses on the latter questions – how textbooks were written to convey "messages" that we often also see in journalism, novels, dramas, and other cultural expressions of the period. Historical and literary studies have told us much about this period; in this book, I hope to add not only detail – important as textbooks are in their own right – but a better sense of the subtle interplay of ideas and social forces in the making of modern Chinese culture. From the Qing, to the early Republic, to the Nanjing Decade: although by the mid-1930s the government exercised unprecedented control over textbooks, a close look at their content reminds us that state-building remained a troubled, tumultuous, and contested process.

In this book I discuss four basic types of textbooks: Chinese language readers, morality and civics textbooks, history textbooks, and geography textbooks. I have looked at but a small fraction of the vast number of textbooks approved for the state school system in this period. Textbooks could be enormously profitable for publishers, and many attempted to get into the business; individual schools and teachers also sometimes printed their own textbooks. The industry was dominated by a few major publishing houses, as I discuss in Chapter 1,

---

[1] Zheng Hang, *Zhongguo jindai deyu kechengshi*.

and I have consulted their major textbook series. Using library collections in China, I have also read some less popular textbooks: I cannot say if these were representative, but they at least show some of the sheer variety of textbooks on the market.

My study covers those textbooks that deal with social and cultural topics, whereas it neglects the sciences. Science education was enormously important, especially at the secondary level where educators sought to train the engineers, agronomists, and researchers of the future, but textbooks in chemistry and mathematics were not directly designed to form *citizens*; even biology textbooks did not speak to the social Darwinism that infected history and geography textbooks (in the following pages I do discuss hygiene, which was treated as an aspect of civics rather than biology). I also neglected teaching materials that were not published as textbooks. I largely neglected textbooks used outside of the state system (private schools and missionary schools) and also the textbooks written expressly for girls. Finally, as suggested earlier, I have tended to read textbooks as pronouncements about socialization and knowledge rather than through the lens of pedagogy and official educational policies.[2] This book is thus not an institutional history, nor a study of student culture.[3]

What I have still done, I hope, is present an overview of the main substance of the education received by most students, exclusive of the sciences. Textbooks are documents of some interest in their own right. They open a window on the tumultuous transformation of the early twentieth century in society and politics and – of special concern in this book – intellectual life. On the one hand, they display a multitude of voices with reference to these changes. And they show how knowledge changed over time. On the other hand, textbooks tended to exclude the most radical and the most conservative views, leaving behind a general perspective best understood as "mainstream reformist." At least until the Nanjing government was able to impose greater uniformity after 1928, textbooks were primarily shaped by the great publishing houses and market forces, individual authors, teachers and principals, and local educational officials, although textbooks were certainly shaped to meet official curricular goals.

---

[2] For pedagogical approaches to history textbooks, see, for example, Carol Morgan, ed., *Inter- and Intracultural Differences*; Volker R. Berghahn and Hanna Schissler, eds., *Perceptions of History*; and Hilary Bourdillon, ed., *History and Social Studies*.

[3] Institutional histories of Chinese education are numerous; some are cited in Chapter 1, where I briefly discuss the curriculum. The political role of students has received much scholarly attention, but examinations of student culture are still a neglected topic; for the late Qing, see Sang Bing, *Wan-Qing xuetang xuesheng yu shehui bianqian*; and for the republican period, Robert Culp, *Articulating Citizenship*. Scholarship on textbooks has just begun to emerge in the past few years. Much of this work has unearthed valuable information about the lives of authors and publishers, the processes of editing and publishing textbooks, the role of government, and so forth; I know of no work that follows the approach I am using here of simply "reading" textbooks.

The historian Ying-shih Yü has emphasized the radicalization of Chinese intellectuals across the twentieth century.[4] But at a time when primary school graduates were considered intellectuals, we must also note that as far as we can tell, most educated Chinese believed what they were taught: China needed to reform its institutions, to steer a course between Westernization and sound moral traditions, and to promote and deserve the loyalty of its citizens. Proud revolutionary notes were sounded in republican-period textbooks but calls for radical or totalistic upheaval were rare.

The truly radical aspect of textbooks lay in the epistemological shifts associated with social Darwinism, utilitarianism, and the reification of the nation-state. Textbooks are tools of socialization comparable to other tools in certain respects, such as parental discipline, peer pressure, and today mass media, social media, and advertising. Textbooks, like parents, may display a cynical intent as well: do as I say, not as I do. Textbooks are also a purgative, first taken and then regurgitated. What is retained from them – how much is "returned to the teacher" – is another question. But through simple stories and direct exposition, repeated often, textbooks make their mark on whole societies. The narrativization of knowledge is emphasized in the pages below. Narrativization is a powerful way of making meaning through the construction of stories – with characters that students may identify with – about daily life, right and wrong, and the actions of great men and even nations.

Textbooks are designed to transmit knowledge, not produce new knowledge. But they may reflect new discoveries quickly or slowly as the case may be. As the following chapters show, Chinese textbooks were often very quick to reflect the new discoveries of intellectuals studying the West or working on problems of Chinese history and geography. Chinese textbooks were thus part of the global circulation of knowledge, refracted through Chinese intellectuals' sense of their nation's needs and functioning as a kind of mediator between cosmopolitan knowledge production and vernacular culture. They reveal what was largely accepted as knowledge at the time, both that which was traditional in nature and that which was unprecedented. Much moral education and a good deal of historical identity as taught in modern textbooks were directly derived from ancient classics. Yet many principles basic to understanding the world were essentially new – racial categories and social Darwinism most prominent among them.

It is true that from the point of view of child development, textbooks are a very small part of the story. Their impact is easily outweighed by the role of parents, community, various school activities, religious institutions, and popular culture. However, textbooks are central to political socialization and knowledge formation in all modern societies, precisely because they represent

---

[4] Ying-shih Yü, "The Radicalization of China."

the best opportunity for state elites to shape children. In the West, compulsory and universal education – and its textbooks – spread with the democratization and industrialization of the nineteenth century. Put cynically, elites wanted youth who could read, do simple math, and follow instructions. A two-tiered educational system (classical education for elites; mechanical training for the masses) made this clear. Put idealistically, elites wanted youth who could become responsible citizens, protected by their education from the tricks of demagogues, and able to become economically productive members of society. Universal schooling for boys was becoming well developed in the North Atlantic world by the mid-nineteenth century, and peripheral regions (central and southern Europe, South America) were not too far behind. In Meiji Japan, a national school system was in place by the 1880s. In this light, China's educational reforms of the late Qing were not too far behind either. The great accomplishment of modern Chinese textbooks was to create a new textual community whose members were able to communicate with one another across dialects and regions. What the classics and the examination system did for late imperial China, textbooks did for the early twentieth century. Students became citizens as they learned the language of nation and civic responsibility.

Chapter 1 describes the construction of the state school system, a project officially begun in 1902, which was led by national and local reform-minded gentry, by government officials, by textbook publishers, and increasingly by professional educators themselves. The goals of these groups did not always correspond, and the Chinese notion of proper childhood development was in constant flux. The remaining chapters take up textbooks in four different subjects. Chapter 2 shows how language readers, which students studied daily, not only introduced them to vocabulary and grammar, but presented lessons on all the other subjects of the school day (except for the sciences, though they included short biographies of famous scientists). Moral lessons took the form of stories about ordinary students who did good deeds and famous cases from the pages of history. Fables with talking animals and tales of generals, emperors, and inventors filled many readers. Language readers conveyed political lessons, sometimes in clear dissent against official views. Even more, they taught students what roles they might fill as they grew up.

Chapters 3 and 4 focus on textbooks that taught self-cultivation, ethics, civics, and hygiene. This was also a subject taught every day. If language readers conveyed lessons through indirection – through narratives that, like all stories, could be read in different ways – ethics textbooks did more to tell students directly how to behave. Ethics and civics textbooks did use stories to gain students' attention, but they also told students what to think. Nonetheless, they also took students into the world of political debates between tradition and modernity, conservatism and progressivism, individualism and communitarianism, though expressed in simpler terms. Chapters 5 and 6 discuss Chinese history textbooks. History and geography were taught on alternate days. It was through history that students learned what it meant to be Chinese – heirs to great racial and cultural traditions that had long flourished and in which students could take pride. Even though the country had seen troubles since the nineteenth century, as history textbooks frankly noted, it was history that taught students their duty to resolve those troubles. Finally, Chapter 7 shows how geography textbooks taught students to think of China as a bounded territory that was composed of diverse – but unified – peoples shaped by a rich land. Geography textbooks defined space by connecting children to circles of community that expanded from neighborhood to nation and the world. If history textbooks rooted Chinese-ness through time, geography textbooks linked Chinese-ness to place.

The chapters that follow point to tensions between the official curriculum and actual textbooks in particular places. But by and large, textbook writers represented mainstream elite views that were not too far off from official views. Indeed, increasingly the official curriculum was shaped by the attitudes of professional educators who were consulted by officials. The basic ingredients of Republican ideology were widely shared: that China needed to survive in an international order of social Darwinian struggle, that a strong state needed a strong citizenry, that a citizenry needed to understand itself both as individuals with rights-and-duties vis-à-vis the state and as members of complex social orders, that patriotism required strong minds and strong bodies, and that women too were citizens – at least to some degree. Chinese intellectuals had begun to propagate theories of citizenship in the 1890s, and these contributed to the revolutionary movement that culminated in 1911 and continued to inform social movements and protests throughout the republican period. Chinese textbooks gave these abstract theories concrete form. Neither the curriculum nor any textbook was politically neutral. They taught the Chinese to be Chinese, but they were torn between competing views of a citizenship that emphasized the people's autonomous participation in the processes of government and a citizenship that emphasized the individual's membership in a political society that was an organic whole.

1   The construction of the state school system

A China Bookstore elementary language reader of 1920 expressed what was a widespread Chinese faith in education:

> People are born entirely ignorant, but if they wish to cultivate their virtue, expand their knowledge, and train their bodies, they must become educated. From youth to maturity we receive education from our families, from society, and from schools, but families and society are not specialized in the task of education. In order to become truly educated, we must attend schools. State schools (*guomin xuexiao*) carry out the education of citizens (*guomin jiaoyu*), and all who are educated in the schools begin to acquire the qualifications of citizenship.[1]

The goal of universal education (or at least universal male education) was not new to Chinese of the twentieth century. At times, it had been supported by Ming and Qing officials, including the first Ming emperor. But it had never been an important goal for the imperial state. Officials and gentry elites did not actively fear that the masses would become educated, as was the case in early modern Europe.[2] But they regarded education as only really important for a small, ultra-literate elite. It was the notion of citizenship in the late Qing that made all the difference. Now, the population had to be mobilized if China was to be saved. Mobilized, but directed. To educate more and more citizens required measures to control them, and hence officials proposed many restrictions on student activities. More central yet to the project of discipline was the great emphasis placed on moral behavior in the schools.

The modern Chinese school system was part of a global and relatively recent creation of mass schooling. The men who founded it were particularly indebted to missionary schools and to the Japanese educational system. Formal schooling, under state auspices, secular, widely available to children: such educational

---

[1] Shen Yi et al., *Zhonghua guowen jiaokeshu*, 10: 1a.
[2] Alexander Woodside suggests that the late imperial state did see that universal literacy would pose a threat to a bureaucracy that depended on a quasi-monopoly of knowledge of the classics – on which basis officials were chosen. Alexander Woodside, "Real and Imagined Continuities in the Chinese Struggle for Literacy." But because education was so thoroughly imbued with moral values and the chances of classical education (rather than basic literacy) becoming widespread were so small, this was a minor concern.

systems began to spread in Western Europe, the United States, and Britain in the early nineteenth century.[3] Over time, such schooling became compulsory and universal. Roughly speaking, this radically new approach to education was a response to the needs of industrializing economies and designed to strengthen nation-states in a competitive international environment. For elites in non-Western nations, it was the survival of the state that prompted efforts to reform education around the end of the nineteenth century. The modern Japanese state school system, on which the Chinese system was initially based, was first established in 1872.

In China until the twentieth century, the civil service examination system was used almost exclusively to choose imperial officials. Although village and clan schools taught basic literacy, education was largely oriented toward classical learning. By the Ming dynasty in the fourteenth century, the exams were based on Neo-Confucian interpretations of classical Confucian texts. Although their form and content changed frequently over the ensuing centuries, the exams dominated education and officialdom.[4] The curriculum was not ostensibly mandated by the state, but in effect it was determined by the questions that officials posed in the civil service exams. However, during the Qing dynasty (1644–1912), something like a two-tiered educational system emerged, with a superliterate elite conversant with the finer points of the classics, history, and poetry at the top of the political and social order, and a minimally literate and numerate body of men able to transact simple business, read simple religious texts, and write simple letters and contracts at a distinctly lower level.[5] The elementary literacy primers were no less orthodox in their teachings about filial piety and obedience to elders and social superiors than were the Neo-Confucian writings themselves.[6]

As foreign pressures and domestic rebellion deepened in the mid-nineteenth century, the Qing court and Chinese literati began to adopt Western military technology and desired to understand the science that underlay it. In the wake of the massive Taiping Rebellion, which devastated the richest parts of central China in the 1850s and 1860s, new Confucian academies were founded with the support of officials and gentry.[7] Many of these schools began to Westernize

---

[3] Francisco O. Ramirez and John Boli, "The Political Construction of Mass Schooling."
[4] Benjamin A. Elman, *A Cultural History of Civil Examinations in Late Imperial China*. "Neo-Confucianism" refers to the interpretations of the Confucian classics (fifth through second centuries BCE) that emerged during the Song dynasty (960–1279).
[5] By the nineteenth century as much as 40 percent of the male population and 10 percent of the female population may have possessed functional literacy, though those figures represent the top end of estimates and still leave the majority of the population illiterate and innumerate. See Evelyn Sakakida Rawski, *Education and Popular Literacy in Ch'ing China*.
[6] Limin Bai, *Shaping the Ideal Child*.
[7] Barry C. Keenan, *Imperial China's Last Classical Academies*. (For government schools, see Knight Biggerstaff, *The Earliest Modern Government Schools in China*.)

their curriculums, very modestly at first, but more radically by the 1890s. A few of them gave rise to new schools when groups of teachers and students broke away to focus more on Western subjects and contemporary affairs. In the surge of reformism after China's defeat in 1895 in the Sino-Japanese War, some of these schools began producing their own simple textbooks.[8] One count of "new-style" schools finds very few before 1890, whereas 104 emerged between 1895 and 1899.[9] The number of students in such schools rose from fewer than 7000 in 1902 to 1.6 million in 1909, and nearly 3 million in 1912. The numbers continued to grow after the 1911 Revolution: 4 million in 1916, approaching 6 million by the 1920s. China may have had some 36,000 schools in 1907, 42,000 schools in 1908, and more than 100,000 schools in 1909, though this number dropped to about 90,000 in the political turmoil of 1911–1912 before expansion resumed again.[10] New-style school students long remained a small fraction of China's school-age population, but they still amounted to a large number of students. Boys predominated, but the number of girls attending schools was also growing. By 1930, the Ministry of Education counted nearly 11.5 million students in state, provincial, local government, and private schools.[11] Of this total, nearly 11 million were enrolled in primary schools (including a small number in kindergartens) and more than 500,000 in middle schools. More than 1.6 million girls and more than 9 million boys were enrolled in primary schools. The figures for middle schools were approximately 75,000 girls and more than 400,000 boys.

Missionary schools played a significant role in bringing Western education to China. Protestant mission schools emerged in some numbers after the First Opium War in the 1840s and enrolled some 6000 students in 1877, which increased to 16,836 in 1890 and 57,683 in 1906.[12] By this time, in addition to basic reading and religion, they also taught sciences, Western geography, politics, and history. Missionary-teachers adopted the subject-based written materials of the West to write the first "textbooks" in China.[13]

Chinese educational reformers learned much from Western missionaries. At the very least, missionaries were a key source of information about Western educational practices, including the role of textbooks. The notion of shaping curriculum to accord with the child's stage of intellectual and emotional development provided a basic mold for textbook writing. However, to Chinese

---

[8] Wang Jiarong, *Minzuhun*, pp. 12–19.
[9] Sang Bing, *Wan-Qing xuetang xuesheng yu shehui bianqian*, p. 2. Such figures cannot be exact, of course.
[10] Marianne Bastid, *Educational Reform in Early 20th-Century China*, pp. 66–68.
[11] That is, estimations. Zhou Bangdao, ed., *Diyici Zongguo jiaoyu nianjian*, vol. 2, pp. 194/518, 423/747; vol. 1, pp. 93/1575, 161/1643.
[12] Paul Cohen, "Christian Missions and Their Impact to 1900," p. 577.
[13] Wang Jianjun, *Zhongguo jindai jiaokeshu fazhan yanjiu*, pp. 13–18, 50–59.

officials, missionaries seemed more like a source of heterodoxy than worthy of emulation. And progressive intellectuals were not much happier than conservative officials at the prospect of foreigners influencing Chinese students through their textbooks.[14] At least ostensibly, Chinese reformers did not seek to model their new-style schools on missionary examples. Rather, especially after 1895, Japanese theories and models (though arguably themselves inspired by continental Europe) became the main inspiration for Chinese educators.[15] The reasons for this included general respect for the Meiji reforms and relative familiarity with Japan and Japanese.

Although conservatives opposed virtually any education in "Western learning," high-ranking reformers like Zhang Zhidong (1837–1909) and Zhang Baixi (1847–1907) appreciated that Japanese education was based on the principles of loyalty to the emperor and Confucian morality even while the Japanese had introduced classes in Western history, politics, and geography, as well as the sciences. By the 1890s what Chinese observers, both official and nonofficial, found in Japan was a young but well-established school system.[16] Japanese educators had required much trial and error – Chinese observers might have taken heart had they known of this. Enrollments rose and dropped in Meiji Japan before rising again, and centralized and localized systems were all tried before a Prussian-style centralized system fell into place and textbooks were slowly brought under government control. The lack of textbooks in the 1870s meant that teachers had to use old or hastily translated materials, and it was probably not until the 1880s that new normal schools had produced enough trained teachers even to use textbooks properly. The Ministry of Education produced a small number of textbooks in the 1880s, but the role of private publishers remained key. The ministry began to censor textbooks in the early 1880s, and a systematic inspection system was in place by about 1886.

The Japanese school regulations of 1881 set up a system of primary schools consisting of a lower level of three years, a middle level of two years, and a higher level of two years. The 1881 regulations stipulated that the lower primary school curriculum was to consist of morality classes, reading, writing, arithmetic, and singing and physical training; morality classes were to stress both patriotism and the Confucian values of loyalty and filial piety. The middle

---

[14] Wang Jiarong, *Minzuhun*, pp. 11–12.
[15] For the Japanese role, see Hiroshi Abe, "Borrowing from Japan"; Marianne Bastid, *Educational Reform*, pp. 44–50; Sally Borthwick, *Education and Social Change*, pp. 66–77; Wang Jianjun, *Zhongguo jindai jiaokeshu*, p. 89. For the general role of Japan in China at this time, see Douglas R. Reynolds, *China, 1898–1912*, esp. chapter 7. However, more research may show that mission school textbooks, as well as Japanese textbooks, did in fact serve as models for late Qing Chinese textbooks.
[16] Michio Nagai, "Westernization and Japanization"; Herbert Passin, *Society and Education in Japan*, pp. 75–85; Kaigo Tokiomi and Naka Arata, *Kindai Nihon kyōkasho sōsetsu*, esp. pp. 14–37.

level added geography, history, art, and sciences (and sewing for girls), while the upper level added more sciences, higher math, and economics (household management for girls).

In rough terms, the Chinese system would follow Japan's example. However, Japan's Imperial Rescript on Education, promulgated in 1890, set Japanese on a path that was in many ways unique, and in any case not entirely suitable for Chinese conditions.[17] The Rescript was timed to coincide with the promulgation of the Meiji Constitution and the beginning of parliamentary politics. Japanese conservatives saw the Rescript as a bulwark against populism: it would tie future generations to the emperor (*kokutai*), but at the same time it ratified the state-building project of the Meiji, which is possibly what Chinese would have appreciated at the beginning of the next century. The notion of *kokutai* or the "national polity" referred to Japan's foundations as an imperial state and to the emperor as the source of morality. This seems to have had little resonance in China, whereas *kokutai* and the Rescript itself were to become central to the developing ideology of the modern Japanese state. The Rescript briefly linked the ethics of Confucian relationships, loyalty and filial piety above all, with respect for the constitution, obedience to the law, and willingness to sacrifice for the state. In the following years, in its name, dissenters were driven out of public life and textbooks were standardized. By the early 1900s, the government had succeeded in its goal to compile all Japanese primary and secondary school textbooks.

Late Qing curricular goals and textbooks

By the 1890s Chinese reformers – usually examination degree-holders but out of office – had founded a number of "new-style" private academies. A few reformers wrote primers to foster the patriotism of children and encourage them to study the new learning in order to strengthen China.[18] They also made use of translated Western books.[19] However, most of these should not be considered textbooks, at least outside the sciences. Western works dealing with politics, history, and geography were largely treatises on specific subjects, and

---

[17] Teruhisa Horio, *Educational Thought and Ideology in Modern Japan*, pp. 70–78; Carol Gluck, *Japan's Modern Myths*, pp. 120–133.

[18] Wang Jianjun, *Zhongguo jindai jiaokeshu*, pp. 83–105. For the case of Lin Shu (1852–1924), who would soon become famous for his literary translations, see Limin Bai, *Shaping the Ideal Child*, pp. 176–183.

[19] Wang Jianjun, *Zhongguo jindai jiaokeshu*, pp. 72–82. It should also be noted that many of the most reform-oriented schools of the 1890s and early 1900s had their roots in the academies founded in the 1860s in the wake of the Taiping Rebellion with the intention of reviving a practical, tough-minded Confucianism. See Barry C. Keenan, *Imperial China's Last Classical Academies*.

even introductory texts were not written at levels suitable for children's comprehension. Rather, they were designed for an audience of young men who were already adept in classical learning.

It was a struggle to write in a way that young minds could fully grasp – the traditional pedagogy had been to begin with rote memorization and worry about understanding later. Yet in the end the new schoolbooks, along with the late Qing proliferation of journals and encyclopedias, gradually acquainted a new generation with the basic forms of Western civilization. Furthermore, textbooks, written for various levels of understanding, began to treat knowledge as cumulative; that is, children were to acquire more and more knowledge in specific stages as they proceeded through the school system. The knowledge conveyed in late Qing textbooks was of immediate import because the venerable civil service examination system was changing. As early as the 1890s, questions on current affairs had begun to appear on the exams; however, successful candidates still required classical training and, to a degree, broad reading in the contemporary press rather than modern schooling. It was in 1902 that the emphasis of the exams shifted from classical exegesis to discussions of Chinese and world history, politics, and technology, in tandem with the creation of a modern school system. It might be said that the reform of the examination system reflected changes in conceptions of knowledge and the goals of education more than it prompted them. Nonetheless, the exams still represented the most prestigious and rewarding path of personal advancement, and student demand would follow. But the exams were abolished in 1905. In effect, the Qing court decided that school-trained elites would be better equipped to lead Chinese governmental and private institutions than the candidates produced by the examination system. The abolition was a major shock to traditionally educated elites and perhaps signaled the passing of an entire knowledge order.

But we are getting ahead of the story. It was in the thoroughgoing reforms collectively called the "New Policy reforms" (*xinzheng*) in 1902 and 1903 that the Qing court began to establish the foundations of a modern state school system. This system was set up through a series of edicts promulgated through 1906.[20] Educational reform did not occur in a vacuum. From the beginning of the New Policy reforms, statesmen such as Zhang Zhidong regarded the prospect of constitutional government and universal schooling as two sides of the same coin.[21] Collectively, the New Policy reforms represented a huge effort

---

[20] For background, see Qiu Xiuxiang, *Qingmo xinshi jiaoyu de lixiang yu xianshi*; Xiong Xianjun, *Qianqiu jiye*; Shu Xincheng, ed., *Jindai Zhongguo jiaoyu sixiangshi*; Li Guojun and Wang Bingzhao, eds., *Zhongguo jiaoyu zhidu tongshi*, vols. 6–7; and Mao Lirei and Shen Guanqun, eds., *Zhongguo jiaoyu tongshi*, vol. 4. For a succinct overview in English, see Marianne Bastid, "Servitude or Liberation."

[21] Guan Xiaohong, *Wan-Qing xuebu yanjiu*, pp. 178–179.

to dramatically expand the size, functions, and scope of government. Taking over the educational system was not the least part of that vision.

The vision of a state school system, radical in conception if slow to take practical form, was the result of several trends that began to coalescence in the second half of the nineteenth century. For a growing number of reformers in and out of government, mass education seemed like a panacea for China's problems. Popular education would not only give Chinese people new sets of skills, but even more basically it would teach the people that they formed a nation: a nation that could be strengthened and made prosperous through their mutual efforts. Reformers looked to Germany and Japan as models for what education of the masses could accomplish. Such reformers were the mainstay of the new schools, and both state schools and private schools (which long continued to outnumber state schools) depended on their support.

In 1902, the editors of the Commercial Press (Shangwu yinshuguan) in Shanghai were quick to see the pedagogical – and financial – advantages of publishing textbooks.[22] The press had begun in 1897 as a small printing operation, moved into translation projects, and finally secured market dominance with textbooks. By the last years of the Qing, its editors included men who were leading intellectuals in their own right, interested in raising the cultural level of the people and looking to education to help solve China's problems. It hired teachers and prominent scholars to work on such subject areas as reading, history, and geography. The Commercial Press also worked closely with a leading Japanese textbook publisher, which was among its chief investors.[23] The results were sets of textbooks called the "most up to date" series in every school subject. Each volume of each series was designed to be used for one semester. Once students started, say, the first volume of the "most up to date" language reader, it was advantageous to continue to use the entire series. Other publishing houses, sometimes formed with more reformist zeal and less business savvy, soon joined the Commercial Press. The most notable of these were the Civilization Press (Wenming shuju) – which had been founded in Shanghai in 1902 by men associated with new-style schools founded earlier in nearby Wuxi, at the height of the reform movement in 1898 – and the Extending Knowledge Bookstore (Guangzhi shuju). Altogether some 40-odd publishing houses had emerged by the end of the dynasty.[24] The Commercial Press, however,

---

[22] Wang Jianjun, *Zhongguo jindai jiaokeshu*, pp. 105–127. An insightful discussion of the origins of the Commercial Press in English is Meng Yue, *Shanghai and the Edges of Empires*, chapter 2. Good introductions to modern Chinese publishing are Christopher A. Reed, *Gutenberg in Shanghai*; and Robert Culp, "Mass Production of Knowledge and the Industrialization of Mental Labor."

[23] Tarumoto Teruo, "Xinhai geming qian de Shangwu yinshuguan."

[24] Wang Jiarong, *Minzuhun*, pp. 37–38, 21.

dominated the textbook industry, set up a national distribution network that included traveling salesmen as well as its own stores in major cities, and was soon publishing an array of journals and trade books. In addition, the government officially sponsored textbooks that were published under the auspices of the Imperial University (forerunner to Peking University), of Nanyang gongxue, an academy first established by reformist officials in Shanghai in 1896, and of the Ministry of Education.[25] Official textbook publishing never got off the ground, however, and the government understood that it simply lacked the resources to meet China's textbook needs directly.

With the New Policy reforms, Qing political elites finally committed the state to the kind of comprehensive educational system that reformers had been urging for over a generation. Research into the history of education thus far does not allow us to reach many conclusions about what actually went on in late Qing classrooms or what students actually absorbed. Be that as it may, textbooks tell us what Qing elites *wanted* children to learn. This is not to say that elites spoke in one voice. Reformers differed among themselves and with officials, and in some respects even the official goals were contradictory. Above all, the demands of creating modern citizens loyal to the nation and identifying as "Chinese" ran counter to the demands of creating loyal subjects of the emperor. Of course, textbooks – subject to censorship and the demands of the market – never openly challenged the legitimacy of Qing rule or, after the 1911 Revolution, that of the Republic. But they reflected the tensions of the period over identity, values, and the pace of change.

Under the general direction of Zhang Zhidong, Qing educators envisioned a process leading eventually to universal, compulsory education. The educational regulations of 1904 stipulated that each prefecture needed a middle school and each county a primary school.[26] A small but functioning state school system could be found in China's cities by the time of the 1911 Revolution. In the countryside, building local schools by confiscating temple lands and raising taxes provoked protests; however, there were also quiet successes.[27] And a large number of village schools and private academies outside of the embryonic state system taught both traditional and modern subjects – and sometimes used state-approved textbooks to supplement the old Confucian fare. Provision

---

[25] Wang Jianjun, *Zhongguo jindai jiaokeshu*, pp. 145–148.
[26] In 1902 the official vision was of eventual universal education for boys. By the last years of the Qing, girls' schools were being built as well; however, the goal of universal education was not reached until after the founding of the People's Republic in the 1950s. For estimates of the reach of state schooling, see Borthwick, *Education and Social Change*, pp. 105–114; and Thomas D. Curran, *Educational Reform in Republican China*, pp. 224–225.
[27] Elizabeth VanderVen, "Village-State Cooperation." A recent overview of the resistance to modern schools is Curran, *Educational Reform*, pp. 235–251.

was made for girls in the 1906 regulations, but boys remained a large majority of students.[28]

The new Ministry of Education set out general goals for the new schools in 1906. This document plunged into the debates of the day, promoting reform on the one hand but criticizing reformist extremism on the other. It was the latter problem that seems to have struck the ministry as especially worrisome; it did not claim that the West set a bad example but that some Chinese did not properly understand the West. Universal education was ultimately a means to inculcate loyalty and inoculate the population against revolutionary "heresies"; it was also a means to strengthen the state by mobilizing the people.[29] This was all in line with Zhang Zhidong's insistence that reform would rest on "Chinese learning for the essence, and Western learning for its utility."

A major concern of the Ministry of Education was that proper policies be established on the basis of China's circumstances and popular customs. Above all, the traditional teaching of the state (*zhengjiao*) rested on loyalty to the emperor (*zhongjun*) and reverence for Confucius (*zun Kong*). What was now needed, in order to maintain these foundational principles, was esteem for public consciousness (*shanggong*), the military arts (*shangwu*), and the practical arts (*shangshi*).[30] According to the Education Ministry – still echoing Zhang Zhidong – although the political forms of Eastern and Western countries differed, all based on their politics on reverence for the ruler (*guozhu*). For example, the recent rise of Germany could be traced to the emphasis its schools placed on preserving the unity of the empire, and Japan's rise had much to do with its schools' emphasis on the unbroken imperial line. The Qing court, in its great beneficence and care of the people, could, according to the ministry, shape its educational system similarly.

Public consciousness, the military, and the practical arts were thus, for the ministry, essentially means to promote Confucianism and loyalism. More specifically, "public" referred to creating a unified populace that was determined and unconquerable.[31] The role of schooling here was essential, the ministry declared, in creating trust and friendship through lessons in self-cultivation, ethical relations, history, geography, and the like: all such courses promoted the cooperative sentiment of students. Patriotic unity, the ministry

---

[28] Girls' education was to emphasize womanly virtues and household management and skills, along with academic subjects and physical education. In the last years of the Qing, women students in fact proved as obstreperous and rebellious as men students. See Paul Bailey, "'Modernising Conservatism' in Early Twentieth-Century China"; Weikun Cheng, "Going Public through Education"; Joan Judge, "Between Nei and Wai"; Judge, "Meng Mu Meets the Modern"; and Judge, "The Culturally Contested Student Body."

[29] Qu Xingui and Tang Liangyan, eds., *Zhongguo jindai jiaoyushi ziliao huibian*, vol. 1, pp. 534–539.

[30] Ibid., p. 535.   [31] Ibid., p. 536.

explicitly noted, should be rooted in childhood, just as Confucius taught that universal benevolence was the extension of more particularistic filiality. Central to this process would be a revival of a "national learning" (*guoxue*) that was in decline. National learning meant not abstract forms of knowledge but – as naturally understood by Confucians – cultivating the self and ordering the family in practice. Also according to the ministry, "public" implied all that which was not private and selfish: the entire range of human communities from village and neighborhood to the world, but especially the Chinese nation. It is interesting to note the government's use of this loaded term. The realm of the people and the realm of the government were both "public" – and for reformers there was, or should be, no distinction between those realms. For reformers, the realm of the individual and the family were suspiciously "private" (*si*) and at least potentially selfish. Zhang Zhidong may have been thinking that "public" signified the legitimacy of taxes and military duty, but more radical intellectuals were suggesting that if the government was truly public, then it should be the realm of the people, and if it was the realm of the people, then the legitimacy of the imperial family could be challenged. But reformers did generally agree on the need for popular enlightenment, which fell under the category of the public.

The ministry's other two legs of the tripod of Chinese schooling were military preparedness and the practical arts, which were of even greater immediate use than public consciousness. The goal was to encourage both a general martial spirit and specific military training. In contrast to the old academies, the new schools would be run in more military fashion: even the youngest children would be lining up to enter and leave classes, and physical education would include military-like drills. If the old Confucian elites had little use for the military and soldiers, this disdain was rapidly becoming approval in the late Qing. The ministry even wanted a curriculum that put military lessons into literature, history, and geography classes – and even into art and music classes.[32] Finally, the idea of practical arts referred not merely to technical crafts and skills but was redolent of a long-standing interest in "substantial learning," as opposed to airy metaphysical speculation and pedantic textual research. It reflected something of the nineteenth century's interest in what was called statecraft: practical knowledge for officials dealing with everything from shoring up irrigation works to dealing with minority peoples of the frontiers.

The ministry acknowledged the deficiencies of the current system in which the common people's knowledge of the nation was limited and their feelings for it indifferent. This was not because the people lacked a conscience, according to the ministry, but because there had been no way to reach or educate them. The spirit of loyalty existed, but it did not function properly. But witness Japan: education reached down to the commoners through elementary school readers,

---

[32] Ibid., p. 537.

and thus everyone learned of the urgent need to erase national humiliations, to understand the happiness of the king as the glory of the nation, and to see the glory of the nation as belonging to oneself. In the ministry's words, this was what was meant by the unity of ruler and people (*junmin yiti*) – a common trope among reformist intellectuals. Following this confident line of thought, the ministry claimed that China, as a nation of ritual propriety and loyalty, could easily develop this identification of individual and nation (and king) through universal education. Textbooks would emphasize the history of the nation: its origins, its development over much time, recent events, the worries of the emperor, and the problems stemming from foreign pressures and domestic issues. In this way, the ministry promised, students would never forget loyalty to the emperor – and, in remembering the great deeds of former heroes and the blessings of the cosmos, would be inoculated against revolutionary heresies.

This document can be read as a conservative manifesto, a finger in the dike blocking the flood of more progressive ideas. Yet the ministry had a point when it emphasized that the West did not always value progress over conservation. This misconception, it argued, led to the denigration of sacred teachings and ethics. Every nation's education was based on its own language, literature, history, customs, and religion to preserve them, and so "all their schools substantially respect the national teaching."[33] In 1906, then, the ministry held up Confucius and the emperor as twin symbols of continuity; if they symbolized conservative values, they also justified the creation of a national school system ultimately designed to create a strong nation.

Official documents naturally ignored the potential conflict between the interests of the imperial court and the nation. The ministry's twinning of loyalty and Confucianism reflected traditional attitudes, but it was also a defense response to the unprecedented pressures facing the imperial state. Officials could no more imagine the monarchy without Confucianism than they could imagine the Three Bonds and self-cultivation without the monarchy – much less a China without the monarchy.[34] Yet by this time revolutionaries had drawn a sharp distinction between loyalty to nation (patriotism) and loyalty to the emperor, so this distinction was not literally unthinkable. Officials, then, hoped the schools would teach that the two kinds of loyalty were mutually supporting. Indeed, the ministry claimed that under the rubric of unity and public-mindedness, schooling would extirpate selfishness, and the people would become prosperous and the country strong.

---

[33] Ibid., p. 535.

[34] The Three Bonds forms an ethical basis of Confucianism, stressing the relationships between parent and child, king and subject, and husband and wife. Self-cultivation was a practice of moral introspection particularly stressed in the orthodox Neo-Confucian school since the twelfth century.

Of the goal of patriotism, there can be no doubt. A key function of lower primary schools was precisely to "establish the foundations for their understanding of proper human relationships and for promoting their love for the nation" – as well as, of course, the imparting of knowledge.[35] Patriotism was a key new element of moral education. The new school regulations defined morality as developing youth's sense of good character, avoiding evil deeds, and learning good habits, partly through the use of historical role models. And not least: "the knowledge of love of the same kind [of people] (*ai tonglei*) at this time [in youth] is the basis for the patriotism of adults."[36]

The 1902 regulations stipulated that four-year Kindergarten Halls (*mengxuetang*), for students starting about age 6, would teach basic skills. The 1904 school regulations modified this; now, students were to begin in grade 1 at age 7 in lower primary schools.[37] The schools' purpose was to instill knowledge and the basis of morality and patriotism, as well as health and development. General science and arithmetic were added to the curriculum, whereas classics and self-cultivation together constituted nearly half of class time (12 classes for classics and 2 for self-cultivation, out of 30 per week).

The 1906 regulations continued to propose that students start formal schooling at age 7. Lower primary schools covered grades 1 through 5; higher primary schools grades 6 through 9; and middle schools (along with parallel vocational and normal schools) grades 10 through 13. Then, higher schools were to provide more specialized university-preparation courses in grades 14 through 17, followed finally by a university or Confucian academy.[38] The curriculum of higher and lower primary and middle schools emphasized self-cultivation and the classics. Chinese classes were designed to equip students to understand the classics as well as the entire literary tradition, and thus give students a sense of the "national essence." Other classes included history, geography, arithmetic, sciences, physical exercise, and perhaps drawing and crafts. Higher primary and middle schools were to provide more specialized scientific or vocational classes (such as agriculture and commerce); middle and higher schools were to offer courses in law, finance, and foreign languages in addition to the basic curriculum and a separate teachers' training program. In sum, although the new schools were to include great clumps of "modern" or "Western" learning – maths, sciences, foreign languages, geography, and history – the officials who

---

[35] In the words of an edict of 1904. Qu and Tang, eds., *Zhongguo jindai jiaoyushi ziliao huibian*, vol. 1, p. 291.
[36] Ibid., p. 294.
[37] Kecheng jiaocai yanjiusuo, ed., *20 shiji Zhongguo zhongxiaoxue kecheng biaozhun*, vol. 1, pp. 20–27; vol. 2, p. 6. Introductions to modern Chinese morality education include Zheng Hang, *Zhongguo jindai deyu kechengshi*; Wang Jiarong, *Minzuhun*, pp. 76–100; and Huang Shuguang, "Jiazhi chonggu yu Minguo chunian zhongxiaoxue deyu kecheng jiaoxue de shenceng bianqe."
[38] For details of the system, never fully implemented, see Shangwu yinshuguan, comp., *Da Qing xin faling*, part 7.

initially designed the school system also wanted to preserve traditional morality. Although subject to frequent changes, some of which will be discussed later, essentially the school week was envisioned as follows:[39]

Lower primary schools, grades 1–5 (30 hours/week)	
Self-cultivation	2
Classics	12
Chinese	4
Arithmetic	6
History	1
Geography	1
Sciences (handicrafts optional)	1
Physical education	3
Higher primary schools, grades 6–9 (36 hours/week)	
Self-cultivation	2
Classics	12
Chinese	8
Arithmetic	3
History	2
Geography	2
Sciences (agriculture and commerce optional)	2
Art	2
PE, military-style drill	3
Middle schools, grades 10–14 (36 hours/week)	
Self-cultivation	1
Classics	9
Chinese	3–4
Foreign language	6–8
History	2–3
Geography	2–3
Mathematics	4
Sciences	2–4
Art	1
PE, military-style drill	2

Outside of the sciences, the Qing system largely produced its own textbooks, although based on foreign models. In the very first years of the new school system, translations or paraphrased versions of Japanese textbooks set a standard for publishers to follow.[40] Japan's defeat of China in the Sino-Japanese War in 1895 did not discourage Chinese reformers, but rather was taken as evidence that Japan's successes should become China's lessons. Japan was also a kind of

[39] Kecheng jiaocai yanjiusuo, ed., *20 shiji Zhongguo zhongxiaoxue kecheng biaozhun*, vol. 1, pp. 23–26, 34–36, 44–46.
[40] Namiki Yorihisa, Ōsato Hiroaki, and Sunayama Yukio, eds., *Kindai Chūgoku – kyōkasho to Nihon*.

window to the West for Chinese, who found it easier to learn Japanese and pursue studies there – and they could communicate with educated Japanese, who read and wrote classical Chinese. Over a decade after reformers began promoting Japanese-style reforms across the board, the Qing court was finally ready to embrace change in 1902. High officials liked the monarchism of Japanese Confucianism and thought it a good basis for the Chinese educational system.[41] They dispatched scholars to study Meiji schools. At the same time, as increasing numbers of Chinese students flocked to Japan, many private translations of Japanese textbooks began to appear. Japan was a model, but one that had to be adapted. In history, although historical studies had long been central to traditional education, the dynastic histories, biographies, and institutional histories written in previous generations were clearly not suitable to the new schools. Zhang Zhidong commissioned the young scholar Liu Yizheng (1880–1956) to translate – or at least adapt – a Japanese general history of China to serve Chinese students.[42] The form of "the story of the nation" has dominated history classes to this day. Similarly, moral education was if anything even more central to traditional primers and Confucian texts, but the idea of self-cultivation textbooks came from Japan.[43] Yet the content of Japanese moral education obviously had to be changed to fit the different conditions in China (which lacked Japan's "unbroken imperial line," for example).

One recent count lists 508 textbooks translated from Japanese between 1890 and 1915.[44] Most of these taught the sciences and mathematics, foreign languages, and the field of education itself. For the content of textbooks in Chinese reading and literature, morality and civics, Chinese history, and Chinese geography, the Chinese relied mainly on themselves. For example, once Liu Yizheng's adaptation of the Japanese-authored general history of China offered a model of national history, Chinese authors could use traditional sources to write their own histories.[45] Translations continued to be used to teach Japanese, Western, and world history, but not Chinese history. In the category of geography, again, most of the translations focused on world geography, whereas Chinese authors used standard works such as local gazetteers to write Chinese geographies. As Wang Jiarong argues, Japanese sources (themselves often reflecting Western scholarship, if indirectly) underwent a process of Sinification in the first years of the twentieth century.[46]

---

[41] Wang Jianjun, *Zhongguo jindai jiaokeshu*, pp. 60–71.
[42] See Tze-ki Hon, "Educating the Citizens," pp. 84–90.
[43] Though perhaps the ultimate origins lay in France. See Paul Bailey, *Reform the People*, pp. 32, 58n.103.
[44] Bi Yuan, *Jianzao changshi*, pp. 246–302.
[45] Although a range of Chinese and Asian history textbooks were translated right about the turn of the century. Li Xiaoqian, "Qingji Zhinashi, Dongyangshi jiaokeshu jieyi chutan."
[46] Wang Jiarong, *Minzuhun*, pp. 38–45.

In 1906, textbooks became subject to the Education Ministry's review and censorship.[47] Before that date, officials had established guidelines for textbooks, but the court had not set up a dedicated inspection office. It was also in 1906 that the ministry also began producing its own textbooks, though these remained limited in number. The ministry's main job was guiding publishers through a process that would result in approval for the use of their textbooks in official schools. Generally speaking, the prospect of professional regulation by the ministry was not seen as a threat to authors' freedom so much as a promise of higher quality. The ministry's standards included not only the general goals outlined earlier, but also consideration of the grade level each textbook was aimed at – although it also frowned on the vernacular, demanding that textbooks be written in standard classical Chinese.[48]

By publishing at least some of its decisions and the reasoning behind them, the ministry offered continuing guidance to publishers. It could approve publication of submitted manuscripts, demand revisions and resubmission, or outright reject a proposed textbook. The ministry certainly kept a watchful eye out for seditious or heterodox ideas. It would not approve talk of "equality" or "freedom of marriage," for example. However, as we will see, this still left room for more subtle forms of dissent. The Commercial Press and the Civilization Press were especially good at getting their books approved. Even they sometimes struggled through negotiations about what would be acceptable before earning the ministry's seal of approval. The ministry envisioned the day it would have the ability to censor all materials published in China, yet not even all textbooks went through its procedures. Both before and after the 1911 Revolution, textbooks continued to be published privately. In theory and practice, private schools could use whatever educational materials they wanted. This only changed toward the end of the 1920s, when the new Nationalist government was able to assert greater control over publishers and schools.

Throughout the last years of the Qing and indeed well into the republican period, private schools of all descriptions continued to flourish, as did a range of quasi-public literacy and vocational schools.[49] They often emphasized traditional texts such as the basic primers, the Confucian "Four Books" and "Five Classics," and the *Classic of Filial Piety*, but they also increasingly mixed these texts with the modern textbooks that the official curriculum mandated.

---

[47] Zhang Yunjun, *Wan-Qing shubao jiancha zhidu yanjiu*, chapter 3; Guan Xiaohong, *Wan-Qing xuebu*, pp. 178–179, 375–385; Wang Jianjun, *Zhongguo jindai jiaokeshu*, pp. 158–190.
[48] Classical Chinese as a written language developing over two millennia had long served as the common means of communication among highly literate Chinese, as well as Koreans, Japanese, and Vietnamese. There was no single vernacular, but regional dialects were spoken across the empire; elite Chinese, whatever their mother tongue, generally learned the "official talk" (*guanhua*), which was essentially the northern Chinese dialect.
[49] Bailey, *Reform the People*, chapter 3.

Although major publishers dominated the market, many teacher-written textbooks were published as well. The case of Liu Shipei is special. Liu (1884–1919) was a precocious scholar – one of the last masters of the textual analysis of the classics that had flourished in the eighteenth century – and anti-Manchu revolutionary.[50] In 1905, during a crackdown against radical activists in Shanghai, Liu changed his name and fled, eventually landing in Wuhu City in Anhui Province, teaching in middle school there. Always prolific, Liu now wrote textbooks on ethics, classics, literature (one of the first of its kind), history, and geography. Liu's textbooks reveal his radical support of nationalism and democracy, but they were based on his deep immersion in traditional writings of all kinds. Most remarkably, perhaps, they were for the most part published serially in the Shanghai journal dedicated to preserving the Chinese cultural tradition, the *National Essence Journal* (*Guocui xuebao*). The *National Essence Journal* was strongly political insofar as it sought to link Chinese culture with the Han people, thus defining the Manchu rulers as non-Chinese. But national essence scholars, including Liu, were as interested in discovering and preserving the finest elements of China's past – even while absorbing certain features of Western civilization – as they were in making revolution. Liu's and other teacher-written textbooks are discussed in the following chapters.

Republican period curricular goals and textbooks

The textbook boom of the late Qing reflected years of work by reformers, the officials, and publishers. These factors also shaped the schools of the republican period. The prospect of constitutional government had inspired elites to concentrate their attention on raising the "quality" of the people. The sudden success of republicanism made this cause seem even more pressing. The numbers kept growing as well. Some 3 million students in state schools in 1912 grew to over 4 million students in 128,000 primary schools and 126,000 students in 1000 secondary schools in 1915.[51] The total approached 7 million students by 1922. By 1930, there were 11 million students in 200,000 primary schools and 500,000 in 3000 secondary schools. By 1936, the total number of students was approaching 20 million. Furthermore, again, the market for textbooks was not limited to state schools or even to students, as there is some evidence that adults bought textbooks to serve as introductions to subjects they were interested in. As well, dozens of Overseas Chinese schools were established across Southeast Asia by the early twentieth century, and those students too generally used

---

[50] In 1907 Liu converted to anarchism, and in 1909 even more dramatically announced his re-found loyalty to the Qing dynasty; he thenceforth largely abandoned political action for scholarship. See Martin Bernal, "Liu Shih-p'ei and National Essence," pp. 90–112; Hao Chang, *Chinese Intellectuals in Crisis*, pp. 146–179.
[51] Wu Binggui, *Minguo chuban shi*, pp. 445–446.

the textbooks published by the major Shanghai houses.[52] In French Indochina, the Dutch East Indies, British Malaya, and other places, the Commercial Press, the China Bookstore, and other publishing companies set up local distribution networks and sold the same textbooks that they sold in China. (They began to compile separate sets of textbooks for Southeast Asian Overseas Chinese in the 1930s.)

In the immediate wake of the 1911 Revolution, the most significant change to the school system was the disappearance of the classics from the curriculum. Morality textbooks and history textbooks were rewritten – or at least sections were added to them – to highlight China's transformation into a republican polity. Republican values were also to affect language readers, but more slowly. The number of students continued to grow, and thus publishers competed for their business. Commercial Press had achieved dominance in the last years of the Qing, but it was nursing in its bosom a revolutionary viper.[53] Secretly preparing new republican textbooks in 1911 even before the revolution broke out, a group of Commercial Press editors was ready to found the China Bookstore publishing company (Zhonghua shuju), as soon as the opportunity presented itself. And because it was able to work with the new revolutionary government in 1912 to set curricular standards, China Bookstore got off to a very good start. The new Ministry of Education prohibited all use of old textbooks in 1912, which was a direct blow against Commercial Press. However, Commercial Press soon repackaged its old "most up to date" textbooks with new covers labeled "Republican Series." While China Bookstore achieved something like parity with the Commercial Press, the World Bookstore (Shijie shuju) and the Enlightenment Bookstore (Kaiming shudian) publishing companies also emerged as major competitors. These publishers, all based in Shanghai, along with smaller rivals, produced thousands of textbooks – well over 4000 multi-volume sets.[54]

A revolutionary "provisional" government was established in Nanjing in January 1912; the fighting was not over, but it was clear that one way or another, the days of the Qing were numbered. The new Nanjing government had little real power, and in March it was superseded by a Beijing regime under the control of a former Qing general, Yuan Shikai. Yuan soon took all power into his own hands, and he suppressed the new parliament. Political chaos and even civil war ensued, and the rise of regional warlord commanders further weakened the central government after Yuan's death in 1916. The Guomindang (Nationalist

---

[52] Robert Culp, "Cultivating Cultural Citizenship."
[53] Zhou Qihou, *Zhonghua shuju*. A brief English-language account of the rise of Zhonghua and the recovery of Commercial Press is Christopher Reed, *Gutenberg in Shanghai*, pp. 225–253; also see Wang Jiarong, *Minzuhun*, pp. 116–131; Wang Jianjun, *Zhongguo jindai jiaokeshu*, pp. 203–217.
[54] Wang Jiarong, *Minzuhun*, pp. 115–116.

Party), based on opposition to warlordism and imperialism, and dominated by Sun Yat-sen until his death in 1925, became a military power in the southeast in the 1920s. Temporarily working with the Chinese Community Party and aided by the Soviet Union, the GMD was able to reunify the national government under its authority in 1927–1928. The Guomindang under Chiang Kai-shek then suppressed the CCP and, with its new capital again in Nanjing, was able to assert real control over the central provinces. Although many of its powers remained limited, it was able to reshape the state school system and severely limit the independence of private schools. The full-scale Japanese invasion of China in 1937 meant the end of the Nanjing government, although the Guomindang survived in the southwest. As we examine the textbooks used in the early Republic, from 1912 to 1937, we will see how the extreme political tensions of the day were reflected both in clear calls for national unity and in disagreements about the nature of the Chinese nation.

Needless to say, the chaotic conditions of the early Republic were not conducive to building a strong and orderly national school system. Nonetheless, the educational establishment continued to grow: not just the numbers of schools and teachers, as we have seen, but also teacher-training programs, specialized journals, and lively debates over pedagogical theory.[55] Although the provisional government of 1912 was short-lived and Yuan Shikai's policies rather more conservative, the revolutionaries still managed to shape the entire Republican educational system. Cai Yuanpei (1868–1940), serving as Nanjing's Minister of Education from January to July 1912, proposed that the new school system focus on five goals: military citizens, practical education, morality, worldview, and aesthetics.[56] Actually, in general terms, this was not much different from the goals of late Qing educators (public consciousness, military arts, and practical arts), which is not surprising because Cai and his associates had been closely involved with late Qing educational reformers. Cai had joined the anti-Manchu revolutionaries but had spent most of the years preceding the revolution studying in Germany. Revolutionaries and reformers had shared his belief that a militarized population was essential in a social Darwinian world. Practical education – that is, a more vocational emphasis – was necessary to prepare individuals for their future careers, careers that would collectively help to strengthen the Chinese nation. Cai's pragmatic emphasis differed from the late Qing schools' more humanistic or classical orientation, but only in degree; furthermore, it reflected the trends of late Qing pedagogical ideals rather than reversing them. Cai's notion of the substance of moral education (discussed

---

[55] Cyrus H. Peake, *Nationalism and Education*, remains a useful overview, based partly on firsthand observation. See also Paul Bailey, *Reform the People*, chapter 4.
[56] Cai Yuanpei, "Duiyu jiaoyu fangzhen zhi yijian," pp. 77–84; originally published in the February 1912 *Jiaoyu zazhi* 教育雜誌, and soon reprinted in *Dongfang zazhi* 東方雜誌. There are numerous discussions of Cai's views and their impact. See inter alia Thomas D. Curran, *Educational Reform*, pp. 185–208.

later) differed fundamentally from that of the Qing, but he was in agreement that "self-cultivation" was essential to schooling. Furthermore, for Cai, moral education would balance utilitarian education, creating modern citizens. Cai's notion of education for "worldview" was ultimately derived from Kant, and he seems to have seen it almost as a substitute for religion: a means of teaching students to appreciate the nonmaterial aspects of life. More concretely, he thought it provided a way to transcend the nationalism inherent in the first three goals of education and teach students to identify with humanity as a whole. The role of aesthetics was to help students find the road to this kind of worldview.

Cai himself regarded his views as diametrically opposed to the late Qing educational system: the Qing was dedicated to ideological indoctrination, he said, whereas "republican education" focuses on the development of each individual student. Cai's pronouncement was exaggerated. Ideological indoctrination did not disappear from Republican schools. Nor could it disappear, as long as schools had to socialize future citizens. Cai's notion of teaching "worldview" was never going to be easy to pin down, and it never found much of a place in the curriculum, though it was eventually reflected in some civics and world history lessons. But educators were increasingly thinking about the needs of children as well as the needs of the state. The Ministry of Education under Yuan Shikai – himself actually a long-time supporter of educational reform – accepted much of Cai's program. In November 1912 it proclaimed:

Special attention should be paid to all matters relating to national morality, regardless of the specific course. Knowledge and skills should be taught in accord with the needs of life, and repeatedly practiced to the point they become automatic. It is hoped that students' bodies are developed in complete health, and teaching must be in accord with the stage of development of students' bodies and minds. As for all boy and girl students, their special characteristics and future lives should be considered in order to give them the appropriate education.[57]

Significant changes to the educational system were ratified. One was coeducation: boys and girls were to attend lower primary schools together. Another was shortening the period of schooling. Lower primary school was made 4 years, theoretically compulsory. This could then be followed by a 4-year higher primary school, which could in turn be followed by a 4-year middle school.[58]

---

[57] Kecheng jiaocai yanjiusuo, ed., *20 shiji Zhongguo zhongxiaoxue kecheng biaozhun*, vol. 1, p. 63.

[58] Lower primary school graduates might also attend vocational schools, and higher primary school graduates might attend normal schools or higher vocational schools. Their curriculums differed slightly and will not be specified here. For normal, or teachers' training, schools, see Xiaoping Cong, *Teachers' Schools*. Late Qing reformers were quick to grasp that a mass educational system needed massive numbers of teachers, who would have be trained quickly. The curriculums of normal schools, except for the addition of classes in pedagogy and educational theory, did not differ much from the regular schools.

Given the weakness of the central government, schools depended on provincial and local initiatives. Conditions thus varied widely by locality, although China always maintained a national educational community linked by educational associations, teachers' schools, journals, textbook publishers, and occasional conferences.

The curriculum of the 1910s assigned hours of class time per week roughly as follows:[59]

Lower primary schools, grades 1–4 (22–29 hours/week)	
Self-cultivation	2
Chinese	10–14
Arithmetic	5–6
Handicrafts	1–2
Art	1–2
Singing and PE	4
Higher primary schools, grades 5–7 (30–32 hours/week)	
Self-cultivation	2
Chinese	8–10
Mathematics	4
History and geography	3–4
Sciences	2
Handicrafts	1–2
Art	1–2
Singing	2
PE	3
Agriculture/needlework	2–4

Higher primary schools also began offering foreign languages in some cases.

Middle schools, grades 8–11 (33–35 hours/week)	
Self-cultivation	1
Chinese	5–7
Foreign language	5–8
History	2
geography	2
Mathematics	3–5
Sciences	3–6
Art	1–2
Handicrafts	1
Music	1
PE	2–3

---

[59] The curriculum differed somewhat according to grade and gender. Kecheng jiaocai yanjiusuo, ed., *20 shiji Zhongguo zhongxiaoxue kecheng biaozhun*, vol. 1, pp. 66–67, 70–71, 98, 103–104.

The final year of middle school was to add a course on law and economics two hours a week. Girls' schools also offered up to two hours a week of classes in household management and gardening, and needlework.

With this curriculum in place, textbook production was fairly stable through the 1910s. At the same time, political chaos provoked intellectuals to ask why the revolution had seemed to fail; several answers emerged in the New Culture movement of 1915.[60] The movement rejected all aspects of "old culture" and was influential in educational circles. By the late 1910s a split was emerging between "liberals," who wished to repair the bleeding republican political system by focusing on long-term and gradualist solutions, and "radicals," who favored direct political street protests and the mobilization of students, workers, and women. But where the two groups overlapped was their interest in promoting "citizenship education" that would enable the people to truly determine their own fates. They shared the view that of the various "lingering poisons" infecting the Chinese, "superstition" and Confucianism were the worst, and that a new ethics was needed. They sought to promote simultaneously a stronger sense of individualism and commitment to the community. Education seemed the one sphere in which they might work without too much interference from warlords, who were intent on their own battles.

The immense intellectual and cultural changes of the late 1910s thus formed the background against which school reforms were pursued in the early 1920s. Educators themselves were beginning to criticize the schools for their isolation from society and their excessive scholasticism. In 1917 Chen Duxiu, then a dean at Peking University, complained bitterly about the state of Chinese education in a talk to the students of Nankai Academy in Tianjin, a progressive school founded by Chinese educators. Chen (1879–1942) began by asking whether any kind of formal education ever had any use.[61] Western educators, too, Chen said, sometimes thought that because whether a person was good or intelligent was determined by birth, schooling had little point. However, he himself thought that although natural endowments might be important, they could still be shaped by education. Chen compared education to wood carving. Only better-quality woods might be carved into roof beams or art pieces, but even the worst wood could be made into something useful. The more important question was whether – and how – China could follow the example of Western education. Of course, Chen condemned conservatives who denied the superiority of Western civilization and wished to continue traditional teachings. But that was not the real problem. Rather, Chen thought too many schools pretended to

---

[60] For the intellectual shift of the 1910s, the classic work remains Tse-tsung Chow, *The May Fourth Movement*. For the impact on textbooks, see Wang Jianjun, *Zhongguo jindai jiaokeshu*, pp. 224–259.
[61] Chen Duxiu, "Jindai xiyang jiaoyu," *Duxiu wencun*, vol. 1, pp. 153–159.

teach Western learning but did not understand its true spirit. Students had to be shown how to actively pursue learning, not passively memorize readings. Teaching had to be tied to secular, practical knowledge – this was the spirit of science, not religion. And finally, Chen said, education had to inspire thinking (not memorizing) and involve the whole body.

Without necessarily swallowing whole Chen's excessively idealized vision of Western education,[62] Chinese educational circles were welcoming a slow but steady return of Chinese students from American universities, where they had fallen under the spell of the progressive school movement.[63] Chinese graduates of Teachers College at Columbia University proved especially influential in promoting school reform. John Dewey himself toured China for two years between 1919 and 1921, as what was originally to have been a brief lecture series became a visiting professorship.[64] Dewey spoke on political theory, science, and philosophy, but above all on education. Chinese educators, including many of his own students, listened intently, and many of Dewey's voluminous writings on education were quickly translated. All of these factors led to a new consensus on school reform, which the presidential office approved in late 1922.[65] Primary school was to be 6 years (divided into lower primary and higher primary segments of 4 years and 2 years, respectively), junior middle school 3 years, and higher middle school 3 years. The Ministry of Education also envisioned that primary school graduates might go on to 6-year normal schools or vocational programs. Students who started at age 6 would graduate at age 18. This was to follow the American model of the day. More emphasis was to be placed on teaching students to work with their hands and become involved in community activities. The curriculum was designed to be taught in a flexible way, and class time was reduced (to as low as 18 hours per week for first and second grades). Schools and teachers were largely on their own in figuring out precisely how many hours to devote to each subject; students were not to take every subject every year. But on average the weekly schedule would have looked something like this:[66]

---

[62] For example, Chen stated that Montessori's methods were universally adopted.

[63] Some of the changes are discussed in Ruth Hayhoe, "Cultural Tradition and Educational Modernization"; and Gang Ding, "Nationalization and Internationalization." See Lawrence A. Cremin, *The Transformation of the School.*

[64] John Dewey's ideas on progressive education were particularly influential in China, because of the general promotion of his thought by the prominent intellectual (and Dewey student) Hu Shi and other educational leaders, and as a result of the popularity of Dewey's extended lecture tour. See Robert W. Clopton and Tsuin-chen Ou, eds. and trans., *John Dewey: Lectures in China*; Barry Keenan, *The Dewey Experiment in China*; and Takada Yukio, "Minkokuki kyōiku," pp. 147–175.

[65] Kecheng jiaocai yanjiusuo, ed., *20 shiji Zhongguo zhongxiaoxue kecheng biaozhun*, vol. 1, pp. 105–107.

[66] The curriculum was officially defined in percentages and credits, from which I have estimated hours. Kecheng jiaocai yanjiusuo, ed., *20 shiji Zhongguo zhongxiaoxue kecheng biaozhun*,

Primary schools, grades 1–6 (approximately 24 hours/week)	
Chinese	6–8
Arithmetic	2–3
Society (hygiene, civics, history, geography)	4–6
General science & gardening	2–4
Handicrafts	1–3
Art	1–2
Music	1–2
PE	1–3
Lower middle schools, grades 7–9 (approximately 30 hours/week)	
Society (civics, history, geography)	4
Languages (Chinese, foreign)	12
Mathematics	5
Sciences	2.5
Arts (art, handicrafts, music)	2
PE (physiology, exercise)	2.5
Optional courses and prep	2+
Higher middle schools, grades 10–12 (approximately 30 hours/week)	
Chinese	4
Foreign language	4
Life philosophy	1
Social problems and social sciences	1–2
Cultural history	2–3
Sciences, math, logic	3–6
PE (hygiene, health, exercise)	2–3
Optional courses and prep	10+

The 1922 presidential order emphasized that schools should meet the needs of social progress, reach the commoners, and develop the individual student, among other goals.[67] It might seem there was nothing new in promoting the "spirit of republicanism" or "populism in education" and emphasizing the practical aspects of education – this was the spirit Cai Yuanpei had championed in 1912. But this spirit was being deepened and broadened. In fact, in the 1920s many schools encouraged students to form their own self-governing organizations and find ways to interact with the community.

As early as the mid-1910s, some textbooks tried to highlight the practical aspects of their subject matter. And not surprisingly, textbook writing gradually became more vernacular, abandoning the sometimes rarefied terminology

---

vol. 1, pp. 108–115. The example of higher middle school used here is the humanistic university-preparation model; other specialized schools variously emphasized sciences, commerce, industry, agriculture, household management (girl's schools), and teacher preparation (normal schools).

[67] Kecheng jiaocai yanjiusuo, ed., *20 shiji Zhongguo zhongxiaoxue kecheng biaozhun*, vol. 1, pp. 105–107.

and grammar of the classical tradition. This process reflected a goal reformers had held since the late Qing, although most textbook writers of the day probably regarded a somewhat plain form of classical Chinese (*guwen*) as the most appropriate medium for transmitting knowledge. It could adopt neologisms when necessary while maintaining a continuity with the long tradition of Chinese learning. Also, classical Chinese maintained its prestige as the mark of the educated person, and we might assume that children's families expected their children to learn classical Chinese. Nonetheless, the trend toward vernacularization was inevitable.[68]

In 1923 the ministry mandated curricular reforms that were meant to help teachers put the new pedagogical ideals into practice. Self-cultivation classes were abolished, replaced by civics (or "philosophy of life" and "social problems" in higher middle school). The plethora of separate subjects were combined into six categories: society, language, mathematics, science, art, and PE.[69] However, although it influenced the way textbooks were written, this was a change that looked bigger than it actually was. For example, "society" (*shehui*) was a key concept in Chinese intellectual life: in the late Qing it was used to signify the organic unity of the nation, whereas in the early Republic it suggested a less hierarchical and more integrated entity in contradistinction to the state.[70] Educational interest in society also reflected growing interest in socialism, but perhaps the place of "society" in the curriculum mostly reflected the movement to integrate history and the social sciences in American educational progressivism. Chinese educators wanted to teach the umbrella category of "society" through topical units such as humiliation days, stories of citizens, and the lives of primitive people.[71] But in practice the society course included civics, history, and geography, and textbooks continued to be written on these subjects. "Art" was divided among visual arts, music, and handicrafts. Biology and physics were still taught as separate courses. And so on. In primary school,

---

[68] I return to the vernacular movement in the next chapter on language readers.

[69] This model refers specifically the lower middle school curriculum, but it applied with minor variations to primary and higher middle schools as well. Kecheng jiaocai yanjiusuo, ed., *20 shiji Zhongguo zhongxiaoxue kecheng biaozhun*, vol. 1, pp. 108–115.

[70] See Kai Vogelsang, "Chinese 'Society,'" pp. 155–192; Jin Guantao and Liu Qingfeng, "Cong 'qun' dao 'shehui', 'shehui zhuyi'"; and Michael Tsin, "Imagining 'Society'."

[71] Kecheng jiaocai yanjiusuo, ed., *20 shiji Zhongguo zhongxiaoxue kecheng biaozhun*, vol. 8, pp. 137–138. Formally, "humiliation day" was May 9th, commemorating the date in 1915 when China was forced to agree to Japan's Twenty-One Demands, seen as a blow against Chinese sovereignty. Other humiliation days commemorated military losses to the Western powers from the nineteenth century onward. In other words, humiliation days were a means of building nationalism through a certain kind of modern historical consciousness, which we examine in later chapters. For early Republican educators' views, see Hou Hongjian, "Guoxue, guochi, laoku," pp. 21–24; and Liang Xin, *Guochi shiyao*; for recent historical overviews, see Paul A. Cohen, *Speaking to History*; and William A. Callahan, *China: The Pessoptimist Nation*.

hygiene was also an integral part of the society curriculum. Geography's position was ambiguous: society or science? But either way, in practice it remained a separate subject. The proportion of class time devoted to each subject also changed little from the 1910s.

The next attempt to rewrite the curriculum came at the end of the 1920s as soon as the Nationalists had formed a new government based in Nanjing. Cai Yuanpei, having served as chancellor of Peking University, now returned to a role in national educational policy. But Cai was mostly interested in universities and research; it was Dai Jitao, Sun Yat-sen's long-time secretary now close to Chiang Kai-shek, who led the effort to "nationalize" and "partify" the schools.[72] "Partification" (*danghua*) required compliance in letter and spirit with Guomindang policies, as explained in official exegesis of the Three People's Principles. These principles had been outlined by Sun Yat-sen and become the heart of the Nationalist ideology: nationalism, democracy, and people's livelihood. These principles had motivated some of the revolutionaries in the years before the founding of the Republic. Nationalism originally referred to anti-Manchuism, on the grounds that overthrowing the Qing and returning power to the Han Chinese people would make China a modern nation-state. Now, however, it referred to anti-imperialist policies designed to rid China of unequal treaties and the foreign military presence.

Nationalism or patriotism was, of course, hardly a new ideology for Chinese intellectuals in the 1930s. Late Qing textbooks already emphasized patriotism (*aiguo*), a sentiment that only intensified in the first years of the Republic and was converted into the language of the "nation" (*minzu*) by the Nationalists. The Guomindang was able to ride the tiger of nationalism to power at the end of the 1920s, but they found the tiger to be a dangerous beast.[73] The American Cyrus Peake, when he visited China in 1928–1929 on a Columbia University dissertation fellowship, concluded that "After 1925 the educational system became permeated with the dogmatic and intolerant spirit of modern nationalism," as seen in attacks on Christian, Islamic, Buddhist, and the old-Confucian style schools.[74] This seems to me not wrong but one-sided, ignoring cosmopolitan aspects of education in the 1920s; but it helps us see two points. First, nationalism was a bedrock goal of educational modernizers from

---

[72] Chiu-chun Lee, "Liberalism and Nationalism at a Crossroads."
[73] Richard W. Rigby, *The May 30 Movement*; and Peter Zarrow, *China in War and Revolution*, chapters 10–11.
[74] Cyrus H. Peake, *Nationalism and Education*; quote from p. xii. Peake's fellowship in China corresponded with a high point of nationalist fervor, which no doubt influenced his interpretation of the course of modern schooling. See "The Reminiscences of Cyrus H. Peake." At any rate, textbooks did not shift from a relatively cosmopolitan approach to a relatively nationalist approach until the end of the decade.

its origins. Second, nationalism in the schools, however defined, was subject to ebb and flow depending largely on outside pressures: it is not that there were clear turning points in the growth of an intolerant nationalism. Conversely, a more cosmopolitan emphasis in education, or what Cai Yuanpei called worldview, also ebbed and flowed. Clearly, nationalism came to the fore under direct threat of Japanese invasion in the 1930s, an invasion that finally took place in 1937.

As for the second of the Three People's Principles, democracy, Sun Yat-sen had spent much of the 1920s explaining that it needed to be modified by the doctrine of "tutelage." Tutelage referred to party dictatorship, under which the people would gradually be prepared to build a fully constitutional order. (In Sun's analysis, the 1911 Revolution had failed because the revolutionaries tried to build democratic institutions too quickly.) As we will see, this gave civics textbooks a schizophrenic quality. The third principle of "people's livelihood" referred to something like state-directed economic development rather than socialism, but it contained socialist notions as well. Much school life in the 1930s revolved around Sun's writings and speeches and the official exegesis of the fundamentally ambiguous notions of the Three People's Principles.

If Sun was China's savior, Dai Jitao was his prophet. Dai (1891–1949) was dubious of the utility or even the possibility of pure scholarship; the first function of primary and secondary schools was political inculcation; the second was training for Chinese conditions. In 1929 he proclaimed that the purpose of education was "to unify millions of people into one person, and to center their attention on commonly shared goals."[75] Dai's vision was of education for the masses that would give them basic skills, strong national identity, and also the qualifications to act as citizens. The primary school curricular goals of 1932 were: "as based on the Three People's Principles and in accord with the educational objectives and executive principles, to develop the minds and bodies of children, to foster the moral basis of national morality and the basic knowledge and skills necessary for life, and to build a citizenry which understands propriety and righteousness and loves its nation."[76]

The content of "party doctrine" classes in primary and secondary schools in the 1930s was initially determined by the Party Headquarters, while the rest of the curriculum remained in the hands of the Ministry of Education.[77] As Robert Culp points out, political education and civics classes fostered a vision of the national society as an "organic totality."[78] And at the head of this social

[75] Cited in Cyrus H. Peake, *Nationalism and Education*, p. 305. See also Huang Jianli, *The Politics of Depoliticization in Republican China*.
[76] Kecheng jiaocai yanjiusuo, ed., *20 shiji Zhongguo zhongxiaoxue kecheng biaozhun*, vol. 1, p. 123.
[77] Ibid., vol. 1, p. 116.   [78] Robert Culp, "Setting the Sheet of Loose Sand," p. 49.

body was the ruling party. Yet, while Sun Yat-sen's Three People's Principles almost dominated school life, the 1920-style civics curriculum was revived by the mid-1930s, suggesting the limits of pure ideology. The Nationalist Decade was in the end less about changing the content of education than gradually asserting central control over schools that had been more or less locally run. Not coincidentally, the government was largely successful in its efforts to abolish missionary and private schools.

The lower and higher middle school curriculum of 1929 gave increased attention to math and science, as well as a full complement of courses in Chinese, history, and geography, while party doctrine essentially replaced civics.[79] It was also to be supplemented by non-credit participation in a Party Scouts movement. The 1932 curriculum represented something of an evolution in the thinking of Nationalist educators:[80]

Primary schools (20–26 hours/week)	
Civics	1
Hygiene	1
PE	2.5–3
Chinese	6.5
Society	1.5–3
General science	1.5–2.5
Arithmetic	1–4
Labor	1.5–2.5
Art	1.5
Music	1.5
Lower middle schools (34–36 hours/week)	
Civics	1–2
PE	3
Hygiene	1
Chinese	6
English	5
Mathematics	4–5
Sciences	2–4
History	2
Geography	2
Labor	2–4
Art	1–2
Music	1–2
	(*cont.*)

---

[79] Kecheng jiaocai yanjiusuo, ed., *20 shiji Zhongguo zhongxiaoxue kecheng biaozhun*, vol. 1, pp. 119–122.
[80] Ibid., vol. 1, pp. 123–131.

Higher middle schools (31–34 hours/week)	
Civics	2
PE	2
Chinese	5
English	5
Military drill (years 1–2)	3
Mathematics	3–4
Sciences	5–7
Chinese history (semesters 1–3)	2–4
World history (semesters 4–6)	2
Chinese geography (semesters 1–3)	2
World geography (semesters 4–6)	2
Art	1–2
Music	1

Options to take a second foreign language – Russian, German, French, or Japanese – were also to be available to students. Higher middle school students were also to take one semester of logic.

The publication of recognizably modern textbooks – that is, devoted to particular subjects and aimed at specific age groups – grew from relatively small numbers through the 1890s to a veritable explosion by about 1906. They were used in official schools and, less systematically, in a variety of private schools. This built a new "textual community" of students and teachers reading the same kinds of materials.[81] By 1906, schools could choose among dozens of competing textbooks in particular subjects (upper primary Chinese history, for example, or middle school physics). This multitude of texts simultaneously represented diversification and standardization. Competing editions by different publishers (or the same publishers in the case of larger companies) reveal some different approaches to the subject matter, as we further explore later in the case of Chinese history – but they also show general similarities.

From the beginning of the modern school system, the different class subjects were conceived as overlapping, or at least as contributing to a general set of goals. Language readers, self-cultivation, history, geography: all were to produce patriotic students who rejected bad customs, contributed to their society, and understood China's place in the world.[82] By the 1920s "citizen morality" rested on familiarity with literary and historical cases that illustrated the origins and development of Chinese culture and the Chinese state, on self-cultivation and knowledge of civics that instilled patriotism, and on knowledge of China's natural resources and of the imperialist incursions made against them. Even

---

[81] James Wertsch, *Voices of Collective Memory*, pp. 27–29, 62–65.
[82] Zheng Hang, *Zhongguo jindai deyu*, pp. 190–198.

sciences were to be taught by using Chinese materials to the extent possible. Sometimes trends within the disciplines encouraged a certain blurring of boundaries.

From 1912 onward, the Republican Ministry of Education maintained the late Qing system of inspecting and censoring textbooks.[83] One of its very first actions in the wake of the revolution was to demand that all manuscripts be sent to it before they could be published. As governments came and went through the 1920s, this principle did not change. It is not clear how strictly the weak governments of the day could enforce their dictates, but perhaps the censorship system contributed to the dominance of the few publishers which, with their large editorial staffs, could consistently work with it. Education officials were at least as concerned about the basic quality of textbooks as the threat of political dissent. Indeed, official educational goals were worded vaguely – republicanism remained the legitimating ideology – and so discussions of democratic spirit, civic morality, and even elections were completely acceptable.

After 1928, the Nationalists were in a better position to enforce their decrees, at least in the central provinces.[84] The new government established a new bureaucracy to inspect textbooks, and its curriculum standards were much more detailed than before. The Nationalists never had the capacity to write their own textbooks, and so the major publishers continued to offer all types of competing series compiled in accord with the curricular guidelines. But now the Three People's Principles were to provide the basis of education. More specifically, aside from ensuring the pedagogical quality of textbooks, the Nationalists' main concern was to foster patriotism and stamp out Communism. A long-popular history textbook had to be revised when it was discovered that it offered modest criticism of Yue Fei (1103–1142). Yue Fei was a loyal but arguably feckless Song dynasty general who had become a symbol of patriotism to the Nationalists. Yue Fei had been a last-ditch opponent of the invading northern Jin, putative ancestors to the Manchus, whose overthrow in 1911 the Nationalists claimed as their historic accomplishment.

As for anti-Communism, a directive in 1932 specified that 30 percent of materials for primary school readers should consist of exposing the crimes of Communism, 30 percent of discussing the Three People's Principles, and 40 percent of ordinary materials.[85] However, it should also be noted that the Nanjing government tolerated and even encouraged a certain style of left-wing thinking under the umbrella of the principle of the people's livelihood. The Nanjing government encouraged textbooks to speak of solidarity with

---

[83] Wang Jianjun, *Zhongguo jindai jiaokeshu*, pp. 259–280.
[84] See Son Ansoku, "Nankin kokumin seifu to kyōkasho shintei."
[85] Liu Zhemin, comp., *Jinxiandai chuban xinwen fagui huibian*, p. 338.

workers. It also sought to use the schools to continue the standardization of written and spoken Chinese, and it forbade nonstandard usages.[86]

In spite of all these regulations, looking at education as a whole in China from the 1910s and through the 1930s, the most remarkable feature of schools was their extreme plurality: rural literacy movements; urban night schools; traditional private schools; vocational education; study-abroad programs; the official school system; and universities staffed by faculty with degrees from the finest universities in the world. The textbooks discussed in the following chapters primarily belonged to the official school system, though they spread more sporadically beyond it as well. As Meng Yue points out, if the state schools remained limited in scope and goals, "It was the compilers of textbooks who performed the role of education reformer."[87] That is, they imbued education with a reformist zeal that officials sometimes disdained. In all, critics of the Chinese educational system both at the time and since have accused it of not meeting China's real needs, of too slavishly imitating foreign models, of focusing on the urban middle classes at the expense of the mass of workers and peasants. The Chinese system produced too many alienated, overeducated graduates and exacerbated the urban-rural split, while failing to give the vast majority of Chinese youth the skills they needed in a society undergoing rapid change. Fair enough, though there is only so much any school system can do in times of political chaos, conflict, and war. In fact, China's schools also contributed to the strengths that allowed the Chinese to slowly modernize their commercial institutions, social structure, and political organization, resisting foreign aggression and building a strong state. Much of this process can be read in the textbooks that were produced by the thousands over the first few decades of the twentieth century.

[86] Ibid., p. 341.   [87] Yue Meng, *Shanghai*, p. 45.

2 Reading modern China

Reading primers dealt with a great deal more than literacy. As The *Most Up-to-Date Chinese Textbook* put it, simply knowing how to read was not "true learning."[1] Rather, true learning had to be based on the foundations of the past, which had to be mastered in order to make truly new discoveries.

Thus those engaged in learning must read books. Books are formed out of words, and so scholars must know how to read words. However, the opinion seen today that knowing how to read is learning – is simply wrong. Words are but a tool used in the construction of learning. They are like the axes necessary for the construction of palaces, but you wouldn't put the axes to one side and say, "here is my palace" without having a lot of people laugh at you. The relationship of words to learning is just like this.

Today's scholars say that if you do not learn to read Chinese, you will have no way to understand the writings of the ancient sages, and if you do not learn to read foreign languages, you will have no way to understand the discoveries of prominent persons of the world. This is true! However, if you only know how to read and do not know how to pursue learning, you will not know how to apply these words to government in a fruitful way, you will not know how to apply these words to skilled arts in a useful way, and you will remain a useless person. We hope that those in pursuit of learning today will not puff themselves up merely because they can read.

The new schools had much to do. They were to produce citizens who were moral persons, but they also continued to promote a vision of the scholar in pursuit of useful learning. Notwithstanding this emphasis on the practical, language readers also tried to make room for play and imagination.

As this chapter shows, while language readers did not offer a grand narrative like the rise of China or its place in the world, or a coherent vision of citizenship, or a clear vision of China's future, they did touch on all these topics and more. They thus served to introduce and reinforce the lessons offered in morality, history, and geography classes. Chinese readers talked about almost everything – Chinese and world history and geography, ethics, political institutions and ideas, economics, biology and the other natural sciences, geology and mining, and hygiene – as well as presenting fiction, poetry, and model letters.

---

[1] Gao Fengjian et al., *Zuixin guowen jiaokeshu*, 1: 42a–b.

They offered numerous biographies of prominent Chinese and Western (and occasionally Japanese) figures in history and culture.

Chinese language readers were published in enormous numbers and variety, perhaps more so than the textbooks of any other school subject.[2] From an educator's point of view, language readers offer a wonderful opportunity to accomplish two tasks. While teaching characters and reading (and grammar and writing), they also provide a medium in which educators can slip in lessons about ethics, history, and social life. This was the case for the last thousand years in China. Elementary primers used throughout the Ming and Qing periods required students to memorize – one by one – roughly 2000 characters. The primers were written in simple sentences, often rhymed couples that spoke of simple moral lessons, historical events, and descriptions of Nature and daily life.[3] The next stage of schooling consisted of the Confucian Four Books and Five Classics. Much learning took place by rote, as students chanted passages they did not understand.

The new state schools founded at the beginning of the twentieth century did not at first make a sharp break with this tradition. In her thorough study of language policy, Elisabeth Kaske concludes that the late Qing schools' emphasis on the classics "led to a neglect of literacy education."[4] This is certainly true compared to the emphasis on basic reading and writing skills in other countries at the time. However, a separate if smaller reading curriculum did equip students with basic literacy. A look at Chinese language textbooks shows that in practice basic literacy was a major concern.

Chinese educators learned much from Japanese language readers. These included materials on all sorts of daily life, Confucian morality, foreign relations, and even translations.[5] Readers at lower grade levels were written in kana, as Chinese characters were gradually introduced. Upper level courses used traditional "Chinese" materials, but readings variously touched on history, geography, the sciences, and business.

As early as 1904, the Commercial Press, which adapted many Japanese readers wholesale, promised to teach basic literacy by introducing first-grade students to 12 new Chinese characters in every lesson (Figure 2).[6] Each lesson was to be taught over two days, giving students a chance to learn how to use the new characters. Character learning was to begin with items of daily life

---

[2] Namiki Yorihisa, "Shinmatsu minkoku kokubun."
[3] Limin Bai, *Shaping the Ideal Child*, chapter 2; Alexander Woodside, "Real and Imagined Continuities." Of the three most commonly used primers, one – the *Hundred Names* – consisted simply of about 400 surnames.
[4] Elisabeth Kaske, *The Politics of Language*, p. 250; see chapter 4, esp. pp. 294–316, for late Qing curriculums and textbooks.
[5] Kaigo Tokiomi and Naka Arata, *Kindai Nihon kyōkasho sōsetsu*, pp. 137–161.
[6] Jiang Weiqiao and Zhuang Yu, *Zuixin guowen jiaokeshu* 2: "Bianji dayi" 編輯大意, 1a.

Figure 2 "Recognizing characters and learning characters; from the simple to the complex" – a late Qing Chinese class.

that students were already familiar with: person, dog, boy, girl, and so forth. Language readers introduced students to the natural world and to society: from spiders and sparrows to swings and sewing. Such information was conveyed piecemeal, but it began to explain as well as name phenomena that were part of children's lives. The earth was round and traveled around the sun, producing the seasons. Dew was formed out of the moisture in the air by temperature differentials. Plants grew from seeds. And as Robert Culp has shown, language readers also adopted new terms associated with political reform (such as "citizen" and "constitution") and the experiences of new phenomena that children might have ("park" and "railroad").[7]

One of the few textbooks ever published directly by the Ministry of Education was the *Easy Character Recognition Textbook* of 1909. Shen Guowei has suggested that the textbook's format – simple declarative sentences to introduce basic vocabulary – was like that of traditional primers, while it also introduced new terms for citizenship training.[8] It spoke of the state's production of its

---

[7] Robert Culp, "Teaching *Baihua*."
[8] Shen Guowei, "Guanyu Qing xuebu bian, *Jianyi shizi keben*."

citizens, and their corresponding duty to pay taxes and serve as soldiers. The overall political tone, however, remained that of Confucian paternalism. The more successful readers produced by private publishers minimized exhortation and maximized story telling. Narratives – stories with a beginning, middle, and end, no matter how short – became the chief vehicle for teaching reading and writing.

The reading and classics curriculum

The regulations for primary schools of 1902 and 1904 proposed that students be introduced to the simpler classics slowly, and given simple explanations of their meanings. Moreover, a separate class four hours per week would introduce the reading and writing of characters, and simple grammar.[9] For example, first-year students were to read or memorize some 40 characters a day, second-year students 60 characters, and so on, devoting nearly half the school day to this purpose. Second-year students were to begin composing sentences, and by graduation in the fifth grade, students were expected to be able to compose simple letters. They were also expected to be familiar with some of the simpler classical poems, including the *yuefu* (a pseudo-folk style), and lyrical poetry of the Tang and Song masters, all of which could be sung or recited as an aid to memory. As in the traditional curriculum, students would spend much time memorizing and reciting essentially sacred texts whose language and meaning were indivisible.

Higher primary school Chinese classes were increased to 8 hours per week, while classics reading was maintained at 12.[10] Students were expected to learn how to interpret classical texts and begin writing in the classical style. They were to learn to write in the regular script, as well as to speak Mandarin (*guanhua* or the "official language"). By the time they graduated, students were to be able to write short essays and also to write in the running style of calligraphy. Chinese classes were also the place to continue the study of poetry, but the overall emphasis was on expository writing – not unlike the kind of essays used in the examination system.

The new primers of the 1890s produced by private schools had been somewhat of a hodgepodge, and some assumed that students were already familiar with basic characters. As Elisabeth Kaske has argued, the late Qing emphasis on classics reading detracted from efforts to impart basic literacy.[11] However, the Commercial Press did begin publishing primers that did not assume any literacy on the part of beginning students as the new school system lumbered into

---

[9] Kecheng jiaocai yanjiusuo, ed., *20 shiji Zhongguo zhongxiaoxue kecheng biaozhun*, vol. 3, pp. 3–7.
[10] Ibid., vol. 3, pp. 8–10.   [11] Elisabeth Kaske, *The Politics of Language*, pp. 250–253.

operation in 1904. Thus the editors worked out their own system. They decided to begin with simple and common characters.[12] Each lesson highlighted new characters, and later lessons repeated them. Illustrations were important, and the editors thought hard about what terms would be most accessible to young readers. As well, as Robert Culp has pointed out, the textbooks combined the classical style with the modern neologisms that constitutional reformers had been popularizing for a decade in order – in higher grades – to talk about "citizens," "democracy," "patriotism," "progress," as well as more ordinary terms like "railroad" and "parks" and the like.[13] Language readers thus, regardless of the expectations of Qing officials, taught both basic literacy and lessons about political reform. The Commercial Press readers with their carefully graded lessons of gradually increasing complexity came to dominate the market. They also pushed educators to devote more hours to basic reading and writing than the official curriculum originally envisioned. Or perhaps they were meeting a growing demand for this.[14] In any case, a new mode of language learning was taking shape.

The late Qing curriculum scheduled middle school Chinese classes three to four hours per week and continued to emphasize writing and grammar.[15] But it was also at this level that publishers in effect began to fashion a new literary canon, as Michael Gibbs Hill has shown.[16] The Commercial Press invited Lin Shu – a well-known, reform-minded, and best-selling translator – to compile a set of middle school readers. These reflected Lin's devotion to a particular genre of classical Chinese, the ancient-style prose (*guwen*), at the expense of prominent writers using other historical genres such as parallel prose. For training students this was a reasonable approach, because ancient-style prose was flexible, could absorb neologisms, and in fact was associated with the late Qing reform movement. However, it also ignored vast swathes of Chinese literature. Indeed, as in the traditional education, the new schools slighted imaginative literature and neglected fiction and poetry.

In the wake of the 1911 Revolution, the new Ministry of Education defined the goals of Chinese (*guowen*) teaching in the primary schools as instilling the knowledge of commonly used characters, promoting the ability to express thoughts, and fostering intelligence and morality.[17] (Self-expression and creativity were not among its goals.) Language readers were to contain "interesting" lessons based on self-cultivation, history, geography, and science, and

---

[12] Jiang Weiqiao, "Bianyi xiaoxue jiaokeshu zhi huiyi," pp. 141–143.
[13] Robert Culp, "Teaching *Baihua*," pp. 7–8. [14] Wang Jiarong, *Minzuhun*, pp. 73–75.
[15] Kecheng jiaocai yanjiusuo, ed., *20 shiji Zhongguo zhongxiaoxue kecheng biaozhun*, vol. 3, pp. 268–269.
[16] Michael Gibbs Hill, "National Classicism."
[17] Kecheng jiaocai yanjiusuo, ed., *20 shiji Zhongguo zhongxiaoxue kecheng biaozhun*, vol. 1, pp. 63–64; vol. 3, p. 11.

other materials relevant to the students' lives. Girls' readers were also to include materials relevant to family life. The ministry stressed the need for materials simple enough for students to understand, but did not specify more exact standards. The middle school Chinese curriculum was a continuation of this approach. Above all, with the abolition of classics classes, more time was created for literacy and literature. By no means did the classics disappear, and a 1916 regulation referred to their twinned uses: conveying the correct doctrines of the sages and instilling the spirit of patriotism.[18]

In 1920, the Ministry of Education formally announced that all primary school textbooks should now be written in the vernacular – that is, "official dialect" (*guanhua*), which was based roughly on Beijing speech but not exactly the common vernacular. This was not a decision that came out of the blue. The last few years of the Qing had seen increasing calls from educational circles to stress basic literacy – vernacular as well as classical – and to reduce or even abolish classics reading in the primary schools.[19] Against conservative opposition, curricular reforms in the 1910s headed in this direction. With the abolition of classics-reading classes, the use of the vernacular had inevitably spread. The "victory" of the Beijing dialect, suitably cleaned up and modified by certain southernisms, was probably inevitable given the centrality of the "official dialect" among Chinese elites for generations. One advantage it offered students was the introduction of punctuation, which was not used in classical writing.

The victory of vernacular over classical in the schools was part of a larger movement. In 1917 the young intellectual Hu Shi had called for "literary reform," demanding that writing be simple, substantial, and straightforward. He did not actually call for use of the "vernacular" at this point (and wrote his essay in good classical style), but he condemned use of classical allusions, stereotypical expressions, and parallel couplets. Hu Shi was not the first Chinese to think that the meanings of literacy and literature must change if China was to become modern.[20] Liang Qichao had advocated "new fiction" in 1902, arguing that the traditionally disdained genre of stories and novels could help "renew" the people, his central concern being to strengthen China by strengthening its people.[21] Liang was confident that fiction – properly written – had the power to educate and morally improve its readers.

Whether Hu's essay of 1917 is seen as a culmination of trends of the day or a new battle cry, its effect was enormous. In the New Culture movement of the 1910s, radicals demanded an entirely "new literature" that would be straightforward rather than flowery, relevant to modern life rather than

---

[18] Ibid., vol. 3, p. 12.   [19] Elisabeth Kaske, *Politics of Language*, pp. 86–94.
[20] See Zhang Zheying, *Qingmo minguo shiqi yuwen jiaoyu*.
[21] See Alexander Des Forges, "The Uses of Fiction," pp. 341–347.

following turgid formulas, and vernacular rather than classical in style. The New Culture intellectuals wanted to promote democracy and universal education, and they instantly saw that vernacular schooling would help them in their fight against Confucianism and old cultural habits. They regarded the classics, with their extraordinarily difficult vocabulary and grammars, as a barrier that prevented most Chinese from fully participating in the life of their community. In this time of enormous intellectual ferment, some proposed that Chinese written characters be abolished and replaced by a syllabary (like Japanese kana) or the Latin alphabet.[22]

It is interesting to note that although the new literature movement was anti-Confucian, it did not sever the link between literature and morality: it merely changed their contents. It may have even inherited traditional attitudes that in some sense we *are* what we read and write. A deeply held presumption of the traditional Confucian view of education was that reading – literature in all its forms and connotations of civilization (*wen*) – was inextricably intertwined with the Way. If children were to be taught that reading was merely instrumental, a means to performing specific tasks, then much of the original significance of *literature* would be lost.

In fact, the vernacular movement faced a tension between the real vernacular languages spoken all over China, often in mutually incomprehensible dialects, and the idea of a unified national vernacular. For many students, the "national language" may have been as foreign as the classical style, or even more so. Nonetheless, by the 1920s textbook publishers were ready to make the switch.[23] Indeed, in practice much of the standardization of modern Chinese depended on the decisions of textbook publishers, as Robert Culp has argued, and not on the Ministry of Education or university-based linguists.

The new "liberal" curriculum of 1923 established the goals of primary school Chinese classes as learning the common language, instilling an interest in reading, cultivating the ability of self-expression, nourishing the children's characters, and inspiring their imagination and intellect.[24] In effect, the definition of literature was broadened to include more fiction, drama, and poetry. In the first grades, learning to read was to be based on children's stories, songs, and riddles; higher grades also moved on to historical tales, fiction, and poetry, and finally some classical Chinese could be taught in the sixth grade. In middle schools, the goals were to give students the ability to freely express themselves, read classical texts, and develop an interest in Chinese literature, while higher middle school graduates were also expected to be able to write in classical

---

[22] These debates are described in John DeFrancis, *Nationalism and Language Reform in China*; and Elisabeth Kaske, *Politics of Language*, pp. 391–458.
[23] Robert Culp, "Teaching *Baihua*," pp. 18–31.
[24] Kecheng jiaocai yanjiusuo, ed., *20 shiji Zhongguo zhongxiaoxue kecheng biaozhun*, vol. 3, pp. 13–15.

Chinese.[25] Hu Shi, for example, expected middle school students to read and write in a variety of genres. Reading materials for lower middle school students included the traditional novels *Romance of the Three Kingdoms* and *Journey to the West*, but the curriculum really focused on contemporary authors, including translations of Western literature. Drama also covered a lot of territory, ranging from Yuan-Ming classics to modern Western plays. Expository writing was not neglected, and assigned readings included essays by such modern masters of the form as Liang Qichao, Zhang Shizhao, and Hu Shi.[26] Higher middle school students were further expected to read the traditional novels *Water Margin*, *The Scholars*, and *Flowers in a Mirror*, as well as a wide range of philosophical works from the ancient to the modern, and the long poetic tradition. Students were expected to be able to discuss aesthetic values, and even comparative philology was to be on the curriculum.

In the area of Chinese classes, the Nationalist curriculum made few changes to their structure but began to politicize their content.[27] The 1929 curriculum was explicit. Schools were not to teach materials contrary to Guomindang principles, and they were to actively seek to raise the national spirit, democracy, and people's livelihood. Readings should be optimistic and liberating, not pessimistic and constraining. They should stress cooperation, courage, labor, and law: not selfishness and laziness. The 1932 regulations for primary schools spoke even more specifically about the need to "use materials that convey the spirit of sacrifice and mutual aid, in accord with Guomindang principles. All materials conveying selfishness, profiting, stealing, fighting, retreating, negativity, constraint, feudal thought, aristocratic tendencies, capitalism, and the like – must be weeded out." Acceptable were materials relating to the life of Sun Yat-sen and the revolution; the flags of party and state and the official memorial days and humiliation days (remembrances of revolutionary heroes and imperialist aggression, respectively); the evils of superstition; national products (reflecting the movement to buy Chinese); and cooperative labor and consumer schemes; and so forth. Middle schools were to add a unit on the need to reform social conditions.[28] In other words, middle school students were being taught to move beyond family and school to the larger society.

In addition to the formal schools, China saw various efforts to teach basic literacy outside the classroom. Chinese governments and intellectuals never assumed that formal schooling would solve the problem of illiteracy. They

---

[25] Ibid., vol. 3, pp. 274–281.
[26] Robert Culp demonstrates that the textbooks produced according to this curriculum did much to establish the writings of the young intellectuals themselves as a new canon – "Teaching *Baihua*," pp. 31–39.
[27] Kecheng jiaocai yanjiusuo, ed., *20 shiji Zhongguo zhongxiaoxue kecheng biaozhun*, vol. 3, pp. 16–29.
[28] Ibid., vol. 3, pp. 282–295.

knew that, public or private, schools for children were elite institutions. As early as 1909, the Qing's Ministry of Education published a literacy manual for adults. This was conceived as part of the move toward constitutional government.[29] In six volumes, this textbook was designed to provide a level of literacy equivalent to that of a lower primary school graduate. By the 1920s, literacy campaigns were conducted as part of popular, vocational, and mass educational efforts, frequently through the private auspices of Chinese educators, the YMCA and YWCA, and in the 1930s the Nationalist government.[30]

To be filial and loyal

Language readers naturally featured numerous stories illustrating filial piety. The Commercial Press's main textbook told of a nine-year-old named Huang Xiang. Huang, in actual fact a Han dynasty official of the second century who had turned up in both the *Twenty-four Filial Exemplars* and the *Trimetrical Classic* – popular texts from the thirteenth century – fanned his father's bed in the summer and warmed it up for him in the winter (Figure 3).[31]

A "Song to Teach Filiality" told of the swallows who assiduously fed their young, flying back and forth to the nest with insects until their poor wings were tired (Figure 4).

Filial piety was not merely a personal virtue: it was a political ethic. The *Elementary Primer* contained a lesson on "heresy" that criticized the ancient philosophers Yang Zhu, who denied rulers, and Mozi, who denied fathers.[32] Students learned that these improper views were in contrast to Confucius, who advocated loyalty to the ruler and filiality to parents. "We respect Confucius as our teacher, and in learning the teachings of Confucius cannot fall into heresy." The reformers behind the *Elementary Primer* wanted neither revolution nor a new morality, however much they supported reform.

Language readers presented filial piety always as an eternal and unchanging virtue. Such was not the case with patriotism, which was always a virtue but one expressed in different ways at different times.

Patriotism and Chinese history

The *Elementary Primer* published by the Sandeng Public Academy of Wuxi, a hotbed of educational reform in the first years of the twentieth century not far

---

[29] Elisabeth Kaske, *Politics of Language*, pp. 283–286; Shen Guowei, "Guanyu Qing xuebu bian *Jianyi shizi keben*."
[30] See Charles W. Hayford, *To the People*.
[31] Zhuang Yu, *Guoyu jiaokeshu*, 1: 58–59. As discussed later, this story was also used in a Commercial Press self-cultivation textbook.
[32] *Mengxue duben quanshu sanbian*, 3: 37b–38a.

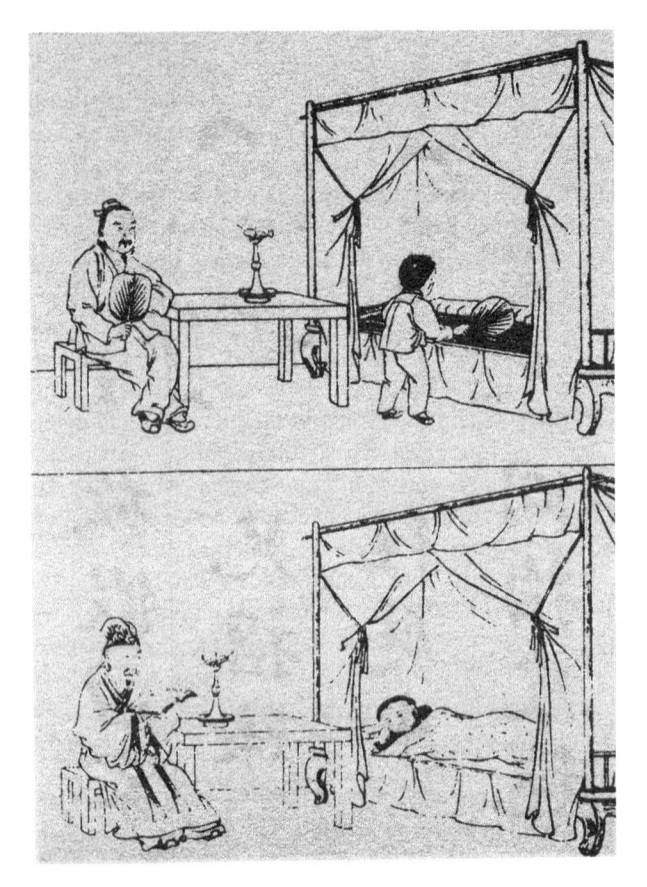

Figure 3 Huang Xiang fans and warms his father's bed. This simple image shows a traditional bedroom of a gentry family.

upriver from Shanghai, reflected reformers' concerns: love of country, strengthening the Qing dynasty, and developing the economy.³³ It began, "Great Qing is the name of state of our dynasty. Our country is located in the southeastern part of Asia," and so forth.³⁴ It taught a song of celebration for China – a "sleeping lion" – that also noted the rise of "imperialism" and the destruction of India and Poland.³⁵ The Qing dynasty was not described as a foreign conquest but the result of the fall of the Ming to banditry, which the Qing was able to repress and thereby finally restore order.³⁶ Moving back to the "origins of Chinese culture," *Elementary Primer* focused on the Yellow Emperor and highlighted the

---

³³ Ibid., 3: *yuezhi* 約悋, 1a–2a. See Wang Jianjun, *Zhongguo jindai jiaokeshu*, pp. 92–105.
³⁴ *Mengxue duben quanshu sanbian*, 3: 1a.   ³⁵ Ibid., 3: 1b.   ³⁶ Ibid., 3: 5a–b.

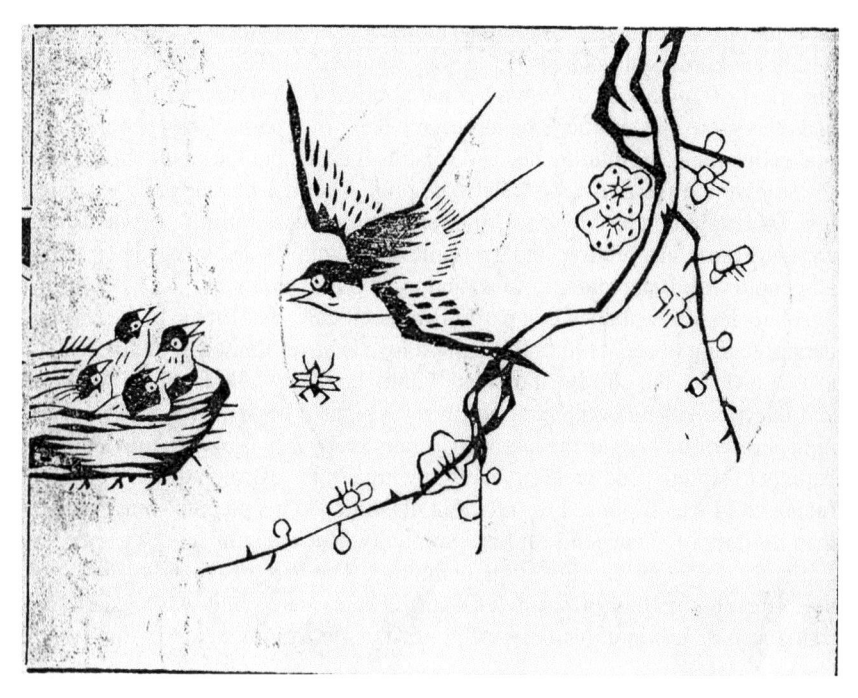

Figure 4 Good parenting is the root of filial piety.

achievements of the whole panoply of sage-kings who created the basic institutions of civilization.[37] It also described the rise of new dynasties in terms of the need to punish evil kings of the previous dynasty and establish justice.

A Commercial Press textbook for upper-level primary students presented a considerably more sophisticated explanation of patriotism. It began with an explanation of "extended love" (*boai*), a term rooted in the Confucian notion of love extending out from family relations and also at this time used to translate the more radical notion of "fraternity" from the French Revolution. The textbook reflected both senses, with a nationalist thrust.[38] The lesson argued as follows. The tendency to love is innate. It takes different forms, such as filial piety toward parents, friendly feelings toward siblings, or trust among friends, but is at root the same phenomenon. As children grow, they learn to extend their love from the family circle to their circle of friends, but this is still a limited form of love. Mencius spoke of the universality of feelings of commiseration, so, in terms of the world, all persons should be treated with this ethic. In terms of the

---

[37] Ibid., 3: 17b–18a.
[38] Gao Fengqian, Zhang Yuanji, and Jiang Weiqiao, *Zuixin guowen jiaokeshu*, 1: 34a–35a.

race, the entire Yellow race should be united in amity. In terms of the nation, all within the borders should be regarded as compatriots. The lesson then offered historical exemplars of an empathy that abolished the boundary between self and others – so that another's pains became one's own pains. Now, people's natural endowments of intelligence and wealth all differ, but the smart should help the stupid, and the rich should help the poor. The true meaning of "extended love" was captured by Mencius, who said that the superior man "treats his parents with familial affection, and treats all people with Benevolence; and treating all people with Benevolence, he is kind to all living creatures."[39]

A later lesson explained that patriotism specifically was rooted in the entirely natural feeling of self-love.[40] But natural love is never limited to the individual self. It includes the child's immediate family and his whole circle of relatives, and the friends who help teach him what is right. The *Most Up-to-Date Chinese Textbook* had begun the lesson in a completely orthodox way, moving from parents to siblings and creating ever-growing circles of community. The Confucian child was supposed to infer that his duties to his parents were stronger than his duties to his friends or his community. However, the reader went on to explicitly deny this interpretation, claiming, "The love of [friends] should be no different from that of family and kin." The modern child was to learn that righteousness lies in defending and protecting the nation.

> Now, the extension of the family is the clan (*jiazu*), and the extension of the clan is the nation (*minzu*). When this happens, government is established to control [the nation], and this is called the state (*guojia*). States are great assemblages of clans. Therefore, the stalwart hero's love of his country is like his love of his family. A humiliation inflicted on the country is a matter of personal shame. A defeat inflicted on the nation is a personal defeat.

Part of the force of this lesson stemmed from the linguistic elements shared among the terms of clan, nation, and state (*zu* and *jia*). It attempted to find a psychological and moral basis for a patriotism sought by late Qing reformers that, they thought, the Chinese people had thus far failed to realize. Whether the family, in particular clan structures, could form the basis of national feeling or in fact hindered its development was to become a matter of debate in the 1910s. The point here, however, is how identification between family and nation leads to a personal sense of humiliation and defeat. The rhetoric of humiliation became ever more prominent in the twentieth century, and we will find it in readers, history textbooks, and morality and civics textbooks.

Language readers could convey a sense of the continuous history of China from ancient times more efficiently than history textbooks, because they could

---

[39] *Mencius* 7A45.
[40] Gao Fengqian, Zhang Yuanji, and Jiang Weiqiao, *Zuixin guowen jiaokeshu*, 2: 1a–2b.

sum it all up in a few words, telling students who they were. China's was a story that began with sage-kings and the gradual construction of civilization: farming, calendars, the Han conquest of the Miao people and rule over the Chinese homeland, peace and order.[41] Over centuries, the feudal dynastic system fell apart, until finally Qin Shihuang united the polity and also centralized monarchical control (221 BCE). Interestingly, the reader broke with traditional Confucian condemnation of Qin Shihuang, instead praising his military achievements in enlarging China. All blame for the collapse of the Qin was placed on the immorality of his successor. Covering the next 2000 years, a list of dynasties and foreign invasions followed; then the Qing arose to suppress the banditry that had spread during the last years of the Ming. Qing territories had steadily expanded until recently, when foreign powers began to occupy frontier regions and threaten the state. In line with reformist goals, the purpose of such passages was to arouse student's energies to defend their country.

The ancient sage-kings were also a frequent topic of language readers. These mythical creatures – which history textbooks began to treat as "legends" rather than purely historical persons by the 1920s – represented the origins of China. A China Bookstore reader described the Yellow Emperor as the first of the lords to be named emperor, upon his conquest of his enemies.[42] The Yellow Emperor also invented boats and carts, clothing, and writing, in this account, while his wife the empress taught the people how to raise silkworms for silk. A later sage-king, Yu the Great, tamed the great floods. So busy was he in this task for some 13 years that even though he passed his own house, he never went in. The sitting emperor, Shun, then abdicated the throne in favor of Yu. Later lessons in the China Bookstore readers returned to Yu to continue the story through the creation of China's first ruling houses.[43] In this version, often taught in late Qing history textbooks as well, upon Yu's death the people wished his son to succeed him, and thus was the principle of inheritance of the throne established. This became the Xia dynasty. But after four centuries, an evil descendant became emperor, and he was overthrown. A new clan came to the throne, establishing the Shang dynasty. But again, this time after six centuries, an evil emperor emerged – killing, torturing, imposing heavy taxes – and he was overthrown and the new Zhou dynasty established.

Language readers could teach patriotism via microhistory as well, for example, offering models for students to admire and perhaps emulate. A China Bookstore language reader told of the general Yue Fei's many victories against the invading Jin people in the twelfth century.[44] In this account, Yue Fei was betrayed by an evil official, his mission failed, and the Jin pushed back the

---

[41] Jiang Weiqiao and Zhuang Yu, *Zuixin guowen jiaokeshu*, 9: 37b–41a.
[42] Shen Yi et al., *Zhonghua guowen jiaokeshu*, 7: 1b–2a.
[43] Ibid., 7: 8b–9b.   [44] Ibid., 11: 6b–7a.

armies of the Chinese Song dynasty. Because the Manchus were not only like the Jin insofar as they were northern invaders, and even claimed descent from the Jin, the Qing dynasty had had little use for Yue Fei. However, he became a hero to anti-Manchu revolutionaries, and the late Qing saw a revival of his cult. Textbooks have continued to burnish his image ever since.

Geography and race

The Commercial Press reader defined Chinese identity in time and space:

This China of ours is located in the eastern part of Asia. It has a temperate climate, a large territory, and numerous people. Five thousand years ago, China's civilization was already advanced, and it was the most well known of all the ancient countries of the world. We have been living here since our ancient ancestors, clothing ourselves and finding food here through the generations. If you are a Chinese, how can you not love China?[45]

A few years later, after the founding of the Republic, the China Bookstore reader contained an almost identical passage. Aimed at beginning third-graders, it went on: "However, in the last century, China became ever weaker and people's lives ever more difficult. Today, political reform for the sake of the people is truly enabling every person to fulfill their duties to their utmost, and future progress will be beyond measurement."[46]

The late Qing *Elementary Primer*, in addition to lessons on world geography, also included a lesson on races that foreshadowed generations of geography, history, and civics textbook lessons on the subject.[47] It linked the five major races of the world – Yellow, White, Red, Black, and Brown – to their native places: northeast Asia, Europe and west Asia, the Americas, the southern oceans, and Africa respectively. It further pointed out that the Red, Black, and Brown peoples had lost their territories, while the White race was on the verge of seizing the lands of the Yellow race. In this way, *Elementary Primer* reflected the general understanding of educated Chinese of the day, who foresaw a great race struggle, certainly commercial and possibly violent, between the White and Yellow races for world dominance. So, too, the Commercial Press' *Most Up-to-Date Chinese Textbook*, which explicitly told students that the Chinese must resist the threat from the White nations.[48]

Various illustrations of the world's "five races" appeared in readers, geography, civics, and history textbooks. In Figure 5, the representative of the Yellow race appears dominant while the three races sometimes dismissed as having no

---

[45] Jiang Weiqiao and Zhuang Yu, *Zuixin guowen jiaokeshu*, 4: 18a–b.
[46] Shen Yi et al., *Zhonghua guowen jiaokeshu*, 7: 1a–b.
[47] *Mengxue duben quanshu sanbian*, 3: 32b–33b.
[48] Jiang Weiqiao and Zhuang Yu, *Zuixin guowen jiaokeshu*, 9: 52a–b.

Figure 5 The world's races by skin color: White, Yellow, Red, Black, and Brown.

future appear in the lower half of the drawing. Readers generally equated the Yellow race with the Chinese and spoke in alarmed tones of the threat from the White race.

In the early Republic, the Chinese people were simultaneously described as one, and as divided among five races or ethnicities: Han, Manchu, Mongol, Hui (Muslim), and Tibetan. A key political slogan defined China as the "unified republic of five races." A China Bookstore language reader included a lesson defining these races in terms familiar in late Qing political discourse.[49] Although dispersed and culturally distinct, the five groups lived together

[49] Shen Yi et al., *Zhonghua guowen jiaokeshu*, 11: 14a–b.

harmoniously, sharing their joys and sorrows, heedless of boundaries. Readers thus used geography to describe the pluralistic unity of China and the threats it faced from outside. A 1927 China Bookstore textbook told the story of little Peng Fu, who happily drew a map of the extensive territories of the old Qing Empire.[50] But his father gave him detailed advice on coloring the map for the present-day: red in the northeast, yellow in the south, blue in the southeast, white for Taiwan, Korea, the Ryukyus and the Pescadores, and black for Macao. Peng Fu happily colored away, but when he asked why, his father just sighed: each color represented a different power that had stolen those territories. After his father had also explained about all the concessions over which China had lost control, Peng Fu felt like crying. But his father said, "Feeling bad is useless and will harm your body, and then you will never be able to recover the lost territories and concessions. You youth all need to make yourselves stronger, more moral, and more knowledgeable to become useful – and then when the entire nation no longer has any weak elements, it will take back the lost territories. This is the responsibility of you youth."

Political values

Language readers of the late Qing were quick to convey new ideas about the nature of the state. A lesson in the Commercial Press's *Most Up-to-Date Chinese Textbook* described the mutual dependence of the people and their political organization. The people establish the state, which they then depend on for their very survival. The state protects the people and deserves their loyalty and even their willingness to sacrifice their lives for it. Ultimately, the lesson concluded, the strength of the state depends on the patriotism of the people. In this way, the reader restated what radical reformers – like the journalist and activist Liang Qichao (1873–1929) – had been saying for 10 years, even using the same vocabulary. These views had once been on the margins of acceptable opinion, for by implication they made the emperor a secondary concern rather than the prime focus of loyalty. But textbooks demonstrate that such views had become mainstream. The very next lesson of the *Most Up-to-Date Chinese Textbook* continued to voice Liang's earlier concerns, in particular the need for unity. To resist foreign pressures and incursions, it implied, mere patriotic sentiment was not enough; rather, "If all the classes united their efforts, then China could hold the entire world at bay."[51] The 1913 edition emphasized that unity was especially important in a republic.

In the late Qing, upper primary and middle school textbooks published selections of past writings, for which students by the sixth grade and up were

---

[50] Li Jinhui and Lufei Kui, *Guoyu duben*, 8: 23–28.
[51] Gao Fengqian, Zhang Yuanji, and Jiang Weiqiao, *Zuixin guowen jiaokeshu*, 2: 3a.

deemed ready. Such anthologies included the writings of reformers since the mid-nineteenth century. The Civilization Press anthologies were quite political. The selections in a reader for upper primary students, for example, featured the relatively cautious reformism of the generation of statesmen who came of political age after the Opium War, but also included critiques of monarchism.[52] Three essays dealt with the notions of natural rights and democracy.[53] They were published without the author's name, but they were translations from the writings of the Japanese liberal Miyama Toratarō. He argued that "popular power" or "people's rights" (*minquan*) rested on the people's natural endowments, which enable their survival. This is why the people possess political powers or rights. Such rights, stemming from birth, are inviolable, and monarchs may not deprive their subjects, nor fathers deprive their children, nor husbands deprive their wives of their rights. In my copy of the reader, a student's hand has scrawled, "Popular power, that is democracy (*minzhu*), also called republicanism." Miyama's essays argued that absolutism inevitably weakened the state because everything depended on the ruler – and many rulers were incompetent. Absolutist systems encouraged the people to regard their ruler as their enemy, and European states had developed systems of "shared rule" (*gongzhi*) that allowed them to break out of the historical cycle of prosperity and collapse and to embark on a road of ever-increasing wealth and power. The implication was that Western constitutional systems were able to harness this popular feeling, whereas Asian despotisms were mired in chaos because of their inability to do so. Of course, what students (and teachers) made of such essays in readers is difficult to say, but it is interesting that in my copy of this particular volume, someone has written more marginal notes on the Miyama essays than on any other essay in the book.

In the first years of the Republic, the Commercial Press's upper primary school reader began with lessons on the structure of government and the significance of China's recent revolution.[54] Its authors described types of government and defined the rights and duties of the people. In absolutist monarchies, they proclaimed, people were merely slaves with neither rights nor duties. The authors linked rights and duties as two sides of the same coin of citizenship, simply not known before the rise of republican thought. Like the morality textbooks of the late Qing that we examine in a later chapter, this reader counted

---

[52] Gu Zhuo, *Guowen duben*.
[53] Ibid., 3: 23b–27b. The essays were modified from Miyama Toratarō's original texts, which achieved wide circulation in Chinese when they were published by Zheng Guanying (1842–1922) in the 1900 edition of his *Shengshi weiyan* 盛世危言 (*Words of Warning to a Prosperous Age*). Zheng probably noticed Miyama's essays when they were first published in Chinese under a title that might be translated *An Outsider's Words of Warning* (*Caomao weiyan* 草茅危言) in Shanghai in 1898 and by Liang Qichao in Tokyo in 1899. See Xiong Yuezhi, *Zhongguo jindai minzhu sixiangshi*, pp. 165–166.
[54] Gao Fengqian, Zhang Yuanji, and Jiang Weiqiao, *Zuixin guowen jiaokeshu*, 1: 1a–5a.

paying taxes, serving as soldiers, and obeying laws as among the first duties of citizens. Educating one's children was also a duty. All these duties contributed to the success of the state. Rights included life, property, reputation, protection of the law, and freedoms of speech and assembly. Such rights were given to all persons, whereas only citizens had the rights to participate in elections and become officials. We should note premises about gender assumed in this reader. The standard notion of a citizen's duty of military service applied to men, not women. Women had participated in the revolution, but after a short debate, the republican assembly restricted suffrage to men. Education, however, was to apply to girls as well as boys.

As for gender roles, a later lesson in the Commercial Press reader spelled out the distinct but complementary roles of men and women:

The human race is divided between male and female just as the body has a right hand and a left hand. Both are hands, and even if the left hand is not as proficient as the right hand, you need the left hand to be a complete person. All are people, and even if the female is less competent than the male, without women it would not be possible to form societies.[55]

The right hand takes food while the left hand holds the bowl, and so the male deals with outside affairs while the female manages the household – or at least this has been the Chinese tradition, this lesson suggested. Actually, the lesson was edging its way to a surprise ending. Just as household duties included accounting, education, and textiles, and so Western women were employed as lawyers and doctors, the apparent gap between the abilities of men and women was shown to be simply a matter of education.

The *Most Up-to-Date Chinese Textbook* described the economy, or China's political economy:

From ancient times it has been said that if a man does not till, he may go hungry, and if a woman does not weave, she may grow cold. Now, a man and a woman are extremely insignificant [by themselves], but whether they are diligent or lazy will affect the entire society. Why is this the case? It is because a person can only engage in one occupation, and that occupation provides a sufficiency [of a particular product] for him and more as well, while that which he still needs must be procured from the people engaged in other occupations. In a given society, this is the case no matter what occupation one engages in. When everyone trades what they have for what they lack, then a rough balance is achieved.[56]

This was to speak of both the division of labor and means of cooperating. Indeed, cooperation was the basis of particular societies, according to the reader, which linked economics back to the definition of a citizen as one who

[55] Gao Fengqian, Zhang Yuanji, and Jiang Weiqiao, *Zuixin guowen jiaokeshu*, 1: 24a–25a.
[56] Gao Fengjian, Zhang Yuanji, and Jiang Weiqiao, *Zuixin guowen jiaokeshu*, 1: 16b–17a.

accepted his responsibilities to the group. (One who refused his responsibilities was simply a parasite).

The reader also presented some of this material in the form of stories. One such story was called "The Advantages of Society."[57] This told of a boy who was a loner. His father warned him, "The survival of a person depends on the group." His son answered that since he couldn't get people to do what he wanted, he preferred to play alone. Furthermore, he would make everything he needed himself: plant his own food, weave his own clothes. His father warned him, however, that it was not so easy. Even if he were to plant his own fields, he would need tools, made out of iron, and "Are you going to open your own mine?" And would he plant his own cotton, set up his loom, use the shuttle? Humans are the most dependent of all the animals, slow to mature, and "isn't the reason why you have been able grow up to this point today, because you have relied on the strength of others?" The boy admitted his defeat and acknowledged the necessity of society.

In contrast to the readers of the Commercial Press, China Bookstore readers for advanced primary students continued to emphasize abstractions such as "liberty." However, this was not to be mistaken for lawlessness. One lesson followed another distinction earlier made by Liang Qichao: civilized liberty is a good thing, but barbarous liberty is not.[58] Civilized liberty consisted in acting within the scope of the law – this was, the reader told children, the true meaning of liberty. Ignorant people excuse their bad behavior in the name of liberty, it said. Liang's fear had been that excessive individual liberty would harm the group; the textbook simplified matters by just telling children to obey the law. In the next lesson, the textbook tried to clarify the concept of "equality."[59] Children should understand that this referred to equality before the law. It did not mean everybody had exactly the same duties and rights, because these depended on the different capacities of individuals. So, too, different achievements merited different awards. Thus to demand equality outside the scope of the law would lead to selfishness and chaos, in this view.

Liberty was thus embedded in the theme of cooperation. A Commercial Press upper primary school reader dealt with this theme in an early lesson on "respect for humanity."[60] In language that turned to the Confucian foundations of personal morality, it said:

As people are born, due to their different natural endowments and their differences in status, differences in rank and wealth are unavoidable. However, they are equally called humans, and so they love their species. If the wealthy oppress the poor or those of high

---

[57] "Hequn zhi li" 合群之利, Gao Fengjian, Zhang Yuanji, and Jiang Weiqiao, *Zuixin guowen jiaokeshu*, 1: 46b–48a.
[58] Shen Yi et al., *Zhonghua guowen jiaokeshu*, 10: 16a–b.   [59] Ibid., 10: 16b–17a.
[60] Gao Fengqian, Zhang Yuanji, and Jiang Weiqiao, *Zuixin guowen jiaokeshu*, 1: 5b–6b.

rank oppress the lowly, the species is harming itself. This is certainly not anything that the benevolent person or the good man can tolerate.

Looking to the future, the reader hoped that the rise of machines promised progress, and condemned the use of humans to pull rickshaws. Furthermore, "the Western countries respect humanity and regard the substitution of human power for animal power in Asia as barbarian and backwards." To look at China through foreign eyes was a typical rhetorical trope of reformist writing.

As the notions of assemblies and parliaments spread in the first years of the Republic, textbooks sought to explain them. A language reader authored by Lü Simian treated the notion not so much in terms of political institutions as a kind of collective thoughtfulness.[61] Lü (1884–1957) is today best known as a historian, but he was a very active educator at all levels of the school system and a prolific editor and textbook author. His lesson on "assemblies" stressed that their advantage came from bringing together a large number of people to consider a question from different viewpoints, but in a spirit of cooperation. "This is why civilized nations esteem assemblies." Lü said that discussions and debates needed to be precise and exhaustive. Given China's problems, "the matters are countless for which it is necessary to rely on the wisdom and strength of the masses." Lü noted that to build the kind of cooperation he had in mind would require a self-restraint on the part of individuals. What Lü had in mind was not a national parliament debating affairs of state, but the people of a neighborhood getting together to figure out how to repair a road. Lü implied that citizenship was to be learned from the bottom up. Lü was hardly a radical scholar by the standards of the day, and his language reflected three strains of thought. It did reflect the populism of the day, while it also reflected the view of late Qing reformers that assemblies were less decision-making bodies than guides to popular sentiment, and it even reflected the officially sanctioned village meetings of imperial China.

A China Bookstore language reader for upper primary students introduced basic economic concepts such as industry, commerce, corporations, and agriculture.[62] Industry here was not defined in terms of mechanized factories but the fundamental process by which human labor transformed natural products into useful items. Raw cotton, for example, must be spun and woven before it can be worn as clothing. But the textbook criticized handicraft industry as slow and difficult, whereas machines make manufacturing efficient. If the Chinese can build more mechanized factories, they will become a wealthier people. Commerce stems from geographical variation – that is, for example, coastal areas and mountain areas produce different things which can be traded for one

---

[61] In Lü Simian, *Minguo guowen keben*, 1: 69.
[62] Shen Yi et al., *Zhonghua (guomin xiaoxue) guowen jiaokeshu*, 11: 9a–12a.

another. "And so as commerce spreads, the people become richer." The textbook emphasized that China's extensive products should put it in a good position in the global trading networks. To do this, however, it was necessary to raise capital, and the corporation was a means to do this. In the case of the unlimited corporation, its shareholders were responsible for all its debts, but they could raise unlimited amounts of money, the textbook explained. In the case of the limited corporation, however, debts were incurred only by the corporation itself, but if these debts amounted to over half of its raised capital, it must declare bankruptcy. With questionable accuracy but in accord with the family orientation of Chinese capitalism, the textbook emphasized the relative freedom of the unlimited corporation.

The China Bookstore language reader also displayed a physiocratic tendency, proclaiming that whereas national wealth depended on manufacturing and commerce, manufacturing and commerce ultimately depended on agriculture. It is thus important to improve knowledge of farming techniques, soil science, botany, hydraulics, fertilizers, chemistry, and the like. Lü Simian also proclaimed that agriculture was the basis of national wealth.[63] He disputed the common assumption that Western nations had become wealthy on the basis of trade; rather, he said, they ceaselessly strove to improve farming techniques. So this is now what China needed to do. However, in a later lesson Lü stressed the importance of industry and the power of machine manufacturing.[64] He took seriously the problem of the relationship between industry and the concentration of capital, and the resulting exacerbation of inequality, but he argued that without industrialization, the entire country was condemned to poverty and would remain vulnerable to outside aggression.

Social etiquette and daily life virtues

Language readers emphasized a range of proper personal behaviors and attitudes that marked the cultivation of the self and benefited society. Such lessons were derived from little stories illustrating proper behavior or, sometimes, improper behavior. The characters in these stories – like the vast majority of students – came from privileged class backgrounds.

One reader explained that when a guest arrived, you should invite him into the house, ask him to sit, and serve him tea.[65] And when he was leaving, you should accompany him to the door, stand outside the door, and bow to him. The frontispiece of the first volume of this China Bookstore series (Figure 6) advertised a book on *Etiquette for Children*, dealing with such questions as "how to be a guest."

---

[63] Lü Simian, *Minguo guowen keben*, 1: 107. [64] Ibid., 2: 83.
[65] Shen Yi et al., *Zhonghua guowen jiaokeshu*, 3: 2a–b.

62   Educating China

Figure 6 "How to be a guest" – China Bookstore publishing company advertisement.

This vision of an afternoon tea party shows a variety of cute and very polite animals sitting on chairs around a dining table by a large picture window. A clearer expression of Westernized middle-class life could hardly be imagined. And the reader went on to suggest that here was a guide to treating foreigners – by way of analogy, foreigners should be treated with all the courtesy due to a guest visiting their homes.[66]

Language readers offered many such lessons in basic propriety. One should, for example, "guard against hastiness."[67] This was illustrated with the famous story of Mencius becoming upset by his wife. In one version, Mencius enters a room to find his wife unclothed. Distressed, Mencius complains to his mother that, "my wife is without propriety." But Mencius's mother says: "It is you who lack propriety. Propriety demands you should ask who is there before entering a room; raise your voice before entering a hall; and lower your gaze when entering a room. This is so that you do not take people unprepared." From this story, the textbook draws the lesson that although husband and wife share a home, behavioral norms cannot be relaxed. The authors emphasized that this is even

---

[66] Ibid., 12: 13b–14a.   [67] Zhuang Yu and Shen Yi, *Xin guowen*, 8: 13b–14a.

more the case when people are not husband and wife, and especially when one is entering another person's house.

Proper public behavior – that is, attention to the needs of others in public venues – was also illustrated by a story about a certain Mr. A.[68] Mr. A was frank and open by nature; he talked loudly and walked big as if there were no one else around him. Mr. B often admonished him. Mr. A says, "This is my liberty. It's of no concern to others." Later, the two men were taking a boat, and the boatmen were making such a clamor that they couldn't hear one another. Mr. A is upset; Mr. B says, "You realize that the noisy boatmen are violating your liberty, but how is your loud talk and arguing any different?" Mr. A says, "I see my mistake." Later, the two men were strolling in a park. Mr. A starts to sing loudly, dancing around. Mr. B says, "Isn't your noise disturbing other people's conversations? And your dancing interfering with other people's walking? Have you forgotten the boatmen?" Mr. A then berates himself.

Gender roles were an important aspect of propriety. Language readers described the activities of girls and women in terms of the family. A China Bookstore reader told of a "mother and daughter in the kitchen," washing the rice and vegetables to make dinner.[69] The Commercial Press illustrated gender and social roles in a story about a mother who wanted to teach her daughter how to cook.[70] The daughter naturally objects that this is servant's work. Her mother replies, "It is the job of women to manage the household. If you do not know how to cook, how can you manage the household?" In another story, the mother tells her daughter that both sexes need to be able to take care of themselves.[71] "Today you don't even know how to weave or embroider – you are really useless. Even if you have lovely clothes and get all dressed up, people who know will look down on you."

Language readers thus made assumptions about the kind of lives that schoolchildren led. They lived with a nuclear family, or at least they could recognize the nuclear family as a model form of the household. They also had servants, as we have seen. A China Bookstore reader told of a boy who abused the family's servant. But his father warned him, "Humans are all equal and fundamentally there is no distinction between noble and base. It is because of poverty that they were forced to become a servant in our family. They work in exchange for payment. This is simply a transaction. How can you mistreat them just because we are wealthy?"[72] This passage was distinctively modern in

---

[68] Ibid., 14a–15a. [69] Shen Yi et al., *Zhonghua guowen jiaokeshu*, 3: 11b.
[70] Zhuang Yu, *Guoyu jiaokeshu* 2: 73.
[71] Ibid.: 2: 89. One lesson in this reader called for gender equality and the independence of women (2: 148–149). Another lesson imparted the message that boys from wealthy families still also needed to be able to take care of themselves, but only lest they squander their patrimony (2: 176–177).
[72] Shen Yi et al., *Zhonghua guowen jiaokeshu*, 6: 20a–b.

its rhetoric ("equality") and its notion of economic exchange as a way of producing equality rather than servitude. If a traditional view of the master-servant relationship valued paternalistic benevolence, the modern view was less about changing proper behavior than offering a new explanation for it.

Numerous lessons in language readers focused on "hygiene," which referred to individual health, public sanitation, and physical exercise. PE classes were closely connected to military drill and the goal of "revering the military." The number of lessons describing boys playing soldiers or practicing military drill is incalculable, but language readers also stressed the medical benefits of exercise.[73] The more you exercise, the better your breathing, the stronger your muscles, and even the higher your intelligence. Contrariwise, if you spend all day hunched over your desk, you will only be able to lift your writing brush.

Hygiene started with care of the self. Language readers described how to get up in the morning; for example, by hanging up your bed curtains, folding your quilt, rinsing your mouth, washing your face, sweeping your room, and wiping off your desk.[74] Few language readers omitted stories about the problems of drink and gambling.[75] The bad effects of tobacco and opium also formed the basis of stories, but less prominently. These were not moral issues so much as simply commonsensical threats to health.

As for PE classes, readers stressed the classical matching of civil and military.[76] As schools in ancient times, it was said, taught archery and charioteering alongside the classic arts, so modern schools teach PE and military drill alongside literature, history, sciences, and math. One lesson went on to complain that for too long Chinese had separated civil and military education, so that scholars were weak while soldiers were ignorant. Today, however, students were to be prepared to defend their country. Another contemporary issue discussed in readers was the problem of footbinding. Although reformers had been criticizing footbinding as harmful to the nation since the 1890s, language readers attacked it for crippling individuals.[77] Fortunately, students were told, the practice was beginning to disappear.

Lü Simian wrote a lesson on the importance of parks.[78] "Civilized nations" all built parks in their cities to give hard-working residents a place to relax and restore themselves. A touch of Nature improved the lives of tightly packed urban residents, but, Lü exhorted, people needed to learn the morals of park visiting. No damaging equipment, no picking flowers, no blowing your nose on the ground, and so forth. Indeed, many language readers contained lessons on public parks, which linked the general theme of hygiene to the concept of

---

[73] Gao Fengjian, Zhang Yuanji, and Jiang Weiqiao, *Zuixin guowen jiaokeshu*, 1: 9a–b.
[74] Shen Yi et al., *Zhonghua guowen jiaokeshu*, 3: 10a.   [75] Ibid., 4: 18b–19a, 10: 14b–15a.
[76] Gao Fengjian, Zhang Yuanji, and Jiang Weiqiao, *Zuixin guowen jiaokeshu*, 1: 28a–29b.
[77] Shen Yi et al., *Zhonghua guowen jiaokeshu*, 6: 10b–11a.   [78] Ibid., 1: 38.

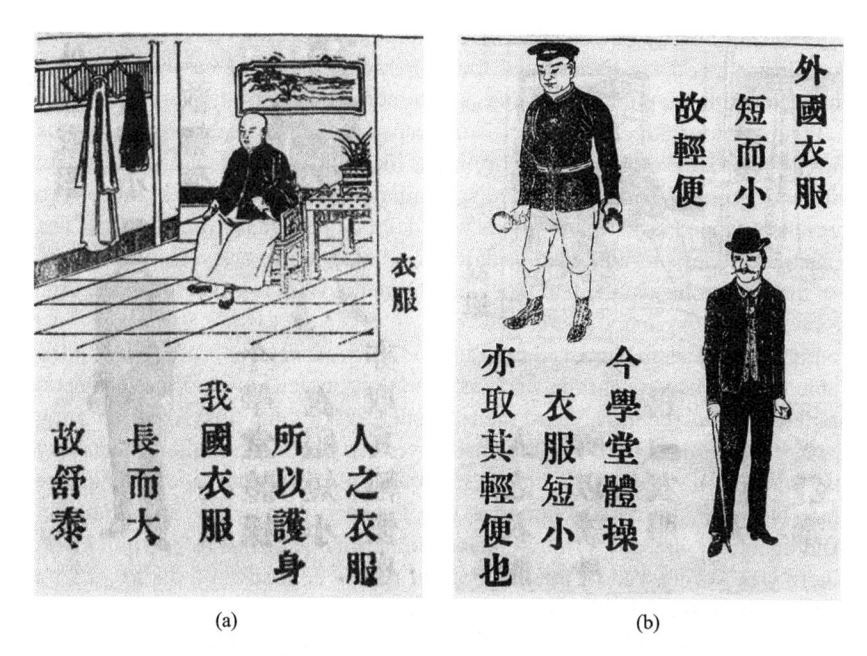

Figure 7 (a) Chinese clothes are comfortable. (b) Western clothes are convenient.

civilization.[79] Parks – as first developed in advanced countries – encouraged healthy outdoor activities that ranged from strolling about and enjoying the flowers to competitive sports. Parks were necessary to provide leisure space for poor urban residents. As symbols of advanced civilization, parks stood alongside libraries and museums – which Lü Simian pointed out were necessary both to advance knowledge and to preserve an ancestral spirit.[80]

As for clothing, a major Commercial Press reader commented that the advantage of Chinese clothing lay in its comfortable roominess (Figure 7a), while the advantage of Western clothing, which fit more tightly, lay in its convenience (Figure 7b).

Students in the lower grades were treated to many pictures of items whose names they were expected to learn. The text here mentions that Western-style clothing is more suitable for exercise.

The Commercial Press' *Most Up-to-Date Chinese Textbook* also provided students with practical lessons understood in terms of economics. For example, "frugality" was an important virtue. But it should not become an excuse

---

[79] For an example, see Shen Yi et al., *Zhonghua guowen jiaokeshu*, 10: 10a–b.
[80] Lü Simian, *Minguo guowen keben*, vol. 1, pp. 92–97.

for refusing charity or contributing to the public good.[81] Properly practiced, frugality is good for society and the individual alike, whereas extravagance threatens both the public good and private benefit, because it eventually leads to the loss of wealth. The reader distinguished among necessary items like the simplest food and clothing, ordinary items like furs and meat, and luxuries like silk and liquor. Whether individuals, families, or whole countries: those who became wrapped up in luxury goods would fall into decadence and decline. The tone of these lessons harkened back to a kind of fundamentalist Confucianism, but they also reflected the fear that China's wealth was disappearing in the urge to buy foreign products.

Language readers conveyed the value of intelligence over brute force. In the fable of the sparrow and the finch, a lesson on prudence was offered.[82] As it started to snow, the finch urged the sparrow to store some food for the coming hard days, but the sparrow said he had never had a problem finding food every day when he needed it. But indeed it snowed for several days, and while the finch had plenty of food to tide him over, the sparrow nearly starved to death. And historical anecdotes from ancient China provided examples of quick wit. There was Master Yan of the kingdom of Qi – who insulted the king of Chu but only within the bounds of diplomatic politesse.[83] When the king tried to humiliate Yan because he was short, Yan said that the kingdom of Qi appointed envoys based on the kingdom they would visit – since he was the most worthless man in Qi, he was sent to Chu.

Numerous stories like these valued cleverness over military might: they showed that even if stratagems could not fully defeat brute strength, they might neutralize it. They also perhaps said something about patriotism. The need to pull together for the sake of one's country was illustrated in the story of the statesman Lin Xiangru and General Lian Po.[84] When the king of Zhao wished to promote Lin over Lian, Lian was angry and humiliated. Lin avoided Lian, but when his underlings asked if Lin was afraid, he said the only issue was how to maintain unity against the threats of Qin. When Lian heard this, he was properly abashed, and the two men became friends.

Stories from the Nationalist government era

The new government established by the Nationalists in Nanjing in 1928 exerted unprecedented control over the school system. Yet textbook publishing largely remained in private hands, and the tensions and ambiguities in the government's

---

[81] Gao Fengqian, Zhang Yuanji, and Jiang Weiqiao, *Zuixin guowen jiaokeshu*, 1: 21b–23b.
[82] Shen Yi et al., *Zhonghua guowen jiaokeshu*, 3: 31a–b.
[83] Ye Shengtao, *Guoyu duben*, 2: 106–107; Wei Bingxin, *Guoyu duben*, 2: 131–134; Lü Simian, *Minguo guowen keben*, 1: 60.
[84] Wei Bingxin, *Guoyu duben*, 2: 140–142.

own ideology allowed for a range of views to be expressed on political, social, and cultural questions. As we will see in later chapters, the ideology of the Three People's Principles as formulated by Sun Yat-sen was heavily inculcated in student's minds. Formally, the three principles were nationalism, democracy, and "people's livelihood" or state-directed economic development. Substantively, the ideology revolved around anti-imperialism and "tutelage" under the vanguard leadership of the Guomindang – Nationalist Party. "Tutelage" referred to the notion that the Chinese people were not ready for democracy, and that the Nationalists would prepare them to assume democratic responsibilities through a period of military and civil training. Educators had long believed their role was to prepare children to become citizens, but not necessarily loyal to a specific government. By the 1930s, however, citizenship was directly linked to the party-state that the Guomindang was building. Publishers continued to use many of the lessons that they had used since the 1920s or even earlier. But they added new ones on the spirit of revolution, the Three People's Principles, the life of Sun Yat-sen, and the symbols of the party-states, such as the flags of China and of the Nationalist Party.

The editors' introduction to a teaching manual for a World Bookstore series of lower primary school readers put the matter this way: the educational systems of all countries rested on a foundation of core principles to unify their standards and provide them with goals; in the case of China, this foundation was provided by the Three People's Principles.[85] And an important tool to carry out "Three People's Principles education" is obviously textbooks, the introduction pointed out, for textbooks influence children's thinking, will, and sentiments. The editors noted that reading classes were the single most important part of the curriculum and promised that their readers were developed with the "spirit of the Three People's Principles." They would foster children's revolutionary ideals by making reading materials that were both child-friendly and literary. Their goals were to influence children's thinking, shape their "revolutionary character," and instill them with bravery and ardor. They promised tales of heroism and martyrdom to accomplish this.

The editors' introduction to a China Bookstore reader also promised to follow the educational ideals of the Three People's Principles, but they did so less fulsomely and spoke first of the pedagogical needs of students.[86] However, another Chinese language reader put out by the same publishers for lower middle schools emphasized that the first goal was to find materials that would arouse the national spirit and inspire political interest in accord with the party principles of the Nationalists, and to show the road to national reconstruction

---

[85] Wei Bingxin and Yin Shuping, "Qianqi xiaoxue guoyu duben jiaoxuefa gaiyao," 1: 1–2.
[86] Fang Qinzhao, Zhu Wenshu, and Yu Shouzhen, *Xin Zhonghua guoyu duben jiaoshoufa*, 1: "Bianji dayi" 編輯大意, 1.

and encourage students to work hard.[87] The second goal was to encourage labor and mutual cooperation in accord with the practical needs of society, to raise spirit of empathy and helping others, and to nourish habits of honesty and trustworthiness. Other goals referred to art and imagination, logic and the scientific spirit, and the need to speak to the experiences of students themselves. The textbook itself used writings ranging from Sun Yat-sen to the ancient philosophers Mengzi and Liezi; the Tang poets Li Bai, Du Fu, and others; and New Culture intellectuals such as Hu Shi and Zhou Zuoren.

A 1932 reader published by the Ministry of Education conveyed a story of China as the victim of foreign oppression from the Opium War onward, and the Chinese as facing perhaps even racial extinction.[88] The orthodox view of the early Republic on the equality of the five races was maintained, in spite of the Han chauvinism of many leading Nationalists. One lesson in the volume reiterated a lament common since the late Qing: China is large and its population great, so it should be the strongest nation in the world, but it is not. "This is because our nation doesn't know how to unite together, so even though we are numerous, we are a sheet of loose sand."[89] Then, following Sun Yat-sen, it argued that nationalism can be built on the foundation of familism and clanism. Chinese devotion to their families and clans can be extended to the nation. Then, the Chinese nation will liberate itself and forge the equality of all its peoples, and then it will unite with other oppressed nations in the world and seek general liberation against the forces of imperialism and build equality among all nations. Another lesson postulated that five main races of the world generally occupied different territory. But, "in today's world, the strongest race is the Whites, who use force to exterminate the other races. For example, the Red and Black races will be extinct soon, and the Brown race is also facing extinction, and we of the Yellow race are also facing extreme oppression. We of the Yellow race should quickly learn how to resist."[90]

Finally, the Ministry of Education reader also emphasized "traditional morality."[91] It gave examples of what it had mind. Loyalty referred to working for the sake of your county, even to the point of sacrificing your life. Filiality referred to devotion not only to your parents but also to your country. Love was exemplified by Sun Yat-sen's determination to sacrifice everything to save the Chinese people. Trust referred to the way Chinese merchants relied on their word; so China would help other countries to resist oppression. Peace was the natural goal of the Chinese people, unlike the case with foreigners. The ministry's elementary reader thus spoke to historical, political, and moral questions that we examine in greater depth in later chapters.

---

[87] Zhu Wenshu, *Xin Zhonghua guoyu yu guowen jiaokeshu*, 1: "Bianji dayi" 編輯大意, 1–2.
[88] Jiaoyubu, *Sanmin zhuyi qianzike*.   [89] Ibid., 2: 12.   [90] Ibid., 2: 9.   [91] Ibid., 2: 32–33.

Left-wing views were expressed in the readers by Ye Shengtao (1894–1988), a famous writer particularly known for his children's stories.[92] He was an editor at the Commercial Press before moving to the Enlightenment Bookstore in 1930. For his primary school readers with the Enlightenment Bookstore, Ye wrote brief stories about children at home, at play, and at school, suggesting proper ways to interact with parents, siblings, friends, and teachers. Ye was concerned with teaching respect for workers. In one story, father asked "us children" what we wanted to be when we grew up. Older brother said he had two hands, and he could work, and so he wanted to become a farmer growing rice and wheat. Big sister said she had two hands, and could work, and wanted to plant cotton and hemp. Little sister said she had two hands, and could work, and wanted to be a machinist. "I" said I had two hands, and could work, and wanted to do construction work. Father said that was good: everybody needs to eat rice and wheat, to wear cotton or hemp clothing; everybody needed machines, and houses to live in. These are important jobs, and "I approve of your becoming farmers and workers."[93]

This story, told in the younger brother's voice, strikes a false note insofar as the future facing most primary-school children was not that of a worker or a farmer. But the dignity of physical labor was important for Ye. With woodblock illustrations by the famous artist and cartoonist Feng Zikai (1898–1975), Ye presented many images of labor, with and without children.

The men in Figure 8 are harvesting wheat: the day is very, very hot; the ripe plants ripple golden-yellow in the breeze; everyone is in the fields scything, sweating under the sun, but working on regardless.

If we contrast Ye's story to a somewhat similar story from a China Bookstore primer, we can see that the difference lies in the subjectivity of the assumed reader. Ye wants children to envision themselves as workers and peasants, or at least feel a kind of acute empathy with them. The China Bookstore story "Refraining from Pride" tells of a boy from a wealthy family who mistreats a visiting peasant.[94] His father admonishes him, "Can you survive without clothing or food? . . . Clothing is made out of cotton and food is made out of rice. Now cotton and rice all come from the peasants. Without the peasants, even if you had gold and silver, and pearls and jade, you would face freezing and starvation." The China Bookstore story was less about empathy than a sense of upper-class obligation.

Numerous hard-working animals like bees and silkworms populated Ye Shengtao's whimsical fables.[95] But also, Ye did not shrink from discussing the

---

[92] See Mary Anne Farquhar, *Children's Literature in China*, pp. 93–115. Ye began publishing his original fairytales in 1921.
[93] Ye Shengtao, *Guoyu duben*, 1: 129.
[94] Shen Yi et al., *Zhonghua guowen jiaokeshu*, 7: 20b–21a.
[95] Ye Shengtao, *Guoyu duben*, 1: 101.

天氣很暖。南風陣陣地吹。田裏的麥熟了,望去只見一片金黃色。

這時候農人很忙。他們都到田裏去,一刀一刀,把麥割下來。太陽曬着。他們不管,只管割麥。

滿頭是汗。他們不管,只管割麥。

割完了麥,你一擔,我一擔,把麥挑回去。太陽曬着。他們不管,只管挑麥。滿頭是汗。

Figure 8 At work in the fields.

terrible events of the day. In late January 1932 the Japanese attacked the Zhabei section of Shanghai, ostensibly targeting Nationalist troops on the grounds that they were failing to protect Japanese civilians (in the wake of the Japanese invasion of Manchuria in September 1931, anti-Japanese boycotts and demonstrations spread across Chinese cities). Although Chinese authorities had agreed to clamp down on anti-Japanese demonstrations, Japan demanded the withdrawal of Chinese troops from Shanghai. Facing unexpected resistance, the Japanese shelled Zhabei intensively; in the end, the entire district was destroyed by firestorms. Ye did not write an emotionally charged account of the incident. He did not frame the Japanese bombing of Zhabei in a direct narrative at all; rather, he described the conditions there in the voice of a young visitor to Shanghai writing a letter to his cousin. The tone was of restraint and determination. "We cannot forget," was the message in so many words.[96]

Determination was the theme of the parable of the foolish old man who moved a mountain, later a favorite story of Mao Zedong.[97] In Ye Shengtao's telling of the story, the foolish old man decides that his family is inconvenienced by the mountain that blocks the path to his house. He gathers his sons and grandsons together, and they enthusiastically agree to dig up the mountain. First, his wife criticizes him, asking how a bunch of men who can't even move a pile of dirt can possibly move a mountain. And where will they put it? In the sea, they answer, though the ocean is far away and it will take a great deal of time. Then a "wise old man" criticizes the impossibility of the task, but the foolish old man replies that his grandsons and descendants beyond will continue the task, so it is only a matter of time. One point of the parable was the limits of intelligence, because the "smart people" are shown to be wrong. More important was the value of persistence even in the face of ridicule. The theme of family continuity is also suggested.[98]

Ye's parables generally had leftist implications. One story (Figure 9) presented the beasts of the forest, all in thrall to their fear of the lion. One day they gather together to talk about how to avoid being eaten.[99] Some say they should run from the lion, some say it is best to climb trees. A wild sheep says the first task is to get used to hearing the lion's roar, so it would not be so intimidating. Once they are used to his roar, the animals will have time to react. The wild horse says the roar is too frightening, but the wild sheep says that courage is

---

[96] Ibid., 2: 35–36.   [97] Ibid., 2: 125–127.

[98] In the version of this story later used by Mao Zedong, the foolish old man and his sons were digging out two mountains. Eventually, God was moved and sent down two angels to aid them. "Today, two big mountains lie like a dead weight on the Chinese people. One is imperialism, the other is feudalism. The Chinese Community Party has long made up its mind to dig them up. We must persevere and work unceasingly, and we, too, will touch God's heart. Our God is none other than the masses of the Chinese people." *Selected Works of Mao Tse-tung*, vol. 3, p. 272.

[99] Ye Shengtao, *Guoyu duben*, 2: 21–24.

72   Educating China

Figure 9 With unity, even lions can be defeated.

a matter of training. First, we all hide by the side of the path when the lion comes roaring by and lose some of our fear. This plan worked, and everyone got braver, even the horse. The deer then asks, what is the next plan? The wild sheep says the animals can now unite in opposition to the lion's oppression: united, we can use our horns and hooves to defeat the lion! And when the lion comes, the animals attack it, and the lion falls bleeding on the ground. The animals thus learned their own bravery and strength. Ye Shengtao's political message was clear enough, but how this may have been discussed in class, we cannot know.

Ye Shengtao's fable of the silkworm and the ants – or, as he called it, "Completely Different" – also spoke to the issue of strength through cooperation. The story began with a "lazy" young silkworm who leaves all his comrades because he does not want to spend his whole life eating, spinning a cocoon, and finally being boiled by humans.[100] He comes across an ant, who – the silkworm assumes – faces a similar fate. The ant, however, is working hard and way too busy to talk with him, but does give him a letter of introduction so he can visit the ants' nest and see how they live. The silkworm then finds a lifestyle that is indeed "completely different." First, the ants all work hard, and no one is lazy or greedy. Second, the ants' communal provisions provide for every contingency. His guide first takes the silkworm to visit the ants' food stores, which are prodigious, with ants everywhere stacking up materials. They then visit the nursery, where caretaker ants are assiduously tending the eggs and the newborns. And finally they go by the road builders, also hard at work, and the silkworm remarks to the ant, "'You are all so happy!' The silkworm thinks a bit, and adds, 'But is there no one who ever comes to attack you?' The guide ant points to all his comrades in the nest and replies, 'You need to understand that everyone one of us is a soldier! If anyone attacks us, we all rush to the defense.'"

The role of moral exemplars in language readers and morality textbooks has never slacked in China. Several late Qing and early Republican readers used the famous story of the youngest son who chose the smallest pear (Figure 10). In this story, when his father brought pears home, 4-year-old Kong Rong insisted on taking the smallest for himself. When his father asked why, little Rong explained that he was the smallest of the brothers, so he should have the smallest pear. Kong Rong (153–208) was a military official in the late Han dynasty and a noted literary scholar and putative descendent of Confucius. The pear story had long been incorporated in the *Trimetrical Classic*. In the twentieth century reader, yielding and harmony are not the only virtues: the equality of all siblings, girls and boys, was also emphasized.

---

[100] Ibid., 2: 54–57.

74   Educating China

Figure 10 Kong Rong takes the smallest pear because he is the smallest child.

In 2012, the Chinese government published the *New Twenty-Four Filial Exemplars* to encourage children to take better care of the growing number of seniors. Reasonable in itself – asking children to take their parents on trips rather than, as in the original version, lying down naked on ice-covered ponds so as to get fish for their parents to eat – it was perhaps part of a larger campaign to support traditional moral standards. Kong Rong was also revived in a new twenty-first century form. Then a small brouhaha erupted over a first-grade class in Shanghai that read the story of Kong Rong. Tested on what he would do if he were Kong Rong, one student said he would not give up his pear. His other answers were all correct, but this answer was marked wrong.[101] His father, a little upset, uploaded a picture of his son's answer sheet (Figure 11) to Sina Weibo (China's most popular social networking service).

Repostings and an excited discussion followed, and the first-grader received much support for his answer. Some netizens simply thought he was being

[101] Li Zheng, "Xiaoxuesheng yuwen shiti daan yin gefan zhenglun."

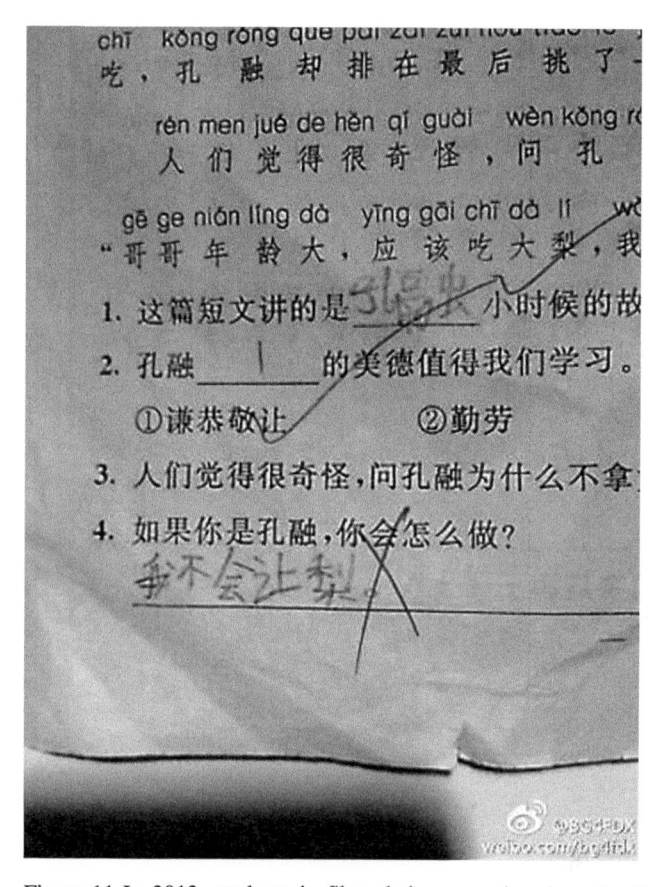

Figure 11 In 2012, students in Shanghai were quizzed on the Kong Rong story. One boy's answer was marked wrong: "If you were Kong Rong, would you give up [the pear]?" "I would not."

honest, and others thought Chinese education in general was too narrowly focused. Voices critical of the boy cited general concerns about contemporary Chinese morality in the age of capitalist competition. According to his father, the boy himself said he thought 4-year-olds would not give up the pear (not that he himself was so selfish). One netizen noted that logically, the answer had to be "yes," because we know that Kong Rong really did give up the pear, so if one were Kong Rong, then one would have to give up the pear. More people, however, felt that there was not really a right or wrong answer to a question like that.

Language readers touch on every conceivable topic, and while students are thinking about how to master reading and writing, they are absorbing images of family life, adult roles, moral behavior, and political concepts. However, more systematic introductions to morality, to society and politics, to history, to geography, and to the sciences required more specialized classes based on specific disciplines of knowledge.

3   Textbook morality, self-cultivation, and civics

What makes a good person and citizen? Is there a difference? If so, is it a radical difference, or do the duties of personhood and citizenship overlap? What were the specific goals of moral and civic education in the first three decades of the twentieth century? This chapter and the next describe the fraught realm where students were told how to behave.

In the late Qing, classes in "self-cultivation" were designed to supplement the moral lessons that educational leaders thought the traditional Four Books and the Five Classics would provide. Textbooks in self-cultivation were to help students practice the principles and models purveyed in much older texts. Yet self-cultivation textbooks – while outwardly teaching seemingly timeless verities about filiality, trustworthiness, loyalty, and so forth – were also beginning to set out how members of a modern nation-state should act.[1] They did not speak of "citizens," because of course they were designed to educate "subjects" of the emperor. But a new view of the virtue of loyalty was emerging: in this view the highest loyalty was not owed to any individual, no matter how august, but to the state, or perhaps even to the nation, the Chinese people.

After the 1911 Revolution, moral education sought to construct the republican citizen by modifying Confucian ethics. Self-cultivation textbooks continued to teach traditional virtues, while simultaneously emphasizing responsibilities to the national community.[2] For the purpose of socializing students into the national community, textbooks largely presented the republican state as the

---

[1] Thus there was no straightforward progress from self-cultivation to citizenship, as in Bi Yuan, "Cong 'xiushen' dao 'gongmin'," pp. 90–95; and see also Huang Xingtao and Zeng Jianli, "Qingmo xinshi xuetang de lunli jiaoyu yu lunli jiaokeshu tanlun," pp. 51–72; and Wang Xiaojing, *Qingmo minchu xiushen sixiang yanjiu*.

[2] For some purposes, the late Qing morality books and the Republican civics books should be considered separate genres, as the official curriculum changed in 1912 (and again in 1923 and 1928). However, content change, while real, was more gradual. See Chen Guanghui, "Qingmo Minchu zhongxuetang (xiao) xiushen jiaokeshu de fazhan," pp. 1–10; and Sheng Langxi, ed., "Cong xiushenke shuo dao gongmin xunlianke." Sheng suggests that self-cultivation remained central from the late Qing into the early Republic and that 1923 marked a real break in terms of a new emphasis on civics, which shifted from moral character to social conditions (pp. 5, 11). Nonetheless, even after 1923, social life was predicated on the inculcation of "good habits" (pp. 12–14), which suggests moral training.

family writ large, clearly adopting the previous notion of the imperial state as a kind of family. One can see here the power of the logic rooted in the ancient classical text (and one of the Four Books), the *Great Learning*, which directly linked social order and political rule to individual self-cultivation. But by the 1920s, this link had been broken. It was broken by clarifying the distinction between private and public, and textbooks played a role in defining this distinction. Private (*si*) now referred to the interests of individuals and families, whereas public (*gong*) referred to the shared interests of the Chinese nation or perhaps humanity as a whole.

The dichotomy between private and public was an ancient one, but it had reemerged with special force by the late Qing.[3] It was necessary to rethink suspicions of the "private" and to define the "public" more precisely. By the 1920s, civics textbooks and the very notion of civic morality were based on this new form of the public/private distinction. This was largely implicit, but it formed the premise of the view that the republican state was categorically different from the family, and that, while traditional virtues had a major role to play in the socialization of future citizens, the rights and duties of citizens also transcended personal virtues. In their private lives, citizens should be filial and loving, but in their public lives, they should put aside all personal considerations and devote themselves only to the public good. Citizens, for example, should vote for the best candidate regardless of kinship ties. The citizen was to have an unmediated relationship with the republican state, no longer dependent on kinship or local networks. Citizens were to supervise officials, even as they were to obey their government.

The citizen as imagined in textbooks was not defined as an autonomous individual but as a member of the national community. Citizenship, therefore, was an identity based on a role vis-à-vis the state.[4] If, as Tu Wei-ming suggests, the view of the self in the dominant Confucian tradition was dynamic and relational – not imaginable as an isolated essence but always "the self as a center of relationships,"[5] then civics textbooks functioned to change the system of relationships but not the traditional view of personhood. Children were to become members of the state, not merely their family. As citizens, then, Chinese were to possess specific rights and duties while remaining firmly embedded in sets of relationships. By the 1920s, virtue-talk and rights-talk had interpenetrated one another. The first acted to socialize, and hence virtue-talk obviously functioned as a means of social control. The second, however, functioned to legitimate

---

[3] See Huang Kewu and Zhang Zhejia, eds., *Gong yu si*; Peter Zarrow, "The Origins of Modern Chinese Concepts of Privacy."
[4] Morality and civics textbooks do not generally seek to construct identity in the way that history and geography textbooks do, but they inevitably assume the existence of a self-other distinction. For an unusually clear case, see Klaus Vollmer, "The Construction of 'Self' and Western and Asian 'Others'." See also Ger-bei Lee, "Values, Tradition, and Social Change," pp. 10–13.
[5] Tu Wei-ming, "Selfhood and Otherness in Confucian Thought."

and even demand the participation of the citizen in public affairs. Voices in the New Culture movement were calling for greater individualism, and the logic of rights-talk was reflected in textbooks' respect for women, youth, and workers. Nonetheless, the child's world in civics textbooks was construed in concentric circles that widened out from family to nation and humankind. The future citizen was to be a person of many roles.

The tension in this message can also be described as that between individual autonomy and independence on the one hand, and devotion to the common good on the other. Textbooks sought to transcend this tension by suggesting, in effect, that the moral ties of nation were no less natural than the moral ties of family. We obviously do not choose our moral ties when we are born into particular families, and so they are rooted in nature. In the political ideology of imperial Confucianism, the family was analogous to the state, and the father to the emperor. In a simplified picture of society, the world was made up of patriarchal nested hierarchies: the set of individuals encompassed by family heads, the set of family heads encompassed by the local "father and mother official," and the set of local officials ultimately encompassed by the emperor. In contrast, Republic civics did not work by analogy but by extension. Moral ties of family led inexorably through school, neighborhood, town, and province, and finally up to the state and even the world. The individual was not so much the basis of a complex set of nested hierarchies as in direct relationship with each level of state and society. Civics textbooks taught that all persons were politically equal, which suggested that society was fundamentally horizontal rather than hierarchical. Civics textbooks merely distinguished between the child, who lacked positive rights vis-à-vis family and school, and the adult that the child would become, who possessed defined rights in the various spheres of political life.

When the Nationalist government came to power in 1928, it attempted to build a curriculum in civics that incorporated Sun Yat-sen's Three People's Principles and his notion of tutelage. This was to emphasize one strand of the civics education of the 1920s: selfless devotion to the public interest. The new Nationalist textbooks also explicitly sought to revive traditional (Confucian) virtues and root loyalty to the new state in the extension of family ties. This move worried liberal intellectuals who understood that appeals to tradition in this context represented attacks on the ideals of individual autonomy and political participation that they believed in. The Nationalists' vision of the political community as a single body nonetheless rested on moral principles that were fairly unobjectionable. Who is really opposed to patriotism, trustworthiness, and cleanliness?

Curriculum development and debates

Notwithstanding a few moralizing passages in the premodern primers used to prepare students for the classics, self-cultivation textbooks were a complete innovation. Late Qing educators first saw them in use in Japan, which of course had adopted them from Western models even while maintaining the centrality of the Chinese classics. Japan's decision to create self-cultivation textbooks largely came about because of the realization that, as schooling began to be made compulsory in the 1870s, the classics did not speak to students' need for "practical morality."[6] At first, self-cultivation textbooks consisted of a hodgepodge of materials put together by local educators as best they could. By the 1880s, the Japanese government had mandated that classes emphasize Confucian benevolence, righteousness, loyalty, and filiality, and the Ministry of Education published its own textbook. Centralization allowed self-cultivation textbooks to be closely linked to history textbooks, so that historical examples could reinforce moral lessons.[7] By the 1890s, curriculum regulations specified a long list of Confucian virtues that were to be taught, and demanded that schools foster a spirit of loyalty to the monarch and patriotism (*sonnō aikoku*). Morality extended from the self through family and community to the nation, and in the 1890s self-cultivation textbooks included discussions of the constitution. One goal of the Imperial Rescript on Education was to guard against the dangers of democratization.[8]

Filiality was central to a Japanese self-cultivation textbook published in 1880; here, the author spoke of service to one's parents and to one's older brother as the basis for establishing the self.[9] The Ministry of Education liked filiality but wanted passages on Japan's unbroken imperial line.[10] By 1900, self-cultivation textbooks began with lessons that described the student's day, such as going to school lessons. Stories of emperors and ministers were used to teach loyalty, say, but loyalty was also to be found in daily life. Patriotism and the flag were added to the more traditional Confucian virtues. Self-control (J. *kokki*; Ch. *keji*) assumed new importance, and all such virtues were mixed together with the notion that "good Japanese" felt deep gratitude for the favors of the emperor and loved their ruler.[11] By this time, the Japanese self-cultivation textbook had assumed the form that would last until the Pacific War. The ministry's textbook spoke of duties, not rights, and the modern nation-state was firmly rooted in the trans-historical empire.[12] Volume 1 began with lessons on studying and orderliness, and also the goodness of parents and brotherly accord. There was also a picture of an imperial procession. Volume 2 did more to explain these themes, highlighting family life, while gradually introducing Chinese characters.

---

[6] Kaigo Tokiomi and Naka Arata, *Kindai Nihon kyōkasho sō*, pp. 47–85.
[7] Nakamura Kikuji, *Fukkoku kokutei rekishi kyōkasho kaisetsu*, pp. 18–19. For the late Meiji, see Wilbur M. Fridell, "Government Ethics Textbooks in Late Meiji Japan," pp. 823–833.
[8] Kaigo Tokiomi and Naka Arata, *Kindai Nihon kyōkasho sōsetsu*, pp. 100–116.
[9] Kametani Seiken, *Shūshin jikun*, 2: 41.   [10] Monbushō, comp., *Shōgaku sakuhōsho*, 2: 181.
[11] Monbushō, comp., *Jinjō shōgaku shūshinsho*, 3: 94–95.
[12] Monbushō, comp., *Jinjō shōgaku shūshinsho: jidōyō*.

Volume 3 included the ever-popular story of George Washington and the cherry tree to illustrate honesty, and also described Empire Day, or the National Foundation Day (February 11, supposedly marking the accession to the throne of Emperor Jimmu in 660 BCE). It defined a "good Japanese" as loyal and filial to his parents, siblings, teachers, friends and neighbors. Volume 4 spoke more of the emperor, the Yasukuni Shrine, propriety, the law, the body (hygiene), superstition (bad), and self-control and establishing one's will (Confucian notions). Volume 5 included many models of exemplary behavior. And volume 6 defined gender roles: the man goes out to work, the wife stays at home; both have duties; both need self-cultivation, but boys strive to become resolute and decisive while girls strive to become agreeable and virtuous.

There was much here that Chinese reformers could use, and much that had to be ignored. Qing educators liked the clear and systematic presentation of moral principles in Japanese textbooks, as well as their use of the classics. Zhuang Yu, who became a prolific textbook editor at the Commercial Press Shanghai, praised Japanese morality primers for their lively writing style and story-telling, which presented lessons that young students could absorb.[13] In 1905 the Civilization Press published a translation of a 1900 ethics textbook by Akiyama Shirō.[14] This was presumably meant to help Chinese educators write their own textbooks rather than directly be taught to students. Its glorification of Japan's unbroken imperial line and uniquely unchanging polity (*guoti*) made it unsuitable to Chinese schools. But it was useful for its emphasis on orthodox relations modeled on father-son and emperor-minister. Interestingly, it began with a description of the state rather than the family. The Japanese state was headed by an emperor who was owed love and obedience (like a father). Akiyama also demonstrated how the concept of "grouping" (*hequn*), which was central to the Chinese reformers' conceptualization of national unity, was compatible with Confucian norms. Thus, "The Japanese polity was formed on the basis of racial unity, and the line of sages [emperors] treated the people as their own children, while the people regarded the sages as their own fathers. This Great Way of loyalty and filiality stemmed naturally from love and respect."[15] Akiyama equated filiality and loyalty, on the grounds that the state was literally, by blood, simply the family writ large.[16] Chinese self-cultivation textbooks of the late Qing would be organized in the opposite fashion – beginning with filial piety and the family – but reach the same conclusion.

When the Qing government first proposed a self-cultivation curriculum in 1902, the very youngest students were to learn filial piety, trustworthiness, ritual etiquette and shame, respect for elders and teachers, and loyalty to the monarch and love of country in their self-cultivation (*xiushen*)

---

[13] Zhuang Yu, *Chuji mengxue xiushen jiaokeshu*, "Bianji dayi" 編輯大意, n.p.
[14] Akiyama Shirō, *Lunli jiaoke fanben*. [15] Ibid., p. 2a. [16] Ibid., pp. 8b–9a.

classes.[17] Even Kindergarten Halls should teach virtues through the examples of the ancients.[18] Patriotic unity, the new Ministry of Education explicitly noted, should be rooted in childhood, just as Confucius taught that universal benevolence was the extension of more particularistic filiality.[19] Central to this process would be the revival of "national learning." Self-cultivation textbooks were initially a mere supplement to the classics, spelling out the virtues students should acquire. Or, in Confucian terms, they should foster children's "moral nature" – that is, a social orientation that they already possessed. As for classics reading, students were to begin with the *Classic of Filial Piety* and the *Analects* (records of conversations with Confucius), and move on to the *Mencius*, and then the *Great Learning* and the *Doctrine of the Mean*. A more traditional moral education curriculum for the twentieth century could hardly be imagined. Upper-level classes were to move on to classics focused on ritual, ethical philosophy, and history.[20]

This curriculum existed mostly on paper, as the actual schools were not yet operating, and it was soon superseded. But it clearly shows that Qing officials believed the heart of self-cultivation lay in the Four Books and Five Classics that they themselves had studied. This approach was encouraged by Japanese educators, who also felt that the classics provided the best moral education for modern imperial subjects.[21]

According to the new school regulations of 1904, which did begin to be implemented, self-cultivation classes were to be held two hours per week separately from classics reading. Their goal was to foster the moral nature of the children, teaching them to avoid bad habits and acquire good ones.[22] Constant restraint but without excessive severity was key. The beautiful words and good deeds of the ancients can be held up for emulation. A sense of justice, unselfishness, and empathy should be taught in youth. Knowledge of the love of one's group in childhood would in adults become the basis of patriotism. In upper primary schools, the Ministry of Education further stressed, teachers faced a problem. Self-cultivation was manifested in practice, not book learning, but there was no way to examine the student's level of self-cultivation except through the (rather crude) instrument of school regulations. Officials noted that the problem was not unique to China: foreign schools also had to teach self-cultivation

---

[17] Kecheng jiaocai yanjiusuo, ed., *20 shiji Zhongguo zhongxiaoxue kecheng biaozhun*, vol. 1, p. 2; vol. 2, p. 3.
[18] For kindergarten education, see Margaret Tillman, "The Authority of Age."
[19] Qu Xingui and Tang Liangyan, eds., *Zhongguo jindai jiaoyushi ziliao huibian*, vol. 1, p. 535.
[20] Kecheng jiaocai yanjiusuo, ed., *20 shiji Zhongguo zhongxiaoxue kecheng biaozhun*, vol. 1, pp. 5–10, 14–17; vol. 2, pp. 4–5.
[21] Bi Yuan, *Jianzao changshi*, pp. 163–164.
[22] Kecheng jiaocai yanjiusuo, ed., *20 shiji Zhongguo zhongxiaoxue kecheng biaozhun*, vol. 1, pp. 22, 32.

through textbooks, even though the point was daily practice, not abstract knowledge.

Classics reading was to focus on relatively brief and simple passages that students could memorize and understand. By absorbing the "right doctrines of the sages," students would be building a foundation for further knowledge. At this point in their education, it was only necessary for students to grasp basic meanings, not the finer exegetical points. Even in upper primary schools, students would understand the deepest meanings of the classics, but they should get in the habit of reading them for their general sense, and teachers would explain them in ways appropriate for the level of the student.

In middle schools, self-cultivation was to be based on the *Five Sets of Bequeathed Guidelines* (*Wuzhong yigui*) of Chen Hongmou (1696–1771), which students would read systematically over five years.[23] Chen's work was an effort to popularize orthodox morality and provide practical guidance for specific classes of people such as women and merchants. The 1904 curriculum continued to emphasize the importance of moral practice as well as book learning – again, "words and deeds must be in harmony." In the middle school curriculum, classics reading was reduced from 12 to 9 hours per week, and a pragmatic tone was emphasized. From ancient historical and ritual texts such as the *Zuozhuan* and the *Zhouli*, students should learn how ancient institutions "nourished and educated the people." In the fifth year of middle school, instruction in politics and economics was to be added three hours per week.

In the first years of building a state school system, many publishers produced morality and civics textbooks that challenged the bounds of official orthodoxy. Reformist interest in concepts of constitutional order and citizenship was coming to the fore, regardless of official hesitation.[24] Self-cultivation textbooks seemed to rate patriotism more highly than loyalty. However, with the system of censorship more or less in place by 1906, the Ministry of Education began to demand that textbooks be modified before they could be published, or withdrawn altogether. Officials understood morality to be absolute and eternal. In 1910 censors rejected a self-cultivation textbook that proposed that the current era was in transition between an old, moribund morality and a new morality that had yet to develop.[25] Censors also condemned the book for its attacks on "superstition," which they feared might lead ignorant people to abandon respect for Heaven and sacrifices to their ancestors. And finally, they insisted, a self-cultivation textbook should begin with filiality. Evidently, this textbook

---

[23] Kecheng jiaocai yanjiusuo, ed., *20 shiji Zhongguo zhongxiaoxue kecheng biaozhun*, vol. 1, pp. 41–46; vol. 2, pp. 131–132.
[24] See Yvonne Schulz Zinda, "Propagating New 'Virtues'"; Wang Jiarong, *Minzuhun*, pp. 86–96; and Joan Judge, "Gaizao guojia."
[25] "Shanghai tushu gongsi cheng chudeng xiaoxue xiushen jiaoshouben ji keben qing shending pi."

represented a reformist viewpoint that was too outspoken for conservative officials. Officials did in fact approve a number of textbooks that included attacks on superstition and began with discussions of the basic structure of society before moving on to filiality, as we will see in the pages that follow. At the same time, in wake of the promises of a constitution that the Qing made in 1906, one of the few textbooks that the Ministry of Education published itself came out in 1910: *Required Reading for Citizens Textbook*.[26] Of course, this "civics" was categorically distinct from self-cultivation, but it dealt with the same question of how to make students fit for society.

Following the 1911 Revolution, the new curriculum's most important move was to drop the classics from primary schools, while self-cultivation classes continued to be taught two hours a week.[27] As Minister of Education under the Nanjing revolutionary government of 1912, Cai Yuanpei proposed a new set of principles to replace the Qing's view of education. Cai saw his principle of civic morality (*gongmin daode*) as a logical heir to the Qing's principle of public-mindedness (*shanggong*). However, he completely rejected the Qing's principles of "loyalty to the monarch" and "reverence for Confucius."[28] The former was obviously not compatible with a republic, whereas the latter was not compatible with freedom of religion. Instead, Cai would teach the French's Revolution's principles of liberty, equality, and fraternity (*qin'ai*). Cai's approach to civic morality junked the traditional "human ethics" of the five relationships, but, whether out of genuine conviction or for strategic reasons, he cited Confucius and Mencius to support the notions of liberty and equality, and various classics to support the notion of fraternity. Thus according to Chen, *yi* (righteousness) represented an indigenous notion of liberty; *shu* (mutuality) equality; and *ren* (benevolence) fraternity.

No doubt, Cai's attempt to link Confucian virtues to the ideals of the French Revolution was extremely forced, but it demonstrated a faith that although what we might call "political Confucianism" had to be ejected from the school curriculum, there was much in Confucianism that was compatible with modern citizenship. The new republican self-cultivation curriculum, like the old, began with filial piety and fraternal duty and conceived of the child's world of concern moving from the family and immediate relatives in ever-widening circles to finally include the nation and the world.[29] For all the radical features of Cai's

---

[26] *Guomin bidu keben*. See Shin Kokui [Shen Guowei], "Shinmatsu no kokumin hitsudoku ni tsuite"; and Shin Kokui and Son Sei [Sun Qing], "Gen Fuku to Shinmatsu gakubu hen *Kokumin hitsudoku kahon shokō*."

[27] Kecheng jiaocai yanjiusuo, ed., *20 shiji Zhongguo zhongxiaoxue kecheng biaozhun*, vol. 2, p. 8. With a reorganization of the system of grades in 1916, self-cultivation classes were to be taught three hours a week to third and fourth year students.

[28] Cai Yuanpei, "Duiyu jiaoyu fangzhen zhi yijian," pp. 77–84.

[29] But see Zheng Yuan, "The Status of Confucianism in Modern Chinese Education," pp. 203–204, for the drastic diminution of Confucianism.

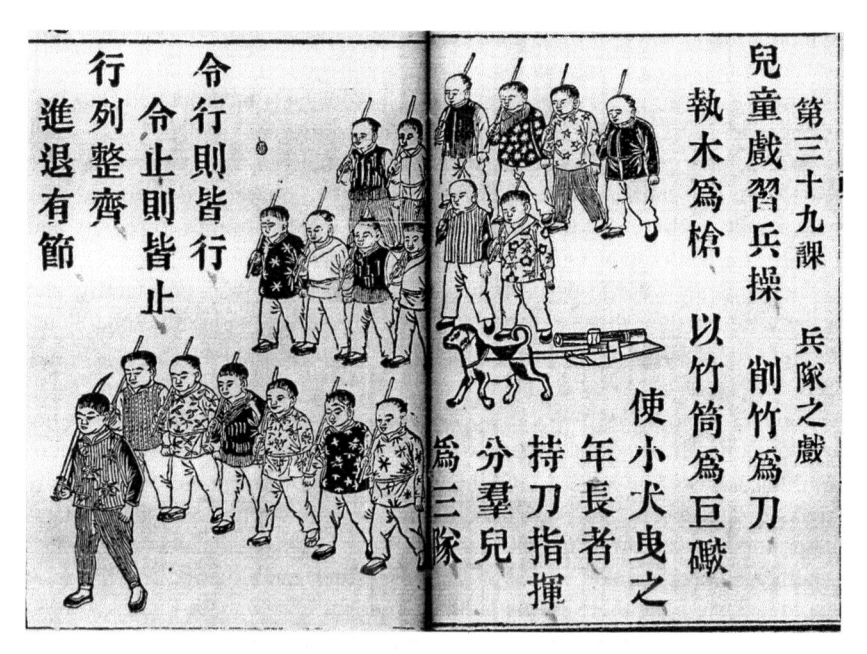

Figure 12 Play drill with bamboo swords and wooden rifles.

ultimate vision of education, his specific ideas about the self-cultivation curriculum were as much as continuation as a break from late Qing practice. In spite of the Qing's official curriculum, late Qing textbooks had either treated "loyalty" as a general virtue or related it to patriotism. In fact, unlike their Meiji predecessors, they scarcely mentioned the monarch at all. Cai's somewhat vague calls for moral education to stress a universal "worldview" (*shijieguan*, *Weltanschauung*) also made room for a "militant citizenry" (*junguomin zhuyi*). PE classes often featured military-style drills for boys (Figure 12). Although Cai possessed a genuinely cosmopolitan and even transcendental vision of humanity, he recognized that education in these principles was based on political education. First the citizen of China, then the citizen of the world.

When Yuan Shikai became president later in the year, he tried to reinstate Confucius's place in the schools, but "reverence for Confucius" hardly formed a significant aspect of self-cultivation classes.[30] No doubt classics-reading classes did not disappear overnight, especially in private schools, but the

---

[30] Yuan resisted efforts to turn Confucianism into a state religion and proclaimed his support for freedom of religion, while treating Confucius as a quasi-sacred founder of Chinese civilization with a special role in schools as China's First Teacher. See Han Hua, *Minchu Kongjiaohui yu guojiao yundong*; also Wang Jiarong, *Minzuhun*, 142–147; and Zheng Hang, *Zhongguo jindai deyu*, pp. 88–95, 129–132.

symbolic importance of their disappearance from the official curriculum cannot be overstated. Throughout the Republic, selections from the classics were – naturally enough, and as Cai himself had advocated – incorporated into language readers.

At the upper primary level, lessons on the republican political system were added, but still students were to begin with filiality, honesty, respect, and diligence, and the like, and then move on to their responsibilities to society and country. Girls should be taught chastity, as well as independence (*zili*). Primary school students were to be introduced to the concepts of school, family, and society, and in their third and fourth years to the state. The middle school curriculum emphasized citizenship in addition to moral thought and practice.[31] Self-cultivation classes were held once a week; in the fourth year, politics and economics were added twice a week. First-year self-cultivation classes were to focus on ethical norms, whereas the second year was to deal with responsibilities to state and society, and the third year with responsibilities to family and self, and to humanity and all things. The special characteristics of Chinese morality were to be taught in the fourth year. Some educators questioned whether it was desirable to use textbooks to teach morality and asked how it could be tested, but there seemed few alternatives.[32]

Civics classes began to replace self-cultivation, at least in progressive middle schools around 1920.[33] Rooted in the patriotic citizenship discourse of the late Qing, by the end strands of New Culture liberalism and populism came together to form a distinct republican ideology in educational circles.[34] Already in 1914 a writer had noted that in foreign countries nationalism formed the core of civics education.[35] Whereas Western nations made civics a required course, Japan taught both civics and morality, he noted. But the issue facing China was particularly urgent, it was claimed, because, having just become a republic, China needed civics education to qualify its people as citizens.[36]

As China descended into warlordism after Yuan Shikai's death in 1916, regional power holders provided little support for schools. Worse, they seemed to promise to keep China in perpetual chaos. Nonetheless, civics replaced self-cultivation in the curricular reforms of 1923. The new curriculum diminished the flavor of Confucianism in the schools, yet did not eliminate it. The goals formulated for primary school civics classes in 1923 were to teach students

---

[31] Kecheng jiaocai yanjiusuo, ed., *20 shiji Zhongguo zhongxiaoxue kecheng biaozhun*, vol. 2, pp. 135–136.
[32] Jia Fengzhen, "Xiushen jiaoshou"; "Taixuan," "Gongmin de xunlianfa"; and Hou Hongjian, "Xiaoxuexiao feiqu."
[33] Yi Zhengyi, "Minguo chunian zhongxue." For notes on curricular changes at this time, see Zheng Hang, *Zhongguo jindai deyu*, pp. 80–85.
[34] Zheng Hang, *Zhongguo jindai deyu*, chapter 4; Bi Yuan, "'Minguo' de dansheng," pp. 42–52.
[35] "Tianmin," "Gongmin jiaoyu wenti," pp. 115–122.
[36] "Tianmin," "Gongmin jiaoyu lun," pp. 43–50.

"to understand the relationship they hold with society (family, school, associations, locality, country, and world), to foster the knowledge and will to reform society, and to encourage habits that are in accord with contemporary life."[37] The basic design of the course was simple. Year 1 focused on family and school and the student's responsibilities thereto, while year 2 dealt with school activities and introduced students to the public life of the community. Year 3 moved on to the economic and social systems of the community, country, and province and introduced school self-government. Year 4 further focused on government, the structure of the nation-state, and the responsibilities of citizens toward the locality and the state, such as suffrage, taxes, and military service, as well as study of contemporary events. Year 5 explored associational life, political life, and citizenship in greater detail; year 6 moved on to more contentious issues such as family, women, and labor. Students were to gain an understanding of their place in society and their responsibilities to its organs such as the family, school, and employers; an understanding of the political system and the operations of elections and assemblies; and ultimately an understanding of what citizenship really was.

The 1923 civics curriculum for lower middle schools reduced the attention paid to moral behavior in favor of more academic understanding of state and society.[38] Curricular goals spoke of the "spirit" of constitutional government and "fostering citizenship morality"; moreover, the standards for graduation included basic knowledge of hygiene, the legal system, and economics and society, as well as the relationship between self and others and the rules for collective living. The topic of "social life" dealt with associational forms: family, school, professions, and the state, as well as "individual habits" such as fairness, sincerity, orderliness, and other qualities of citizens. "Constitutional government" highlighted not only political organization but also the people's rights and liberties and their duties to the state. A unit on social problems dealt with contemporary issues, whereas international affairs included the problem of inequality among states. At the same time, a unit on "philosophy of life" was to bring self-cultivation back into the curriculum at an advanced level.[39]

The upper middle school "social issues" curriculum of 1923 focused on controversial questions concerning the family, demography, the economic system, and social problems, concluding with a brief introduction to the discipline of sociology.[40] Such "social issues" reflected debates going on at least since the 1910s. The clear intent of the curriculum was reformist. Meeting three hours per week, classes were to use materials from these contemporary debates. The family unit dealt with questions of forced marriage, early marriage, divorce,

---

[37] Kecheng jiaocai yanjiusuo, ed., *20 shiji Zhongguo zhongxiaoxue kecheng biaozhun*, vol. 2, p. 11–12.
[38] Ibid., vol. 2, pp. 137–139.   [39] Ibid., vol. 2, pp. 140–141.   [40] Ibid., vol. 2, pp. 142–143.

patriarchy and filiality, inheritance, the women's movement, and "ancestral worship and superstition." The demographic unit focused on China's overpopulation problem. The economics unit focused on China's underdevelopment, capital and labor, and socialism. A social problems unit discussed poverty and crime.

Also, in 1923 the "society" curriculum was developed as an interdisciplinary approach that would treat society as both an object to be studied and a kind of spirit to be fostered in youth.[41] The actual subject matter over four years of primary school was much like that of morality and civics classes, although somewhat more anthropological and historical. In addition to family, hygiene, and citizenship, it added basic geography and historical lessons, and units on primitive and foreign peoples. Students were to learn something of how societies evolved. Memorial days or humiliation days and holidays were to receive due attention, in effect punctuating the school year with markers of historical and cultural identity. As with civics classes, students were expected to acquire a basic knowledge of how their society functioned and their duties to family, school, hometown, and country.

As we will see in the next chapter, under the Nationalists starting at the end of the late 1920s, "civics" materials were reshaped to fit into classes on the "Three People's Principles" and "Party Principles." The Nationalists changed the rubric back to "civics" in the early 1930s.[42] Nonetheless, regardless of the name of the course, the importance of citizenship training only increased under the Nationalists. The curriculum included materials on the life of Sun Yat-sen – again we see the importance of models to be emulated as well as admired from afar. And it included various versions of Sun's writings. These were packaged to bring out a variety of themes ranging from old reformist causes like the importance of building national spirit to newer concerns such as fostering economic development through state investments and assuring equality of the sexes. Following Sun Yat-sen, the Nationalists also tried to make room for the good aspects of "traditional morality" in building their new China.

"To enable students through actual life experiences to understand the relationship between self and society and to foster the moral qualities of cultivating the self and serving others." This was the first curricular goal listed in the 1932 civics standards for lower middle schools.[43] The Three People's Principles came second and traditional morality last. There was a Deweyan tone to the emphasis on actual life experiences. None of this constituted revolutionary change to the existing curriculum. If the Nationalists brought back "loyalty and

---

[41] Ibid., vol. 8, pp. 137–138.
[42] Robert Culp, "Setting the Sheet of Loose Sand"; Zheng Hang, *Zhongguo jindai deyu kechengshi*, pp. 279–304; Deng Yuhao, "Sun Zhongshan sixiang."
[43] Kecheng jiaocai yanjiusuo, ed., *20 shiji Zhongguo zhongxiaoxue kecheng biaozhun*, vol. 2, p. 149.

filiality," they emphasized that this was loyalty to the nation, to the people, and not the traditional "loyalty to the monarch." The result was to sharpen lessons directly inculcating patriotism through, for example, teaching respect for symbols of state and party. (Society then became an object of reform, not an ideal.) To demand loyalty to the "party-state" created a new, arguably perverse, form of patriotism, but to regard history, geography, and civics as a general training ground for patriotism was hardly new.

This chapter now turns to the self-cultivation and civics textbooks used in the late Qing and early republican periods.

Citizenship in late Qing self-cultivation textbooks

Probably the most widely-used morality textbook of the last years of the Qing was that of the Commercial Press, the *Up-to-Date Self-Cultivation Textbook*, first published in 1906.[44] It conveyed moral messages through stories, mostly derived from historical examples, of good character and deeds. Though not without progressive elements, this textbook, resting as it did on classical stories, largely assumed the legitimacy of the existing social and political systems. As Cai Yuanpei once commented, although norms certainly changed over time, morality textbooks could not get too far ahead of generally accepted standards.[45]

But if the Commercial Press textbook stood as a monument of orthodox moral learning tempered with a mildly progressive program, shorter textbooks emphasized citizenship and individual autonomy in more explicit terms, and even spoke of the public nature of the state. Liu Jianbai's *Self-Cultivation Textbook for Primary Schools* of 1903 effectively represented reformist opinion. Liu began:

First, there are people, and then there is the state. If the people of the state are all good people, then the state will be strong and civilized. It is not that people of a strong and civilized state are all born perfect, but that they can become good through their own efforts. Who does not wish the country in which they live to be strong and civilized? If everyone can strengthen himself and can become civilized, then a weak country can strengthen itself and an uncivilized country become civilized. The responsibility to strengthen the country and create a civilized state lies not in outsiders but in the citizens (*guomin*) themselves. But if citizens lack the capacity to become strong and civilized, then their country will fail these tasks as well. We want the people to urgently engage in self-cultivation... The [ancient] Chinese sages and worthies understood that self-cultivation was the foundation for ordering the family, ruling the state, and pacifying the empire.[46] All the states of the Orient and the West alike take self-cultivation as a branch of

---

[44] Gao Fengqian, Cai Yuanpei, and Zhang Yuanji, *Zuixin xiushen jiaokeshu jiaoshoufa*. A good analysis is Yvonne Schulz Zinda, "Propagating New 'Virtues'."
[45] Cited in Wang Jiarong, *Minzuhun*, p. 83.   [46] From the *Great Learning* (Daxue 大學).

learning. Thus while there are people who fail at the task of self-cultivation, there is no one who has become cultivated without engaging in self-cultivation.[47]

Liu told students in effect that China depended on every one of them to achieve moral perfection – not for the sake of their families or the emperor but to strengthen China and make it "civilized," meaning modern. This was to reposition the role of the individual and self-cultivation in society. At the same time, Liu's basic approach, once past the first lessons on patriotism, was perfectly orthodox, with chapters on filiality, friendship, loyalty, trustworthiness, righteousness, generosity, and so forth.

So far, so Confucian. But when Liu treated "universal fraternity" (*bo'ai*) as a kind of cosmological principle, he pushed beyond Confucianism.[48] For Liu, universal fraternity should be extended to all humanity, even to everything in the world. Granted, the sphere of family love was distinct from the sphere of universal fraternity, but Liu was not referring to the Confucian notion of graduated love extending out from the family as it diminished in strength; rather, family love was private and practiced in daily life, whereas universal fraternity was a matter of "public interest." And for Liu the traditional virtue of "friendship" became not merely a matter of mutual learning, respect, or assistance, but the basis of "grouping" (*hequn*) or unifying, a goal of reformers since the 1890s. Even more remarkably, Liu described marriage as an equal relationship, including marriage under the category of friendship. Husbands and wives were to read and discuss all matters together, and manage the household together.[49] Liu's treatment of "loyalty" was also in line with reformist ideals. "Loyalty," Liu said, did not necessarily refer to loyalty to the emperor but was a general virtue that could be applied to parents and friends as well.[50] The ancient meaning of "loyalty," Liu maintained, referred to a view of others as important as oneself. Achieving this, one would certainly be loyal to the country and the people, and Liu did not again speak of the emperor. To call the "people" the foundation of the state was not a radical move, but to speak of the need of rulers to be "loyal to the people" was part of the democratizing movement of the late Qing.[51] While discussing aspects of loyalty, Liu effectively separated the state, which was necessary, from the emperor, who, if only by implication, was not. And his writing on the "public" included the following reformist-inflected swipe at the monarchy:

The empire is not the private property of one or two persons but rather the public property of the millions and millions of people. The state is also not the private property of one or two persons but rather the public property of the millions and millions of people. Since they are public property, all that is within the empire and the state is also public

---

[47] Liu Jianbai, *Xiaoxue xiushen jiaokeshu*, pp. 1b–2a, 3b–4a. I have here strung together the texts of lessons 1–3 without ellipses.
[48] Ibid., pp. 19a–21a.   [49] Ibid., p. 19a.   [50] Ibid., pp. 27b–28a.   [51] Ibid., pp. 29a–b.

property. Therefore, anyone who seizes the public property of the empire or the state and privatizes it is a public enemy.[52]

Whether the *Self-Cultivation Textbook for Primary Schools* was entirely comprehensible to primary school students is doubtful. Two years later, the Civilization Press published Li Jiagu's *Beginning Self-Cultivation Textbook*, which was deliberately written at a simple level and covered three years of classes.[53] Following a more or less Confucian framework, the *Beginning Self-Cultivation Textbook* was organized around four major topics: "establishing the self" (*lishen*); "maintaining the self" (*baoshen*); "treatment of others" (*dairen*), which included filial piety; and last, "living in the world" (*chushi*), which brought political issues into third-year classes. Li's very first lesson stated, "As a person, I am a complete citizen (*wanquan zhi guomin*), and this complete citizen is a noble status and indicates high morality, [and so] the self must be protected without any flaws or injuries."[54] This lesson is not remarkable for its stress on selfhood, but for directly linking the practice of selfhood to citizenship. Li rooted selfhood in personal virtues ranging from trustworthiness and caution in speaking to frugality and courage. He spoke of the importance of liberty (*ziyou*) – but only within the law and based on the self-control (*zizhi*) that is provided by self-cultivation.[55] "Thus the person who is most capable of self-control is the person who is freest."

When he turned to the treatment of others, Li naturally began with the moral necessity of filial love, obedience, and respect, before moving on to the relations among brothers, friends, and finally strangers, the last of which brought him back to the importance of unity among fellow countrymen.[56] However, it was the final section on living in the world that served as a proto-civics textbook. Beginning with the example of two persons, Li emphasized the importance of mutual respect.[57] Extending this to larger groups, Li emphasized the importance of following the general consensus even at the expense of one's own ideas. His logic would seem to have been the necessity of what he called "grouping" (*hequn*) or "society" (*shehui*): alone, one could accomplish little.[58] Li was moving his argument from the informal group to the nation. A fundamental duty of citizenship was to protect one's "region," just as family members protected their family.[59] Li described the essence of the constitutional political order as obedience to the law as determined democratically:

The foundation of the state lies in the law, and in a constitutional state the laws are that which are recognized [as such] by the people. To disobey the law is thus to betray the people. How can it ever be right to betray the people? When all the people of a

[52] Ibid., p. 47b. [53] Li Jiagu, *Mengxue xiushen jiaokeshu*, "Bianji dayi" 編輯大義 (n.p.).
[54] Li Jiagu, *Mengxue xiushen jiaokeshu*, p. 1a. [55] Ibid., pp. 26a–b.
[56] Ibid., pp. 27b–28a. [57] Ibid., pp. 30b–31a.
[58] Ibid., pp. 31b–32a. [59] Ibid., pp. 32b–33a.

given state follow the laws, the state is ordered. When all the people of a given region obey the laws, that region is ordered. Thus those who do not obey the laws are the public enemies of the state or the region... There is no state in the world that is without governance, but governance that is not in accord with justice (*gongli*) is the same as being without governance. Thus, within a polity, the majority of the people have to agree before policies are made.[60]

As opposed to emphasizing individual morality, the *Citizen's Required Reader* of 1905 focused almost entirely on the nature of the state, citizenship, and conditions in China.[61] It was written in a simple vernacular style by Gao Buying (1873–1940) and Chen Baoquan (1874–1937), but its content was quite sophisticated. Both Gao and Chen had studied in Japan, were of reformist bent, and were about to take jobs in the Ministry of Education, where they stayed on after the revolution. Gao and Chen began by stressing that the people should regard the affairs of state as their own business. The meaning of citizenship, that is to say, lies in the identification of the citizen with the state. This view was diametrically opposed to long-standing Qing doctrine that political questions were off limits to ordinary people. Yet the *Citizen's Required Reader* was published just as the court announced its intention to promulgate a constitution, at least someday. Gao and Chen emphasized the equal status of all Chinese as citizens, regardless of position or wealth.[62]

The *Citizen's Required Reader* called for a "militarized citizenry" (*junguomin*).[63] All citizens should learn the military arts. One model was ancient Sparta.[64] But that was a barbarous system. More relevant were Prussia and Japan. They illustrated military success in the modern world – a world where "international law cannot be relied on; only 'iron and blood' can be relied on." So Gao and Chen stressed that in the case of Japan, primary school textbooks taught "love of country and reverence for the king," as well as glorifying the military.

Gao and Chen began their second volume by saying that a great nation depended on a great citizenry, and a great citizenry could only be produced by great schooling.[65] "Every civilized country in the world today emphasizes

---

[60] Ibid., pp. 34b, 35b.
[61] Gao Buying and Chen Baoquan, *Guomin bidu*. This is not to be confused with the official Qing publication with the same title.
[62] Ibid., 1: 28a. [63] Ibid., 1: 9a–10b.
[64] Gao and Chen later noted a Chinese precedent from, again, the Spring and Autumn period, but whether the farmer-soldiers of that period could be regarded as a militarized *citizenry*, they did not say. *Guomin bi du*, 1: 12a–b. They did insist on China's historical "reverence for the military," citing Confucius: "if on the field of battle a man not brave, he is not filial" (actually a quote from Confucius's disciple Zengzi, who was listing various forms of unfilial behavior, the earliest version of which is probably the "Jiyi" 祭義 chapter of the *Liji* 禮記, c. fourth century BCE). But then they admitted that this was a tradition that had been long lost. *Guomin bi du*, 1: 14a–16b.
[65] Gao Buying and Chen Baoquan, *Guomin bi du*, 2: 1a–2b.

education, and indeed the distinction between 'civilization' and 'barbarism' lies precisely in whether or not they provide education."

There is an aboriginal group in the Americas that in its extreme barbarism regards slaughtering people as virtuous and practices cannibalism. Now, when a family member dies, the relatives and friends all come to divide up the meat; and if no one comes, it will be said that the deceased had not lived virtuously and had been unable to affect people. How can we not laugh at this kind of custom? But it was mostly because of their lack of education, that when they met up with White people, not only were they unable to protect their territory, but they couldn't even preserve their own race.

One or two heroes cannot rescue a nation; its level of civilization depends on the whole people. Thus, education, which the *Citizen's Required Reader* divided into three realms: physical, mental, and moral. A single thread ran through the specific virtues that the rest of the volume promulgated: the extension of care and compassion from individual and family to society and state. In effect, this was to deny the possibility of conflict between the state – at least as properly constituted – and groups within it. Gao and Chen found much to praise in traditional morality. As for filiality, even a parent's unreasonable orders should be obeyed; of course, all parents must be cared for in their old age.[66] Nonetheless, Gao and Chen steadily moved from family ties to the national community. Their lesson on "self-government" was in line with their concept of a militarized citizenry, or at least a citizenry military-like in its respect for order and law. *After* that was in place, "then all persons can order themselves; and a small group of persons can order a family; and if this is extended to some dozens or hundreds of people, they can order a district; and several thousands and tens of thousands of persons can order a state."[67] Ordering (*zhi*) was the same principle in all cases. No doubt, Gao and Chen were deliberately echoing the *Great Learning* in its recipe for an individual paterfamilias to move from self-cultivation to world-ordering.

Major scholars turned their hands to morality textbooks. Cai Yuanpei's textbook for middle school students in effect universalized the concept of filiality and put it in a new context of rights and duties. Cai began: "The sages of China took filiality as the basis for all their affairs. In small affairs this was a matter of private morality; in great affairs, of citizen's justice."[68] All the duties of citizens are included in the scope of morality. Cai ran through the basics of self-cultivation: exercise, health, and hygiene; good habits; diligence; self-control; courage; and so on and so forth. Such virtues are simultaneously inner-directed and outer-directed, to family and society. Cai stated that the basic virtue of youths was filiality; of spouses was harmony; and of individuals in society was

---

[66] Ibid., 2: 11a–13a.   [67] Ibid., 2: 16b.
[68] Cai Zhen [Cai Yuanpei], *Zhongxue xiushen jiaokeshu*, 1: 1.

trustworthiness; whereas the virtue of the citizen was patriotism.[69] This was for Cai, perhaps, a recipe for ensuring both order and liberty.

The family, for Cai, was the basis of both society and the state, and so the latter depended on the morality of the family. This was to say that family morality was a necessary but not sufficient condition for a successful state. Cai's views of family morality were clearly derived from Confucianism and emphasized the mutual responsibilities of distinct roles: for example, the duty of the husband to love his wife and the wife to obey her husband.[70] This already would have sounded reactionary to radical intellectuals, but Cai was at least as interested in how husband and wife could achieve perfect "intimacy" in a companionate marriage based on their complementary natures (generally speaking: strong-gentle, smart-dull, outer-inner).

Cai defined "society" as a group of persons whose interests were intertwined but that remained separate from the state.[71] Society could refer to a group as small as a neighborhood or as large as the world community, for example: Beijing society, Chinese society, Asian society, worker society, student society, and so forth. The state, for Cai, is a different kind of grouping, marked by shared blood and territory, and under unified rule, and so constituting a special type of national society. The state thus stands above society, in sole possession of sovereignty. Each national society has its own morality based on its particular climate, race, customs, and history. Ultimately, society is the product of the human propensity to cooperate for mutual benefit. Whereas social morality applies to members of society, the law applies to members of a state, and morality merely supplements the law (as the law supplements society), Cai said. It is the law that demarcates the boundary between state and society. As members of society, people were bound by justice and civic virtue.[72] Justice referred to respect for the rights of others, in particular their life, property, and honor. This was, however, merely a negative form of morality. Positive morality consisted in universal love or fraternity (*bo'ai*). Yet, civic virtue, in Cai's view, consisted of more than, say, acts of charity; rather it involved the perpetual improvement of society and benefit to humankind.[73] Justice is a matter of the law, whereas civic virtue is necessary for a complete morality.

Not surprisingly, Cai defined the state, at least analogously, as the family writ large.[74] As the family had a head (in his patriarchal view), so the state

---

[69] Ibid., 1: 36. Cai was in effect modifying the traditional Three Bonds of Confucianism (parent-child, husband-wife, emperor-subject) to the needs of a republic.
[70] Ibid., 1: 52–55.   [71] Ibid., 1: 60–63.   [72] Ibid, 1: 63–66.
[73] In a later chapter, Cai defined fraternity more expansively: a sense of empathy for all creatures that might be rooted in family but was not limited by boundaries of kinship or nation; not just doing good, but leading people to do good, and furthermore planning for its systematic expansion (such as founding schools and hospitals). Ibid., pp. 78–85.
[74] Ibid., pp. 89–91.

had a leader. As family members had to work together, so citizens could not simply pursue their own interests without regard to the greater good. Rights entailed duties, which were, Cai argued, something like two sides of the same coin. Our right to dispose of our property entails our duty to not stop others from disposing of theirs as well. The state's duty to protect its people entails the right to take necessary actions, whereas our right to the protection of the state entails duties to the state. What Cai stressed here was the equality of rights: no one possessed special privileges. A key role of the state was to protect individuals' rights and indeed to prevent people from using the excuse of defending their rights to take action on their own. Cai thus concluded that in this sense the state was founded for the sake of rights. Shifting the perspective, these rights were also the duties of the state and of its people. (Cai also emphasized the duties of obeying the law, paying taxes, and serving as soldiers.) He did not discuss the morality of overthrowing a government, even though this might seem a natural topic for (former) revolutionaries.

Another prominent scholar, Liu Shipei, wrote his *Ethics Textbook* (*Lunli jiaokeshu*) while briefly teaching middle school in 1905, though he also published it in the *National Essence Journal* in Shanghai.[75] The *Ethics Textbook* is a complex work that paid little attention to the official curricular goals of the Ministry of Education, but there are several features it shared with more ordinary textbooks of the day. Most obviously, Liu himself said his goal was pedagogical, and that schools must teach the principles of ethics, without which there was no basis for correct practice.[76] Furthermore, he saw his work as offering students an overview of the Chinese moral tradition, though he criticized aspects of it. Finally, Liu sought to "arouse the spirit of the Chinese people so that they may rise up," a partly veiled reference to his revolutionary nationalism.

Liu offered something of a history of Chinese moral thought, but he also spoke of the theory and disciplines of self-cultivation; the meaning of virtue; the notion of sociability; "esteem for the military," as suggested by the Qing curriculum; the bonds of father-son, brother-brother, and husband-wife; establishing the will; reverence; benevolence; righteousness; and other

[75] Citations here are from Liu Shipei, *Lunli jiaokeshu*, vol. 4. For Liu, see Chapter 1; this work has been read more as a cutting-edge treatise in the history of Chinese moral philosophy than as a typical textbook. The philosopher Stephen Angle has called it "a much more systematic presentation of an ethical theory than any we find in earlier centuries" – "Did Someone Say 'Rights?'" p. 626. Angle goes on: "Liu's ethical theory is shorn of much of the metaphysical apparatus that accompanied earlier Neo-Confucian ethical teachers, and ... Liu's ethics is deeply indebted to strands of the Neo-Confucian tradition, and reads like a conscious updating of the Confucian ethical worldview." Nonetheless, in my view, much of Confucianism is here so thoroughly reworked by Liu that, at least from the perspective of his views of the just society, "updating" is not the best metaphor for a more syncretic and radical process. The historian Hao Chang has further suggested that Liu's very first writings already reflected his "moral quest for the just society and the virtuous man" – *Chinese Intellectuals in Crisis*, p. 150.
[76] Liu Shipei, *Lunli jiaokeshu*, p. 123 (1: 1a–b).

Confucian virtues. In effect, Liu argued for the existence of deep connections between individual virtues and "social ethics," which he said the Chinese still needed to develop.[77] Liu discussed topics that had been raised repeatedly by Chinese thinkers over the centuries, as well as some new ideas from the West – he had a particular interest in Rousseau. A general theme to which Liu constantly returned is the natural origins of morality in the inherently social nature of life, an arguably Confucian view but perhaps also reflecting Rousseau's social contract, on which Liu had written extensively. What moral education could culminate in was the "complete person" (*wanquan zhi ren*) and the "complete society" (*wanquan zhi shehui*).[78] Completeness in this sense was certainly derived from the Confucian tradition, but Liu's historicization of morality moved it away from the cosmological realm of Confucianism to a realm that humans made for themselves. He thus attacked the Three Bonds as oppressive; on ethical grounds he advocated an egalitarian society composed of autonomous individuals.

Good children in Republican textbooks

In the wake of the 1911 Revolution, the Commercial Press repackaged its old product as a *New Self-Cultivation Textbook* for primary schools.[79] First-year students were presented with pictures designed to show such virtues as punctuality, orderliness, personal cleanliness and public hygiene, honesty, diligence, respect for guests, respect for elders, and also charity and "public morality." Such lessons were repeated in more sophisticated versions in later semesters through more advanced texts. But in the first year, teachers were to explain the pictures by telling stories about them. In Figure 13, for example, a picture of a bird feeding its nestlings, accompanied by a second picture of fledglings taking their first flight, turns into a story about "parental love," which is presented as the basis of filial piety.[80] As long as the baby birds are too small to fend for themselves, the mother bird flies off to find food for them, brings it back to the nest, and feeds her babies. Time and time again she does this, softening the food so they can eat it. Then the exhortation: "You students, think about the babies in the nest with their heads sticking up waiting to be fed, and the mommy bird flying back and worth, never resting: how great is her toil and suffering?"

And finally the meaning of the allegory:

You students need to know that the love of the mommy bird for her babies, enormous as it is, is nothing compared with the human love for their babies. How can you not always be thinking about the enormous love your parents have for you?... Now you students

---

[77] Ibid., p. 169 (2: 49b).
[78] E.g., ibid, pp. 126–127 (1: 6b–7a), 169 (49b); see the discussion in Hao Chang, *Chinese Intellectuals in Crisis*, pp. 149–170.
[79] Qin Tongpei, *Xin xiushen jiaoshoufa*.   [80] Ibid., 2: 6b–7a.

Textbook morality, self-cultivation, and civics 97

Figure 13 From right to left: nestlings and fledglings illustrate the meaning of filial piety.

have started school and you are no longer just two-year-old babies, but you still depend entirely on your parents for all your food, all your clothing, and all your housing. Here you can see the enormous love of the human species for its young ... Perhaps you merely take for granted your parent's love and have not really thought about it. But now that it has been explained, if you have any human feeling, you must feel very moved. As you are moved and understand it now, you must constantly keep it in mind.[81]

Teachers were to impress on students that the loving care of parents is the basis of filial obligation. But filial obligation was not merely to obey one's parents; it was to care for oneself, to stay healthy, and to study hard. For slightly more advanced students, stories were often derived from historical cases or *The Twenty-Four Filial Exemplars*. As we have seen, language readers told the story of Huang Xiang, who fanned his father's bed in the summer and warmed it in the winter. The *New Self-Cultivation Textbook* described numerous ways Huang cared for his parents.[82] And based on this story, teachers were to explain the practical aspects of filial service.[83] Even young children should be able to anticipate the desires and needs of their parents. Like Huang Xiang, you merely

[81] Ibid., 2: 8b–10a.   [82] Qin Tongpei, *Xin xiushen jiaokeshu*, 3: 7b–8a.
[83] Qin Tongpei, *Xin xiushen jiaoshoufa*, 3: 11b–12b.

need sincere filiality. Parents do not need the best food or the finest clothing, but if you fulfill their basic physical and emotional needs, you have been filial. Thus you should not let them get too hot in summer or too cold in winter (like Huang Xiang); you should give them food that is tasty and nourishing; you should take them out in nice weather and amuse them at home; and you should try to fulfill their hopes for you.

Another case, this one derived from the *Latter Han History*, was of the 15-year-old Peng Xiu, who was traveling with his father when they were attacked by bandits. He raised his sword, intoning, "If a father is insulted, his son must die. Today is the day of my death." The bandit leader was so impressed that he let them both go.[84] Though it might seem that the story could have ended less happily, the teacher was to explain that Peng's survival was not merely a matter of luck.[85] Rather, Peng thought only of his father and not of himself; since the father-son relationship is rooted in Nature, it is simply morally wrong for a son to think only of himself. It is, however, not necessarily "natural" behavior, since in times of crisis people do sometimes forget the knowledge of ethics, which is what separates us from the animals. It was because Peng was armed with great righteousness, not his sword, that he moved even a thief. As well, students should note: Peng was not only filial but quick and intelligent.

A picture of boys drilling with the 18-star army flag (Figure 14) illustrated respect for the military, exemplifying continuity with the ideals of a militant citizenry that had begun in the late Qing.

In this picture, the boys are marching in uniform behind the new Republic's war flag, which had originally been raised by army rebels in 1911. Eighteen gold balls around a black star represented the 18 provinces of China. The teacher's manual stressed that the larger value to be impressed on students was a kind of natural spiritedness or courage. Children naturally respect soldiers, as their play makes clear, it noted. But training future soldiers requires discipline, not just play.[86] This lesson was also designed to point out a difference between people and animals. Animals carry their weapons in the form of claws and talons and fangs, whereas people are smart enough to make weapons. And unlike animals, or so teachers were to suggest with some poetic license, people did not merely defend themselves as individuals but knew how to group together.

A story of birds cooperating to build their nests was in effect a parable of the efficiency of the division of labor, which came about through cooperation and ultimately universal love (*bo'ai*).[87] As Figure 15 shows, some birds carry twigs and some mud; the individual bird is weak, while collectively the birds

---

[84] Qin Tongpei, *Xin xiushen jiaokeshu*, 5: 6b–7a; *Xin xiushen jiaoshoufa* 5: 13b–14a.
[85] Qin Tongpei, *Xin xiushen jiaoshoufa*, 5: 13b–14a.
[86] Qin Tongpei, *Xin xiushen jiaoshoufa*, 2: 17b–19a.   [87] Ibid., 3: 18a–19a.

Figure 14 The military arts.

are strong; the individual bird works slowly, but the collective works quickly. So the school was built through the cooperative efforts of carpenters and masons and stoneworkers. So, in terms of behavioral norms, students should learn to participate in group projects, to ask for help when it is needed, and to give help when it is needed. "All public tasks must be seen as more important than private affairs, and all must try their hardest to help." The broader lesson was that these were virtues to be taught, but also reflections of natural compassion or empathy.

School and family remained the focus of the early volumes of the series. The centrality of hygiene to self-cultivation textbooks is striking. Hygiene seems both a personal virtue and also a matter of public morality. One picture-story

Figure 15 Building the nest together.

early in the series told of brothers who exercised diligently to make their bodies strong, and another told of a boy who bathed frequently and washed his clothes.[88] Later lessons reinforced the importance of exercise and generally healthy habits through the ancient exemplars Ge Hong (283–343) and Hua Tuo (c. 140–208).[89] Moderation in food, clothing, work, and leisure, when combined with basic hygienic habits, preserved body and mind.

The first lesson of the last volume of the Commercial Press series of self-cultivation textbooks consisted of a key to the entire project: introspection (*zixing*). Take the Song dynasty statesman Fan Zhongyan (989–1052), who

---

[88] Qin Tongpei, *Xin xiushen*, 3: 2b–3a; *Xin xiushen jiaoshoufa*, 3: 2a–4b.
[89] Qin Tongpei, *Xin xiushen*, 5: 5a–6a; *Xin xiushen jiaoshoufa*, 5: 10a–b. Ge was a literatus noted for his long life; Hua was a famous physician.

Textbook morality, self-cultivation, and civics 101

reviewed the events of his day every night before he went to sleep.[90] If he had been good, he could sleep; but if not, he would toss and turn all night. Teachers were to use this text to emphasize the importance of self-control (*keji*). Like this: introspection serves as a kind of mirror. We cannot see our own face as we see the faces of others, so we use a mirror to know if we are dirty. It is also easier to see the moral faults of others than of ourselves, but introspection allows us to compare ourselves to the virtuous people of the past, and then to root out our own faults. The moments before bed are a good time for self-reflection, a chance to look back on your behavior during the day, judge it according to your conscience, and try to reform. Through constant introspection and reform, you can improve your instincts, but you can never abandon introspection lest faults creep back in. For students, the questions to reflect on include these: Do you understand everything you are reading? Are you lazy about learning characters or math problems? Do you fail to follow the rules when playing games? Are you in harmony with your parents and siblings? Do you wash regularly and follow hygienic practices?

Pro patria

By the 1920s, homely virtues were supplemented by systematic education in citizenship knowledge (*gongmin zhishi*).[91] The Commercial Press' new civics textbook series offered analyses of society and the state. A repeating motif of the failures and limits of the Chinese people served as a spur to improvement, and also, perhaps, as a sign that improvement would come about at the hands of the next generation.[92] The first volume of the series dealt with a combination of individual virtues and social knowledge or manners: orderliness, hygiene, self-help, public property, the spirit of obedience, empathy for the less fortunate, and the like. Many of the stories of the 1910s self-cultivation textbook were recycled here. The second volume discussed society and introduced the topic of government, while continuing to emphasize individual morality. And the third volume focused entirely on the nation-state, its political structure, and the rights and duties of the people.

In this spirit, moral values become the virtues of citizens. Students should learn to become self-sufficient, for example, so that they need not depend on others.[93] Teachers were to emphasize that this personal and practical goal – independence – could not justify selfishness, nor did it mean students could not ask others for help when they needed it. But "when everyone is independent,

---

[90] Qin Tongpei, *Xin xiushen*, 5: 1a; *Xin xiushen jiaoshoufa*, 5: 1a–2a.
[91] Wan Liangjun, *Xinxuan gongmin jiaoshoushu*, 1: 2.
[92] Andrew F. Jones, *Developmental Fairy Tales*, esp. chapter 3.
[93] Wan Liangjun, *Xinxuan gongmin jiaoshoushu*, 1: 11–12.

102   Educating China

country and society will also receive blessings." Indeed, this applies to all good habits, such as orderliness, trustworthiness, cleanliness, respect, modesty, and yielding. When students learn such habits in school, they will carry them over to the benefit of society.[94]

The lesson on obedience (*fucong*) began with the natural obedience of children to their parents, their older brothers and sisters, and their teachers. There was a distinction, according to the teacher's manual, between conscious (*youyishi*) obedience and unconscious (*wuyishi*) obedience. The former refers to obedience when the reasons are correct; but when we simply obey without thinking, even if the reasons are improper, this is unconscious obedience. The text concluded that unconscious obedience should be avoided. One example of unconscious obedience was worshipping the Buddha with one's mother – because this is "superstition" that should be avoided. Teachers were to point out that conscious obedience covered behavior that the law demanded, and also prohibitions on causing a disturbance or violating the rights of others. But should one obey mother's instructions to worship Buddha or not? The manual did not help teachers here.

Whether primary school students were really expected to engage their parents in the dialectic, they were expected to engage each other. In addition to generalizations about communal life, empathy, and the inviolability of public property, lessons dealt with student associations and the principle of representation. First, rules for meetings.[95] In the narrative frame of the lesson, a father explains to his son that he needs to arrive punctually, one person should speak at a time, and decisions are taken by majority vote. Teachers were to prod students by noting that Chinese failure to respect these rules of order is the reason why so many public meetings end in chaos. But by encouraging students to learn to organize youth citizen assemblies now, they will develop better behavior. Also, the minority must give way to the majority on any given issue; however, because the majority is not always correct, both sides should listen to one another respectfully. The next lesson went on to describe a fictional youth citizen assembly that resolved by majority vote to tell the local police office that the students wished to help clean up the trash in the school's neighborhood.[96]

The China Bookstore's civics textbook brought the Republic of China into an early lesson via the morning bow to the flag, but in all it had less to say about the state or even society.[97]

In Figure 16, showing the beginning of the school day, students and teachers bow to the national flag, whose five colors represented the five major peoples of China. Instead of discussing society, the textbook focused on behavioral norms.

---

[94] Ibid.,1: 17–18.   [95] Ibid., 1: 29–31.
[96] Ibid., 1: 32–33.   [97] Dong Wen, *Gongmin keben*, 3: 2b–3a.

Textbook morality, self-cultivation, and civics 103

Figure 16 Bowing to the national flag at the beginning of the school day.

"Society" in the early civics lessons of the Commercial Press textbook remained fairly vague, and efforts to explain it systematically could not take narrative form. The second volume of the series described the different occupations of people, networks of transportation and communication, laws, and various levels of government. But according to the textbook, more important than knowledge of the "forms" of government was the "spirit of public-mindedness" (*gonggongxin*).[98] It is not the organs of government, or the specific officials, or even clean elections that make for self-government, but rather the public-mindedness of the people. Without it, even good officials will be hamstrung – as in the case of public hygiene that depends on the cooperation of all. Teachers were to emphasize the bottom-up nature of society:

[98] Wan Liangjun, *Xinxuan gongmin jiaoshoushu*, 2: 47–48.

The state is founded on society, while society is formed out of groups. If the people lack civic virtue, then their groups will be unstable, society will fall apart, and so state itself will be threatened. Thus the importance of civic virtue is enormous, and we should encourage children to develop these kinds of good habits from a young age.[99]

The elements making up "community life" (*gongtong shenghuo*) were the individual, the society composed of individuals, and finally the state, which was effectively treated as a natural expression of society. One way of thinking about society was through the roles of its members. Hence, the textbook urged, finding an occupation was key to independence (a virtue already established as desirable, as we have seen). One's job was also a way to exercise the body and mind, and to contribute to society and to human flourishing.[100] The textbook went on to explain government as a kind of representative of society that should be chosen by society. The key to "self-government" was, of course, elections. And the key to elections was, again, the people themselves, not the officials or the government.[101] The goal of elections was to choose officials who possessed the best morality and ability. For this to happen, the people needed to reject all temptations of bribery and bonds of kinship. The notion of representation was also explained – the Chinese were simply too numerous for everyone to participate directly in making laws, so they chose representatives. Now, these representatives, because they spoke for the people, could also bind the people to the laws they passed.[102] Interestingly, there were to be school elections to give students practice in these arts.[103] Similarly, as a government needed to conduct censuses to understand the people's needs, students could conduct a census of the school neighborhood to acquire data on gender, age, education, occupation, and the like.[104]

What were laws? They were like school regulations, but at the level of society.[105] "However, while school regulations are determined by teachers, the laws that people obey are determined by the people." This is because students are immature. According to the civics textbooks, it is because people make their own laws (at least through their representatives), that they must obey them. Such laws are designed both to maintain order and to further the common happiness. All laws are derived from the constitution, but they consist of two types: public, such as administrative, criminal, and procedural laws; and private, such as civil and commercial law. So-called international law is really not law but a set of conventions settled among countries. Teachers were to bring out the double-sidedness of the "law": in a broad sense, the general norms of

---

[99] Ibid., 2: 53.   [100] Ibid., 2: 1.   [101] Ibid., 2: 45–46.
[102] Ibid., 2: 68–69; 3: 3–4; 3: 36–37.
[103] See also Robert Culp, *Articulating Citizenship*, esp. chapter 3.
[104] Wan Liangjun, *Xinxuan gongmin jiaoshoushu*, 2: 49–51.   [105] Ibid., 2: 67–69.

organized societies; but more particularly, provisions passed by the Assembly and promulgated by the government. Teachers were to explain that it is law that protects and even creates liberty. Disobedience of the law was not a form of liberty; rather, cheating and stealing and the like disturb social order and peace.

The textbook explained that there were two types of duties. Legal duties included tax payment, military service, and compulsory schooling, whereas moral (but public) duties included voting. And also, one had a moral duty to obey the spirit and not just the letter of the law.[106] The notion of "rights" was introduced in terms of the need to "respect the rights of others."[107] Take student Deng, who frequently "borrows" the books and other items of his classmates, sometimes damaging them. One day on his way to school, another classmate takes one of Deng's books and tears its cover. Deng, furious, complains to a teacher, who tells him:

Now, you finally know that taking or damaging other people's stuff is wrong. You must understand that everything has its owner, and this owner has rights over his property; without good reason, other people cannot take it. If you don't want other people to violate your rights, how could it be that other people want you to violate their rights? "What you do not want done to yourself, do not do to others." From now on, you should know how to behave. Furthermore, the rights of others are not only to be respected in school, but in the future, as you serve society, this spirit is especially important. Since society is based on people associating together, social peace can only be secured when everyone is able to respect others' rights. If everyone in society is violating each other's rights, society will fall into tumult and confusion, and then what kind of peace will be possible?

While the MacGuffin of this story is the boy's book, or property, which reinforces the bourgeois spirit of the civics curriculum, the book primarily serves as a concrete example, suitable to children's understanding, of the larger point: respect for rights is simply another way of speaking about the necessary conditions for community life.

The next lesson defined the state (*guojia*). The goal of the lesson on the state was to develop patriotism.[108] The text defined the state abstractly, in terms taken from late Qing law books: people plus land plus sovereignty. The civics textbook lamented that Chinese sovereignty, however, was compromised. "Sovereignty" is when the government can freely act. China is superficially sovereign but in fact partly subject to other countries. The Chinese people need to recognize the importance of national sovereignty and strive to restore it. Teachers were to explain how territorial concessions, tariff regulations, and extraterritoriality all limited China's sovereignty. The leased concessions, for example, were officially Chinese territory, but in fact they were colonies. The

[106] Ibid., 3: 18. [107] Ibid., 2: 62–64. [108] Ibid., 2: 64–67.

teacher's manual also urged teachers to highlight infringements on sovereignty in their particular locality.[109]

The theme of territorial integrity was drummed into students.[110] National territory was defined as the land under the sovereignty (*zhuquan*) of a particular state: that is, where the states exercise powers over both natives and foreigners (excepting only foreign leaders and diplomats as provided by international convention). Clearly, extraterritoriality harmed China's sovereignty, and "we must struggle against it." The concessions were another obvious blow to China's sovereignty, and teachers were encouraged to get students talking about the infringements of sovereignty both nationwide and in their own particular districts. As for the precise extent of China, the textbook differentiated between two categories of the territorial state: the twenty-two provinces and the vassal states of Inner and Outer Mongolia, Tibet, and Qinghai. However, it did not define vassal state (*fanshu*), nor did it provide maps, which were left to history and geography textbooks.

Civics classes did complicate the definition of sovereignty, suggesting it was something more than the exercise of state power. For the other side of the coin of sovereignty, as it were, was self-government. The state could not be separated from the people. The goal of the next lesson was "to explain how the people of the nation can achieve true sovereignty."[111] The lesson explained: "Since China is a democracy, sovereignty lies in the whole body of the people."[112] However (as students might remember from previous lessons), not literally everyone can participate in governance, so the people entrust political powers to parliamentary representatives. The point to be stressed about popular sovereignty was that, for all the responsibilities of the people's representatives to act selflessly in considering the public good, it was the people's responsibility to select good representatives.[113]

> Thus although sovereignty resides in the people in name, it does not reside in the people in practice, but is exercised merely by a small minority. Therefore, if one wishes to support the principle that sovereignty resides in the people, one must carefully select representatives, and also constantly inspect them, so that the national assembly becomes an organ that truly represents the popular will, follows the demands of the people, and decides various policies [accordingly].

Teachers were to emphasize that although the Chinese liked to criticize the government and complain about their assemblymen, the real responsibility for

---

[109] Ibid., 3: 2–3.   [110] Ibid., 3: 1–3.   [111] Ibid., 3: 3–5.
[112] Who were the people? The next lesson described the nationality law, which rested on a jus sanguinis definition of citizenship. Ibid., 3: 8–15. The implication was that overseas Chinese (*Huaqiao*) remained citizens or at least "Chinese" (*Zhonghua renmin*) through eternal generations through their father's line.
[113] Wan Liangjun, *Xinxuan gongmin jiaoshoushu*, 3: 3–4.

these affairs lay with the people themselves. If children could be brought to understand this, they would become more capable citizens.

But the textbook also noted a problem.[114] "If China is a democracy and national sovereignty lies in the people, then according to logic everyone should directly possess governing authority. But since the Chinese population approaches some 400 million, if everyone wanted to govern directly, the situation would obviously be impossible." And so the people elect representatives who directly govern through the national assembly, as we have seen; here, however, the textbook stressed that elections and assemblies alone do not make for democracy. What is needed is the genuine spirit of representation. The representatives themselves need to remember that their role is to think of the good of the whole people. The government needs to report to the assembly and carry out the laws it passes. And, not least, the people need to maintain supervision over their representatives and also support for them. Again, teachers can point out that students should be involved in school elections. Repeatedly, this civics textbook emphasized the importance of the people to the political system, not to idealize the system but to get it to work. "Good government" depends on the quality of the people.[115] It is necessary but not sufficient to get rid of corrupt officials. It is necessary but not sufficient to have good laws. Only "a good people" – displaying their constant concern with public issues and closely supervising representatives and officials – serve as the motive force for good government. To this textual bromide, teachers were to instruct their students that the Chinese of today have given up their rights. Under these circumstances, to sit back and hope for good government was worse than futile.

As for the rights and duties of the Chinese, the textbook turned to the constitution.[116] First, public rights include political rights such as suffrage and holding public office, and also include "liberty rights" (*ziyouquan*). Liberty rights are further subdivided between those basic liberties such as physical freedom, movement, occupation, property, speech, and religion, on the one hand, and, on the other hand, supplementary rights such as freedoms of publishing and association. Second, the rights of the people (presumably, here was meant "private rights" as opposed to public rights) include equality before the law, privacy of mail, the right to petition, and the like. Again, the text noted that rights are limited by the needs of the public good, while teachers were to make clear that not all Chinese possessed political rights – because suffrage was limited. Furthermore, rights could not be granted to children or the insane. Finally, teachers were to note that the constitutional system just described had not, in fact, been completely carried out because of political instability.

The lesson on duties explicitly noted that rights and duties were twinned norms.[117] As we have noted, the text distinguished between legal and moral duties. It also pointed out that – beyond morality and beyond law, as it

---

[114] Ibid., 3: 36–38. [115] Ibid., 3: 52–54. [116] Ibid., 3: 15–17. [117] Ibid., 3: 18–19.

were – people had the duty to respect the powers of the state. These powers may indeed restrict the rights of individuals, but such restrictions directly benefit society and indirectly benefit the individual. Therefore, people should be willing to obey without resentment: "this is also a kind of moral duty." Not surprisingly, the next lesson dealt with the law.[118] Here, the text was not descriptive but returned to a narrative strategy. The story was of Henry V of England. When he was a wild young prince, a judge sentenced him to prison, saying, "In applying the law, judges do not consider royalty or rank to reduce the sentence." Henry, however, continued his wild ways, got into more scrapes, and even attacked the judge. The judge then had him seized again, saying, "The crimes of the prince deserve punishment; these crimes do not lie in insulting me but in disobeying the law," and he directly told the prince: "One day your majesty will be the King of England. If your majesty cannot uphold the law today, how will you later rule over the people?" Needless to say, Henry was suitably chastened, vowed to reform, and became a good king. The teachers' manual spelled out the lesson that everyone must obey the law.

Society

The "society" curriculum of the 1920s overlapped with self-cultivation and civics textbooks. Interest in society is amply documented in the preceding pages, and it had long been a focus of late Qing intellectual interest via Herbert Spencer and to some extent Comte and Marx.[119] The rise of the discipline of sociology in Western universities at the beginning of the twentieth century attracted a new generation of Chinese intellectuals. But Chinese educators were probably most influenced by the role the "study of society" assumed in civics education in the United States in the 1920s. American educators decided that studying government was not sufficient to produce good citizens. One major textbook defined civics as the study of social relationships; government was still important but was only one form of social life.[120] Another spoke of the concept of "community civics," defined as "an interpretation of the *community character* of national and international life equally with that of town or neighborhood."[121] Society is based on cooperation, and government is an agency to secure cooperation, but presumably not the only such agency, nor

---

[118] Ibid., 3: 20–21.
[119] For the concept of society, see Kai Vogelsang, "Chinese 'Society'"; and Michael Tsin, "Imagining 'Society' in Early Twentieth-Century China"; for the social sciences, see Yung-chen Chiang, *Social Engineering*; and Arif Dirlik, Guannan Li, and Hsiao-pei Yen, eds., *Sociology and Anthropology*.
[120] R. O. Hughes, *A Text-Book in Citizenship*, foreword.
[121] Arthur W. Dunn, *Community Civics and Rural Life*, p. iv. See also R. O. Hughes, *Community Civics*.

does it determine the common goals of community life. In the words of a major textbook, "The teaching of the mechanics of government is not enough; the children must learn how people live together in communities and how they may best share in the activities arising from this life together."[122] Even textbooks that stressed traditional civics noted the need for students to have some understanding of economics and sociology. Textbook authors also placed a good deal of stress on the need to get students participating in group activities outside the class. These could be Deweyan social welfare projects.[123] Or they could be school governments, for students "must have a chance to form *habits* of good citizenship if we are to develop intelligent, enthusiastic, helpful members of the community."[124]

In 1924 the pioneering sociologist Tao Menghe (1887–1960) wrote a middle school textbook focusing on a range of social issues but concentrating on the problem of poverty.[125] Tao obtained his Ph.D. from the London School of Economics and in the 1920s was teaching at Peking University. He defined the study of society as knowledge of the nature of "community life," a field of knowledge that had much in common with history, politics, and economics, but that also spoke scientifically to the question, how can we improve society?[126] Tao insisted that people are inherently social: there is simply no such thing as the isolated individual. For example, it is no use running a hygienic household if the streets are unsanitary because the city government is corrupt. At the same time, the individual cannot blame society for its faults as if it were an external force. Tao argued that individuals constituted and affected society. "Society" was no more an abstraction divorced from the individual than the fantasy of the isolated individual divorced from society. He also believed that attempts to solve social problems – perhaps even attempting to maintain society itself – required scientific understanding of the nature of society. Tao was implying that neither random charity nor blindly led revolution could solve China's problems.

Tao tended to define society as a web of relationships that surrounded every individual. Such relationships were "social relationships" and constituted society.[127] Tao used both the metaphor of a net composed of interwoven relationships and the metaphor of a living organism whose parts exercise mutual influence on one another. Tao's point here was to deny that the individual and society constituted a kind of binary relationship.[128] For individuals did

---

[122] Edgar W. Ames and Arvie Eldred, *Community Civics* (New York: MacMillan Co., 1921), p. v.
[123] Thomas Harrison Reed, *Loyal Citizenship*, pp. v–vi.
[124] Charles Edgar Finch, *Everyday Civics*, p. vi.
[125] Tao Menghe, *Shehui wenti*. Though writing with reformist intent, Tao claimed that the field of social knowledge was not "propaganda," but rather was as objective as knowledge of the natural sciences. As the natural sciences led to the ability to control natural phenomena, so the social sciences could lead to the ability to control social phenomena.
[126] Ibid., *Xu* 序.   [127] Ibid., pp. 1–3.   [128] Ibid., pp. 3–5.

not make society; it was social relationships that made society. What appears to be "individual behavior" was in fact a product of social forces. Basing his ideas on broadly Durkheimian premises, then, Tao did not deny the existence of the individual, but rather the notion of a binary opposition of individual and society, which forgets that individuals are always everywhere embedded in society. Tao concluded that what made this common mistake possible was the extraordinary complexity of modern society.

The task facing middle school students, then, was to gain understanding of the interconnectedness of everyone in their society, which would lead to a certain kind of solidarity. For example, a beggar may be a parasite on society, but one cannot deny one's relationship to the beggar. The beggar's failure to contribute to society increases the contributions needed from everyone else.[129] Tao saw poverty to be the single most basic social problem facing China, either causing or closely linked to many other problems, such as robbery and begging.[130] The causes of poverty were complex: what, then, was to be done? Roughly speaking, and putting aside such important (and complex) questions as education, politics, law, and public health, Tao suggested two main reform programs.[131] First, control over nature, which essentially referred to economic development through more productive use of natural resources and to measures to ameliorate natural disasters and improve public health. Second, the ordering of economic and social conditions to produce an equitable distribution of wealth through a few relatively simple steps: increase workers' wages; regulate and tax business owners; stabilize the conditions of production with limits on competition; and, finally, protect the rights of women and children, that is, provide support for child-raising and education.

Tao's views obviously placed him among the progressives of the 1920s. But in addition to repeatedly reminding students that there were no simple solutions, he took an essentially apolitical approach to China's problems. Indeed, for Tao, society was not only complex but an organic whole. Thus if one part was diseased, the entire body was threatened, even if parts of the social body seemed prosperous at the moment. The metaphor of organic disease implied that social reformers needed to be expert professionals, like doctors,[132] and indeed, that an unprofessional approach would simply make matters worse. Western nations, Tao noted, had produced material plenty without solving poverty and unemployment. The socialists, he concluded, saw the problem, but their proposals were too idealistic to be practical. Nor did the materialist conception of history provide an adequate explanation of the way society operated. In other words, Tao attacked Marxism for its economic determinism, which he

---

[129] Ibid., pp. 8–10.   [130] Ibid., pp. 174–175.
[131] Ibid., pp. 177–191.   [132] Ibid., pp. 14–17, 27.

thought neglected the complexity of the various causal factors shaping the relationship between political and economic questions. Sometimes, Tao said, economic development really does lead to political change, but sometimes political development leads to economic advances.[133] Indeed, such feedback loops (a metaphor not available to Tao) were very tangled: only through thorough knowledge of society could one escape from causal traps. For example, China needed to develop education in order to create a better republic, which better citizens could construct. But to develop education, we first need to reform government. But to reform government, we need to eradicate military interference. But to eradicate the warlords, we must abolish warlord system politics – but to do that, we need well-educated citizens with the capacity for self-government, and we are back where we started. For Tao, evidently, the role of students was not to take to the streets today, but to prepare themselves with the expertise to cure China's social problems tomorrow.

Self-cultivation and civics classes were central to the school curriculum, but they were not the only "morality books" (*shanshu*) on the market. Indeed, of nonfiction, religiously inflected morality books, including reprints of late imperial editions, were probably produced in greater numbers than any other genre. They came in many varieties but basically taught that traditional Confucian ethics were compatible with modernization – indeed, essential for making China both strong and good while avoiding the ills of the modern era.[134] Unlike textbooks, morality books were generally grounded in a theory of karma whereby good deeds would be rewarded in this life or the next, and bad deeds punished. Both textbooks and the morality books emphasized filiality and the importance of family relations, but textbooks dealt in greater depth with the meaning of citizenship. Repeatedly, textbooks stated or implied that the Chinese people had failed to hold power holders to account. This view reflected in part the New Culture movement's analysis of the failures of republican institutions. Textbooks did not accept the radicals' slashing critique of Confucianism, but they did accept the view that republicanism, though undoubtedly necessary, required certain cultural foundations that the 1911 Revolution had not erected. It was thus pointless to go around blaming warlords, factional interests, or even foreign imperialists, for these were like beasts who simply did what came naturally to them. It was necessary, rather, that children learn a particular set of civic values and "habits" in order to become good citizens. Once China had enough such citizens, they could take care of its problems.

Writing in the mid-1920s, Tang Zhansheng was one of a number of educators, inspired by John Dewey, calling the old self-cultivation curriculum

---

[133] Ibid., pp. 23–24.   [134] Jan Kiely, "Shanghai Public Moralist Nie Qijie."

outdated.[135] It emphasized, Tang charged, the "static morality" of self-control and neglected study of active participation. Its narrow scope left it unable to form the basis of "new knowledge, new skills, new appreciations, new attitudes, and new ideals" needed today. Chinese "psychology and customs" had not kept up with the massive changes China had undergone in the previous few years. This has given rise to unease and tensions. Now, "The citizens of a democratic state must certainly be molded by democratic principles (*pingmin zhuyi*) and must possess the spirit of cooperation, mutual aid, self-government, and responsibility and the like, but due to historical conditions, the Chinese lack the capacity to fulfill these tasks."[136] The solution lay in civics education. However, Tang was not satisfied with the kind of "civics knowledge" that was limited to discussions of liberties, rights, suffrage, and the operations of government. Rather, a broader definition of civics should focus on all-round insight, empathetic morality, and healthy bodies.[137] Tang maintained that civics education should focus both on service to society and on autonomy and self-respect.

Key to Tang's thinking was the question of the quality of Chinese people. Though this specific language was not yet widespread, his premise was widely shared: that the people's customs, habits, and knowledge were deficient for advanced or civilized democracy. The conclusion that New Culture intellectuals drew was not that any problems lay with democracy, nor even that the masses were fundamentally flawed. Rather, precisely because people were inherently social creatures, by instilling democratic principles in the broadest sense, schools could foster the development of complete persons. But the conclusion that the Nationalists drew was different. Accepting that the Chinese people were not ready for democracy, they sought to create new citizens simultaneously capable of self-control and active participation – but participation only within the bounds drawn up by the Nationalists. The next chapter describes the Nationalist program.

---

[135] Tang Zhansheng, *Xiaoxue gongmin jiaoxuefa*. See Bi Yuan, *Jianzao changshi*, pp. 187–188; Zheng Hang, *Zhongguo jindai deyu*, pp. 241–247.
[136] Tang Zhansheng, *Xiaoxue gongmin jiaoxuefa*, p. 1.   [137] Ibid., pp. 5–7.

4 Good citizens

The Nationalist government of 1928 inherited the curriculum reforms of 1923. Reviewing the development civics curriculum six years into the Nationalist period, the educator Sheng Langxi (1901–1974) still highlighted the significance of the 1923 curricular reforms.[1] Sheng seemed to imply that relatively speaking, at least, the partification of the curriculum between 1928 and 1933 was not as far-reaching as sometimes pictured. He framed the 1923 reforms as a rejection of the narrow "self-cultivation" emphasis on self-control in favor of a broader "civics" knowledge of self and society, practical reforms, and habits suitable for modern life.[2] Classes in Party Principles and the Three People's Principles acted more to supplement and update the civics curriculum than replace it in any fundamental sense.[3] Nonetheless, in the wake of the founding of the Nanjing government in 1928, civics education, like other school subjects, was subjected to "partification" (*danghua*). In the extensive curriculum reforms of 1932, teaching materials on the Three People's Principles were now to be incorporated not only into civics, but also into classes in Chinese, society, and other subjects, while civics classes also returned to moral education. The "citizenship training" standards for primary schools, seen in retrospect, foreshadowed the New Life movement. The New Life movement was a nationwide effort at spiritual regeneration, undertaken in early 1934, to strengthen the morale of the people to oppose communism.[4] Under Chiang Kai-shek's direct leadership, the movement stressed behavioral norms in the name of Confucianism and put much emphasis on hygiene. These goals can be seen in the earlier Nationalists' school curriculum.

The subject of hygiene shows how intertwined were questions of individual virtue and social morality, as well as knowledge and practice. The emphasis placed on personal hygiene and public health from the very beginning of the modern school system was remarkable. Hygiene was central to self-cultivation

---

[1] Sheng Langxi, ed., "Cong xiushenke shuodao gongmin xunlianke."
[2] Ibid., pp. 5–11.   [3] Ibid., pp. 11–14.
[4] See Arif Dirlik, "The Ideological Foundations of the New Life Movement"; Federica Ferlanti, "The New Life Movement in Jiangxi Province."

and civics textbooks, because it was central to all nationalist discourse.[5] Textbooks effectively told students that strong bodies made strong citizens, and strong citizens made strong states.

"Hygiene" (*weisheng*) referred to anything related to personal health, from cleanliness to eating habits to exercise, and everything related to public health, from sanitation infrastructure to infectious diseases to pest-killing campaigns. Lessons about opening windows for ventilation and killing mosquitoes were endless. Here was a clear overlap between personal morality and civics. In other words, hygiene was centrally important as both a personal virtue and a public necessity that citizens were duty-bound to pursue. Hygiene even became an independent subject of coursework in primary schools in 1923, though classes devoted to physical education and military-style drill had existed since the late Qing.[6] The goal of hygiene class was threefold: personal health, public health, and prevention of contagious disease. In the first year, the curriculum was to cover the body (including appropriate ways to blow the nose and defecate), clothing, and houses (ventilation, for example). In the second year, eating and sleeping habits were covered; in the third, traveling in a hygienic way; in the fourth, dealing with wounds and trauma, vectors of contagion, and prevention of consumption; in the fifth, common diseases and their prevention, as well as emergency first aid; and in the six, basic first aid and nursing skills, as well as the public health concerns of the local district. The curriculum also noted the need for teachers to inspect children for cleanliness and to make sure they were developing good habits.

In 1932, the curricular goals were reframed slightly, to instill hygienic habits for personal health, hygienic knowledge for personal and public health, and hygienic enthusiasm to encourage thinking about healthy environments in family, school, and society.[7] The first years focused on habits of cleanliness. Also, attention should be paid to safety: cross at the green light, don't play on railroad tracks, avoid people who are coughing or otherwise appear diseased. And public health and safety: don't spit or defecate outdoors, litter, or write on walls. More advanced students were to focus on regular habits (sleeping, defecating); to learn some physiology, nutrition, the medical system, and dangers in the environment (from mosquitoes to sewage); and to participate in community

---

[5] Ruth Rogawski has argued that hygiene was central to the entire project of Chinese modernity – *Hygienic Modernity*, esp. pp. 1–18; see also Angela Leung and Charlotte Furth, eds., *Health and Hygiene in Chinese East Asia*. Huang Jinlin has put the argument in slightly different terms, emphasizing that disciplining the body was central to the modern state-building project – *Lishi, shenti, guojia*. And John Fitzgerald has highlighted hygiene and etiquette in the views of Sun Yat-sen and in the New Life movement – *Awakening China*, pp. 9–14, 104–105.

[6] Kecheng jiaocai yanjiusuo, ed., *20 shiji Zhongguo zhongxiaoxue kecheng biaozhun*, vol. 1, pp. 108–110; vol. 8, pp. 217–219.

[7] Ibid., vol. 8, pp. 220–224.

Good citizens 115

improvement projects. Girls were to learn about childcare. Teachers were to rank students according to their cleanliness.

According to a "society" textbook from the 1920s, the most important priority of local government was public health.[8] This was because, the text explained, most people were woefully ignorant of hygiene. It was important to build clinics on healthy ground; provide running water or wells; establish food markets that are open to inspection; regulate toilets, dung heaps, and trash piles; and conduct a census to discover local mortality and disease rates.

Citizenship under the Nationalists: the first phase

The idea that Guomindang educators would teach "Sunism" was in place well before the Nanjing regime was established in 1928. Sun died in 1925 but left in place a party with a growing military wing and ties to vibrant political movements. Ensconced in Guangzhou by the mid-1920s, the Nationalists were able to publish textbooks that created civics in the image they preferred.[9] The *New Citizens' Reader* was written to explain "the struggles of Sun Yat-sen and the successes he achieved, and what kind of thought developed in response to which historical moments, as well as the value of Sun Yat-sen's thought amid the trends of today."[10] This volume marks the beginning of what would become a long effort to systematize Sun's thought for public consumption. Most of Sun's political ideas had been expressed in speeches to general audiences and party members in a somewhat scattered manner. The process of reducing them to the Guomindang's needs in the late 1920s lay not in simplifying them but in ironing out the contradictions.[11] The *New Citizens' Reader* opened with a picture of Sun Yat-sen in death and quoted his final words: "The revolution is not complete. Our comrades must continue the struggle." The editor's note then forthrightly declared, "We believe in Sunism as the only doctrine of national salvation . . . We think that it is necessary to train up a new citizenry in order to built a new China, and that only Sunism can serve as the basis of training up a new citizenry."

Sun Yat-sen had repeatedly proclaimed that the world was divided among three types of persons. First were fore-knowers, who made new discoveries and inventions (such as himself); second, those who followed and imitated them; and third, the rest, who were profoundly ignorant. For Sun, fore-knowers were

---

[8] Ding Xiaoxian and Chang Daozhi, eds., *Shehui jiaokeshu*, 8: 9–10.
[9] Dai Jiyu, ed., *Xin'guomin duben*, vol. 1.
[10] Ibid., frontispiece. This volume might be seen as a kind of pamphlet describing Sunism, but it was written in the style and format of a textbook, and the editors said their audience included upper primary and middle school students and students in workers' schools (*pingmin xuexiao*).
[11] A great deal has been written about Sun's life and thought; a good introduction is Marie-Claire Bergère, *Sun Yat-sen*.

an "intelligent and capable" minority, natural leaders, and should form the revolutionary and political vanguard. The *New Citizens' Reader* hoped it would convince "followers" and "the ignorant" to accept Sun Yat-sen's guidance. Of course, what the editors really meant was Sun's posthumous guidance as interpreted by fore-knowers (or at least followers) such as themselves.

The *New Citizens' Reader* presented Sun as an intelligent and progressive-minded youth who grew up to overthrow the Qing dynasty, though only after many tribulations and defeats.[12] Faced with the betrayal of the Republic by Yuan Shikai, Sun redoubled his efforts, and his revolutionary endeavors to unite China continued until Sun's death in 1925.[13] In the eyes of the textbook, Sun's nationalist revolution had succeeded in 1911, but chaos followed the rise of militarists and warlords. At any rate, even if not fully successful, here was a man to be admired and a model for students to emulate. And in terms of his thought, no man before Sun, East or West, has so succeeded in showing the way to fulfill the goals of natinalism, democracy, and social welfare[14]: that is, the Three People's Principles. The Guangzhou textbook represents the beginning of a cult of Sun, whereby, for example, schools held weekly memorial services performed before Sun's picture and the Chinese and Guomindang flags.[15]

In today's world, according to *New Citizens' Reader*, the weak were fighting for liberation.[16] This is seen in the struggles of the people against their rulers and the struggles of the working class against the capitalist class. "On the one hand are weak and small nations fighting to achieve independence in the world of the competition for survival, and on the other hand are strong and great nations seeking to invade and colonize in accordance with the principle that the strong survive and the weak perish." Democracy has been spreading at least since the French Revolution, but this was a democracy limited to the propertied classes, while workers remained oppressed. The English, American, and French revolutions represented the overthrow of monarchs and aristocracies by propertied classes. But today, the textbook went on to suggest, the "social revolution" represented the struggle of the proletariat or property-less classes (*wuchan jieji*) against the propertied classes. It had thus far achieved success only in Russia. The *New Citizens' Reader* lauded the virtues of nationalism. But nationalism has two faces. The successful unifications of Germany and Italy and the Meiji reforms in Japan show its strength. But the French conquest of Vietnam, the British of India, and the Japanese of Korea, as well as the carving up of Poland by Russia, Austria, and Germany, all show the oppression of weak and small peoples by the great nations.[17] The tasks of the revolution

---

[12] Dai Jiyu, *Xin'guomin duben*, pp. 1–13.   [13] Ibid., p. 16.   [14] Ibid., pp. 26–27.
[15] Robert Culp, *Articulating Citizenship*, pp. 228–230.
[16] Dai Jiyu, *Xin'guomin duben*, pp. 17–19.
[17] For this trope, see Robert J. Culp, "'Weak and Small Peoples'."

were to liberate the Chinese people (*minzu*) and to bring equality to all the peoples (*minzu*) within China's borders. Or in other words, "to organize a free and united Republic of China."[18]

The *New Citizens' Reader* listed the threats and problems facing China. Warlords, bureaucrats, local bullies, and compradors – and above all imperialism – were the enemies that good Sunists had to defeat. Indeed, the first four might be regarded as mere symptoms of the real disease, imperialism.[19] In the eyes of the *New Citizens' Reader*, the warlords were brutal extortionists wreaking havoc on the nation, which is precisely why they needed to rely on the support of the imperialist powers to survive. The imperialist powers and warlords had forged a mutually beneficial relationship at the expense of the people. Under these circumstances, Chinese officials, as well as "local bullies" (*tuhao*) are not public servants but form an oppressive class in alliance with the warlords feeding off the people for the benefit of the imperialist powers. So, too, the compradors, Chinese businessmen who directly work for foreign interests. Naturally, imperialists seek to prevent the rise of the Chinese farming and working classes lest their control of the economy be broken.

Thus did the *New Citizens' Reader* seek the cause of China's dire situation and turn at last to imperialism.[20] The Nationalists' commitment to a new, "national" Chinese revolution is clear here, and this commitment was based on an analysis of imperialism as rooted in global capitalism. The textbook listed the threats facing China today and the losses of territories of yesterday. There was a real threat that the foreign powers would simply conquer China, the textbook urged. And China's economic position was not better than its military one. Financial instruments, imports and trade, taxes, and various forms of exploitation rob the Chinese of "at least 1.2 billion yuan" per year. If this situation continued, the *New Citizens' Reader* threatened, the state would collapse and the people become extinct. And finally the textbook warned of demographic oppression: China's population was being out-produced by the imperialist powers.

Reformers had for decades been pointing to the threats of outright colonization and of racial extinction. They had seen China's large population as a strength, but seldom worried about fertility rates. However, the idea that China was losing the race for reproduction was a theme that Sun Yat-sen had emphasized. The *New Citizens' Reader* argued that European overpopulation led to colonialism, while China's population was shrinking. Foreign powers were jealously eyeing China's good climate and natural resources, and as their populations grew, they would be in an even better position to invade in full force.

---

[18] Dai Jiyu, *Xin'guomin duben*, p. 26.   [19] Ibid., pp. 29–33.   [20] Ibid., pp. 31–43.

All of this did not mean, as commonly thought, that China was a "semi-colony," according to the *New Citizens' Reader*. No, it was a "sub-colony," worse off than even actual colonies. Again, this was to echo a prominent theme of Sun Yat-sen's speeches. Sun said that whereas colonized peoples were slaves of the country that had conquered them, the unequal treaties made Chinese the slaves of not one, but all the powers.[21] "Citizens! Knowing the dangers facing China in the international sphere, we must achieve unity, utilize the spirit of struggle, the determination of sacrifice, and the means of revolution to break our shackles, demand equality, raise our international position, and cleanse away the shame of being a sub-colony." Although schoolchildren were probably unaware of the semantics of semi-colony versus sub-colony, they represented two different sets of political analysis. Following the Comintern, Chinese Marxists – and a good many generic leftists – considered China to be a semi-colony that retained sovereignty as a legal fig leaf but was effectively under foreign domination. (This was obviously true.) The political point for Marxists was that the working class that would eventually lead the Communist Revolution needed to unite with native bourgeois elements in a cross-class united struggle against imperialism before socialist construction could begin.[22] Sun's objection to the term "semi-colonial" was primarily that it was not strong enough. Sun insisted that China was worse off than an actual colony because it was prey to the various powers all at the same time and was therefore *more* oppressed than most colonies. The strategy associated with the formula of sub-colony was one where strong political leaders led the unified Chinese masses to defeat imperialist forces, not one that recognized class contradictions.

Patriotic appeals aside, the *New Citizens' Reader* taught that nationalism (meaning anti-colonial nationalism) was an ongoing movement around the world, not yet successful. Meanwhile, the systems of democracy or welfare had not entirely been instituted even in the West, either. The point of these observations was twofold: first, that Sun Yat-sen's political thought was in accord with the trends of the times; and second, that Sunism represented the solution to humanity's problems, not just Chinese problems. The *New Citizens' Reader* explained Sun's view of the forces of history.[23] The basic motive force of progress lies in the satisfaction of people's economic needs. It is through the development of people's livelihoods that civilization is developed, economic organization improved, and morality enhanced. If the students reading

---

[21] Ibid., pp. 44–45.
[22] Chinese Marxists did not speak with one voice on the meaning of the formula "semi-colonial, semi-feudal," and Guomindang intellectuals also took part in these debates (which, however, lie outside the scope of this work). See Arif Dirlik, *Revolution and History*, pp. 81–84; Rebecca E. Karl, "On Comparability and Continuity."
[23] Dai Jiyu, *Xin'guomin duben*. This section of the textbook was chiefly derived from Sun's last "Three People's Principles" lectures of 1924.

this knew anything about the Marxist view of historical materialism, which is possible, they would have seen that Sunism did not regard class struggle as the motive force of history, nor did he analyze different modes of production.[24] But, at least according to the *New Citizens' Reader*, Sun saw that the history of humanity was the history of struggle and war. Although struggles against nature and theocrats had marked human progress, today's struggle, at least for the Chinese, had to be focused against the forces of imperialism. Here, the textbook cited one example of Sun's thought that ran against the progressive cultural currents of the day – that is, his faith that nationalism could be based on the Chinese family system. Radicals had criticized the patriarchal family as inherently repressive, preventing individual fulfillment, encouraging selfishness, and obstructing patriotism. But Sun thought feelings of identification could be extended from individual, to family, and to state, and that Chinese patriotism could be based on the unification of family loyalties.

As for the form of state, the *New Citizens' Reader* accepted that this was the age of democracy.[25] However, there was a critique: in Western countries where democracy was not well developed, the government was very strong, whereas where democracy was developed, the government's powers were limited in various ways. This tension between democracy and strong government must be resolved, but Western thinkers have not yet been able to do so. This is the task remaining for the Chinese.

The civics curriculum of 1932 stipulated that behavioral standards were to be based on a mixture of "China's innate moral virtues" and the virtues of certain foreign models.[26] The former included loyalty, filiality, benevolence, love, trustworthiness, righteousness, and peace; the latter were unnamed. For citizenship, physical training lay in hygienic habits and a happy spirit; moral training in ritual propriety and shame, love and sincerity; economic training in frugality and labor, and the skills of cooperative production; and political training in respect for the law and love of country and people. The curricular standards clearly linked personal virtues to citizenship, though here citizenship was treated as a passive state. No mention was made of rights, and not much

---

[24] Indeed, the *New Citizens' Reader* explained that Sun did not believe China had a "very rich" or capitalist class but only some people who were not as poor as others. The economic problem was how to raise productive capacity, not redistribute what little there was. This textbook favored immediate land redistribution because of the possibility that, given the major economic changes of the day, today's "small landlords" could become oppressive capitalists as in the West. Land should be redistributed and limits placed on capital. Ibid., pp. 24, 26.

[25] Ibid., pp. 23–24.

[26] Kecheng jiaocai yanjiusuo, ed., *20 shiji Zhongguo zhongxiaoxue kecheng biaozhun*, vol. 2, pp. 13–15. Whether this amounted to a revival of Confucianism in the school system, as Zheng Yuan has suggested, is another question. See Zheng Yuan, "The Status of Confucianism in Modern Chinese Education," pp. 208–211. For an excellent overview, see Robert Culp, "Setting the Sheet of Loose Sand."

more of duties. Rather, the individual was treated almost entirely as a member of the organic whole. According to a pledge to be recited every week: "I will attain the qualities needed to be a citizen of China, maintain a healthy body and perfect virtue, become a good citizen of China, and prepare to serve society and country."

As the list of 32 standards to be met by citizens of China makes clear, citizenship was an all-encompassing project that required personal dedication in the four fields of physical, moral, economic, and political training. It would be tedious to list all 32 requirements, but they represented a new pedagogical interest in the concrete and specific. Rights were matched with duties (item 29), but no examples were given. More concrete were the expected behaviors mandated for each grade.[27] In years 1 and 2, students were to learn not to pick their noses; have regular bowel movements; clean their fingernails; smile often; queue in an orderly fashion; and respect the flags of party and country. In years 3 and 4, students were to exercise daily and get outdoors; rinse their mouths after eating; be happy; reject belief in ghosts; and join school-based associations and vote for the people they admire. Years 5 and 6 students were to wash their faces in cold water; enjoy gardening; face up to challenges and frustrations; protect the liberties and rights given to citizens by the law; be willing to sacrifice themselves for love of country; pay attention to public affairs; and sympathize with oppressed people and countries. And so on.

One of the virtues children were expected to acquire in higher primary school was self-control (*zizhi*). Acquire how? By never borrowing money, or moving people's stuff without their permission, or playing inappropriate games, or pestering parents to buy things – not to mention resisting temptation and staying calm in the face of danger. And so forth. In all, Nationalist pedagogy insisted that to be a citizen of China required strength, cleanliness, joy, liveliness, painstaking effort, mental agility and attentiveness, honesty, fairness, consideration of others, and benevolent spirit, mutual cooperation, courtesy, obedience, responsibility, honor, courage, chivalry, determination, lawfulness, productivity, public-mindedness, and the public good. To name a few.

Is this the language of citizen training? The emphasis on economic productivity is reminiscent of bourgeois values, but the even more relentless emphasis on the collectivity is not. It this then the language of fascism, with its rejection of interests outside of the state? The tempering of nationalism by universal values such as the Confucian benevolence (*ren*) and internationalism suggests a corporatist vision that acknowledged good beyond the state. In any case,

---

[27] Kecheng jiaocai yanjiusuo, ed., *20 shiji Zhongguo zhongxiaoxue kecheng biaozhun*, vol. 2, pp. 15–24. I count a total of 267 items divided among 32 categories. Wang Jiarong counted 257 items, wryly noting that this was the most detailed set of curricular guidelines in history – *Minzuhun*, p. 156.

state-building in the guise of the party-state was certainly a key civic virtue. The 1932 curricular reforms for the "society" course gave greater emphasis to the Three People's Principles and anti-imperialism to the course, though Japanese encroachments were not mentioned.[28]

The more conservative tone of the 1932 civics curriculum for lower middle schools can be seen in the twinned appeals to traditional morality and the Three People's Principles.[29] The implication was that something had been lost and needed to be restored, even as something new was created through Sunism. Civics classes were to focus on the law-abiding character and other straightforward behavioral norms. "Independence" and "liberty" were ascribed to the state, not the individual: imperialist aggression and the unequal treaties were the target. Students were to learn something of democracy through participating in school-based organizations and carrying out concrete social surveys. Part of this emphasis on surveys reflected the late Qing interest in empirical "facts," and part reflected the Nationalist state's faith that social surveys would aid in state-building.[30] Students were to be trained in survey techniques from an early age. Upper middle school students went on to learn in more detail how it was that that the political principles of the Guomindang were the only means of reconstructing China and solving its social problems.[31] Knowledge of social life would equip them to serve society, and what they learned of "philosophy of life" classes was paired with the responsibility to restore the nation.

The Three People's Principles: nationalism

Pictures were used to focus the youngest students' attention on the symbols of Chinese identity.

On the right-hand side of Figure 17, the celebratory parade features pictures of Sun Yat-sen, as well as various flags of the Republic, including the Guomindang flag of the central white sun, twinned with the flag of the Republic of China. The Nationalists discarded the old five-color flag in favor of the "Blue Sky, White Sun, and a Wholly Red Earth," which echoed the party flag. Parades and speeches captured much of the spirit of citizenship that the Nanjing regime

---

[28] Kecheng jiaocai yanjiusuo, ed., *20 shiji Zhongguo zhongxiaoxue kecheng biaozhun*, vol. 8, pp. 145–149. See Wang Jiarong, *Minzuhun*, pp. 158–159.
[29] Kecheng jiaocai yanjiusuo, ed., *20 shiji Zhongguo zhongxiaoxue kecheng biaozhun*, vol. 2, pp. 149–153.
[30] Tong Lam, *A Passion for Facts*.
[31] Kecheng jiaocai yanjiusuo, ed., *20 shiji Zhongguo zhongxiaoxue kecheng biaozhun*, vol. 2, pp. 154–159. The 1936 curriculum regulations for upper and lower middle schools added references to the New Life movement but otherwise changed little – ibid., vol. 2, pp. 160–167.

122   Educating China

Figure 17 "National Day Has Arrived."

had inherited from the very first years of the Republic.³² As a later lesson on flag-raising stressed:

The national flag is a representation of the country. All citizens should love their country and respect its flag. When we are raising or lowering the national flag, as soon as you hear the signal, you should stand up and salute. This way, you not only demonstrate your own patriotism but can also arouse the patriotism of others.³³

A China Bookstore teacher's guide suggested that teachers explain the colors, significance, and uses of the national and of party flags – how to "love the national flag and the party flag."³⁴ There was a story for younger students. Li Ming's father took him to the Sun Yat-sen Hall. Ming was happy to see the big handsome flags on the wall, though he didn't entirely understand them. His father explained, adding, "Little Ming, you are a Chinese, you should love these two flags; I am also a Chinese, and I also love these two flags. All Chinese

---

[32] Henrietta Harrison, *The Making of the Republican Citizen*, esp. chapter 3; David Strand, *An Unfinished Republic*.
[33] Zhang Gengxi et al., eds., *Zhongguo gongmin*, 4: 19.
[34] Zhonghua shuju, comp., *Gaoji xiaoxueyong geke jiaokeshu jiaoxuefa*, 1: 62–63.

people, everyone should love these two flags." In essence, Little Ming learned, the ROC flag's red background represented the unity of the Chinese people, while the white sun in the blue sky represented the party, which was the only source of national salvation.[35] The following lesson focused on the National Day – which could be explained like a kind of birthday – and which turned into a history lesson on Qing oppression, foreign imperialism, and the revolution.[36]

On the upper left of Figure 17 a co-educational commemoration assembly prominently features both the party and national flags, as well as the obligatory picture of Sun Yat-sen. Perhaps most interesting is the lower left-frame picturing a middle-class family celebrating National Day at home. The window is open on this autumn day (October 10), providing the ventilation so stressed in hygiene lessons. The gramophone suggests both the family's class status and the modernity of the scene – also seen in the children's clothing, toys, and the fact that this is a nuclear family. The treats on the table, even though this is not mealtime, further suggest the celebratory nature of the day. In all, this was a picture many students who could afford to attend school could identify with.

Once established in Nanjing in 1928, the Nationalist government sought to instill a new and stronger sense of patriotism across the entire nation. The schools were soon filled with a variety of textbooks on Party Principles, Three People's Principles, Civics, and Society. There was a good deal of overlap among these genres. Generally, Party Principles represented an attempt to systematically inculcate students with the Nationalist ideology. This consisted of five main elements. First were the Three People's Principles of Sun Yat-sen, with a particular emphasis on national unity and anti-imperialism. Second was the five-power constitution, which was still theory rather than fact but offered a particular vision of the relationship between ruler and ruled. Third was Sun's notion of the relationship between knowing and doing, and the role of a tiny minority of "fore-knowers" as natural leaders of society. Fourth was the theory of tutelage, whereby the Nationalists would train the people in citizenship until they were ready for the final phase of the ongoing revolution, full constitutionalism. And fifth was the revival of traditional Confucian morality.

There was less variety in content among the different editions produced by China's various publishers on this subject than any other. No doubt, this was because no subject was more thoroughly vetted by the censors, including National Party organs as well as the Ministry of Education. It was also because all the textbooks were based on a limited set of writings by Sun Yat-sen from his later years. The textbooks offered, in my view, a very fair summary of Sun's ideas. These ideas were smoothed out but not distorted. The single most important source for the textbooks was the set of rambling lectures Sun Yat-sen gave for the party faithful on the "Three People's Principles" (*Sanmin zhuyi*) in 1924.

---

[35] Ibid., 1: 63–67.   [36] Ibid., 1: 68–74.

Sun spoke at length but with few notes and when he was already ill with the cancer that would kill him the following year. Other sources for the textbooks included the more polished *A Plan for National Reconstruction (Jianguo fanglue*, 1917–1921) and *Principles of National Reconstruction (Jianguo dagang*, 1924).[37] Given the strong similarities among these textbooks, this section does not discuss a sample of the textbooks one by one, but is organized around the elements of the Guomindang ideology. I note a few variations in interpretation and tone.

Textbooks taught that the Three People's Principles was simply a recipe for saving the nation, and the first principle was nationalism.[38] Nationalism had an inward-directed face and an outward-directed face. Outwardly, it would lead to abrogation of the unequal treaties and required equality for China in the world. Inwardly, it referred to the equality of all the peoples within China's borders – Han, Manchu, Mongol, Hui, Tibetan, Miao, and every minority – and hence their unity. This also meant the nation would flourish and the people be happy. Textbooks stressed that nationalism was a *natural* phenomenon resulting from blood ties of kinship, fundamental living styles (such as farming), language, religion, and customs and the like.[39] This was in contradistinction to states, which are the result of coercion. When authors discussed "statism" they were critical: the 1937 civics textbook by Zhang Kuang essentially equated statism with imperialism.[40] Statism represented the expansion of one state at the expense of others, creating injustice and a world of inequality. But nationalism! Nationalism liberates peoples and, through self-liberation, seeks the equality of all peoples, in Zhang's fervent urgings. The equality achieved within the true nation-state is expanded to the international state system. Thus "cosmopolitanism" (*shijie zhuyi*) could take either the form of imperialism or the form of utopian "Datong" harmony. Although calls for the Datong, the ancient vision of Great Unity that had been revived at the end of the nineteenth century, were rare in textbooks, all discussions of Chinese nationalism treated the liberation of China as the first step in the liberation of all colonized peoples.[41]

"Statism" was not good, but textbooks praised the idea of the nation-state. Again following Sun Yat-sen, textbooks claimed that China possessed a unique

---

[37] There are a number of translations of Sun's major works. For background, in addition to Marie-Claire Bergère, *Sun Yat-sen*, an important analysis is David Strand, *An Unfinished Republic*.
[38] Wei Bingxin, *Sanmin zhuyi keben*, 1: 1–2, 5: 25–30; Lü Boyou, *Xin Zhonghua dangyi keben jiaoshoufa*, 3: 10–13; Wei Bingxin, *Chuzhong dangyi zhidaoshu*, 2: 127–130.
[39] Wei Bingxin, *Sanmin zhuyi keben*, 1: 7–29; Wei Bingxin, *Chuzhong dangyi zhidaoshu*, 1: 2–5; Lu Shaochang, *Xin Zhonghua sanmin zhuyi keben*, 1: 1–14; Zhang Kuang, *Gaoxiao gongmin keben jiaoxuefa*, 1: 87–106; Jiang Jianqiu, *Chuxiao changshi keben jiaoxuefa*, 7: 79–82; Lü Boyou, *Xin Zhonghua dangyi keben*, 1: 27–41; Zhao Tizhen and Ma Pengnian, *Xiaoxue shehui keben jiaoxuefa*, 6: 120–122.
[40] Zhang Kuang, *Gaoxiao gongmin keben jiaoxuefa*, 1: 97–106.
[41] For the revival of "Datong," see Kang Youwei, *Ta t'ung shu*.

relationship between nation and state: the Chinese were not merely a nation (*minzu*), but also a state-nation (*guozu*). This was because – in Sun Yat-sen's somewhat convoluted reasoning – at least since the Qin-Han period (221 BCE), the Chinese state had been formed by only one nation. Other countries were populated by a variety of nations (peoples), or sometimes a single nation was divided among various states. But for 2000 years the Chinese nation and the Chinese state had been one. True, there were minorities. But with more than 400 million Han and fewer than 10 million minorities, essentially the Chinese were all Han. And anyway, the minorities were all assimilating into the Han race. Or so textbooks claimed, when they were not proclaiming the mutual respect and equality of the different peoples of China.

To speak of the equality of the peoples of China was to speak of the need for their unity. The need for unity was based on the need to resist imperialist aggression and oppression. The crimes of the imperialist powers against China were many, from the opium of the nineteenth century to the troops patrolling the Yangzi River. Extraterritoriality, the tariff system, the concessions: above all, the "unequal treaties" came to symbolize the aggression of the various powers against the Chinese people.[42] China's losses from economic imperialism were as real as its territorial losses, but somehow "invisible."[43] A little story explained Sun's theory of the sub-colony. Pingsheng said to his father, "Korea and Vietnam are colonies of other countries. That's so humiliating!"[44] But his father replied, "There is no need to speak of others! They are only the colonies of one country, while we Chinese are the colony of just about every country! We are at a lower level than they!" Analyses of imperialism in reference materials for teachers, if not for direct consumption of students, accepted that the nature of the beast had changed. As fearsome as enemy troops were the monopoly capitalists dividing up the Chinese market. Following a well-known left-wing analysis, a China Bookstore teacher's manual defined imperialism as the final stage of capitalism.[45] Defiantly calling China a semi-colony, it traced the development of imperialism back to the rise of monopolies as capitalism developed, which created an international cabal of plutocratic countries that were dividing up the world. China was an attractive target because of its rich resources. The manual highlighted imperialism in the political realm, such as the concessions; in the economic realm, such as tariffs and railroad companies; and also in the cultural realm, as in missionary schools.

Notwithstanding the narrative of victimization, textbooks also told a story of triumphant resistance. Students were to celebrate the May Fourth movement

---

[42] Dong Wang, *China's Unequal Treaties*.
[43] Lu Shaochang, *Xin Zhonghua sanmin zhuyi keben*, 1: 5–11.
[44] Lü Boyou, *Xin Zhonghua dangyi keben*, 5: 6–10.
[45] Zhao Tizhen and Ma Pengnian, *Xiaoxue shehui keben jiaoxuefa*, 6: 115–116.

of 1919 and the May Thirtieth movement of 1925, both essentially nationalist mobilizations led by students. One set of teachers' reference materials from the early 1930s smuggled in a left-wing analysis of the ongoing Chinese revolution by citing an article from the Shanghai newspaper *Shenbao*.[46] In this view, May Fourth was a natural successor to both the 1898 reform movement and the 1911 Revolution. This view is striking because in the usual revolutionary narrative, 1898 was forgotten. But according to the *Shenbao* article, the 1911 Revolution was itself severely limited. Sun Yat-sen had also come close to calling 1911 a failure, but he never subjected it to class analysis. In the *Shenbao*'s view, the revolution failed because Chinese capitalism was still embryonic and the bourgeoisie too weak to overthrow the country's feudal forces. As capitalism became stronger, it raised Chinese national consciousness, liberalizing the culture by promoting vernacular literature and science and by criticizing traditional morality, and supporting the twinned voices of anti-imperialism and anti-feudalism. A statement like this implicitly criticized Sunist contempt for the New Culture movement; it also entirely neglected the issue of the Guomindang's relationship to Chinese capitalism.

A *Party Principles* textbook from the early 1930s offered a different explanation of imperialism.[47] Here, too, imperialism was invading "small and weak countries" by arms, capital, and propaganda. Today's world was thus in a counterrevolutionary phase, marked by capitalism, bureaucratism, and militarism. These forces depended on a kind of individualism, in this analysis, but the ideologies of counterrevolution were statism, conservatism, interventionism, and protectionism (and not individualism as such). These are what the Three People's Principles must oppose. One theme of this *Party Principles* was the competition of nations, which depended on the strength of their individual members.[48] The rhetorical trope here was more Liang Qichao than Sun Yat-sen, though of course Liang's social Darwinism had been thoroughly absorbed across Chinese society. So, students were asked if they could fight back when they were bullied. At the same time, strength came from unity. It was no use having such a large population, no matter how strong its individual members, if they could not unify. Again the textbook repeated Sun's fears that the Chinese were not reproducing at the same rate as other nationalities.[49]

Teachers were encouraged to get their students talking about these issues: Who first advocated nationalism? (Sun Yat-sen, was the answer). Who were the Chinese? How does imperialism harm China? And so forth.[50] Chinese nationalism was to progress, as we have seen, from unity and struggle against

---

[46] Ibid., 6: 120–147; citing "Jingzi" 靜子, "Jinian wusi" 紀念五四, *Shenbao* 申報, 4 May 1933, p. 16.
[47] Tao Baochuan, *Dangyi*, 2: 1–36.   [48] Lü Boyou, *Xin Zhonghua dangyi keben*, 1: 27–41.
[49] Ibid., 4: 1–5.   [50] Jiang Jianqiu, *Chuxiao changshi keben jiaoxuefa*, 7: 79–82.

imperialist oppression, to equality in the world of states, to aid for other "small and weak peoples." But – and this was a big "but" – textbook authors were afraid that the Chinese had still not taken the first step. Yes, there was some resistance against imperialism that was a cause for pride, and also the previous generation's overthrow of the Manchus. But the real spirit of nationalism had yet to be embraced by a backward people.[51] So textbooks hectored.

All nations, said one textbook, have their own character. Germans possessed iron will, Anglo-Saxons possessed cool-headedness, while Japanese were narrow-minded and Latins were hot-headed – and Chinese were peaceable and tolerant.[52] The point was not to engage in national stereotyping for its own sake, but to rouse the Chinese to be *less* peaceable and tolerant, at least when facing injustice. So what should Chinese actually do here and now?

One set of lessons revolved around the importance of buying domestic products in place of imported goods.[53] Textbooks taught that since the late Qing, treaties had prevented Chinese governments from using tariffs to product domestic industries, and so cheap goods had flooded in, pushing out traditional handicraft workers. Teachers were to explain that this was a major cause of China's poverty. One civics textbook offered a story for primary school students.[54] The boy Ping'er wanted new clothes, and so his mother took him shopping. He looked at lots of clothes in every color, but he finally said: "These are all foreign made, and I don't want them. I want to buy Chinese clothing." He finally found something he wanted, and his mother asked him why he chose that clothing. Ping'er replied: "Chinese clothing is very durable, and using domestic products is a sign of our patriotism. This is because if everyone used domestic products, then our money will not flow out to foreign countries – and then won't China have no need to fear that it will fail to become righteous and strong?" Ping'er's mother was very happy to hear this.

Another set of lessons revolved around the need to revive traditional morality (*guyou daode*). I have listed this earlier as a major feature of Nationalist ideology because of the emphasis it received in textbooks. Sun Yat-sen had seen traditional morality as a means of reviving China's nationalist spirit. It was inherently Chinese and superior to other moral systems, and its revival would mean the revival of China itself. The tropes of revival, recovery, and return appeared in most discussions of traditional morality. Sun had been highly critical of at least "excessive" forms of individualism and liberty promoted in the New Culture movement of the 1910s. Textbooks, rather, harped on the link

---

[51] For example, Wei Bingxin, *Sanmin zhuyi keben*, 1: 10–11, 28–29; Lu Shaochang, *Xin Zhonghua sanmin zhuyi keben*, 1: 11–12.
[52] Zhang Kuang, *Gaoxiao gongmin keben*, 1: 88–95.
[53] For example, Yang Shuming, *Minzhong changshi keben jiaoshoufa*, 1: 7–11.
[54] Zhang Gengxi et al., eds., *Zhongguo gongmin*, 5: 10–11.

between traditional morality and the spirit of the nation.[55] What was traditional morality, exactly? Textbooks said it consisted chiefly of these values: loyalty-filiality; benevolence-love; trust; and harmony. This could turn essentialist, by associating Chinese with morality and foreigners with amorality (Chinese as peace-loving and foreigners as war-loving), but by and large it was an attempt to forge a middle path between total rejection of the tradition and actually returning to the tradition. Textbooks denied the conservative charge that the Republic had destroyed all morality. On the contrary, with the emperor gone, loyalty found its true focus in the nation. Traditional morality could even lead to self-critique: textbooks pointed out that foreigners with their schools and hospitals and orphanages seemed to practice love-benevolence rather better than most Chinese. Nonetheless, textbooks said, there was something especially Chinese and especially noble about ideals such as filial piety, and to revive their practice would revive the nation. Eventually, textbooks promised, China would set an example for foreign nations as well.

In his teachers' notes, Wei Bingxin suggested that the problem was that the old morality had declined faster than the new morality was able to take its place.[56] The decline of the old morality was due more to economic oppression and material needs than republicanism. In a possibly incoherent but certainly ecumenical spirit, Wei wanted to support the new morality while reviving the old. For Zhang Kuang, traditional morality was more: it was life itself.[57] Loyalty he defined as fulfilling to the utmost one's responsibilities to the state, its people, and also to oneself. Filiality – a special virtue of the Chinese – is simply the utmost in care for one's parents. Love or fraternity is best seen in those who sacrifice themselves for the sake of the whole community, such as martyrs who sacrifice for revolution or for religious ideals. Zhang's nonetheless remained a patriotic lesson, not so much because these virtues were specifically Chinese (though that was a point) as that they were a recipe for national salvation. In a later section on "revolution and China's traditional morality" for teachers to consult, Zhang wrote:

We are Chinese, and we seek to reform China, but if everything about China was really completely worthless – if Chinese culture has nothing to offer world culture and if the Chinese people are incapable of creating culture – then the Chinese should simply die. What would be the need for revolution? The first reason why we want revolution is that we need revolution, and the second is that we see we are capable of making revolution. However, the starting point of revolution certainly lies in the development of our nation's traditional capabilities and the preservation of our nation's traditional morality. If we

---

[55] Zhao Tizhen and Ma Pengnian, *Xiaoxue shehui keben jiaoxuefa*, 6: 120–125; Wei Bingxin, *Sanmin zhuyi keben*, 1: 24–27; Lu Shaochang, *Xin Zhonghua sanmin zhuyi keben*, 1: 14; and see the following two notes.
[56] Wei Bingxin, *Chuzhong dangyi zhidaoshu*, 1: 2–3.
[57] Zhang Kuang, *Gaoxiao gongmin keben jiaoxuefa*, 1: 65–86.

reject traditional Chinese culture, morality, and capability completely, then that is as unreasonable as saying that the Chinese nation has no right to exist in the world.[58]

The notion of recovery or return was also applied to China's "inherent intelligence" or what Zhang Kuang referred to above as its traditional capabilities.[59] Textbooks said the Chinese had to learn some things from foreigners, but also had to rediscover their own tradition of invention. Some spoke of the Chinese inventions of the compass, gunpowder, printing, and silk production, not to mention porcelain and tea. Some spoke of the political wisdom of the ancient *Great Learning*, which taught students how to proceed from self-cultivation, to managing a family, to ruling a state, to pacifying the world. It is worth noting that the textbook authors of this period belonged to a generation that had received a solid education in the classics, even if not the full-bore classical education of the previous generation.

The Three People's Principles: democracy and livelihood

Nationalist-era textbooks often explained the principle of democracy or literally "popular power" (*minquan*) in terms of the two Chinese characters for "the people" (*min*) and "power" (*quan*).[60] Power meant something like the force of a machine. Such is the power of the people to control state affairs. But what was so good about democracy? Weren't textbooks repeatedly saying the Chinese people were backward? Wasn't it another foreign import? How could the people be given power without it all ending in disaster? In effect, textbooks answered these questions by positing that democracy was an ancient idea, seen in the texts of Confucius and Mencius and practiced in a limited way in ancient Greece and Rome. Today, as we learned from Rousseau, the social contract, and natural rights, democracy's time had come. Theocracy and monarchy were valid forms of government in previous ages, but no longer. Following Sun closely, textbooks told students that several institutions would make democracy safe (safe from anarchy and chaos) and effective (in the hands of wise governors). The government should be strong, but completely controlled by the people so that it worked for the people.

We can analyze how textbooks did this in schematic fashion. Textbooks did not always present the material in this order, but they had to cover four issues.

---

[58] Ibid., 1: 113–114.
[59] Ibid., 1: 97–109; Wei Bingxin, *Sanmin zhuyi keben*, 1: 24–29; see also Wei Bingxin, *Chuzhong dangyi zhidaoshu*, 1: 2–3; Lü Boyou, *Xin Zhonghua dangyi keben jiaoshoufa*, 4: 6–11.
[60] Zhao Tizhen and Ma Pengnian, *Xiaoxue shehui keben jiaoxuefa*, 7: 87–121, 7: 162–174; Wei Bingxin, *Sanmin zhuyi keben*, 2: 1–16, 4: 1–30; Wei Bingxin, *Chuzhong dangyi zhidaoshu*, 1: 2–5; Jiang Jianqiu, *Chuxiao changshi keben jiaoxuefa*, 7: 167–178, 7: 192–206; Lü Boyou, *Xin Zhonghua dangyi keben*, 7: 5–16, 8: 41–46, 8: 72–77; Zhu Bingu, *Dangyi keben*, pp. 36–40.

First, students were to understand the position of "fore-knowers" and the relationship between knowledge and practice; second, the stage of political tutelage; third, the distinction between power and capability; and fourth, how the "five-power constitution" would guarantee safe and effective democracy.

1. "Fore-knowers" simply referred to the small minority of human beings who deeply understood the world and could create new ideas and institutions. This vision of the world was further associated with the theory that "to do is easy, to know is difficult." Fore-knowers were the natural leaders of society. How to combine this view with egalitarian democracy was a balancing trick that textbooks, following Sun, tried to perform. These principles, though not specifically political and certainly not egalitarian in tone, formed the basis of the following three points and ultimately legitimated the rule of the Guomindang.

2. Sun Yat-sen had said the Chinese revolution should proceed through three stages: revolutionary military rule, political tutelage, and constitutionalism. Textbooks of the 1930s taught that China under the Nanjing government was undergoing political tutelage. Textbooks told students that they were part of a vast effort to raise the level of the Chinese people so that China could practice democracy. The 1911 Revolution had failed because it jumped from military government to constitutionalism too quickly: the people had not yet acquired the capacity for democracy. Some textbooks here pointed to the need for surveys of population, property, and resources, much like the civics textbooks of the 1920s. Others described how officials, having passed exams to show their capability, will prepare the people for self-government. (Whether officials would have to pass exams once the stage of constitutional government was reached was always left a little vague.) Meanwhile, even in the period of tutelage, citizens possessed rights as well as duties. Rights included political equality, and also freedoms of belief, association, expression, and so forth. Duties included paying taxes, working on public infrastructure projects when necessary, and obeying officials as long as they were acting lawfully. Whereas school textbooks presented a balanced picture of rights and duties, adult education textbooks tended to emphasize duties, including the duty to educate one's children.[61]

In theory, the tutelage stage would see the spread of self-government from the local level, to the provincial level, to all of China, at which point the constitutionalist stage would be at hand. The *Revitalized Citizen's Textbook* described the institutions of local government.[62] Town, city, and district governments were to conduct censuses of the population and land and to provide police, schools, hygiene, roads, and similar services, as well as "train the populace" in

---

[61] For example, Yang Shuming, *Minzhong changshi keben jiaoshoufa*, pp. 92–96.
[62] Lü Jinlu et al., eds., *Fuxing gongmin jiaokeshu*, 1: 7–19. ("Revitalized" was the name of a set of textbook series, not specifically referring to citizenship.)

Good citizens 131

Figure 18 Local self-government: "Municipal election assembly."

its duties to enable it to assume its rights. A lesson on "The Rights and Duties of the People in Regard to Their Locality" explained how the people could elect their local council representatives, county magistrates, mayors, and township heads, and recall them and vote on initiatives and referendums – as pictured in Figure 18.[63] The duties of the people were to obey the law. This textbook did not argue that obedience was owed, because the people themselves made the law. Rather, it simply noted, "All [laws and regulations] should be strictly followed, and it is not permissible to disobey on the grounds you disagree with them." Other duties include contributing labor to public projects and taking on public responsibilities when chosen to do so.

[63] Ibid., 1: 19–20.

In fact, the most prominent new feature in this introduction to local government was the *baojia* mutual surveillance system, though, as the textbook insisted, its roots lay in the Song dynasty. Ten households were to form 1 *jia* and 10 *jia* 1 *bao*, amounting to a district or township, and functioning as a self-protective organization below the level of local government. The *baojia* were supposed to maintain infrastructure such as roads and canals, pursue criminals, and collect funds. Modern social scientists have seen the *baojia* system as a brutal but not necessarily successful form of social control on the part of the Nanjing government.[64] It can also be seen as a symbol of the limits of the state, which lacked agents capable of real penetration into local society. For the *Revitalized Citizen's Textbook*, however, *baojia* was simply a part of the set "self-government" instruments that operated all across the local levels of Chinese society.

Three People's Principles textbooks, like the civics textbooks of the 1920s, included lessons on how students should hold their own meetings and establish organizations. Often, they pointed out that such meetings and organizations were training for democracy. Students would discover how to elect a chair and a secretary, how to write a charter, how to deal with motions and discussions and voting (students needed to listen respectfully when someone was talking, and speakers needed to be succinct and disinterested). This was "beginners' democracy." As before, it was the upper primary school textbooks that really introduced students to the ways government worked (at least ideally) and how society was structured. The Commercial Press's *Revitalized Citizen's Textbook* explained how meetings were run.[65] The point was simple: "We have many classmates in school, and if we can organize groups, then we can not only engage in all kinds of group activities, but also we will improve our organizational abilities and in the future we will certainly be able to cooperate with others for the sake of society and the state." And good groups depend on good meetings to run correctly. The *Revitalized Citizen's Textbook* then explained how to get your group going, form provisional rules, draw up membership lists, choose committees, and determine procedures for making and passing motions.

Students might infer that such organizational meetings were the foundation of active citizenship. This was much like the approach taken in civics textbooks in the 1920s, though limited to "local government." And the *Revitalized Citizen's Textbook* went on to explain not only voting and local government but also the "four powers" of citizens that students should begin exercising in their own organizations. Aside from voting, this included recall, initiative, and

---

[64] See, e.g., C. K. Yang, *A Chinese Village in Early Communist Transition*, pp. 103–107. In practice, *baojia* did perform militia functions; see Hans J. van de Ven, *War and Nationalism in China*, chapter 4.

[65] Lü Jinlu et al., eds., *Fuxing gongmin jiaokeshu*, 1: 1–5.

referendum.[66] Thus was Sun Yat-sen's vision of democracy to be translated into school life. Or, as Wei Bingxin put it, calling for students to study politics: "People are political animals. If we do not act in the political realm, the political realm will act on us."[67]

3. The distinction between power and capability could be analogized to either a company or a steamship. Basically, textbooks, faithfully following Sun Yat-sen, told students that the people in a democracy possessed power like the stockholders of a company, while the managers of the company possessed the capability to actually run it. Or, the people were like passengers on a steamship, deciding where they wanted to go, while the engineer ran it. Or perhaps most succinctly of all: after the master (the people) selects his chauffeur (the government) and tells him where to go, he must leave the driving to the chauffeur. This distinction could be seen in students' meetings as well as the national government. Wei Bingxin insisted, "The school is like the country; and the school's self-government assembly is like a government. The officers of the self-governing assembly should have sufficient ruling powers to take care of its business, while their classmates as a whole, like the citizens of a country, should have sufficient governing power to supervise [the work of the] self-government assembly."[68] Other textbooks noted that regardless of the differences in people's natural abilities, all were equal in the political sphere. And conversely, if the goal of democracy was equality, true equality also depended on democracy.

4. In Western democracies, textbooks assured students, the people are dissatisfied and their officials incompetent. People there want to control the government but don't accept that the government must control them as well. In China, the five-power constitution would guarantee that the people held (ultimate) power and would not become dissatisfied, just as their officials would be competent and expert. Textbooks said that Sun Yat-sen's addition of the examination and oversight branches of government to the three branches of the legislative, executive, and judicial would create a kind of governing "machine" that would "harmonize liberty and rule." Based on the civil service examination system and censorate of the imperial government, the addition of these two branches would make the Republic's political system both stronger and more Chinese. Textbooks explained that the examination branch would ensure the quality of officials, while the oversight branch would root out corruption. Ultimate power would reside in the people, because they would have the rights of suffrage, recall, referendum, and initiative. But here, several textbooks noted, there needed to be limits placed on excessive liberty; people needed to give up some of their liberties so that the state could be strong. Textbooks could cite Sun's own words to warn students that liberty was not unrestrained.

[66] Ibid., 1: 5–7.   [67] Wei Bingxin, *Chuzhong dangyi zhidaoshu*, 1: 4.
[68] Wei Bingxin, *Sanmin zhuyi keben*, 3: 32.

The ideal of democratic equality included women. Textbooks all stressed this.[69] The Chinese tradition of male supremacy was a bad tradition, they warned. Women may be physically weaker, they admonished, but were essentially the same as men. Their accomplishments may not look like much, but this was because until the reforms of the Republic, the environment did not let them flourish. Biological differences do not justify different treatment in the social or political realms. Textbooks asked boys to check if the performance of their girl classmates was lacking in any way, and to ensure that their sisters did not undergo footbinding. Looking at the position of women from a cosmopolitan viewpoint, textbooks pointed to World War I as a turning point: brought into factories and offices, women proved their abilities. The women's suffrage movement is sweeping the world. (In fact, women's suffrage made great strides in China in the 1930s, although at the national level women only got the vote in 1947.)

The third of the Three People's Principles was also something of a balancing act. "Livelihood" essentially mixed notions of state-led economic development and economic egalitarianism.[70] Following Sun, textbooks might offer students a rather philosophical approach to the question of livelihood through discussions of the human instinct for survival and a kind of anthropological history of food, clothing, and shelter. They asked whether Marx's materialist concept of history was correct (no, it wasn't) and whether capitalists were exploitative (yes, but not entirely, because it is not only workers who contribute to society). On the subject of equality, Sun had repeatedly stressed the notion of equal political and legal rights, and equal opportunity, but had just as fiercely criticized any form of egalitarianism that suppressed talent.

To explain the origins of the principle of livelihood, Wei Bingxin spoke of Sun Yat-sen's experiences of the West.[71] Here, the point was that Sun saw not only the strength of the Western powers but also the problems they faced, particularly the conflicts between rich and poor. Thus Sun came to understand the importance of a revolution of "livelihood" as well as revolutions of nationalism and democracy. Wei implied that a history of the West showed that although the English, American, and French revolutions of the seventeenth and eighteenth centuries had been successful national revolutions, they had limited democracy to the bourgeois property owners. Workers remained oppressed, though Wei was a little vague about whether they were still so oppressed. Apparently, he thought of unionization and the socialist movement of his day (in the West) as an ongoing livelihood revolution – a sign of the conflicts within Western

---

[69] Lü Boyou, *Xin Zhonghua dangyi keben jiaoshoufa*, 3: 28–32, 6: 42–47; Yang Shuming, *Minzhong changshi keben jiaoshoufa*, pp. 156–160.

[70] Lu Shaochang, *Xin Zhonghua sanmin zhuyi keben*, 3: 3–9; Wang Jianxing and Zhu Liangji, *Sanmin zhuyi keben jiaoshoufa*, vol. 2; Wei Bingxin, *Sanmin zhuyi keben*, 1: 19–34; and Wei Bingxin, *Chuzhong dangyi zhidaoshu*, 1: 2–5.

[71] Wei Bingxin, *Sanmin zhuyi keben*, 1: 2–6, 2: 16–18.

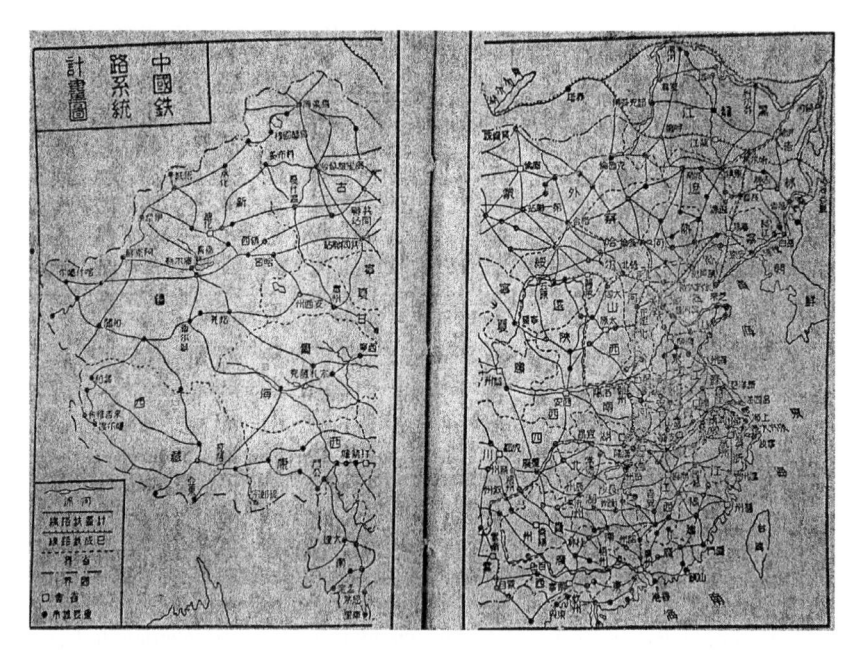

Figure 19 "Rail system planning chart."

society but also of the future path the world would take. Meanwhile, Wei told students, the West's national revolutions themselves had produced both unity at home and expansionism abroad. In the cases of the more recent unification reforms of Germany, Italy, and Japan, Wei saw self-strengthening at work. But these countries had also joined the ranks of the imperialists. And industrialization had created a rich capitalist class and a poor class of workers who had been pushed out of their traditional crafts jobs. Now the imperialists were bringing this problem to China. Vicious economic imperialism was victimizing Chinese workers and peasants. "Therefore, before capitalism is completely developed [in China], we should take preventative steps and must advocate people's livelihood, and only then will we be able to prevent future class struggle and solve the social problem." The Chinese needed to carry out national, democratic, and livelihood revolutions all at the same time. Above all, China needed economic development.

Sun Yat-sen was personally interested in railroads and had even been enticed – briefly – into working for Yuan Shikai as head of railway development. It may be that the lines Sun enjoyed drawing on maps of China did not take into account topographical features such as mountains that trains would have to go over, through, or around, but this imaginary map of Chinese railroads (Figure 19) also symbolized national unity. Sun's vision of a China united by rails finally came into existence at the beginning of the twenty-first century.

The China Bookstore's *Civics Textbook for Primary Schools* declared that Sun himself had equated his principle of livelihood with socialism.[72] Socialism in this view was simply a means of resolving the "social problem" that a large number of people were living without sufficient food, clothing, shelter, or transportation.[73] Livelihood thus referred to the "livelihood of the people, the survival of society, the budget of the state, and the very existence of the masses." It could be achieved by adjusting the economic profits of society as a whole, and particularly through equalizing land rights and regulating capital. But whence the problem of poverty? The *Civics Textbook* explained that the industrial revolution had caused widespread poverty as machines replaced people, who were thrown out of work.[74] The *Civics Textbook* also noted that the industrial revolution vastly increased the power of capitalists, as production moved from household and workshop to factories, eventually creating a conflict between workers and bourgeoisie.

Written during the Great Depression, the *Civics Textbook* understandably focused on the question of unemployment, blaming it on the effects of imperialism in weakening the entire economy, and on the unwillingness of capitalists to cooperate with the demands of labor.[75] As for the disintegration of the rural economy, the *Civics Textbook* blamed economic imperialism for the collapse of household handicrafts, which had provided a necessary supplement to farming income.[76] But it also cited technological backwardness; the rise of usurious lending practices by landlords; and out-migration from villages as men joined armies and bandit gangs or sought menial labor in the cities. Villages were thus increasingly unable to deal with drought, flood, and disease. On a more optimistic note, the *Civics Textbook* suggested that solutions did exist, and these ranged from universal school and encouragement of enterprise to village banking cooperatives and infrastructural improvements.[77] Its suggestion that frugality would help farmers save for emergencies was perhaps more a gesture toward traditional morality than a practical step, given its own description of the rural poverty. And, in good Sunist fashion: "As for the basic measure to be taken, of course it lies in practicing the principle of people's livelihood."

In general, primary school students were to understand that economics was the foundation of social life, because it was the study of the goods that made life possible.[78] "Economic behavior" could be divided among four categories: production, exchange, consumption, and distribution (meaning the outcome of economic processes). The *Civics Textbook* also introduced the concept of the division of labor, based on the fact that no one can be self-sufficient. All goods are produced through labor, but at least since the industrial revolution, the relations between capital and labor have been fraught. But if the *Civics Textbook*

---

[72] Zhao Lüqing et al., eds., *Gongmin keben*. [73] Ibid., pp. 2–4. [74] Ibid., pp. 1–2. [75] Ibid., pp. 18–19. [76] Ibid., 19–20. [77] Ibid., 19, 21. [78] Ibid., pp. 4–8.

Good citizens   137

blamed the industrial revolution for poverty, it did not want to turn the clock back but to increase scientific production. This view reflected the Nationalists' call for cooperation between labor and capital. The *Civics Textbook* emphasized that the distribution of wealth must be fair and suggested that this goal might be achieved by a competent public agency.[79] By acting in a disinterested fashion, such an agency could eliminate a potential source of division between rich and poor. The textbook did not suggest that "fairness" meant absolute equality, but it implied that current conditions were not ideal. Echoing Tao Menghe, it urged that decisions should be made only on the basis of scientific investigation of China's conditions.

In a break from the traditional view that merchants were not productive members of society, the *Civics Textbook* pointed out that trade was inherent in the processes of production-distribution-consumption, because of the division of labor.[80] In accord with much discourse of the day on the social position of intellectuals, the *Civics Textbook* noted that "labor" was not merely physical but could be mental as well.[81] Of course, many jobs require both, and the *Civics Textbook* proclaimed: "All jobs, no matter what they are, are of benefit to society; are equally important, and are of equal value; they cannot be distinguished between high and low or noble and base. Only roaming tramps who refuse to work are social parasites."[82] However, for young students, perhaps more interesting than such fine sentiments were the array of jobs that the textbook laid out – from the restaurant trade to law and nursing, and suggestions on how to find the right job for you.[83] Your individual capacities, interests, and training were key. Farmers should have scientific knowledge and appreciate the simplicity and natural beauty of rural life. Workers should learn to be meticulous and appreciate aesthetics and creativity. Merchants need to be agile and decisive and to exhibit trustworthiness and understand social conditions.

Against this background, the *Civics Textbook* described the good citizen:[84]

> Citizens are nationals who possess public rights, and since they possess public rights, citizens are [in this capacity] not private persons, not the children of family heads, nor yet the heads of families with children. Rather, in terms of the nation, the citizen is one member of the entire nation; in terms of the state, the citizen is one member of the state; in terms of society, the citizen is one member of society. Therefore, insofar as we are citizens, our identity is a public one.

It follows, the textbook goes on to explain, that citizens have duties to the public. These include duties to the nation: to protect it, help it recover, strengthen it, and help it flourish. Duties to the government are that, because the government represents the state, its orders should be obeyed, its laws followed, and its taxes

---

[79] Ibid., p. 12.   [80] Ibid., pp. 7–8, 10.   [81] Ibid., p. 6.
[82] Ibid., p. 13.   [83] Ibid., pp. 14–18.   [84] Ibid., pp. 22–23.

paid; however, when the government makes mistakes, citizens should correct it. And duties to society include, especially, to have a proper job. Thus did the *Civics Textbook* turn the economic actor and the social being into the citizen.

A 1937 civics textbook treated both family and society as natural and indispensible for human survival.[85] Beginning, of course, with the Sunist belief that national identity could be built out of family identity, it implied the nation was equally natural. "From birth to death, we all live social lives; and regardless of who we are, we cannot leave society and live independently."[86] The division of labor is necessary to meet the needs of humans, and conversely, everyone has the duty to work at a job and contribute to the larger society. This was a vision of cooperation, not competition. Students were told that Sun Yat-sen had said that the very intelligent people would work for the whole society, while people of less intelligence could still work for some other people. Even children can contribute to society, by killing pests, promoting national products, and joining literacy campaigns. The teachers' reference notes offered a more technical definition of society as systems of commonly shared social relationships. The implication was that societies operated at various levels, the national society only being one sort of society, but the following discussion suggested that it was the key sort. This was because societies had to be held together, and the discussion of social glue sounded much like discussions of national glue. This civics textbook held that although the predisposition to cooperation was natural, societies were also held together by sanctions that included public opinion, the law, religion, customs and manners, and even art, which appeals to the emotions by offering images of the good and the beautiful. These sanctions, we may note, included all the elements defining the nation except language.

In general, Three People's Principles textbooks proposed dealing with China's "social problem" in the following terms. First was equalizing land rights and raising money through a tax on the increase in the value of land (which was due to general economic development and not the landlord's efforts). Second was encouraging but limiting and directing private capital. Third was improving technology for the production of basic needs such as food, clothing, and shelter. And fourth was building up the infrastructure, especially railroads. Wei Bingxin's was not the only textbook to complain about foreign capitalists or to notice the growing problems of landlordism and landless

---

[85] Zhang Kuang, *Gaoxiao gongmin keben jiaoxuefa*, 1: 7–24.
[86] Ibid., 1: 11–12. It is interesting to note that in its reference materials for teachers, this textbook offered a balanced appraisal of whether small families or large families were better. In contrast to progressive views of the 1920s, it suggested that although the large family was associated with the patriarchalism of the earlier age of autocracy and stifled the development of its members, nonetheless it offered a greater sphere for mutual support. The small family was more hygienic and egalitarian, but also possessed fewer resources to take care of its children, produced fewer children to take care of the older generation, and might lead to extreme individualism.

peasants. But the problem was not that landlords were evil, or even the evil of foreign capitalists, but rather that a system needed to be set in place that would constrain them.

Having said that, textbooks emphasized that peasant poverty had reached crisis levels, and students should visit rural areas to see it for themselves. The reasons for this crisis are various, involving imperialism, natural disasters, and the government failure to maintain basic infrastructure such as waterways. Zhao Tizhen and Ma Pengnian in their reference materials for teachers again used an article from *Shenbao* to show how imperialism and "feudal forces" acted together to create the rural crisis.[87] As we have seen, Sunism emphasized the role of imported products in the collapse of rural handicrafts. What the *Shenbao* article added was an emphasis on the role of taxes, rents, and interest rates – exploitation by "feudal forces" such as warlords and landlords – in pushing peasants over the brink. Furthermore, the rural depression had lowered wages across China and shrunk markets.

Sunism and the New Life movement

Textbooks began to explicitly promote the New Life movement in the mid-1930s, but they advocated what would become its major planks from the very beginning of the Nationalist regime.[88] If New Life movement propaganda focused on public behavior, textbooks continued to emphasize personal morality. The story of George Washington and the cherry tree was recycled to show the importance of honesty.[89] The old lessons on need to treat servants well – with some empathy – were retaught. For example, Caiying ordered her servant to pick some radishes, even though it was a cold winter's day with driving snow.[90] When the servant came back with a basket of radishes, her face was frozen blue and red; Caiying was ashamed of herself and vowed, "I will not ask others to do what I do not wish to do myself." The *Revitalized Citizen's Textbook* retold a brief version of the orthodox story of Lao Laizi from the *Twenty-four Exemplars of Filial Piety*. Though elderly himself, he kept his aged parents happy by pretending to be a little boy and clowning around.

The issue of civic virtue (or "public morality," *gongde*) also continued to be discussed. This could be a matter of spitting in the streets and picking the flowers in the park, but it could also be a question of serving one's country, following

---

[87] Zhao Tizhen and Ma Pengyuan, *Xiaoxue shehui kegben jiaoxuefa*, 6: 160–164, citing "Cong nongcun jingji bengkui shuodao dushi shangye xiaotiao" 從農村經濟崩潰說到都市商業蕭條, *Shenbao yeyu zhoukan* 申報業餘周刊, 28 May 1933, p. 1 (unsigned editorial).
[88] Explicitly: Zhang Kuang, *Gaoxiao gongmin keben jiaoxuefa*, 1: 37–60; implicitly: Yang Shuming, *Minzhong changshi keben jiaoshoufa*, 72–89; Lü Boyou, *Xin Zhonghua dangyi keben jiaoshoufa*, 2: 34–38, 7: 1–4; Wei Bingxin, *Chuzhong dangyi zhidaoshu*, 2: 116–120.
[89] Lü Jinlu et al., eds., *Fuxing gongmin jiaokeshu*, 4: 9.   [90] Ibid., 5: 24–25.

the rules of the associations one belonged to, and generally taking care of public property. Some textbooks said there was no problem with the "private morality" of the Chinese, but only their public behavior. Several cited stories Sun Yat-sen used to tell of Chinese behavior that earned foreign contempt. These revolved around not peasants but men of high status spitting in first-class ship's lounges, or Chinese businessmen farting in restaurants and bars. Such behavior naturally led to foreign contempt for the Chinese, Sun had remarked, and sometimes Chinese were even banned from restaurants and hotels. Textbooks presented even the burning down of Chinatowns abroad not as an example of Western prejudice and violence but an understandable public health measure. Textbooks urged students that through self-cultivation, Chinese need to learn proper habits, and then foreigners will respect us. Such lessons may seem odd in an era of heightened anti-imperialism that was fully shared by the Guomindang. However, textbooks reflected Sun's views in this regard, which belonged to an earlier generation and its acceptance of certain foreign standards of deportment.

Like the concern with hygiene, the anti-superstition lessons in the textbooks of the 1930s were not new, but they were relentless.[91] Sun Yat-sen's youthful exploits made a nice story. In fact, Sun did break a temple statue in his home village after his secondary schooling in Hawaii. In the textbook mythology, he was destroying Buddhas at age 10. Educated persons not only cannot believe in "superstition," they have the duty of destroying the superstitions of others. Textbook said superstitions were a waste of time and money, served as obstacles to getting at the truth, and could even kill. Many traditional customs were good. The tomb-sweeping festival in honor of the ancestors, for example; and, after all, sweeping was hygienic. But extravagant weddings and funerals were bad. Students can create a chart of local customs and discuss how they could be improved.

The *Revitalized Citizen's Textbook* told a story of two students playing in a temple.[92] Qinger saw a statue of a god and said, "This is Pusa – we should venerate him." Xiangsheng said, "What is this Pusa? He is only a molded and carved icon thing." Qinger said, "You have insulted the god and he will punish you." Xiangsheng laughed heartily, replying, "I don't believe in ghosts and spirits; they are only a superstition of idiots. How can there be such things?" (Figure 20). Students were asked why stupid people believed in spirits, and why they themselves did not believe in them. The *Revitalized Citizen's Textbook* suggested students could organize an anti-superstition propaganda team and perform skits.

---

[91] For example, Lü Boyou, *Xin Zhonghua dangyi keben jiaoshoufa*, 6: 26–30. See Rebecca Nedostup, *Superstitious Regimes*.
[92] Lü Jinlu et al., eds., *Fuxing gongmin jiaokeshu*, 5: 30–31.

Good citizens 141

Figure 20 "I don't believe in ghosts and spirits."

Textbooks reiterated Chiang Kai-shek's desire for people to live more rational lives. People should be respectful, diligent, filial law-abiding, and so on and so forth. They should not insist on their rights but yield to others, not be afraid of hard work but serve the masses. Teachers were advised that the New Life movement was designed to cure the Chinese people's hypocrisy, greed, decadence, corruption, indifference, indiscipline, self-indulgence, and various base behaviors. Students were to learn to make their lives more military, productive, and aesthetic. To aestheticize referred to living without vulgarity, more modestly and simply (the textbook helpfully added that art was a lifestyle in the sense of the ancient six arts: rites, music, archery, charioteering, calligraphy, mathematics). More specifically, students should learn to eat at regular times and chew their food quietly; to wear ordinary clothes (and Chinese-made clothes), wash them often, and darn them when necessary; to help the aged and to let women and children into streetcars first, to keep to the left, and to hold out your chest and look ahead.

Although ridiculed for these seemingly trivial dictums, the New Life movement was but the latest phase of a program to remake the Chinese people into citizens that had really gotten underway in the last years of the Qing. Elites saw that the best way to do this was to begin with children. In a republic, citizenship was not about belonging to a state but becoming a disciplined member of a "shared life." This was a vision of individuals, each learning to be strong, then coming together. However, textbooks of the 1930s reflected not general elite attitudes, or not only those attitudes, but the needs of a centralizing government. Thus the legitimacy of the "party-state" was as much a part of the New Life movement as proper nose-blowing. Turning Sun Yat-sen into a symbol of the state on a par with the flag was part of the legitimation process. Although the Three People's Principles textbooks did not quite speak of Sun in every lesson, many lessons held him up as a model to be emulated.[93] As a small child he was already happy to help with father with the farm chores. Amid the long turmoil of revolution, Sun held the party together – all groups need a leader, after all: schools had their principles and families their heads. He made the 1911 Revolution, and he cleared the way for the Nationalist government to eventually emerge. Thus Sun is the one and only "premier" (*zongli*) of China: the title is reserved for him in perpetuity. Textbooks described the Guomindang as open to all regardless of gender, based on local branches in a hierarchy through distinct and provincial levels up to the central party, each with its representative assembly. Wei Bingxin asserted that the Guomindang is the center of political life.[94] Youth should have revolutionary spirit, he said, but revolution cannot be accomplished through romantic longings. Rather, it is accomplished through discipline, leadership, and experience: the Guomindang. Students need to "pledge their loyalty to the party-state."[95]

Educators under the Nationalist regime, like their predecessors, recognized that evaluating the morality and civics of students was highly subjective.[96] Confucian education held that having students follow ritualized behavior patterns led them to internalize certain values. The Nationalists inherited the move to replace self-cultivation with civics, that is, a more practical pedagogy. The notion of the "citizenry militant" placed more emphasis on competition, courage, and spiritedness, to some extent at the expense of the deference and "yielding" of the older, more Confucian curriculum.[97] Regardless of how much "traditional morality" was retained, by the 1920s educators were simultaneously moving in two directions. One was to give more room to individualism and engage in child-centered pedagogy. The other was to turn to "society" and "civics" to alter the balance in favor of public life. The emphasis of the schools

---

[93] Lü Boyou, *Xin Zhonghua dangyi keben jiaoshoufa*, 1: 1–9; Zhao Tizhen and Ma Pengnian, *Xiaoxue shehui keben jiaoshoufa*, 5: 130–134; Zhu Bingu, *Dangyi keben*, pp. 2–4.
[94] Wei Bingxin, *Chuzhong dangyi zhidaoshu*, 1: 2–5.   [95] Ibid., 2: 127–130.
[96] Ding Zhongxuan, "Zeyang kaocha ertong de coaxing yu gongmin xunlian," pp. 47–54.
[97] Bi Yuan, *Jianzao changshi*, p. 182.

Good citizens 143

on student organizations and outside activities was a way to combine theories of sociality with concrete behaviors.

Although the Nationalist curriculum of the 1930s represented a conservative reaction, it was also firmly rooted in the turn to the "public" that had taken place in the 1920s or even earlier. The paradox of the 1920s was that the sweet ideals of civics class were played out against the background of imperialism, banditry, and warlordism. The paradox of the 1930s was that the Nationalist government wished to prevent people from interfering in political decisions even as they sought to mobilize the people. Liberal intellectuals favored political participation (up to a point, anyway) but were more skeptical of mobilization. Yet liberal distrust of politics perhaps helped to prepare China for the Nationalists.

In their "bird's eye" view of citizenship training written for the *Educational Journal* in 1936, Wu Jiazhen and Gao Shiliang traced a more or less continuous development of civics from the morality classes of the late Qing.[98] Their main point was that gradually but steadily, the curriculum came to construct the ideal citizen. This is not to say that all was well – indeed, the Chinese people remain "ignorant, poor, selfish, weak, and chaotic."[99] A lifelong educational program is needed; schools can provide the basis but not the whole program. First, Wu and Gao argued that moral education and citizenship training were two sides of the same school coin. Echoing the Nationalists' neo-traditionalism, they posited that students could simultaneously learn loyalty, filiality, benevolence, and the like along with a resolute spirit and law-abiding habits. In other words, good persons made good citizens. And vice versa. Wu and Gao stressed the Nationalists' vision of partification, especially important for civics classes, which were to be ultimately evaluated by educators who were members of the Guomindang.

But second, Wu and Gao also emphasized broader forms of civics education, including the New Life movement, the *baojia* mutual surveillance system, and special thought reform programs in areas that the Communists had infiltrated.[100] Wu and Gao, good moralists, began their analysis with the decline of standards and the moral corruption of the day.[101] Thus the need for a comprehensive program of reform – not centered on the schools, because society-wide, but not ignoring the schools either. With the New Life movement, concerns long central to the civic curriculum were now to be spread across the nation: hygienic practices, propriety and good manners, and a sense of shame. Wu and Gao saw participation in the Boy Scouts and military drilling not as extracurricular activities but as inherently part of the civics curriculum.[102] Youth Services Associations were to involve themselves in everything from general exhibitions of the New Life movement to inoculation and rat-catching

---

[98] Wu Jiazhen and Gao Shiliang, "Xianjieduan Zhongguo gongmin xunlian," pp. 43–56.
[99] Ibid., p. 53.   [100] Ibid., pp. 50–53.   [101] Ibid., pp. 50–52.   [102] Ibid., pp. 46–47

campaigns.[103] Finally, "symbolic stimulation," Wu and Gao claimed, could nourish people's faith and unify their will.[104] Symbols such as national flags, commemorations, music, and architecture were major features of nation-states around the world, including China.

Wu and Gao show the vast hopes being placed in civics education. It was nothing less than the remaking of the scattered masses, as Sun Yat-sen and others had conceived of the people since the late Qing, into a unified nation. The language of patriotic citizenship was becoming ever more deeply entrenched. This was a process that began with the first textbooks of the late Qing. Tsuchiya Hiroshi has recently argued that late Qing self-cultivation textbooks were designed to produce the "national" (*guomin*) and not the "citizen" (*gongmin*).[105] This distinction implicitly acknowledges the difference between the traditional subject and the modern national, while explicitly it distinguishes between the national defined in terms of duties and the citizen defined in terms of rights. Tsuchiya points out how traditional concepts were used to produce a modern national identity that was shaped by the crises of the late Qing. Citizenship education in China emerged only with the birth of the Republic, and only partially. Although the new morality textbooks rejected "loyalty to the emperor" and spoke of rights and liberties, the centrality of statist doctrines continued to limit the scope of the notion of citizenship.

I am largely in agreement with this argument, but I would modify it in two ways. First, I regard the distinction between national and citizen as extremely porous. They are almost two sides of the same coin: the former refers to the identity of the member of a modern state, and the latter to the political role of the member, however heavily that role is restricted in theory and practice. It will not do to idealize the conception of citizen. Second, the late Qing self-cultivation textbooks in effect argued for the compatibility of patriotic education and Confucianism, and patriotism inevitably implied a degree of citizenship. This approach continued in the first years of the Republic, when textbooks were quick to say more about the specifics rights and duties of the people.[106] In textbooks if not political reality, rights in fact found a major place. But, again, citizens certainly have duties, which mark their identity as members of the political community. It may be, as Wang Jiarong suggests in his general study of modern Chinese textbooks, that the late Qing self-cultivation textbooks were not necessarily suitable for the grade level they aimed at, nor even that most lessons did a good job of illustrating the particular virtues that they

---

[103] Ibid., pp. 50–51.   [104] Ibid., pp. 52–53.
[105] Tsuchiya Hiroshi, "Shinmatsu no shūshin kyōkasho to Nihon."
[106] See also Wang Jiarong, *Minzuhun*, pp. 152–153. Wang suggests that the new curriculum's attention to "national affairs" marked a major break with the Qing's attitude that national affairs belong solely to the emperor. However, if that distinction was true at the level of official pronouncements, late Qing textbooks had already legitimated the people's interests in the nation.

were designed to convey.[107] But given the assumption that most students would have already been acquainted with some of the traditional primers, this may not have mattered so much. It was, after all, the first foray of authors and publishers into this realm.

It is certainly the case that the emphasis on duties over rights continued into the republican period, as Zheng Hang concludes.[108] And we should also note the elitism that permeates civics textbooks.[109] It is never clear how far "down" citizenship really extends. If the model of citizenship was the educated and probably propertied ethnic-Han male, then the status of peasants, workers, women, minorities, and children was forever ambiguous. But *any* talk of citizenship and of rights was significant in changing the field of discourse to one of constitutional norms rather than an imperial imaginary. And citizenship is not exclusively about rights. The effort of the Nationalists in the 1930s to revive "traditional morality" did not show that all such virtues had disappeared, but that political leaders thought they had. Actually, this effort confirmed the adaptability of certain strands of Confucianism – but not the whole cloth – to the needs of a modernizing nation-state.

The modern nation-state promises a certain equality among citizens, before the law if nowhere else, even if it rests on social and economic hierarchies no less than did traditional states. Robert Culp has rightly pointed to a tension in the 1930s between the revival of Confucianism norms resting on hierarchical relationships on the one hand and insistent social egalitarianism on the other.[110] What both visions shared was a sense of state and society as an organic unity resting on the devotion of individuals to the whole and the virtues of cooperation, for example between capital and labor. Morality-civics textbooks in China in the early twentieth century sought to teach students about this vision of the state and, more importantly, how they could fit into the modern nation and contribute to it. Self-cultivation soon became not a goal in itself but a means to produce citizens: half cog in the machine and half autonomous individual. If political disillusionment – first with empire and then with the outcome of revolution – was a theme of Chinese politics, perhaps civics and society classes acted to re-enchant the political realm. At least they presented an ideal to strive for.

Morality-civics textbooks attempted to make children into virtuous beings. They were texts, but they wrote about practice. They advocated practice, but they conveyed knowledge. In virtuous behavior lay identity. Here by "identity" I mean something like role: student of a specific school, child of specific parents,

---

[107] Wang Jiaorong, *Minzuhun*, p. 86.
[108] Zheng Hang, *Zhongguo jindai deyu kechengshi*, pp. 103–104.
[109] Bi Yuan, *Jianzao changshi*, pp. 184–185.
[110] Robert Culp, "Setting the Sheet of Loose Sand," pp. 45–90.

resident in a specific neighborhood, and so on, and finally to citizen of a specific state and member of the world community. The larger the scale, the greater the imaginative effort involved. The youngest children were reminded to wash their faces, while older ones were located in their communities. The state was made visible across the curriculum and everywhere in the physical space of the school: from history lessons to flags. But it was explained in civics classes.

5 The national subject in time

Of the various knowledge disciplines adopted by the new school system, only history was a traditional discipline. For example, though discussed in different ways, ethics, sociology, literature, and certainly chemistry were not autonomous bodies of theoretical and empirical work. History had long been an important discipline, providing a "mirror" for rulers based on its profound ethical purport. History did not try to describe progress but the relationship between human actors and the Dao, or ethical cosmic order. Although it did not quite provide a foundation of Chinese identity for the gentry class in the way the classics did, history illuminated the classics, which described a perfect, or nearly perfect, social order that later rulers should strive to emulate.

However, the main function of history in twentieth-century China was not to describe standards of perfection reached in the past but to show the way toward building the nation. Textbooks thus reflected the "new historiography" that had just adopted the goal of writing the history of China as the evolution of the nation. Liang Qichao was the most prominent of those who wanted to make the "nation" into the prime historical subject. He promoted the idea of progress and tried to conceptualize history as linear development, using social Darwinism to explain progress. And he condemned the voluminous dynastic histories – the 24 official histories – as simply the "genealogies of twenty-four families."[1] This was to largely accept the premises of Western historiography as it had developed by the nineteenth century as it, too, was closely tied to nation building. At the same time, a final function of history textbooks was to convey a sense of continuity with the past that provided students' identity in the present.

Textbooks presented many familiar stories, but they framed these old historical data in a new way. Not only did they promote a new story of the "rise of China" as one nation-state among others – to which it needed to catch up – but they were written in an entirely new style. Instead of annals that proceeded

---

[1] Liang Qichao, "Xin shixue," *Yinbingshi heji*, wenji 9: 1–32. The new historiography movement has been extensively discussed; see inter alia Huang Jinxing, "Zhongguo jindai shixue de shuang-chong weiji"; Wang Fansen, "Wan-Qing de zhengzhi gainian yu 'Xin shixue'"; and Peter Zarrow, "Old Myth into New History."

from one date-event to the next date-event, history textbooks used a "chapter and sections" style that emphasized a more or less single narrative. In this sense, content and style were inseparable, and the new style integrated political developments in a way that conveyed that very idea: development.[2]

Like the history textbooks of other countries, Chinese history textbooks taught that national identity was based on race and culture, but Chinese textbooks also – and especially – based identity on political unity forged over centuries. History textbooks were implicitly based on three kinds of time. First was the essentially eternal: at least from the founding, a kind of essential China had never disappeared and never would. Second was the cyclical: the rise and fall of dynasties, unity and disunity, order and disorder, but always return to unity. In this sense, the Republic, for all its uniqueness, was a restoration not only of the Han race but of the eternal underlying order. And third was the evolutionary: history showed progress, the advancement of culture and civilization, the improvement of society, and a kind of culmination of political progress in republicanism. In the progressive view of time at least, China was not isolated but integrated into world trends. One lesson that could be drawn from this view was that facing European imperialism from a position of weakness, China must absorb European civilization precisely in order to resist its imperialist onslaught.[3] Chinese children must learn to keep the country open and struggle economically. Youth needed to be taught practical business skills to make the country strong and wealthy. But was this the task of history?

Throughout the republican period, history educators asked, "What is the goal of teaching history?" They did not necessarily believe that the official curriculum answered this question. And to discover the goal of teaching history, they had to ask, "What is history?" Many educators did not want to focus on the names and dates of political leaders. They saw the goals of history education in terms of the "evolution of ways of living" (*shenghuo yanjin*) and "global trends" (*shijie qushi*).[4] This would equip students with proper life attitudes (*rensheng guannian*). Whether textbooks were the best way to meet these goals was a question. In 1925 the noted historian He Bingsong sharply complained that textbooks were dominating history teaching.[5] He suggested that an overemphasis on textual learning resembled nothing so much as the old examination system. He repeatedly emphasized the use of pictures and charts but thought

---

[2] An overview of the changes to historical thinking through the republican period is Brian Moloughney and Peter Zarrow, "Making History Modern." See also Tze-ki Hon and Robert J. Culp, eds., *The Politics of Historical Production*; Prasenjit Duara, *Rescuing History from the Nation*; and Q. Edward Wang, *Inventing China through History*. For the late Qing, see Tanaka Hiroshi, "Tsukurareru dentō."

[3] See, e.g., Ding Baoshu, *Mengxue Zhongguo lishi jiaokeshu*, pp. 2a–b.

[4] For example, Wang Zhijiu, "Xiaoxue lishi jiaoxue shangque," p. 2.

[5] He Bingsong, "Lishi jiaoshoufa."

the way textbooks presented them – in tiny formats with no explanations – was useless. For He Bingsong, history teaching should keep in mind the range of resources already available in schools: maps, models, reference works, and pictures. He wanted students to begin studying history by focusing on resources for their local history: including textual resources but also old steles and buildings nearby, and trips to historical sites and museums. As well, students could learn from models of historical objects and pictures, charts, and maps, as long as a good teacher made these objects come to life.

Clearly, He Bingsong wanted to make learning history as hands-on as possible. This did not mean he entirely dismissed textbooks. He approved of textbooks as one of several means of teaching history, but he did not think students should simply memorize them. Rather, they should be just one tool given to students to make their own discoveries about history. What kind of textbooks should be used depended on the resources of the school and the level of the students – it was the responsibility of the teacher to select the best textbook for a particular class. In a school with a good library, a textbook that merely outlined major events would suffice, and the teacher could assign supplementary readings. In a poorer school, a more comprehensive textbook would be better. In any case, teachers had to make sure that their students could comprehend the assignments.

Looking back nearly a century later, we can find justification in He Bingsong's criticisms. Republican-era education was excessively devoted to mindless memorization, and textbooks were a major part of this style of education. Nonetheless, history textbooks presented a formula of linear progress determined by the "rules" of social Darwinism. In the 1920s they came to reflect the new interest in social history, and in the 1930s they explored new research on China's place in a global system of capitalist imperialism. All such narrative frameworks are subject to later modification and even rejection, but the point here is that, for all their faults, Chinese history textbooks offered students ways of making sense of the world.

After a discussion of the changing history curriculum and periodization debates, this chapter focuses on textbook treatments on the origins of Chinese civilization and the dynastic period up to the modern era; Chapter 6 focuses on textbook treatments of the Qing (1644–1912), the problem of the foreign, and the Republic.

The curriculum: defining and framing history

"The study of the past is the only route to understanding contemporary society," a history curriculum of 1929 somewhat arbitrarily pronounced.[6] But was

---

[6] Kecheng jiaocai yanjiusuo, ed., *20 shiji Zhongguo zhongxiaoxue kecheng biaozhun*, vol. 12, p. 37.

history a field of objective knowledge about the past, or was it a source of moral instruction? Late Qing educators of course saw that history classes could be both. Officials perhaps tended to emphasize its moral qualities, whereas reformers turned to history as a source of identity. In the 1904 curriculum, the aim of history was to convey the "great and virtuous deeds of the sage rulers," so students learned the origins of Chinese culture and the sacred governance (*shengdezheng*) of the "present dynasty" in order to nurture the wellsprings of national loyalty (*guomin zhongai*).[7] Although the ministry may have sought to finesse any potential conflict between loyalty to the dynasty and loyalty to the "nation" (patriotism), the term "national" or "citizen" (*guomin*) was itself a break with the past. Referring to young students, it proclaimed: "The knowledge of love of the same kind [of people] (*ai tonglei*) at this time is the basis for the patriotism (*ai guojia*) of adults."[8] At the same time, in addition to China, the histories of other Asian nations and Western nations were also to be taught, though with more emphasis on the modern period.[9]

For their first two years, students studied stories of their hometown, especially famous local persons. (Again, we see the importance of exemplary models.) In years 3 and 4 they moved on to learn of the specific dynasties and reigns and the great deeds of the sacred rulers, and in year 5 they learned of the founding of the Qing and the good government of its various sage-rulers.[10] Perhaps national consciousness and moral rectitude were two sides of the same coin. Late Qing teacher's manuals spread the word. Through familiarity with their nation's history, students would develop into loyal citizens.[11] The implication was that because each country possessed its unique character (J. *kokutai*, Ch. *guoti*), it was the history teacher's responsibility to make sure students understood their own country's character, which was based on its historical experiences. The national character is not only a product of historical development but is discovered through history.

Upper primary school history classes were to revolve around the stories of dynastic rise and fall – the alternations of order and chaos – since the Yellow Emperor (Huang Di) and Yao and Shun.[12] Still, overall, the curriculum for Chinese history was designed to convey an impression of continuity. Middle school history too was to use the "great events of dynasties and reigns" to narrate, first, the Qing's own "royal sacred government and inexhaustible

---

[7] Qu Xingui and Tang Liangyan, *Zhongguo jindai jiaoyushi ziliao huibian*, vol. 1, p. 295; Kecheng jiaocai yanjiusuo, ed., *20 shiji Zhongguo zhongxiaoxue kecheng biaozhun*, vol. 12, p. 5.
[8] Qu Xingui and Tang Liangyan, *Zhongguo jindai jiaoyushi ziliao*, 1: 294.
[9] Kecheng jiaocai yanjiusuo, ed., *20 shiji Zhongguo zhongxiaoxue kecheng biaozhun*, vol. 12, p. 7.
[10] Qu Xingui and Tang Liangyan, eds., *Zhongguo jindai jiaoyushi ziliao*, 1: 294–295.
[11] See, e.g., Bai Zuolin, trans., *Xiaoxue geke jiaoshoufa*, 4: 1a–b; and *Xiaoxue geke jiaoshoufa*, 1: 75, which cited the ministry's regulations.
[12] Shangwu yinshuguan, comp., "Jiaoyu yi," "Seventh category," in *Da Qing xin faling*, 1: 81b.

virtue" and the great events of the previous century; the stories of loyal and good scholars; the ups and downs of scholarship and technical skills; the rise and fall of military strength; changes in government; the progress of agriculture, industry, and commerce; changes in customs; and so forth.[13] Then students were to learn the history of Asian nations and finally Europe and the United States. In general, the history curriculum at this level was supposed to show students the relations among facts and the different origins of various cultures. In this way, students would come to an understanding of the reasons why some countries were strong while others were weak – the key question confronting Chinese reformers for three generations at this point. Again, the ultimate purpose was frankly didactic if less narrowly focused than the self-cultivation curriculum: to raise the resolve and character of the people.[14]

The Japanese influence on late Qing history textbooks was especially strong.[15] First, traditional Chinese dynastic histories were divided into separate units such as annals and biographies, as well as essays on particular institutions, but they offered little of an overall narrative of major events, even from the court's point of view. Meiji historians, themselves following Western historiographical trends, had begun to write national histories that basically narrated major events chronologically. This became known in China as the "chapters and sections" style.

Second, Meiji historians wrote national history. The Chinese still had to work out exactly what the history of the nation was, as opposed to a history of a few emperors and generals, but that there was a *nation* waiting for historical discovery seemed a huge break with traditional historiography. Indeed, the very first general histories of China used in Chinese schools were paraphrastic translations of Japanese histories of China. A key case was Liu Yizheng. His 1902 *Brief History of Past Dynasties* was commissioned by Zhang Zhidong.[16] Liu made some changes to the original and added sections on more recent history. But he maintained the original's periodization of Chinese history into ancient, middle, and modern and the original's organization into chapters marching along chronologically. This also provided a model for Xia Zengyou's *Most Recent Middle School Chinese History Textbook*.[17]

No wonder the reformer Ding Baoshu, a founder of the Civilization Press, argued that the Chinese people needed to develop their own "historical point

---

[13] Ibid., 1: 73. [14] Ibid., "Jiaoyu yi," 1: 74.
[15] See Tze-ki Hon, "Educating the Citizens," pp. 84–95; Q. Edward Wang, "Narrating the Nation," pp. 103–133; Li Xiaoqian, *Xifang shixue zai Zhongguo de chuanbo*, chapter 1; and Li Xiaoqian, "Qingji Zhinashi, dongyangshi jiaokeshu jieyi chutan."
[16] Liu Yizheng, *Lidai shilue*. Liu's Japanese source was *Shina tsushi* 支那通史 by Naka Michiyo 那珂通世 (1851–1908).
[17] Xia Zengyou, *Zuixin zhongxue Zhongguo lishi jiaokeshu*.

of view."[18] Their failure to do so, he charged, had resulted in their forgetting the origins of the "ancestral nation." Ding compared the narration of the affairs of the nation to a grandson narrating the meritorious deeds of his father and grandfather to encourage clan solidarity, and so Chinese needed to write their own history. Modern history education in Japan in the 1870s was itself based on paraphrastic translations of Western textbooks to teach foreign history, which influenced the production of Japanese history textbooks.[19] These, however, continued to be organized along the lines of imperial reign periods for some time. The pattern was to begin with the "age of the gods" and then turn to the ancestral emperor Jimmu; all later emperors descended from Jimmu, himself descended from the sun goddess. By the 1880s textbooks sometimes divided Japanese history into periods of ancient-middle-modern – helping to create a more coherent narrative of the nation. By the 1900s, when Chinese began paying closer attention, Japanese history textbooks were fairly standardized. They told the stories of emperors and other great personages, and they worked in tandem with self-cultivation textbooks to foster a Japanese identity that revolved around the national polity with the emperor at the center. Of course, this did not preclude any attention to social and cultural change, "civilizational" development, and sophisticated discussion of geographical factors. The Ministry of Education's regulations of 1891 stipulated that primary students should begin historical studies with local history (a practice followed by Chinese educators), along with "teaching the institutions of the founding of the country, the inexhaustibility of the imperial line, the great accomplishments of the emperors throughout the ages, the deeds of the loyal and sagely men, the loyalty of the people, and the origins of culture, and so forth."[20] Nonofficial textbooks that ignored or slighted mythical stories were marginalized in the 1890s and displaced entirely in the 1900s.[21] By 1903 only the textbooks compiled by the Ministry of Education were permitted.

The ministry's 1908 "ordinary history textbook" may be taken as representative of what Chinese educators found.[22] It presented a triumphal story, especially celebrating the Meiji Restoration and the rise of Japanese power that culminated in the annexation of Korea. It spoke of a Japan that stood in equality with the world power and of a people united in loyalty to throne and country. It also began with the age of the gods and the founding of the imperial state by Jimmu. Perhaps Chinese exaltation of the Yellow Emperor as the founder of the Chinese state, which we examine later, was based on the example of Jimmu.

---

[18] Ding Baoshu, *Mengxue Zhongguo lishi jiaokeshu*, p. 1a.
[19] Kaigo Tokiomi and Naka Arata, *Kindai Nihon kyōkasho sōsetsu*, pp. 435–496.
[20] Cited in Yasuda Motohisa, "Rekishi kyōiku to rekishigaku," p. 13.
[21] Nakamura Kikuji, *Fukkoku kokutei rekishi kyōkasho kaisetsu*, vol. 1, pp. 8–31; see, e.g., Ijichi Sadaka, *Kogaku Nihon shiryaku zennisatsu*, in ibid., vol. 18, pp. 261–262.
[22] Monbushō, comp., *Jinjō shōgaku Nihon kokushi*.

Be that as it may, when the new Chinese Republican government set standards for the history curriculum at the end of 1912, little seemed changed on the surface, beyond the mere fact of a new government. The Ministry of Education proclaimed that primary school history classes should "instill a deep commitment to the moral standards of citizenship."[23] Students were to understand how the Yellow Emperor founded the state, the words and deeds of great men over the ages, the origins of East Asian civilization, the establishment of the Republic, and China's foreign relations over the last century. The goals of middle school history perhaps reflected Chinese republican nationalism in more obvious ways. Students were to understand the progress of the "nation" (*minzu*) – a reference to ethnic identity long favored by revolutionaries – and especially to learn of the change of political system (*zhengti*) and the foundations of the Republic.[24] But this was not a narrow nationalism, and the middle school history curriculum was also expanded to include world history.[25]

The 1923 curricular reforms attempted to integrate Chinese history and world history.[26] If carried out, the middle school history curriculum would have attained Cai Yuanpei's dream of worldview education. Students were to study the changes in the living conditions of all humanity in order to help them adapt to their own environment and deal with natural forces, and to learn empathy toward humanity in order to develop their spirit of fraternity and mutual aid. Of course, Chinese history should receive special emphasis, but students should understand it in the international context and gain an appreciation of the common progress of humanity as such. Units of study, then, would bounce back and forth between different regions – for the most part civilizational units such as China, ancient Egypt, Renaissance Europe, and also Japan. More emphasis was to be placed on environmental factors and cultural history.

However, it is not clear if any history textbooks were actually written along these lines.[27] It was not only difficult to integrate the histories of different cultures but might contradict the goal of nation-building. In any case, the Nationalist curriculum of 1929 again separated Chinese and foreign history, while granting importance to their interactions.[28] According to this provisional curriculum, the purposes of history education in lower middle school included an understanding of China's political and economic conditions, as well as the recent attacks of the imperialist powers on the Chinese nation (*minzu*), in order to arouse students' "national spirit" and "awaken them to an awareness of their responsibilities to the Chinese national movement." For the Guomindang,

---

[23] Kecheng jiaocai yanjiusuo, ed., *20 shiji Zhonggu zhongxiaoxue kecheng biaozhun*, vol. 1, p. 64; vol. 12, pp. 10–11.
[24] Ibid., vol. 12, p. 11. [25] Ibid., vol. 1, p. 69. [26] Ibid., vol. 12, pp. 14–20.
[27] See Robert Culp, "'China – The Land and its People'," pp. 20–21.
[28] Kecheng jiaocai yanjiusuo, ed., *20 shiji Zhongguo zhongxiaoxue kecheng biaozhun*, vol. 12, pp. 21–42.

history was less about past glories than present-day threats. The study of foreign histories was to inculcate a kind of internationalist sympathy, but the Ministry of Education warned against excessive idealism, lest students forget the need of the Chinese nation to defend itself. History was to help students understand current conditions with a mix of alarm and optimism. True, this was not to neglect the usual stuff of history – change over time – but it was to look for particular stories such as the rise of democratic thought, achievements in culture, and economic progress. And the Guomindang considered that by lower middle school, at least, history would equip students to contribute to society.

The Nationalist upper middle school curriculum similarly emphasized imperialist aggression against China to "arouse students' spirit of struggle." At the same time, students were to first understand how the Chinese nation developed, as well as the historical roots of the Three People's Principles. Outlines for history classes became ever more specific. Chinese history classes were to begin with clear statements of their relevance to current conditions and definitions of the Chinese nation. Foreign history classes were to focus on Europe, but not entirely neglect other regions. This international history was to show how the "development of capitalist imperialism in recent times has led to the oppression of small and weak nations and laborers." World revolution was fine, but Nationalist educators were first interested in strengthening China.

The 1936 curriculum for lower middle schools saw a new emphasis on the historical glory of the nation, which was added to discussions of imperialist aggression against China "in order to arouse the goal in students of national revival and to nourish their confidence and consciousness of self and exalt their spirit."[29] At this moment, when Japan threatened the military conquest of all China, students were to learn of China's contributions to world culture, and their knowledge of contemporary world conditions should enable them to participate in China's national movements. The upper middle school curriculum was roughly similar, though emphasizing the need for students to understand the modern period's imperialism, anti-imperialist national movements, and the role of the Three People's Principles.[30] Students should be equipped to promote a free and equal international order and participate in the improvement of Chinese culture. Yet in spite of goals that spoke of contemporary conditions, the actual history curriculum maintained the long-standing stress on ancient and medieval history.

The Nationalists' 1929 curricular standards even established the periodization system that history textbooks were to follow. Previously, textbooks authors could make up their own schemes, or use no periodization at all. Most followed a scheme adopted from the West via Japan: ancient, medieval, and modern. However, because this was difficult to apply to Chinese history, the exact dating

---

[29] Ibid., vol. 12, p. 43. [30] Ibid., vol. 12, p. 50.

of each epoch was subject to much variety. By the republican period, textbooks tended to follow a modified periodization scheme consisting of five stages: high antiquity from the very origins of the Chinese through the Qin unification (221 BCE); middle antiquity from the Qin-Han through the fall of the Tang (907 CE); late antiquity from the Five Dynasties through the Ming (1644); modern as the Qing; and contemporary as the Republic (1912–).[31] But how were these periods substantively different from one another? One textbook from 1930 stressed that early antiquity was marked by the spread of agriculture, state formation, and the development of Han culture;[32] middle antiquity by racial struggles and power struggles until power was gradually monopolized by the emperor; and the modern by China's openness to the world, which led the authors to conclude that Chinese modernity began in the Ming, rather than the Qing, when the Jesuits had arrived.[33] Warnings against periodization were also heard during the Republic. In their lower middle school textbook, the prominent historian Gu Jiegang and Wang Zhongqi pointed out that efforts to divide history into periods were always artificial.[34] Cause and effect were ongoing processes, and attempts to trace the causes of any historical phenomenon always keep receding into the past. Doubly mistaken is the attempt to link periodization to dynasties rather than more fundamental changes in peoples (the country's racial make-up), political forms, society, and scholarship. Nonetheless, Gu and Wang concluded that periods did possess their own spirit, a spirit that differentiated them from other ages. In his *Vernacular Chinese History* of 1923, Lü Simian also indicated doubts about the reliability of periodization, regarding it at best as a rough guide to making study more convenient. He warned against regarding periods as distinct units of time, and even showed some skepticism about a teleology of progress.[35]

In 1932, the Ministry of Education promulgated standards for history classes that ratified the standard fivefold scheme treating the Qing as modern and the Republic as contemporary.[36] The "contemporary" was not a politically neutral category. By claiming that the 1911 Revolution marked the turning point into the contemporary, the Nationalist government was emphasizing that modern Chinese history culminated in its own achievements: first the 1911 Revolution and then the unification of China in 1928. Above all, by treating the Republic as

---

[31] E.g., Chen Qingnian, *Zhongguo lishi jiaokeshu*; Hu Chaoyang, *Diyi jianming lishi qimeng*. From the tables of contents.
[32] Zhu Yixin et al., *Chuzhong benguoshi*, 4: 94–95.
[33] Ibid., 3: 1–11. However, in their concluding remarks, the authors link the period to continued racial struggle, the florescence of scholarship, and territorial gains, adding that imperial power expanded to the point it became unstable: ibid., 4: 96.
[34] Gu Jiegang and Wang Zhongqi, *Benguoshi*, 1: 16–22.
[35] Lü Simian, *Baihua benguoshi*, p. 10.
[36] Kecheng jiaocai yanjiusuo, ed., *20 shiji Zhongguo zhongxiaoxue kecheng biaozhun*, vol. 12, pp. 43–47.

156   Educating China

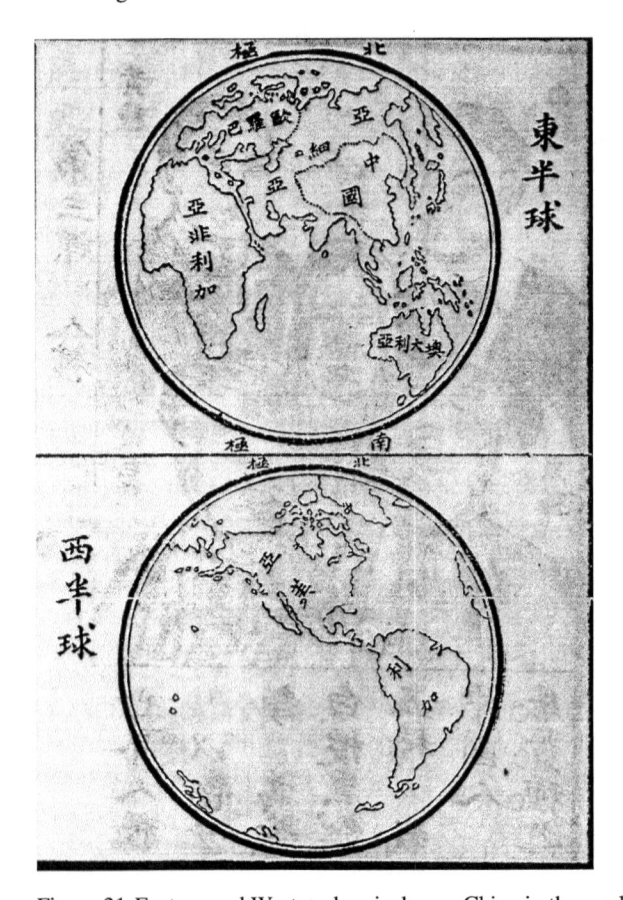

Figure 21 Eastern and Western hemispheres: China in the world.

contemporary, textbooks not only highlighted its temporal position opposed to the Qing's (failed) modernity, but suggested it was in greater accord with world trends, a clear sign of progress, and even the culmination of China's history.

Origin myths in late Qing textbooks

Late Qing, early Republican, and Nationalist textbooks all tended to begin with the origins of China, naturally enough. Some began with the stories of the peoples of the place that became known as China. Some first located China's place in the world.

The global map in Figure 21 shows China as a great landmass on a par with continents rather than other countries. It shows that China is not isolated in central grandeur but that China might dwarf any other individual country. History textbooks also described the place of the Chinese among the races of the world. China was composed of sub-races of the Yellow race, and history textbooks used drawings of the major world races like those used in language readers (see Figure 5 earlier). At the heart of the Chinese people, however, was the Han race. The notion of a population, mostly farmers, that was identified as Han – as distinct from other populations identified as Manchu, Mongol, Tibetan, Miao, and other peoples – was not new. But the racial science that equated genealogy with biological destiny, and the historical myths discussed below: these were new in the late Qing.[37] Racial science amounted to a new imaginary of Chinese identity. A sense of cultural continuity – even with racial aspects – had long coexisted with dynastic loyalties and identities, and in a sense transcended them. But late Qing history textbooks implied the primeval creation of a Chinese nation that was not only distinguishable from a dynasty, but from any particular state or cultural formation. And it was this nation that progressed through time. Happily trapped in the new historiography, as it were, Republican textbooks largely continued to promote these themes, though they began to acknowledge that the legends of the ancient past could not be verified historically.

Essentially, history textbooks used the tools of race and geography to turn traditional stories of the "sage-kings" (*shengwang*) into stories of nation founders. The sage-kings were traditionally not regarded as founders of China but of culture and civilization, though that was perhaps considered much the same thing. They personified the inventions of fire, farming, houses, writing, silk making, and the like. In the late Qing, in the pantheon of sage-kings, the Yellow Emperor *Huangdi* rose to even greater prominence than he had before. He became the conqueror of the lands of the Han race, beginning with the Wei and Yellow River valleys, and even the progenitor of the Chinese people. Where had the Yellow Emperor come from? He and the Han race were explained by the "Western origins" theory. In the late nineteenth century a French scholar, Terrien de Lacouperie, proposed that the Han people originated in Mesopotamia as a wandering tribe called the Bak. The myth of the "Yellow Emperor" was derived from a Mesopotamian god, he argued, and represented a Mesopotamian tribe moving east out of the Babylonian sphere of civilization.[38]

The Yellow Emperor was pictured in various ways, and in this particular view (Figure 22) appears to be a highly civilized king. His headdress confirms his royalty.

---

[37] For "Han," see Thomas S. Mullaney, ed., *Critical Han Studies*; and Peter Zarrow, *After Empire*, chapter 5.
[38] Tze-ki Hon, *Revolution as Restoration*; Ishikawa Yoshihiro, "20 seiki shotō no Chūgoku ni okeru 'Kōtei' netsu"; Son Kō [Sun Jiang], "Renzoku to danzetsu"; and Jiang Sun, "Continuity and Discontinuity."

158   Educating China

像 帝 黃

Figure 22 The Yellow Emperor.

As a putative tribal leader, he did not always look so prim and proper, but one way or another he was a ruler. On the one hand, the "Western origins" theory tied early China into global movements, creating a kind of parity with Europeans, who also derived from Babylonian civilization. On the other, it created a racial-style genealogy of the Han people. The theory intrigued Japanese scholars and was enthusiastically taken up by revolutionary intellectuals such as Zhang Binglin and Liu Shipei, before it dissipated for lack of evidence in the 1910s. The Han were not the original inhabitants of China, in this view, but they were its first conquerors and in a sense the first Chinese. They enslaved or pushed out the Miao people. The Yellow Emperor established a powerful state, and founded an imperial line.[39] In this story, the Miao were either pushed south or turned into a labor caste.

In Figure 23, the Yellow Emperor sports more barbarian facial hair and looks altogether tougher. The late Qing educational reformer Ding Baoshu, who published a elementary history textbook with this picture, was himself something of an artist. Sun Jiang suggests that Ding derived this particular portrait of the Yellow Emperor from the publications of revolutionaries.[40] According to Sun,

---

[39] Shen Songqiao, "Wo yi woxie jian Xuanyuan"; and Luo Zhitian, "Baorong ruxue, zhuzi yu Huangdi de guoxue."
[40] Jiang Sun, "Continuity and Discontinuity," pp. 188–196.

Figure 23 The Yellow Emperor, Conqueror of the Tribes.

although the Yellow Emperor here is wearing the royal headdress, his appearance of strength and power suggests his pre-imperial role as tribal chieftain and conqueror. We might see the Yellow Emperor here as a liminal figure. Whether Ding Baoshu himself supported the revolution is currently unknowable, but the image of the conqueror, representing a virile and uncowed people, was at least as important to reformers as to revolutionaries. Thus it was certainly possible to picture the Yellow Emperor more as a close military leader than a distant emperor, bedecked with weapons and armor (Figure 24).

Inevitably, history textbooks began in one form or another with founding stories of the Chinese nation. The late Qing *Primary Reader in History* attempted to define the Chinese in racial terms.[41] They were members of the Yellow race like Japanese, Koreans, Tartars, and other groups. Their specific subgroup was that of the Hua (*huaren*), who were in turn defined circularly as those who developed China. ("Hua" and "Han" were effectively synonyms in the late Qing.) "China" in this sense was a spatial concept: this people originally moved out of the northern plains, but what marked them as historically Chinese was their settling around the Yellow River Valley and then moving into central and southern China.[42] Culturally, they were marked by scholarship, the educated classes following Confucianism while the ignorant followed Buddhism

---

[41] Xia Zengyou, *Xiaoxue duben shi*, pp. 4a–5a.
[42] Obviously, this story does not accord exactly with the "Western origins" theory that specified Central Asia, but it does maintain the notion of the migration of the (future) Chinese into "China" from the outside.

Figure 24 The Yellow Emperor.

and Daoism. In this sense, identity was defined through race, geography, and culture. Yao Zuyi's *Upper Primary Chinese History Textbook*, published by the Commercial Press in 1904, began with a brief cosmogony, referring to a Great Mist that was succeeded by Pangu and the Three August Ones and the Five Emperors (*sanhuang wudi*).[43] Yao thus generally followed the account in Sima Qian (145–90 BCE) in referring to the August Ones of Heaven, Earth and Humanity (*tianhuang, dihuang, renhuang*) and attributed the inventions of civilization – fire and housing – to this extremely ancient and little-known period. However, it is worth noting Yao Zuyi emphasized that the ancient world consisted merely of tribes or villages, and that it evolved into a unified state. In all, "China" had remained unified through fourteen dynasties.[44] These dynasties stretched back to the second millennium BCE and advanced to today's Qing dynasty. Yao was following traditional lists of legitimate dynastic succession (*zhengtong*), but he was also giving students a sense of national identity that depended on the unified imperial state. In this way, Yao accepted the legitimacy of the Qing, though it was founded by Manchu "invaders" in the seventeenth century, as he accepted the legitimacy of the Yuan dynasty, founded by Mongol invaders in the thirteenth century. More importantly, while obviously not

[43] Yao Zuyi, *Zuixin gaodeng xiaoxue Zhongguo lishi jiaokeshu*, 1: 2a.
[44] Ibid., 1: 1a. Yao did not deny the fact of periods of political disunity but implied the normative nature of unity, which was maintained at the cultural level regardless of political disruptions.

denying Chinese identity to those unfortunate enough to lives in times of disunity or chaos, he bound that identity to the ideal of the unified imperial state.

Other textbooks, however, simply plunged into China's history, beginning at the beginning. The beginning in this sense – the beginning of a recognizable nation – was again the Yellow Emperor. One version noted earlier has him leading a kind of invasion of China. In another version, Qian Zonghan's *Illustrated Vernacular History of China*, various tribes moved into the Yellow River region out of the west.[45] Eventually, these tribes amalgamated and from their various chiefs came a supreme leader: the Yellow Emperor. Establishing a kingdom that stretched from north of the Yellow River to south of the Yangzi, the Yellow Emperor marked the start of true rulership. He was the "first ancestor of us, the Chinese people" (*women de Zhongguoren de touyige zuzong*). He also created written characters and invented carts and ships. Qian Zonghan thus concentrated all these markers of civilization on one historical figure. Before the Yellow Emperor: primitive tribes perhaps with some skills like hunting, fire, even agriculture (in other accounts this is made clearer), but not a unified people. After the Yellow Emperor: in effect, the Chinese nation.

Qian was not alone in attributing both rulership and ancestry to the Yellow Emperor. Ding Baoshu's *Elementary Chinese History Textbook* took a slightly different course in specifying pre-existing "Han tribes" (*Hanzu*) that moved into the Yellow River region out of the northwest.[46] As its population grew, various separate tribes emerged under local chiefs. This was an age of fishing, hunting, planting, medicine, and weaving. There were no supreme rulers (*junzhu*). Then, in Ding's narrative, the Yellow Emperor arose as a conqueror, uniting the tribes under his rule and extending his kingdom to the Yangzi region.[47] In this account, too, the Yellow Emperor created Chinese characters, invented carts and boats – and "established the basis for a unified Chinese polity." In other words, even if "Han" identity of some sort preceded the Yellow Emperor, the Han were but one tribe indistinguishable from many others. Ding's emphasis on the beginning of rulership was essential for a distinct Han identity. So, too, in Zhao Zhengduo's *Upper Primary History Textbook*. Zhao began with the successful spread of the Hua race (*Huazhong*) from out of the West into the upper Yellow River valley and beyond: so that China (*Zhongguo*) has been called Zhonghua ever since.[48] And for Yao Zuyi, the Yellow Emperor represented nothing less than the institutionalization of the bureaucratic system and "improving the lives of the people through civil rule."[49]

---

[45] Qian Zonghan, *Huitu Zhongguo baihua shi*, p. 1a.
[46] Ding Baoshu, *Mengxue Zhongguo lishi jiaokeshu*, p. 1a.   [47] Ibid., p. 1b.
[48] Zhao Zhengduo, *Gaodeng xiaoxue lishi keben*, pp. 1a–b.
[49] Yao Zuyi, *Zuixin gaodeng xiaoxue Zhongguo lishi jiaokeshu*, 1: 2b–3a.

At the same time, the basic story of the evolution of civilization and the organized state could also be told without over-emphasizing the role of the Yellow Emperor. The *Primary Reader in History* pointed out the unreliability of records pertaining to the "Three August Ones and the Five Emperors" while also noting a series of inventions associated with various versions of their names.[50] Essentially, this textbook repeated familiar legends. Taihao (i.e., Fuxi) invented the eight trigrams, hunting nets, ritual sacrifices, and marriage; Yandi (i.e., Shennong) invented the plow and taught the people farming, medicine, and markets – while next on the list the Yellow Emperor made tools, currency, boats and carts, clothes, cities, and ordered the creation of written characters and the stem-branch calendrical system, and his empress taught the people to raise silkworms. These inventions, along with houses, fire, clothing, and the like distinguished the civilized Huaxia from barbarian groups, according to this textbook. The Huaxia's leaders were termed Sages. Yet the *Primary Reader* also pointed out that the inventions of civilization did not all come from one man or one sage: they were the product of hundreds of people's efforts and adapted over generations.

This view, rarely expressed in the late Qing, came close to turning the anonymous collective Chinese people into the agent of historical progress. Civilization took generations to build. The *Primary Reader* also traced the rise of an organized polity to the arrival of the Huaren in what was to become China. Expelling the native inhabitants (barbarians), they established cities and eventually a "huge empire" divided into the nine districts (*jiuzhou*), an ancient term for the lands under the emperor. Unlike most other textbooks, the *Primary Reader* suggested that not until the reliable records of Yao and Shun could one speak of individuals, but it conveyed a similar sort of political identity.

But most typically, a narrative of the traditional Five Emperors was combined with a new emphasis on the Yellow Emperor. Fu Guangnian's *Simple History Textbook* posited an evolutionary process from small tribes to more complex, higher-level social organization.[51] He thus traced an age completely without rulers (*junzhu*) to purely local chiefs, and finally to assemblages of tribes – which marked the origins of the emperorship (*diwang*). Fu Xi invented writing and Shennong medicine, but it was still the Yellow Emperor who defeated his enemies on the battlefield, created a polity – including the well-field (*jingtian*) system – and fathered the entire Yellow race. (In the legendary well-field system, eight plots of land were divided among farmers and one planted for the feudal lord, as represented by the Chinese character for "well." By the late Qing, well-field had became a way to speak of a loosely socialist egalitarianism, but it also represented the epitome of feudal order.) An even stronger position was staked out by Zhao Zhengduo, who dismissed Fuxi and Shennong as mere tribal

---

[50] Xia Zengyou, *Xiaoxue duben shi*, pp. 10a–b.   [51] Fu Guangnian, *Jianyi lishi keben*, p. 1a.

chiefs, although he credited them with the usual inventions.[52] In this way Zhao gave even greater emphasis to the Yellow Emperor as China's first real ruler. The people thus called him, according to Zhao, the "Son of Heaven" (*tianzi*), and he became the founder of the imperial system (*junzhu zhengzhi*).[53]

Almost as important as the Yellow Emperor were not his predecessors but his great successors, Yao and Shun. Not the founders of the imperial state, they came to define its ideal essence. Late Qing history textbooks, following traditional mythology, treated Yao and Shun as exemplars of imperial virtue. Qian Zonghan described Yao as devoted to the people, laboring every day, and establishing the calendar.[54] The main themes here were their good deeds, their abdications of the throne, and the flood stories, which explain the rise of a third exemplar of imperial virtue, Yu the Great. Here, then, is a mix of foundation myths concerning the institutions of civilization on the one hand and personal moral attributes on the other. To late Qing reformers, the traditional stories of "abdication" were a kind of foundation for modern constitutionalism. Textbooks held that an aging Yao, learning of Shun's great reputation for filial piety, first turned over responsibilities to Shun and then, once Shun had proved himself, formally abdicated the throne. In Qian Zonghan's view, Shun's rule was marked by good administration: not only did he work hard personally, but he promoted good officials and demoted bad ones. Again, finding his own son inadequate to replace him, he abdicated to the virtuous Yu, who had quelled the floods after immense and lengthy labor.[55]

Other textbooks added more detail, but although cautiously warning that the records were sparse, nonetheless mixed the flood themes of origins mythology with more prosaic administrative accomplishments.[56] For Ding Baoshu, Yao possessed the "kingly virtue of the great sage."[57] For Zhao Zhengduo, Yao was "humane and virtuous" (*rende*), honoring frugality and simplicity.[58] Also, Yao and Shun continued the military conquest of China,[59] as well as inventing the calendar and astronomy – which were possibly symbols of modern scientific knowledge to late Qing reformers but which were also traditionally the jealously guarded purview of the emperor.[60] These were of course traditional markers of dynastic founders as well as the building blocks of civilization. Shun's virtue was defined more precisely than Yao's. In effect, Shun needed to prove

---

[52] Zhao Zhengduo, *Gaodeng xiaoxue lishi keben*, pp. 1b–2a.   [53] Ibid., p. 2b.
[54] Qian Zonghan, *Huitu Zhongguo baihua shi*, p. 1b.   [55] Ibid., pp. 1b–2a.
[56] However, records pertaining to Yao and Shun were seen as more reliable than accounts of earlier leaders; indeed, several textbooks convey a sense that proper records began with Yao. See Fu Guangnian, *Jianyi lishi keben*, p. 1a.
[57] Ding Baoshu, *Mengxue Zhongguo lishi jiaokeshu*, p. 2a.
[58] Zhao Zhengduo, *Gaodeng xiaoxue lishi keben*: 2b.
[59] Fu Guangnian, *Jianyi lishi keben*, p. 1a
[60] Xia Zengyou, *Xiaoxue duben shi*, p. 11b; Ding Baoshu, *Mengxue Zhongguo lishi jiaokeshu*, p. 2a.

himself worthy: not only did he take care of his parents, but he managed to keep his entire criminally minded family out of trouble. The cycle of flood myths was of course associated with Yu rather than Shun, but in these historicized accounts, it was Shun who appointed Yu as Minister of Public Works, giving him bureaucratic responsibility for controlling the floods. Shun was also no mean administrator, using ritual to command. He put the lords on a schedule of court visits (prefiguring the later Zhou dynasty's enfeoffment system), and he developed a system of rewards and punishments for aristocrats and commoners alike.[61]

Origin myths in republican-period textbooks

Early Republican textbooks continued to speak of Huaren or Hanren in racial terms, but they also emphasized that the "Chinese" (Zhongguoren) were a product of racial mixing. In the words of the *Chinese History* published by the Commercial Press in its "Republican series" of textbooks for middle schools: "Ever since the historical beginnings of the Chinese races through all the various relations and all the various organizations, they have united to form a great national association."[62] Of course, the first of the major groups constituting the "Chinese" was the Han, and among the Chinese ethnic or racial differences did not simply disappear. Nonetheless, "Since the Republic was founded, all the people within its borders are equal. From now on, without distinction as to race, class, or religion, all these boundaries will be merged as the people work to bind themselves together to construct this great association."[63] Furthermore, the *Chinese History* authors noted that a melding of the races already took place after the period of the Yellow Emperor. In other words, for all of the importance of "origins," later developments were equally determinative. First, the *Chinese History* said, in the time of Emperor Yao, tribes joined together to enhance cooperation. Second, the warfare of the Spring and Autumn period and the Warring States period (eighth to third centuries BCE) resulted in interbreeding; this in turn resulted in cultural exchanges and the formation of a new social organization. In the third stage, the struggles between the Xiongnu and the Han dynasty (206 BCE–220 CE) further encouraged the different peoples within China to unite to face the outside threat; then, as China's borders were expanded, the Xiongnu were gradually "assimilated" (*tonghua*). Finally, in the fourth stage after the Han dynasty, the rise of other barbarian conquerors and the reemergence of the Xiongnu led to new threats to Chinese culture. Some of the traditional culture was indeed lost, but cultural interchange led to gains as well, and "our nation advanced a further step."[64] This early-Republican

---

[61] Xia Zengyou, *Xiaoxue duben shi*, pp. 12a–b. [62] Zhao Yusen and Jiang Weiqiao, eds., *Benguoshi*, 1: 2
[63] Ibid., 1: 2–3.   [64] Ibid., 1: 48–50.

discussion of ancient China did not deny the significance of origins of the Chinese, but it considerably complicated the story. The Chinese race and Chinese culture developed through mixing. Yet China remained distinct from the peoples surrounding it. This notion that the Chinese were not purely descended from the Yellow Emperor did not threaten Han-centrism. Republican authors still maintained that 90% of the Chinese population was "Han." However, "Han" was defined not as an "essence" or a single bloodline, but as a historical development. At the same time, "Chinese" was defined as more than Han: still centered around Han and still distinguished from surrounding "others" but not entirely reducible to Han. However, like late Qing textbooks, early republican-period textbooks still insisted on the importance of the ancient origins of the Chinese in order to define the identity of the Chinese today.

In Zhao Yusen's teacher's manual for the Commercial Press, little had changed from late Qing textbooks. Zhao's *New History Teachers' Manual* followed the "Western origins" theory, while the teacher was to point out that these tribes, Hua or Han, were victorious due to their superior culture, a culture that was perfected over thousands of years and thus can represent the entire country.[65] As late as 1923, Lü Simian still accepted the Western origins theory.[66] For his part, Zhao Yusen did not explain exactly what cultural superiority consisted of, but he emphasized the importance of continued progress. So the lesson of the past – victory of the superior – was still applicable today. Zhao's *New History* credited the Yellow Emperor with not only military and political achievements, but also with "opening up" the country.[67] More notably, and continuing a line of thought going back to the early writings of Liang Qichao, Zhao charged that China's failure to further progress lay in the institutionalization of the hereditary monarchy in the Xia dynasty under King Yu. Stagnation was the result of this "privatization" of the empire.[68] And naturally in turn evil rulers gave rise to revolts and eventually new dynasties. Then, for Zhao, the rise of the Shang dynasty under Tangwu – "Tang the martial" – who overthrew the evil Xia ruler in the seventeenth century BCE was a kind of foreshadowing of the righteous Revolution of 1911. "Question: What is revolution? Answer: The people eliminating that which harms them. Question: What harms the people? Answer: Autocratic rulers."[69] The term "revolution" (*geming*) traditionally referred to a change of mandate – that is, dynastic change – but here children are being taught its new meaning. Because the monarchy is inherently autocratic and inevitably gives rise to harms, it can never be allowed to reestablish itself. Still, Zhao found potential models for strengthening and enriching the nation in the struggles of the various Chinese kingdoms of the Spring and Autumn

---

[65] Zhao Yusen, *Xinlishi jiaoshoufa*, 1: 2a.
[66] Or proto-Miao. Lü Simian, *Baihua benguoshi*, 1: 1–3.
[67] Zhao Yusen, *Xinlishi jiaoshoufa*, 1: 4a–b.   [68] Ibid., 1: 6b–7a.   [69] Ibid., 1: 8a–b.

period; if the relevance of hegemons (*ba*) for the young citizens of a republic was not entirely clear, there could be no doubt of the importance of "martial spirit."[70] The collapse of the Zhou "feudal" system allowed Zhao to celebrate progress in the form of the death of the aristocracy.[71]

Zhao seemed to find much to admire in Qin Shihuang, who defeated quarreling feudal lords in 221 BCE and enabled a unified China to face internal and external threats. Just as siblings in a family should get along, so too should the citizens of a state. "Ubiquitous warfare and the slaughter of people, compatriots killing compatriots: this is the same as suicide. The unification of the state is thus of the greatest benefit."[72] At the same time, however, Zhao found all the evils of autocracy in Qin Shihuang. The great tragedy (at least by implication) was that although Mencius had already showed the way toward democracy, Qin Shihuang blocked it. The lesson: autocracy was unnatural and students needed to maintain the Republic.[73]

Zhao praised the Han dynasty for expanding Chinese territory and reestablishing unity – a unity that today's students needed to preserve.[74] And as the collapse of the Han demonstrated, disunity provokes outside attack – so the five races of the Republic need to be harmonious.[75] Given Zhao's emphasis on the harmony of the five races, it is not surprising the *New History* treated neither the Mongol-Yuan nor the Manchu-Qing dynasty as particularly "foreign." Indeed, Zhao credited the Yuan as the period of the greatest extent of Chinese territory, though it was too big to avoid dismemberment.[76] It fell to the Ming not because it was headed by foreigners whom the Chinese wished to expel, but because complacent emperors ignored the suffering of the people.[77] So, too, eventually, the Ming itself. Meanwhile, like the old constitutional reformers of the late Qing, Zhao argued that Manchus were one of the five races of the Republic because Manchuria had been part of China during the Zhou, Qin, Han, Wei, Jin, Sui, Tang, and Yuan dynasties, as well as the Ming itself.[78] Historically, then, Zhao implied that the rise of the Qing was nothing unusual, whereas in terms of contemporary politics the lesson was that Manchuria was intrinsically Chinese. Indeed, the distinguished scholar-official Wang Rongbao (1878–1933), in his thorough study of Qing history, claimed that Manchuria was an ancient state that had paid tribute to the Zhou.[79]

If late Qing textbooks tended to recount the achievements of the Three August Ones and the Five Emperors as fully historical figures, early Republican textbooks tended to be more skeptical. They called stories of the earliest

---

[70] Ibid., 1: 12a–b.   [71] Ibid., 13b.   [72] Ibid., 1: 20a, 30b.
[73] Ibid., 1: 22b–24b, 27b, 30b.   [74] Ibid., 2: 5b–6a.   [75] Ibid., 2: 9a–b.   [76] Ibid., 3: 4a–b.
[77] Ibid., 3: 10a.   [78] A debatable but patriotic proposition. Ibid., 3: 37a–b.
[79] Wang Rongbao, *Qingshi jiangyi*, 1: 1.

period "legends" (*chuanshuo*) and cited the lack of evidence for the period preceding the Yellow Emperor, or even Yu the Great, and they generally implied that the legends of prehistory traced the evolution of civilization from the most primitive conditions. True, a number of textbooks continued to give apparently matter-of-fact accounts of the sage-kings and their singular accomplishments.[80] Chaoshi invented shelter; Suiren discovered fire; Fuxi taught people how to use nets and raise animals, and so forth. But it seems these stories, narrated as fact, were used at the elementary level and for "mass education," whereas more advanced textbooks offered more sophisticated strategies for understanding such stories. The *Chinese History* textbook by Zhao Yusen and Jiang Weiqiao, for example, emphasized that although north China had been populated for 5000 years and we have "legends" of that period, reliable evidence of specific persons and events exists only from the Yellow Emperor onward.[81] By "evidence," most authors meant written accounts, because archeology was not yet developed. The view that evidence existed of Yao and Shun, much less the Yellow Emperor, seems naïve today, but it was part of the textual tradition in which textbook authors had been educated.

It was challenged by Gu Jiegang (1893–1980), who led a "doubting-antiquity" movement that challenged traditional historiography in the early Republic. Gu's attacks on the historicity of the sage-kings influenced the middle school textbook that he co-wrote in the 1920s.[82] Gu and Wang believed that the central task of teaching history was to arouse the imagination of the students.[83] But imagination had to be backed by evidence. The Gu-Wang *Chinese History* actually spent little time debunking the sage-kings and more on attempting to illustrate the complex, multi-ethnic evolution of the Chinese. It is worth noting that Gu and Wang did not hesitate to call a foreigner a foreigner (*waizu*): namely, the Wu Hu, Liao, Jin, Yuan, and Qing dynasties. And although they never claimed the Manchus were evil as a race, they did term the 1911 Revolution a "restoration" (*guangfu*).[84] They began by stating that "legends" traced social developments from the most primitive state. Development represented countless achievements of anonymous people over thousands of years, but the *Chinese History* was not entirely immune to the appeal of the "Yellow Emperor," who did possibly represent in some way an actual ruler of the ancient period.

---

[80] Zhou Chuangui, *Minzhong lishi keben jiaoxuefa*, p. 5; Hu Chaoyang, *Diyi jianming lishi qimeng*, pp. 5a–b; though also the middle school textbook of Cheng Qingnian, *Zhongguo lishi jiaokeshu* 1: 1–2.
[81] Zhao Yusen and Jiang Weiqiao, *Benguoshi*, 1: 4. Zhu Yixin et al., *Chuzhong benguoshi*, pp. 24–25, credit Shennong with unifying the tribes to make the first Chinese state.
[82] Gu Jiegang and Wang Zhongqi, *Benguoshi*, 1: 23–24.   [83] Ibid., 1 (preface): 2.
[84] Ibid., 3: 29, 3: 109 (for the Yuan's discriminatory practices, see 2: 50–53). See Mary Mazur, "Discontinuous Continuity," pp. 131–136.

The Gu-Wang *Chinese History* was banned by the Nationalists in 1929, but its basic approach – taking the legends of the sage-kings as symbolic representation of social development – was widely copied.[85] A teacher's manual published by Commercial Press in 1935 noted that a major issue in teaching ancient history was to give students the "proper attitude." On the one hand, students needed to understand that "most of the ancient history that has been handed down was recorded by people who lived after the events, and these records are inevitably speculative."[86] Only material evidence derived from archeological digs is completely reliable. On the other hand, students also need to recognize that the ancient myths and legends did have a historical component and should not be completely rejected.

The ambiguous nature of doubting antiquity while simultaneously doubting doubt may have been confusing for students. But it was also sophisticated history that treated myths as objects worth studying – as reflections of the cultures of the peoples who produced them. If some of the confusion over competing stories of different god-kings could be explained by their origins in the different ethnic groups of the central plains, then they could even serve as evidence of the gradual amalgamation of a single Chinese people. The 1935 Commercial Press manual still insisted on the ancient origins of the "Han" in the Yellow River basin and rescued the Yellow Emperor from the historical oblivion of mere myth.[87] But it rejected the old idea of "Western origins" or the story that the Han race emerged out of Babylonia, instead insisting on its indigenous Chinese origins. What this teacher's manual did not do was explain *how* the various ancient tribes, including the Han, became the "Chinese people" (*Zhonghua minzu*) whose origins students were supposed to understand. The expansion of the Han dynasty in the third century BCE, however, illustrated the concept of a "renewed amalgamation" of groups distinct enough to create a new nation in ethnic or racial terms, but nonetheless marked by the dominance of Han culture.[88]

One way or another, Commercial Press managed to preserve the old myths of the sage-kings. So too China Bookstore. A 1934 teachers' manual by Fan Zuoguai insisted that the Yellow Emperor was both the First Ancestor of the Chinese people and the great unifier of warring Han tribes.[89] A 1937 teacher's

---

[85] See, e.g., Zhu Yixin et al., *Chuzhong benguoshi*, 1: 19–21; Wang Yunwen and Lou Sanli, *Xiaoxue shehui keben jiaoxuefa*, 1: 189–202. Conversely, for skepticism of skepticism (amounting to agnosticism on the question of the historicity of sage-kings), see Luo Xianglin's middle school textbook, *Gaozhong benguoshi*, 1: 57–60. The Nationalists' banning of Gu and Wang is briefly summarized in Laurence A. Schneider, *Ku Chieh-kang and China's New History*, pp. 107–108.

[86] Zhou Jinglian, *Benguoshi jiaoyuan zhunbeishu*, pp. 1–2. [87] Ibid., pp. 10–17.

[88] Ibid., p. 138. This was not to say that all groups were successfully assimilated into a homogenous ethnic slurry: some, like the Xiongnu, remained outside, but the overall image is of fluid ethnic lines.

[89] Fan Zuoguai, *Xiaoxue lishi keben jiaoxuefa*, pp. 1, 7–8.

manual co-authored by Fan and Han Feimu similarly recounted the "legends" of Chaoshi, Suiren, Fuxi, Shennong, and the other inventors of civilization.[90] The Yellow Emperor was on this list too, coming toward the end as an inventor of clothing. Yet the manual also pointed out that such inventions were not really the achievements of a few people but the long-term products of the efforts of the many. It then went on to describe the Yellow Emperor's conquest of the warring tribes of the Yellow River valley.[91] There are several points in this account worth noting. First, although this is still "legend," there seems no reason to doubt its essential historicity. Second, the Yellow Emperor is a conqueror but also a "good guy," rescuing tribes from less welcome conquerors such as Yandi and Chiyou. And most important, the state he created marked the origins of the unified Chinese nation, a nation at peace. "Our Chinese national territory was based on these areas [of the Central Plains], and then gradually spread out from then to today."

Even as "legends," these stories, coming in the first chapters of history textbooks, worked to establish a kind of genealogy through which the Chinese nation (*Zhonghua minzu*) emerged 4000 years ago. The thoroughgoing historical skepticism of the 1920s was replaced in the 1930s by a return to legend, not because of the excesses of skepticism, but because of the need to assert national identity in the face of Japanese pressures. Nonetheless, a 1937 teacher's manual published by China Bookstore discussed the origins of the state in a purely secular and cosmopolitan fashion. The point of ancient history was to understand, not the origins of China, but the evolution of social organization itself.[92] By the 1930s, Chinese intellectuals had adopted the notion of feudalism as a universal historical stage, so the story basically worked like this: In the beginning human life was precarious, threatened on all sides by dangerous beasts, and small clans lived together for mutual protection. Out of such clans formed larger tribes better suited to raising animals and farming, which in turn supported larger populations. Tribal chiefs marked more complex societies, and in time as tribes struggled among themselves, the stronger absorbed the weaker, giving rise to the first states. In this process, the chiefs of large tribes evolved into kings while the chiefs of smaller tribes became their lords: the feudal (*fengjian*) system had arrived. Teachers could lead the discussion on to the specifics of the Chinese case. The manual also offered teachers reference notes on the class nature of imperial and feudal systems. Whereas tribal societies were more or less egalitarian, the first states were divided between the propertied and the property-less classes. Such coercive societies, like ancient Egypt, might include numerous ethnic groups and consist of priests, warriors, merchants, and slaves. Feudal societies, too, were based on exploitation, but they were more complex,

---

[90] Fan Zuoguai and Han Feimu, *Gaoxiao lishi keben jiaoxuefa*, 1: 9–10.
[91] Ibid., 1: 16–24.   [92] Jiang Jianqiu, *Chuxiao changshi keben jiaoxuefa*, 7: 147–154.

consisting of many social layers from the king all the way down to the peasants. Here, the manual proffered the Yellow Emperor as the founder of Chinese feudalism, which culminated in the enfeoffment system of the Zhou. This system collapsed in the Spring and Autumn period and was formally abolished with the unification of the Qin (221 BCE). Whereas Marxist interpretations might insist on the essentially "feudal" nature of imperial Chinese society, Nationalist teachers took the traditional view that China had created central government long before European states. The teacher's manual did not ask whether this was a good thing, but it did want students to discuss why feudalism was inappropriate for today's society.

The dynastic state and Chinese identity

Yu the Great, who quelled the floods, was one of the iconic sage-king founders of civilization in the popular memory. Late Qing and early Republican textbook treatments of him reflected such mythical elements as his construction of nine rivers to the sea, but differed on the ultimate significance of his turn to the hereditary kingship. After the abdications of Yao and Shun, according to legend, Yu did not abdicate and pass the throne to the best man in the empire: he passed it on to his son. In his early textbook for the Commercial Press, Yao Zuyi emphasized Yu's casting of the nine bronze tripods, which was to say his creation of imperial power, as well as his establishment of a tribute or tax system and his administrative organization of the empire.[93] But the real point was that while previous sage-kings had chosen the best man in the empire to succeed them, Yu chose his son as his successor, creating China's first dynasty, the Xia. In Zhao Zhengduo's account, it was the people themselves who wanted Yu's son to succeed him, thus establishing the hereditary kingship (*junzhu shixi zhi zhi*) of the dynastic state in what might be seen as a quasi-democratic way.[94] Other accounts attributed the decision to Yu; in any case, the first family dynasty was thus established. In another Commercial Press text, Fu Guangnian noted that Yu had already expanded imperial power and reported that people said Yu's virtue had decreased.[95] This was why he was called "king" (*wang*) instead of "emperor" (*di*). Fu's was certainly a minority view in regard to Yu, but it may have represented reformist critique of imperial aggrandizement. More common in the late Qing was the view, presented in the *Primary Reader*, for example, that Yu's title as "king" was a mark of special respect. The Nationalist textbook writers Fan Zuoguai and Han Feimu simply held that all the clan

---

[93] Yao Zuyi, *Zuixin gaodeng xiaoxue Zhongguo lishi jiaokeshu*, pp. 3b–4a. See also Xia Zengyou, *Xiaoxue duben shi*, pp. 13a–b.
[94] Zhao Zhengduo, *Gaodeng xiaoxue lishi keben*, p. 3b. This was also the view of a "masses history textbook" of 1930: Zhou Chuangui, *Minzhong lishi keben jiaoxuefa*, p. 18.
[95] Fu Guangnian, *Jianyi lishi keben*, pp. 1a–b.

The national subject in time   171

chieftains chose to make Yu's son emperor (*tianzi*) upon Yu's death.[96] Neither late Qing nor certainly Republican textbook writers presented the principle of hereditary kingship as natural or moral. If Yu's son was virtuous, his grandson was immoral and lost the empire.[97] True, another heir of Yu was able to restore the Xia, and, in all, the dynasty lasted some 400 years under 17 generations of Xia kings. Yet finally, and with some seeming inevitability, the utterly evil King Jie was overthrown by Tangwu, who founded the Shang dynasty.

Textbooks thus described the first dynastic cycle, which was to structure the rest of their historical narratives. As Zhao Zhengduo pointed out, if Yu had been the first emperor to transmit the throne to his son, Tang had been the first to seize the throne by violence.[98] However, this did not imply moral culpability on his part. Jie was immoral and had lost all popular support.[99] Tang was wise and kind – indeed some textbooks treated him not as a military conqueror at all but as winning the support of all the lords, who pronounced him Son of Heaven.[100]

So, too, with the Zhou that overthrew the Shang, and after the Zhou's prolonged decline, the Qin, and so forth down to the Qing dynasty. In 1937, Fan Zuoguai and Han Feimu described the rise of the Shang and the Zhou in these terms: "Both were following the popular will in overthrowing tyrants. This kind of action was different from the earlier abdications [of Yao and Shun], and is called 'revolution' (*geming*)"[101] Teachers were to make plain to students that the concept of revolution was not unique to the Republic but had emerged with the Shang.

Although history textbooks certainly recognized the pivotal nature of the Qin unification of China in 221 BCE, as a matter of political history they treated the Qin as successor dynasty to the Zhou. The historical events of the next two millennia that textbooks described in some detail must be ignored here for want of space. Each historical incident they described was unique, but all fell into a cyclical rise-and-fall narrative structure. History textbooks were not *directly* concerned with the nature of the Chinese people, the legitimacy of the imperial state, or, for the most part, making explicit judgments about the morality or even the competence of historical actors. Their emphasis on events meant that textbooks did not treat the nation (or people) as a unitary historical subject evolving through time – though they at least made greater reference to this "nation" as historiography developed in the republican period. Relatively

[96] Fan Zuoguai and Han Feimu, *Gaoxiao lishi keben jiaoxuefa*, 1: 40.
[97] Xia Zengyou, *Xiaoxue duben shi*, p. 13b; see also Fu Guangnian, *Jianyi lishi keben*, p. 1b; Hu Chaoyang, *Diyi jianming lishi qimeng*, p. 7b.
[98] Zhao Zhengduo, *Gaodeng xiaoxue lishi keben*, p. 3b.
[99] Yao Zuyi, *Zuixin gaodeng xiaoxue Zhongguo lishi jiaokeshu*, p. 2b.
[100] Qian Zonghan, *Huitu Zhongguo baihua shi*, pp. 2b–3a; Xia Zengyou, *Xiaoxue duben shi*, pp. 14a–b.
[101] Fan Zuoguai and Han Feimu, *Gaoxiao lishi keben jiaoxuefa*, 1: 42.

little social history was presented in primary and secondary history textbooks, especially after "origins" talk of the mixing of races.

Thus, although history textbooks offered some broader perspectives on long-term developments, especially of culture and institutions, the separate dynasties tended to dominate the story. History textbooks offered political narratives, focusing on court politics, foreign relations, military events, rebellions, and the like, sprinkled with occasional summaries of developments in scholarship, religion, and the arts. Nonetheless, beyond this kind of historical "data" certain themes did emerge: these were like repeating motifs seen in many if not all dynasties. For example, several textbooks stressed the dangers of court infighting – particularly the threats posed by eunuchs and women (a highly traditional theme).[102] Almost all textbooks treated the Zhou as the single best image of a Golden Age, whereas later emperors were subject to more purely political analysis.

For Liu Shipei, the golden age of the Zhou was not golden because it represented the ideal of Confucian kingship. Rather, in his 1906 *Chinese History Textbook*, he treated the Western Zhou (c. 1046–771 BCE) as a kind of proto-democracy.[103] In spite of the book's title, Liu took the story of China only up to the Zhou, using established Qing philological techniques to reinterpret ancient literary sources. His secular approach turned the sage-kings into tribal chieftains. A prominent proponent of the Western origins theory, Liu focused on the development of the Han race and its social and political institutions. Although Liu saw the Western Zhou as tending in an autocratic direction, he insisted that the emperor's role was limited to executing decisions actually made by his subjects.[104] Furthermore, the judiciary was in the charge of special magistrates, so the emperor remained subject to the law. Thus did Liu adopt Montesquieu's notion of the separation of power, which had so attracted Chinese reformers in the 1890s, to explain the ancient world – a world soon to be lost as the Zhou decayed. Liu's writings were widely known through the *National Essence Journal*, and possibly Liu's views continued to be influential into the republican period.[105]

During the late Qing, as the autocratic nature of imperial government came under attack precisely in the name of the nation, the historical role of Qin Shihuang, the man who finally unified China in 221 BCE after centuries of Zhou

---

[102] Zhao Zhengduo, *Gaodeng xiaoxue lishi keben*, pp. 14b–15a; Fu Guangnian, *Jianyi lishi keben*, pp. 5b–6a, 7b; Zhao Yusen and Jiang Weiqiao, *Benguoshi*, pp. 30–31, 156–157, 161–163.
[103] Liu Shipei, *Zhongguo lishi jiaokeshu* in *Liu Shipei quanji*, vol. 4, pp. 275–370. For an analysis, see Yuan Yingguang and Zhong Weimin, "Liu Shipei yu 'Zhongguo lishi jiaokeshu'"; Tze-ki Hon, "Educating the Citizens," pp. 95–102.
[104] Liu Shipei, *Zhongguo lishi jiaokeshu*, vol. 4, p. 325 (2: 23a).
[105] See, for example, the references to ancient "democracy" (*minzhu*) and "republics" (*gonghe*) – though the terms actually had completely different meanings in the original texts – in Zhao Yusen and Jiang Weiqiao, *Benguoshi*, p. 38.

The national subject in time 173

Figure 25 Qin Shihuang.

dynastic decline and incessant warfare, naturally came into question. A traditional Confucian view treated Qin Shihuang's famed cruelty as a moral failing that directly led to the fall of the Qin dynasty. History textbooks in the late Qing were concerned less with morality and more with politics. Zhao Zhengduo, for example, criticized Qin Shihuang's policies, not the man: burdens he placed on the people contributed to the uprisings that occurred after his death.[106]

One image of Qin Shihuang (Figure 25) shows him with royal regalia such as his headdress but indicates something of his wild features. Aside from his facial hair, the First Emperor's eyes and eyebrows indicate his remarkable nature.

Another image (Figure 26) shows Qin Shihuang as a more conventional and civilized emperor, with a more elaborate headdress, neatly combed beard, and what appears to be a heavily embroidered cloak. Writing in the republican period, Hu Chaoyang recounted Qin Shihuang's various harsh deeds, summarizing his rule as "tyrannical and inhumane."[107] But this language was still not as harsh as the language applied to the last kings of the Xia and Shang dynasties. Furthermore, the point was still not that Qin Shihuang's evil made him unfit for the throne, but rather that his deeds provoked rebellion.[108] Republican

---
[106] Zhao Zhengduo, *Gaodeng xiaoxue lishi keben*, pp. 11b–12a; see also Fu Guangnian, *Jianyi lishi keben*, p. 4a.
[107] Hu Chaoyang, *Diyi jianming lishi qimeng*, p. 15b.
[108] Zhao Yusen and Jiang Weiqiao, *Benguoshi*, p. 21,

Figure 26 Qin Shihuang.

textbook authors thus maintained the relatively non-moralistic approach of late Qing authors. Of course, the dynastic system whereby emperors succeeded to the throne through birth inevitably produced some bad rulers.[109] But textbook analysis stopped there.

Politically, what then defined the successful dynastic state? The great models of the Han and the Tang, and to some extent the Yuan and the Ming, featured military strength. Unity at home and, above all, the ability to maintain peace along the frontiers emerged, at least implicitly, in history textbooks as core political values. The Yuan was not a "Han" Chinese dynasty, of course, but it was a success in military terms, at least for a century.[110] That the Yuan unified China after a period of disunity (even if that disunity was caused to a degree by the Mongols themselves) marked its legitimacy. Even Republican-period textbooks noted in tones of approval the large extent of Yuan territorial claims across Eurasia, which opened the continent to new flows of communication and trade, and they also emphasized that the Yuan basically adopted the Chinese system of government.[111] Hu Chaoyang noted that the Mongols'

---

[109] Fan Zuoguai and Han Feimu, *Gaoxiao lishi keben jiaoxuefa*, 1: 44.
[110] Fu Guangnian, *Jianyi lishi keben*, pp. 11a–b.
[111] See, e.g., Hu Chaoyang, *Diyi jianming lishi qimeng*, p. 39a; Ding Baoshu, *Mengxue Zhongguo lishi jiaokeshu*, pp. 47a–b; Fu Guangnian, *Jianyi lishi keben*, pp. 11a–b.

conquest of nearly all of Asia was a feat "Chinese" (*woguo*) emperors had never achieved.[112] Whether this was good or bad, Hu refused to admit the Mongols into full Chinese status, referring to their "taking command of China." And as the Yuan collapsed from its overextension and internal tensions, heroes of the Han people (*Hanzu qunxiong*) rose up and contested for power; Zhu Yuanzhang's Ming dynasty represented the "restoration of the Han" (*Hanzu fuxing*) – a term frequently used in the course of the 1911 Revolution.[113] Textbooks noted that the Yuan bureaucratic system discriminated against Han people and that it was unpopular. It survived, after all, only 100 years, though its own internal rifts explained much of its weaknesses. Furthermore, some textbooks said, Mongols were primitive pastoralists, racially related to the Turks, both groups being descended from the Xiongnu.[114] With disapproving tones, Ding Baoshu called the Mongols a race of nomadic herders.[115]

However, much about the Yuan looked like an ordinary, legitimate dynasty. Chinese were not all that much interested in Mongol activities in central and western Asia, leaving the theme of the unification of China in place. In a word, according to textbooks, the collapse of the Yuan largely fit the usual pattern of the dynastic cycle. By the end, emperors were incompetent (even if this was a special problem for the Yuan because they lacked an orderly rule of succession); there was corruption and cruelty; and taxes were too high and so the people became restless. And so the Ming represented renewed unity. From this point of view, the Yuan conquered China militarily, and so did the Ming. The Song dynasty had decayed, and the Yuan reunified China. When the Yuan dynasty decayed, the Ming reunified China. As the Commercial Press's main republican *Chinese History* put it, Zhu Yuanzhang, founder of the Ming, early on began establishing "the foundation for unification."[116] And eventually when the Ming decayed, the Qing reunified China.

As the map in Figure 27 indicates, the Ming was bordered by the Great Wall in the north and mountains in the south (and west – the sources of its great rivers). Interestingly, Shanghai is one of the few cities shown, though it was in fact a relatively insignificant fishing port during the Ming.

In late Qing and early Republican history textbooks, the Qing conquered China militarily like other dynasties – pouring through the pass indicated in Figure 27 at the eastern end of the Great Wall. However, textbooks also made it clear that the Ming had first self-destructed and the Qing's military machine was more a mopping-up operation against bandits and rumps of the Ming court.

---

[112] Hu Chaoyang, *Diyi jianming lishi qimeng*, p. 39a. [113] Ibid., pp. 39b–40a.
[114] Xia Zengyou, *Xiaoxue duben shi*, pp. 5b–6a.
[115] Ding Baoshu, *Mengxue Zhongguo lishi jiaokeshu*, p. 44a.
[116] Zhao Yusen and Jiang Weiqiao, *Benguoshi*, p. 90.

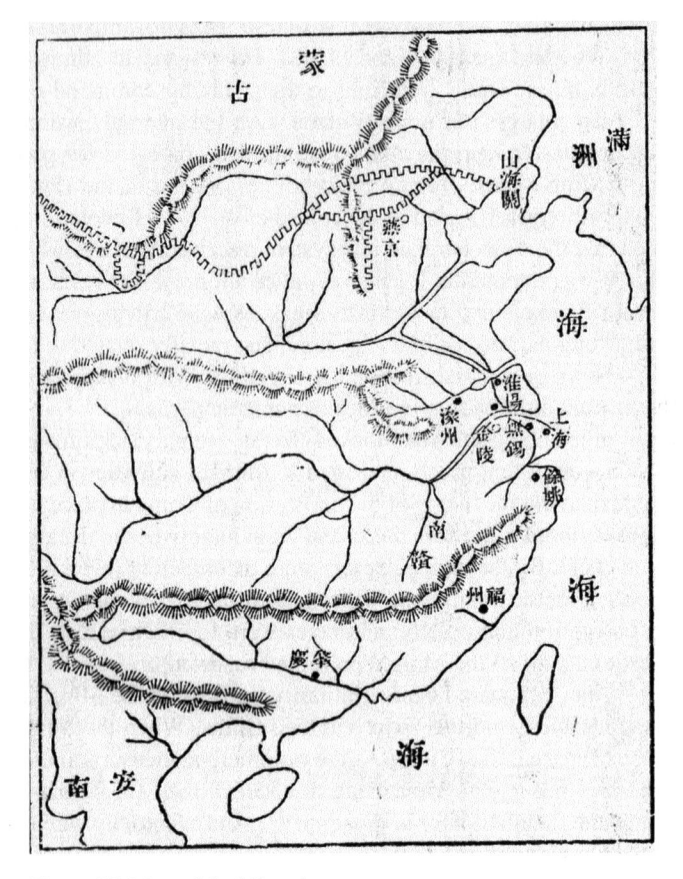

Figure 27 Map of the Ming dynasty

For the Ming had long been under military pressures from the northern tribes and eastern pirates. Perhaps late Qing textbooks tended to downplay the role of the Manchus in inflicting these pressures in the first place, but they were not ignored. A republican-period textbook included references to Tartars as one of the problems facing the Ming and described these people in a section entitled "Invasion of the Bandits."[117] However, even in this account, the Qing's conquest of China occurred only after the Ming had already collapsed because of its own incompetence. The Ming, in this view, collapsed amid factionalism and eunuch maneuvering and finally the rise of vast bandit armies from central China. Meanwhile, the Great Qing had already taken shape in the Northeast as

---

[117] Zhao Yusen and Jiang Weiqiao, *Benguoshi*, 1: 117.

the Aisin-Gioro clan began to conquer and unify neighboring tribes.[118] Having moved into Korea and the Liaodong Peninsula, a process that involved struggles with Ming troops to a degree, the Great Qing was in effect poised to take over China by the 1640s. Textbook accounts, however, make it plain that the late Ming emperor hanged himself when (purely Chinese) "bandits" led by Li Zicheng took over Beijing. This was, aside from being technically accurate, part of the pattern of the dynastic cycle. In other words, textbook authors were not here engaged in Qing propaganda, nor did they present the conquest that was soon to come as in any way friendly to the Ming (as had some Qing propaganda of the seventeenth century). Rather, it was precisely a conquest and a restoration of order. Textbooks treated the emperors Kangxi, Yongzheng, and Qianlong, who collectively reigned from 1661 to 1796, in the heroic mode. Zhao Zhengduo emphasized that these emperors not only defeated all opposition, they established superior government, rectifying the Ming's mistakes.[119] By the eighteenth century the treasury was full and the people prosperous. Ding Baoshu emphasized that the Qing conquered new territories, so that power was spread to its maximum and the arts of government flourished.[120]

The *Primary Reader* accepted racial terms of analysis but argued that the Manchus had become assimilated. The "Manchu race" (*Manzhouzhong*) was itself a subgroup of the Donghu race, but since entering Chinese territory, their ceremonies and customs had been Sinified. Indeed, present-day China benefited from the good points of both Manchus and Han. The groups' powers might differ, but both rested on the foundation of classical learning.[121] The textbook thus admits the limits of assimilation, referring to the political supremacy of the Manchus, while still arguing that culture trumps race. And when the textbook turns to historical discussion proper, it grants the Qing legitimacy from the very fact of dynastic change – or more specifically the "national unity" (*tongyi Zhongguo*) imposed by the imperial state.[122] This was a unity that had existed cyclically for thousands of years.

Textbooks naturally told the story of the rise of the Qing as a triumphant narrative. (Stories of tragedy and violence – rape and slaughter and exile – found no place in textbook narratives.) Yet what were authors to do with the defeats the Qing had suffered since the nineteenth century? Should they be played down to shore up the prestige of the dynasty? Should they be played up to foster patriotic anger? How could they be explained? Who was at fault?

---

[118] Yao Zuyi, *Zuixin gaodeng xiaoxue Zhongguo lishi jiaokeshu*, pp. 13a–b. Ding Baoshu, *Mengxue Zhongguo lishi jiaokeshu*, pp. 54a–55b; Fu Guangnian, *Jianyi lishi keben*, pp. 13a–14a.
[119] Yao Zuyi, *Zuixin gaodeng xiaoxue Zhongguo lishi jiaokeshu*, pp. 13b–14a; see also Fu Guangnian, *Jianyi lishi keben*, pp. 14b–16b.
[120] Ding Baoshu, *Mengxue Zhongguo lishi jiaokeshu*, p. 58b.
[121] Xia Zengyou, *Xiaoxue duben shi*, p. 5b.   [122] Ibid., p. 7a.

In the case of Ding Baoshu, this material is handled very dryly and succinctly. If there was a first cause, it was Qing domestic disorder: the White Lotus uprising.[123] Several textbooks noted that the Qianlong Emperor was not at his best in his old age. British opium imports were increasing, and the court seemed to have little option but to try to prohibit the drug. In Ding's account, the Opium War contributed to the Taiping Rebellion; the Qing was forced to give up Hong Kong and open ports to trade. During the British-French expedition against Beijing during the Taiping Rebellion, the emperor was forced to flee while new peace terms were worked out. This brought Russia onto the scene even as the Qing managed to defeat the Taipings. Ding seems to emphasize the lost suzerainty over the nations of southeast Asia, Korea, and the Liuqiu Islands as much as direct attacks on China itself, a point of view somewhat distinct from modern nationalist feeling. Ding's textbook ends abruptly with the loss of the Sino-Japanese War of 1895 and the postwar proliferation of Western leaseholds. Not only was Taiwan ceded to Japan permanently, but soon Russia, France, Germany, and Britain were all carving out pieces of China proper. Ding ends his textbook on this utterly bleak note without further comment.

Other authors, while maintaining a sober, objective tone, added more telling detail. Zhao Zhengduo jumped from the glory days of Qianlong to the Opium War, and in addition to China's territorial losses, recounted each indemnity "extorted" from the Qing: 21 million taels of silver after the first Opium War, 16 million after the second opium war, 200 million after the Sino-Japanese War (increased by another 30 million after the Triple Intervention), and no less than 450 million in the wake of the Boxer Uprising.[124] Unlike Ding's textbook, in Zhao's account, there is little hint of domestic trouble before Britain started the first Opium War and the foreigners began opening China's ports, taking control of China's traditional dependencies (Vietnam, Korea), and seizing Chinese territory. There is no doubt of the foreigners' aggression, though Zhao, like Ding, refrains from moral or even strategic discussions. Why the foreigners behaved the way they did is not Zhao's concern, though he does note that the Japanese had long coveted Korea, and students are left in little doubt of the foreigners' commercial interests – at least their desire to profit from the selling of opium. Moving beyond Ding's chronology, Zhao discusses the Russo-Japanese War, highlighting China's neutrality, and concluding that although Manchuria remained officially Chinese, real power had passed into Japan's hands.[125] Nonetheless, Zhao ends his textbook on an optimistic note. The disaster of the Boxers had inspired Chinese reformers (though he avoids the

---

[123] Ding Baoshu, *Mengxue Zhongguo lishi jiaokeshu*, pp. 60b–69a.
[124] Yao Zuyi, *Zuixin gaodeng xiaoxue Zhongguo lishi jiaokeshu*, pp. 14b–16b.
[125] Ibid., p. 17b.

controversy of the 1898 reforms), and Japan's defeat of Russia seemed to confirm the effectiveness of constitutional government. China was now preparing for a constitution, which, Zhao promised, boded well for the national future.[126]

Fu Guangnian, too, effectively began the story of Qing decline – not that the term was used – with British opium. He only then turned back to White Lotus Rebellion, which, after all, had been suppressed.[127] But by the mid-nineteenth century, both foreign pressures and domestic turmoil were taking their toll. Fu described the setbacks to the Qing in much the same terms as the other authors, though he added a chapter on the 1898 reform movement. Again without passing judgment, he noted that in the wake of the Sino-Japanese War the emperor had been attracted by Kang Youwei's notions of self-strengthening and institutional reform. The empress dowager, however, accused the reformers of plotting rebellion and countermanded the reforms. Soon, the Boxer disaster broke out, but in its wake the court turned to the New Policy reforms: a second round of institutional reform.[128] This allowed Fu to end his textbook on a note of optimism: the triumphal abolition of the traditional examination system and the promise of a constitution in the future. On the other hand, Yao Zuyi, whose textbook generally stresses loyalism and the Qing point of view, painted a bleak picture of the nineteenth century and ended with the briefest of notes on the promise of the New Policy's school system to strengthen China.[129]

Surely frank discussions of the defeats inflicted on the country over the last half century conveyed the sense of "national humiliation" (*guochi*) that was common parlance in the last years of the Qing.[130] The picture of emperors fleeing to Rehe and Xi'an was hardly edifying. The key, if hidden, issue was not the Qing's foreignness but its competence. Today's struggle set the Yellow race against the White, as Ding Baoshu, echoing much rhetoric of the period, frankly stated in his preface. Several textbooks pointed out that of the various dynasties with foreign elements (including even the great Tang), all these foreigners had at least belonged to the Yellow race. The implicit argument, in terms of debates known to the textbooks writers if not all their young students, was that the various peoples of China needed to unify – through serious governmental reform – to meet the new threat from the West (that is, the White race).

As the map of the Qing shows (Figure 28), here was an empire far vaster than that of the Ming, extending well north of the Great Wall, far west into Central Asia and Tibet, south into today's Burma and Vietnam, and encompassing Butan and Nepal, as well as Korea, Taiwan, Hainan, and the Ryukyus.

---

[126] Ibid., 18a. [127] Fu Guangnian, *Jianyi lishi keben*, pp. 17b–18a.
[128] Ibid., 21b–22a. [129] Yao Zuyi, *Zuixin gaodeng xiaoxue Zhongguo lishi jiaokeshu*, 4: 63a.
[130] See also Xia Zengyou, *Xiaoxue duben shi*, p. 3b. For intellectuals' concerns over the issue, see Paul A. Cohen, "Remembering and Forgetting National Humiliation."

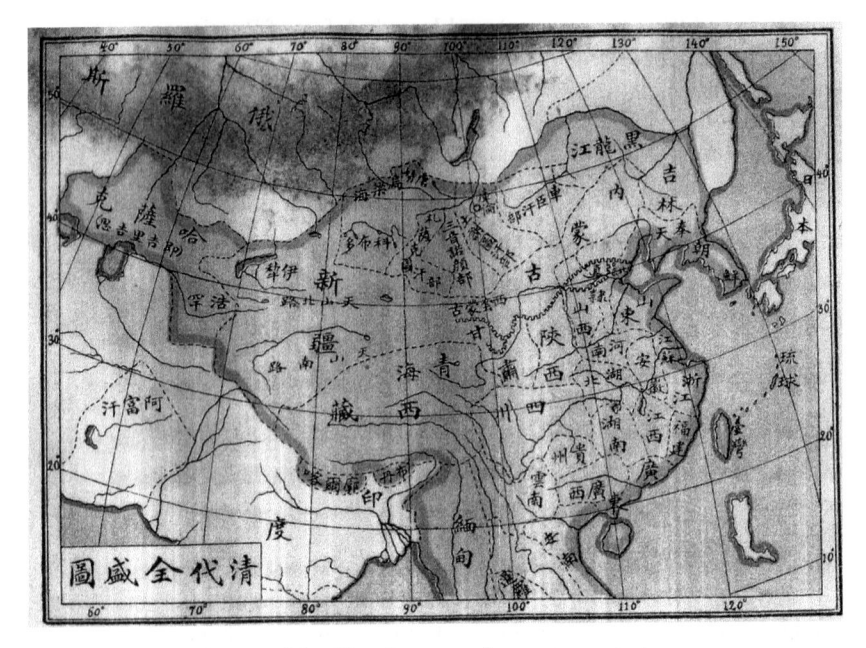

Figure 28 Map of the Qing dynasty at its greatest extent.

In sum, textbook writers valued the dynastic state when it protected – or expanded – the borders. This was of course a historical theme with contemporary implications. Ding Baoshu was unusual in his willingness to make relatively explicit historical judgments, but other history textbooks conveyed the same ideas by implication. Ding found faults with Qin Shihuang, but noted the emperor unified and expanded the empire, thus protecting the "race" (*zhongzu*).[131] If the early Zhou, for Ding, represented the perfection of government, it was apparently an unrecoverable perfection. However harsh, the centralization put into place by the Qin, and even strengthened by later dynasties, at least served to keep the barbarians at bay. Indeed, several textbook writers emphasized orthodox Confucian approbation of the "hegemons" of the Spring and Autumn period on the grounds they protected the borders. Similarly, for Ding, the military expansion of China's borders under Han Wudi (r. 141–87 BCE) created problems for his successors, yet this emperor "protected the race and advanced state power" by defeating the dreaded Xiongnu.[132] And Ding

---

[131] Ding Baoshu, *Mengxue Zhongguo lishi jiaokeshu*, pp. 10a–b; see also Qian Zonghan, *Huitu Zhongguo baihua shi*, p. 9b.
[132] Ding Baoshu, *Mengxue Zhongguo lishi jiaokeshu*, p. 16a; see also Fu Guangnian, *Jianyi lishi keben*, p. 4b.

credited Tang Gaozong (r. 649–683) with the "protection of the race and the extension of state power" in his discussion of the great but scarcely perfect Tang dynasty.[133]

Origin stories seem to hold a peculiar grip on the imaginaries of most human societies. Myth or history, they answer the critical question, "where did 'we' come from?" The question is critical because its answer at least partly defines identity – who we are – in a logic parallel to the acorn already containing the oak. The origin stories recounted in late Qing history textbooks in no way differed from versions in the classics and Han-period textual redactions. Yet a new political and institutional context gave them new significance. They now spoke not merely to flexible ways of distinguishing "us" from "them" through ethnicity and culture but also to the early growth of a specific "Chinese" nation that – by implication – grew like the tree from the seed into today's Chinese nation. The late Qing's unprecedented need for national identity led to the recasting of ancient myths and histories into coherent narratives in which contemporary Chinese could find themselves, or at least their ancestors. A map of the "nine districts" (*jiuzhou*) from the time of the mythical Yu the Great who quelled the floods (supposedly around 2100 BCE) marks a territory, though without precise borders, that looks closer to the Qing than the Ming (Figure 29).

There was no getting away from the most ancient visions of China. It may be that the prominence given the Yellow Emperor reflected a deep-seated orientation in Chinese culture toward ancestors. But perhaps the reshaping of the Yellow Emperor as conqueror and ancestor owed something to the Meiji Japanese reshaping of Jimmu – although Chinese history texbooks created a genealogy of the Chinese people, not merely an imperial line.

However, Chinese history was obviously more than its origins, and in fact textbook authors had to deal with the less-than-ideal dynastic states that in fact formed the heart of the historical record. After origins, textbook authors had to discuss development. This created a problem, because both the traditional moral condemnation of Qin Shihuang and the modern demand for progress suggested that the last 2000 years of Chinese history had not lived up to its earlier achievements. Constitutionalism and republicanism fulfilled China's teleological promise, but textbooks did not always glorify the long dynastic period.

History textbooks recruited history to the nation-building cause, even if not as consistently as they would during the republican period. Yet history classes still emphasized the deeds of individuals: emperors, their ministers, generals, and a few thinkers, beginning with Confucius. Where was the collectivity? Who were the much-vaunted Chinese people or *guomin*? The people generally appeared only in crowd scenes, passive recipients of history, not its makers.

---

[133] Ding Baoshu, *Mengxue Zhongguo lishi jiaokeshu*, p. 30b.

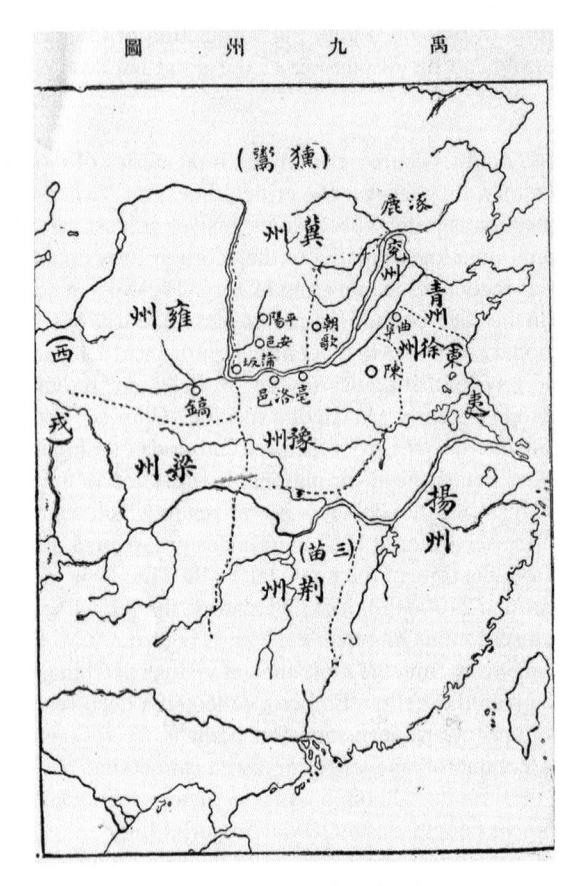

Figure 29 The Nine Districts of Yu the Great.

And where was "progress" in these textbook accounts of various dynasties? The narrative template of dynastic rise and fall left little room for the evolution of the nation. In the late Qing, textbooks naturally did not challenge the Qing's legitimacy, but, overall, they strongly implied the Qing had to earn the loyalty of the people by better protecting the nation. After 1906 many found hope in the promise of constitutional government. After the 1911 Revolution, republican history textbooks literally had new chapters to add to the Chinese story; some attempted to rethink the entire past, but the approaches pioneered in the late Qing were maintained as well.

History textbooks written in the late Qing and early Republic thus reflected the ideals of nationalist intellectuals. But they did not convey moral or political messages in specific ways, and so seem to have been less subject to censorship than language readers or morality textbooks.[134] From another perspective, we can see that history and geography were protected by the professionalization of their disciplines. These disciplines also met the need of the state to define itself. In teaching history as a modern form of knowledge, the first history textbooks were configured to tell the story of China from the ancient period through to the contemporary.

From the beginning of the modern school system, Chinese identity was rooted in Chinese history. The Revolution of 1911 did not much change the new views of historiography that were formed in the last decade of the Qing, but it did change views on the meaning of Chinese history. The Republic gave new meaning to all of Chinese history by allowing it to be interpreted precisely as a path toward republicanism. The national story had a real teleology. The ancient ways culminated in the modern Republic. At the same time, however, the revolution only highlighted the tasks of maintaining the borders and keeping the country unified. And it may be that by the 1920s, disillusionment with the political fractiousness of the Republic led to some textbook authors to treat the Republic not unlike a dynasty beset with problems – or at any rate, not a matter for glory and celebration. Other authors, however, were more hopeful and alert to the unprecedented nature of the Republic.

---

[134] Guan Xiaohong, *Wan-Qing xuebu yanjiu*, pp. 375–385; Wang Jianjun, *Zhongguo jindai jiaokeshu*, pp. 158–190.

6 A usable past

History textbooks, as we have seen in Chapter 5, were quick to reflect the "new historiography" of the late Qing: to at least attempt to shape their narrative structure around the development of China from its origins to the emergence of constitutionalism and republicanism. By the 1920s new historiographical currents were making their way into textbooks: particularly social history and principles of empirical verification. These currents were slower to make themselves felt than the nationalist concerns of the late Qing, but a new interest in social formations and class analysis, also influenced both by progressive American pedagogy and by Marxism, can be seen in textbooks. The trend to distinguish the "legends" of antiquity from actual historical events continued in upper-level classes.[1] This chapter focuses on how history textbooks published in the 1920s and under the Nationalist government in the 1930s dealt with the question of what made modern China modern.

Defining Chinese identity historically was both an obvious project and a tricky one. Ancient China could be a source of pride and even inheritance; it had always been a font of wisdom. But did Chinese of the twentieth century live in a time when the achievement of the ancients had stagnated? We have seen in Chapter 5 that textbooks put the Qing dynasty in a long tradition of the dynastic state using a narrative framework that revolved around political cycles. Second, textbooks often categorized the Qing as marking the "modern" phase of China's historical progress. They did so implicitly in the larger narrative framework based on a periodization scheme that moved from late antiquity or the medieval to the modern; or, increasingly by the 1920s, they did so in explicit terms, particularly describing how China's contacts with the outside world grew at this time. And third, textbooks sometimes treated the Qing as a "foreign conquest" dynasty, but did not always do so.

---

[1] A "masses history textbook" told the story of the "intelligent men of old" – the ancestors of the Chinese people – who invented fire, houses, and farming and so forth. Zhou Chuangui, *Minzhong lishi keben jiaoxuefa*, p. 5; see also Yang Shuming, *Minzhong changshi keben jiaoshoufa*, pp. 96–104.

A usable past

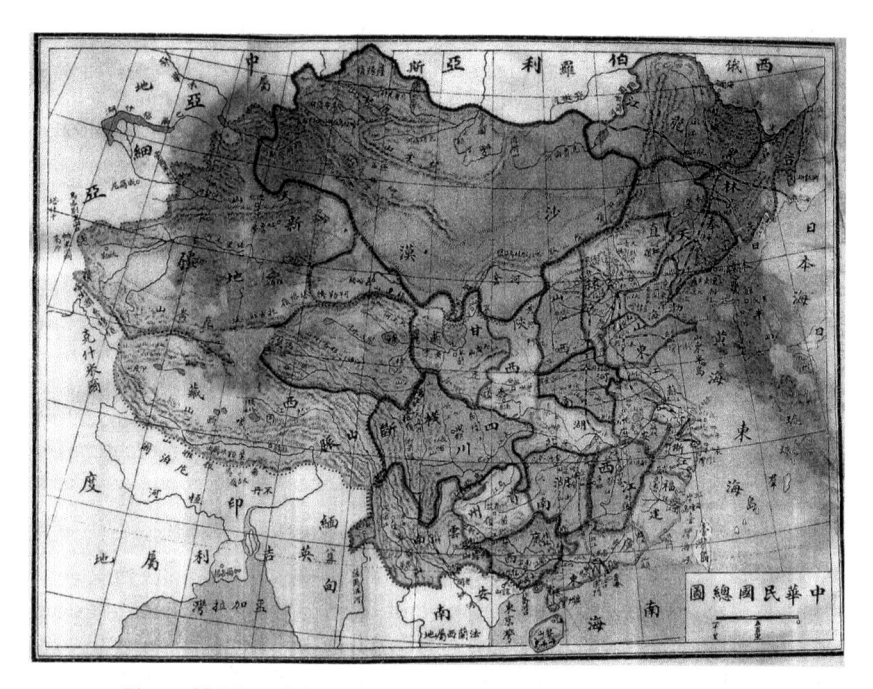

Figure 30 Map of the Republic of China.

The Republic of China, as the map in Figure 30 shows, was marked by clearer borders with surroundings countries than the old Qing Empire had possessed, even while claiming sovereignty over almost all of the imperial territories.

Coming to terms with the Qing and foreign Chinese

Republican textbooks had to find ways to position the Republic vis-à-vis the Qing. That is, was the Republic a radical new political form that rejected the Qing and regarded the dynastic system as its enemy? Or was the Republic a continuation or even culmination of trends and historical processes already in place in the preceding centuries? History textbooks in the early Republic showed no radical break with their late Qing ancestors. Revolutionary propaganda of the previous decade that painted all Manchus as dogs and the imperial system as irredeemably evil had no place in textbooks. Even the textbooks of the China Bookstore, which was founded by men committed to the revolutionary movement, regarded the Taipings and other rebellions of the mid-nineteenth century as a source of "chaos" (*luan*); by using this term, they delegitimized the rebels.

However, the tone of republican-period textbooks did change. For example, they did not elide all the cruelties of the Manchu Qing conquest of the seventeenth century, which had been a staple of revolutionary propaganda since at least the 1890s. The *New-Style History Textbook* by Zhuang Qichuan and Lü Simian discussed the forced adoption of Manchu male hairstyle and the Qianlong literary inquisition.[2] The major Commercial Press textbook by Zhao Yusen and Jiang Weiqiao also criticized the literary inquisition of the Qianlong period, which, they charged, "bound and gagged" the Chinese people, with deleterious consequences for the nation.[3] The literary inquisition had been a common target of anti-Qing propaganda for 20 years, condemned as despotic and even racial oppression.

In his Commercial Press teacher's manual of the early Republic, Zhao Yusen told teachers how to present the story of the Qing through to the "unification" of the 1911 Revolution. Zhao thus gave the Qing considerably more detailed coverage than earlier dynasties, while he envisioned the Republic as a new kind of dynasty, or at least recovering the ancient political value of unity. The Manchu conquest, Ming loyalist resistance, and the gradual establishment of political control were all presented in objective terms: Zhao admired the anti-Manchu resistance leaders of the seventeenth century,[4] but he perhaps had even more admiration for the Qing emperors Kangxi and Qianlong. Kangxi not only completed the conquest in the late seventeenth century but also ordered the realm.[5] His son Yongzheng and especially his grandson Qianlong continued the conquest, establishing the territory of today's Republic. So today, "the citizens of the Republic must always preserve this perfected territory."[6] Zhao also praised the Qing's policies of racial equality (!), which laid the basis of the unity of the five races of the Republic. Zhao did not refer to any privileges reserved for Manchus under the Qing, but he criticized Qianlong's faults, in particular the limits on freedom typical of autocratic systems.

The China Bookstore teacher's manual of 1920 foreshadowed the foreignness of the Qing by emphasizing the foreignness of the Mongol Yuan dynasty (1271–1368). But its authors, Zhuang Qichuan and Lü Simian, also taught that the great strength of the Chinese people was its ability to assimilate foreign groups, not concerned about racial purity but devoted to maintaining the state. The critical issue concerning the Yuan, therefore, was not one of illegitimate conquest, but of how to establish order.[7] That the Yuan ultimately stemmed

---

[2] Zhuang Qichuan and Lü Simian, *Xinshi lishi jiaokeshu*, 6: 16a. *Xinshi lishi jiaokeshu*, 11b, 12b.
[3] Zhao Yusen and Jiang Weiqiao, *Benguoshi*, 2: 35. Advanced textbooks often noted the anti-literati bias of Ming Taizu, however, as well. The inquisition is described and implicitly condemned but without explicit comment on its consequences in Fu Yunsen, *Xin lishi*, 6: 12a–13a.
[4] Zhao Yusen, *Xin lishi jiaoshoufa*, 4: 1b–2a; 4: 4a–b.
[5] Ibid., 4: 7a–b.   [6] Ibid., 4: 19a, 21a, 22b.
[7] Zhuang Qichuan and Lü Simian, *Xinshi lishi jiaoshoufa*, 6: 13a–15a.

from the unification of the disparate Mongol tribes far to the north at the hands of Chinghis Khan (1162?–1227), whose descendants conquered virtually all of Asia and eastern Europe, and who then divided the empire into four great khanates: this was simply historical fact. But for Zhuang and Lü, the Yuan's problem was that struggles over imperial succession through the fourteenth century led to political chaos. (If students had to memorize all the names of the various back-stabbing princes, one feels sorry for them.) However, the basic historical lesson was clear: "As a foreign race, the Mongols conquered China without fully understanding Chinese institutions. They were only interested in seizing the wealth of the people for their own profit."[8] Responding to oppression and heavy taxes, this textbook stressed, "Chinese heroes" rose up in rebellion. Still, Zhuang and Lü gave at least as much attention to institutions as race. Teachers were to ask students to consider the role of the feudal structure (or enfeoffment system) of the Yuan in its collapse.

As for the fall of the Ming three centuries later, Zhuang and Lü provided a list of domestic disruptions and foreign pressures including but not limited to the rise of Manchu power in the northeast.[9] Though indisputably Chinese and not so oppressive, the collapse of the Ming was not that different from the fall of the Yuan. For Zhuang and Lü, the story of dynastic decline was always that of decay at the center of the polity, though the specifics differed in each case. In the case of the Ming, a vicious cycle emerged when military expenses necessitated increasing taxes, which caused domestic unrest, which created new military expenses and weakened the borders. Zhuang and Lü mentioned that the Manchus were descended from the Jurchens, another northern tribe, and that the conquest of China followed from the unification of the various Manchu tribes and their victories in Korea and eastern Mongolia, from whence they eventually expanded into Central Asia and Tibet.[10] The fault, if teachers were to take up the inference of blame, lay in the Ming: "Unceasing domestic disturbances inevitably led to foreign incursions." Zhuang and Lü did not directly cast any aspersions on either the fallen Ming or the triumphant Qing, though they did not say much about the Qing's achievements before moving on to the disasters that began at the end of the eighteenth century – the massive corruption and misrule of the imperial favorite He Shen and the spread of rebellion around 1800.[11] This led Zhuang and Lü to the Opium War and the Taiping Rebellion in the mid-nineteenth century, and the long, torturous decline that followed. Students were to compare the Qing and the Yuan, which would draw out the implications of foreign conquest. But they were also to compare He Shen with Yan Song, a massively corrupt Ming prime minister. Students were also asked

---

[8] Ibid., 6: 14b; also it is later remarked that the Yuan tax system was based on that of the Tang – ibid., 6: 20b.
[9] Ibid., 6: 18b–20a.   [10] Ibid., 6: 24a–26a.   [11] Ibid., 6: 27a–28b.

to think about whether the early Qing's policies designed to make their rule legitimate in the eyes of the Chinese were successful or not.

Zhuang and Lü presented the last years of the Qing as a contest between reformers and conservatives as the government lost control over its borders.[12] Of course it also suffered from rebellions. Rebellion was on the one hand an understandable reaction to government depredations and social decay, and the actions of an ignorant and superstitious populace on the other. In this account, the Qing's promise of a constitution came too late, and the 1911 Revolution reflected the "popular will." For Zhuang and Lü, the last years of the Qing were proof enough of the evils of autocratic government. However, the implication remained that had the Qing sincerely sought constitutional reform, that would have sufficed – but in the event it did not do so, and so revolution emerged as the only solution that most people could accept. Thus China became a republic for the first time in its history. There was perhaps a tone of regret in the observation that the Qing had actually committed "suicide."

Yet in their optimistic conclusion, Zhuang and Lü found that the essence of the Chinese state survived the rise and fall of all dynasties, while the national character of the Chinese people remained strong and firm.[13] Thus were even foreign conquerors assimilated, enriching the Chinese national race, and the state reestablished. However, today's threat is unprecedented: previous threats came from small kingdoms or nomads, whereas today's threat comes from politically sophisticated and culturally advanced foreigners.

Nationalist-period textbooks show a clear shift of emphasis. Textbooks sharpened the distinctions between foreign and Chinese. When the Nationalists came to power in 1928 and founded the Nanjing government, their legitimacy was rooted in their claims to inherit the mantle of Sun Yat-sen and the unfinished tasks of the 1911 Revolution. For the Nationalists, the legitimacy of the Republic depended, in a sense, on the illegitimacy of the Qing. Nonetheless, even in Nationalist textbooks, the weight of the traditional view of the orthodox succession of the dynasties meant that the Qing's accomplishments could scarcely be ignored. Furthermore, facing Japanese invasion in the 1930s, the government naturally returned to the ideology of the "unity of the five races" and the shared identity of all the "Chinese people" (or "peoples," in a language that lacked inflected plurals).

Generally speaking, Nationalist-period textbooks were rather more successful than their late Qing or even early Republican predecessors in telling the story of the "nation" – that is, the formation and progress of a people, as well the social, political, economic, and cultural changes that shaped it – rather than focusing merely on dynasties. This is what the editorial preface of Xie Xingyao's 1933 World Bookstore middle school history textbook

---

[12] Ibid., 6: 29a–30b.   [13] Ibid., 6: 37a.

A usable past 189

promised.[14] Xie also noted that China's traditional origin stories were legends or myths, and even the origins of the Han people could not be known for sure.[15] Xie was skeptical of the "Western origins" theory, but suggested that the "Chinese people" did in ancient times move east from the Kunlun Mountain ranges to the Yellow River valley. These were the Han. Xie's summary of the Yellow Emperor myth suggested a link among the concepts of political organization (that is, the first state), nation, and ethnic identity.[16] He took an utterly secular approach to the stories of the sage-kings and the founding of the Xia and Shang dynasties, which he regarded simply as a question of military conquest. Thus the triumph of the Shang over the Xia and then of the Zhou over the Shang should not be regarded as "popular revolution" in the present-day sense but merely as an aristocratic revolution, or dynastic change.[17] As for the nation, Xie also treated the Han as militarily stronger than their opponents. Xia described distinctions between Han and "barbarian" but also wrote of the intermingling of peoples and the cultural assimilation of outside groups as the Chinese states expanded.[18] This intermingling could be seen from the beginning of Chinese history but was especially clear by the Spring and Autumn period. Xie described the Mongol Yuan dynasty as the first case of a foreign conquest of China, but also as a unification of China (*tongyi Zhongguo*), a phrase with positive connotations.[19] However, there was no doubt about the oppressive nature of the Yuan, especially toward Chinese commoners. To reward their followers and stamp out any chance of Chinese rebellion, the Mongols ruled through non-Chinese ethnic groups. Ironically, this soon led to the rise of a "revolutionary spirit" on the part of the Chinese, easing the way for the rise of the Ming. So, too, in adult education classes of the 1930s, where Zhu Yuanzhuang, founder of the Ming, was presented as the "first ancestor of the Chinese national revolution."[20]

The 1930 "masses history textbook" of the World Bookstore also condemned the Yuan for its oppressive nature, and treated the Ming as a "revival" of the Han people. Another World Bookstore history textbook went further in characterizing the anti-Yuan uprisings of the fourteenth century as a reaction against racial oppression and nothing less than a "national revolution" (*minzu geming*).[21] The Ming "recovered" China from the Mongols, but eventually lost it again

---

[14] Xie Xingyao, *Chuzhong benguoshi*, 1: 1.   [15] Ibid., 1: 7.   [16] Ibid., 1: 7–9.
[17] Ibid., 1: 10–13. The 1930 "masses history textbook" published by the same press also called the Shang and the Zhou "aristocratic revolutions," because the populace was still powerless and needed the strength of the aristocrats to bring about a change in government. Yet the aristocratic founders of the Shang and the Zhou seemed to be representing the popular will in this account – Zhou Chuangui, *Minzhong lishi keben jiaoxuefa*, p. 18. The contrast was to the "commoner revolution" when the Han, led by a commoner, overthrew the Qin (206 BCE) – p. 21.
[18] Xie Xingyao, *Chuzhong benguoshi*, 1: 54–55.   [19] Ibid., 2: 86–98.
[20] Yang Shuming, *Minzhong changshi keben jiaoshoufa*, p. 130.
[21] Zhu Yixin, Huang Renji, and Lu Bingqian, *Chuzhong benguoshi*, 2: 49, 60–62.

to another "foreign race" (*yizu*).²² The Qing was thus the second time foreigners conquered all of China. Yet the Qing was by any standards a more long-lived and stable dynasty.²³

One might ask, if the Mongols and the Manchus were so clearly foreign, how did they become "Chinese"? Textbook writers were in no doubt that they had done so. The answer lay in the long history of the merging of peoples and their assimilation into Han culture. Published in the Commercial Press's "national revival" series, the teacher's manual by Wang Zhicheng and Fei Xiewei taught that the very first Chinese emerged out of a commingling of tribes in the Yellow River valley some 4000 years ago.²⁴ Wang and Fei cited archeological evidence to show that through trade and conquest, distinct peoples became one, explicitly drawing an analogy to the unification of the "five races" in the Republic. They referred to the merging of peoples with the conquest of the Qin and Han empires of southern and western realms, as well as invasions of China by foreigners.²⁵

Writing on the eve of Japan's full-scale invasion, Wang and Fei were as interested in the theme of patriotic resistance as in the question of ethnic mixing. How to explain the rise of the Khitans and the Jurchens in the twelfth century? The key was not the new state formations of these tribal peoples but rather the domestic divisions and rebellions facing the Chinese Tang and Song empires. Here, Wang and Fei implied that students should model themselves on the resistance efforts personified by men of the twelfth century, whose efforts may have been in vain at the time but remain inspiring²⁶ – men like Chen Dong, who led a "popular national salvation movement," and the "national heroes" Yue Fei and Wen Tianxiang, "who fought and sacrificed their lives for their nation-state." Wang and Fei, then, did not present the Yuan dynasty as a "unification" of China, but rather used these terms: "China fell completely under Yuan rule, which set the first historical precedent for the foreign conquest of [all of] China."²⁷ The victory of Ming Taizu represented the "return of Han rule in China" and a "revolution" of the Han.²⁸ Then, discussing the conquest of China by the Qing, Wang and Fei emphasized the resistance to the Manchus caused by the order for Chinese men to shave their foreheads and queue their hair in the Manchu style.²⁹ Why did the Qing issue this order, and why had the Chinese not resisted earlier? First, Wang and Fei suggested that the order was a deliberate attempt to destroy Han racial consciousness. Second, initial resistance was

---

[22] Ibid., 3: 20.
[23] Zhu Yixin, *Lishi jiaoben jiaoxuefa*, 2: 29; Zhou Chuangui, *Minzhong lishi jiaoben jiaoxuefa*, pp. 64–68. The latter work was part of a series for "mass schooling" under the rubric of Three People's Principle's education.
[24] Wang Zhicheng and Fei Xiewei, *Lishi jiaoxuefa*, 1: 22–25. The idea of 5000 years of Han presence in the upper reaches of the Yellow River valley was also heard; e.g., Jin Zhaozi, *Xin Zhonghua benguoshi jiaokeshu*, 1: 2.
[25] Wang Zhicheng and Fei Xiewei, *Lishi jiaoxuefa* 1: 87–88.   [26] Ibid., 2: 9–10, 15–16.
[27] Ibid., 2: 23.   [28] Ibid., 2: 31–32.   [29] Ibid., 2: 37–41.

muted because of the corruption and disorder of the last years of the Ming, even while the the Manchu forces initially spared central China. But finally, given the order to change thousands of years of customs on pain of death, resistance was only natural. This was especially the case because "Han racial consciousness had been strengthened ever since the Yuan dynasty followed policies of oppression."

Having labeled the Qing as oppressors and culture-destroyers, Wang and Fei went on to note that the period was one of renewed commingling of peoples. This could even be regarded as the basis of today's "Chinese people."[30] Yet the Qing deserved little credit for this outcome, which came about in spite of official policies. Qing policies, according to Wang and Fei, favored Mongols, Hui, and Tibetans at the expense of the Han. The Qing sought to oppress Han simply because they feared Han national consciousness, which was less of an issue in regard to relatively backward peripheral groups such as Mongols, according to a teacher's note. (Historians today have come to a nearly opposite conclusion: that the Qing, while maintaining Manchu military supremacy and final decision-making authority in the court, brought Han elites into the government of China proper, while allowing considerable autonomy to the frontier peoples.)

The Commercial Press textbook of 1937 by Fan Zuoguai and Han Feimu recounted the attack of the Jurchen Jin state on the Song Empire in 1127, forcing the court to flee south.[31] Fan and Han devoted an entire chapter to Yue Fei, who was for them a general of high moral virtue and military skills destroyed by a scheming prime minister. In spite of this stab in the back, or because of it, students were to learn that Yue was a "national hero." Yet they were also to learn that the Northern Song did not fall simply because of treachery; rather, especially when compared to the Han and the Tang dynasties, the Song had always been militarily weak. Even Yue's execution could be explained partly by an institutionalized distrust of the military, as the court was from the beginning fearful of the kind of military rebellion that had so damaged the Tang dynasty. The Fan-Han account was thus sophisticated and clearly relevant to the militarization of China in the 1930s.

Fan and Han noted that the Jurchens were of the Eastern Hu race (*Donghuzu*) of the northeast, and spoke of the Jin "state" rather than "dynasty." Meanwhile, Chinggis Khan was uniting the Mongol tribes into a great fighting machine.[32] Khubilai, in this account, succeeded in "unifying China" by defeating the Southern Song, and creating the Yuan dynasty, which encompassed most of the rest of Asia and eastern Europe as well, though this soon turned into four khanates. Although they distinguished between Chinese territory and outer

---

[30] Ibid., 2: 46–48.
[31] Fan Zuoguai and Han Feimu, *Gaoxiao lishi keben jiaoxuefa*, 2: 149–160.
[32] Ibid., 2: 169–180.

territory, Fan and Han also remarked, "This was truly the period when the powers of the Chinese people were at their strongest, and the dynasty under which the extent of Chinese territory was at its greatest." The distinction between Mongols and Chinese was not ignored, but the Yuan dynasty was named as such and treated as a Chinese dynasty. Nonetheless, the Yuan was not a good dynasty but an oppressive one.[33] This provoked popular uprisings, of which the most prominent was led by the future founder of the Ming dynasty. In the Fan-Han account, there was no hint of racial or ethnic antagonism on the part of the Ming, only the last Yuan emperor being pushed back into Mongolia. However, their teacher's notes suggested that teachers should explain that the Yuan was so oppressive because of the resistance of the Han people to being assimilated by foreign conquerors.

Fan Zuoguai and Han Feimu took an equally orthodox view of the rise of Qing power, which they paired with the political decadence and corruption of the Ming.[34] Fan and Han clearly stated that the Ming was overthrown by bandits, with the Qing taking this opportunity to take the capital in 1644. They told this story, however, from the point of view of the Ming loyalists such as Shi Kefa and Zheng Chenggong (Koxinga), who continued to resist the Qing onslaught – men whom teachers were told to label "national heroes" and hold up as models of courage and loyalty. Fan and Han highlighted analogies between the Qing and the conquests of the Five Barbarian Peoples of the fourth century, the Khitan Liao dynasty, the Jurchen Jin dynasty, and the Mongol Yuan dynasty. Similarly, Shi Kefa and Zheng Chenggong were comparable to men like Yue Fei of the Song.

But who were the Qing, exactly? Fan and Han essentially answered that they were the heirs of the Jin, which had been conquered by the Mongols, forced back into the northeast. There they had separated into distinct tribes, some of whom accepted tributary status under the Ming and considered themselves fellow enemies of the Mongols. Fan and Han did not, however, here distinguish the Qing leaders or armies on ethnic grounds by calling them Manchus. In discussing the Qing state itself, they described its conquest of surrounding realms and emphasized its great size.[35]

Fan and Han essentially treated the Qing in pre-national terms: it was a ruling house which had pacified Mongols, Hui, and Tibetans, as well as Han and Manchus. This tone was in harmony with the Republic's motif of the "unity of five races" that was revived to combat Japanese aggression in the late 1930s. Indeed, teachers were to make a special point of emphasizing "the origins of the amalgamation of the Chinese people." But how did this amalgamation come about? Teachers were to note:

---

[33] Ibid., 2: 189–201.   [34] Ibid., 3: 35–47.   [35] Ibid., 3: 47–62.

A usable past

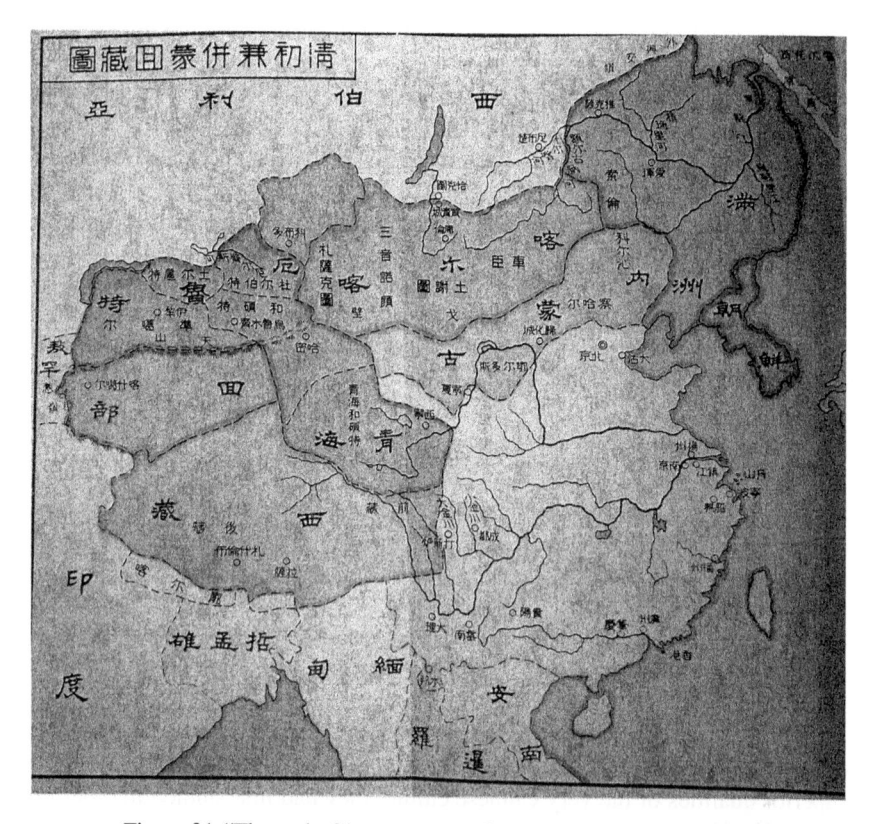

Figure 31 "The early Qing conquest of Mongolia, Turkestan, and Tibet."

There has never been a period in Chinese history without contention between various peoples, as you can see from our previous lessons. Their fights were like the great fighting scenes in operas – the Han race held the leading role while other races had secondary parts. But when did these great fighting scenes finally get played out to their end?

During the Qing, of course. Fan and Han thus overturned the standard Nationalist interpretation of the Qing, which saw it as an apartheid regime like the Yuan and held that only the Republic could have united the various peoples of China.

As the map in Figure 31 indicates, that the Qing was a conquest dynasty was never in doubt. Nor in doubt was that it had come out of the northeast. The question was whether it had become Chinese enough so that the modern, mostly Han Chinese nation should take pride in its imperial reach and lay claim to its territories – land that the Ming had never held. This map implies Qing possession of Korea and Taiwan, as well as Mongolia, Inner Asia, and Tibet, but not most of Southeast Asia. Imperial reach, however, was not the same as direct bureaucratic rule. In the terminology of the twentieth century, this might be conceptualized as the distinction between sovereignty and suzerainty, but this was not a distinction that was meaningful to Qing rulers.

In any case, most textbooks treated the rise of the Qing in matter-of-fact terms – nothing succeeds like success. The expansion of Qing power to Mongolia and Central Asia through the eighteenth century was recounted, along with the spread of enfeoffment procedures or suzerainty to Korea, Burma, Vietnam, and other peripheral states. These were, in effect, China's accomplishments. And equally frankly, textbooks recounted the setbacks and defeats of the Qing in the nineteenth century. This approach fit the narrative arc of rise and fall that emphasized Qianlong's achievements, especially territorial expansion, and found that problems began only at the end of his reign, with popular rebellion and the corruption of high officials.

In the 1930s, however, the Qing was more often pictured as oppressive to the core. Jin Zhaozi, for example, insisted that not merely the conquest but the entire period of Qing rule rested on a system designed to maintain Manchu supremacy.[36] Aside from ruthless military suppression, literati were "caged up," and even routine scholarship, such as compiling dictionaries and bibliographies, was distorted to help the Manchus eliminate any references to Han nationalism in Chinese culture. Jin charged that the Qing's policies of Manchuization, such as requiring Chinese men to wear their hair in the Manchu style, were harsher than anything even the Mongols had done. Yet in the end Jin generously granted that the Manchus eventually became Sinified, attracted by the superior qualities of the very Chinese culture they had first studied in order to control the Han.

History textbooks consistently paid a great deal of attention to borders; here, the Qing (seen as a Chinese dynasty) got high marks for territorial expansion, though, again, perhaps a little less credit in China Bookstore accounts than others. Maps were of course a useful way to give a quick sense of Qing China's vastness. Maps showed borders but did not necessarily delineate clearly what lay inside and outside the nation.[37] Yunnan and Vietnam had their own borders,

---

[36] Ibid., 2: 60–63.
[37] For example, Zhao Yusen and Jiang Weiqiao, *Benguoshi*, between 2: 34–35; on the other hand, their map of the Ming showed a clearly delineated space (including Korea) (ibid., 1: 108–109). Other examples may be found in Zhu Yixin et al., *Chuzhong Zhongguo benguoshi*, 4 vols. The map in Hu Chaoyang, *Di yi jianming lishi qimeng*, is particularly ambiguous as to borders: the symbols for "foreign borders" and "internal borders" are indistinguishable, p. 46a. At least one Zhonghua Bookstore account failed to map the Qing at its fullest extent. See Zhuang Qichuan and Lü Ximian, *Xinshi lishi jiaokeshu*, 6: 10b for the early Qing, which would appear to include Korea but not Vietnam or other parts of Southeast Asia, and 6:12b for the late Qing, which is somewhat shrunken, especially to the north and west. Other textbooks marked borders more clearly with the use of color (see Gu Jiegang and Wang Zhongqi, *Benguoshi*, 3 vols.).

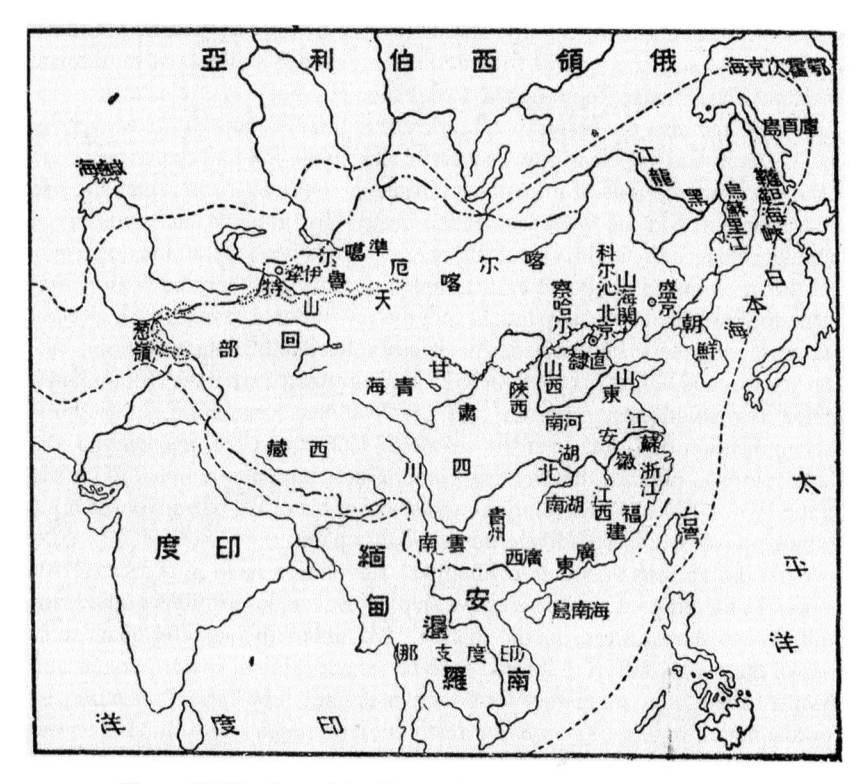

Figure 32 "Borders of the Qing at its greatest extent" [contrasted with contemporary borders].

but both might appear to lie within the Qing, along with, say, Korea, Tibet, and today's Kazakhstan. Numerous nationalities were all considered to be Chinese as the Republic laid claim to the frontier lands of the Qing.

With a sweeping dashed line, the map in Figure 32 shows the theoretical extent of the Qing Empire (somewhat exaggerated) far into Inner Asia and Southeast Asia. For most Republican elites, aside from any questions of national pride, strategic necessity meant that they needed to claim as much of the Qing territory as possible; however, as the dash-dotted line shows, the Republic of China's claims were reduced, leaving out Southeast Asia, Taiwan, and various border regions.

Qing decline

As we have seen, in histories written immediately after the 1911 Revolution, the new Republic of China was not described as a complete break with the past, but rather the culmination of a long national history. Textbooks thereby produced a narrative of struggle against tribulations that reached a climax with ultimate triumph. The Chinese Republic was simultaneously a new and wonderful political form, and also the result of centuries of national becoming. However, by the 1920s it was not clear how successful the revolution had really been: the continued depredations of imperialist powers, new threats from Japan, the rise of warlordism and the weakness of the central government, and widespread popular revolts and banditry – the old specter of "domestic rebellion and external threat" – raised doubts about triumphal narratives. When the Nationalists came to power in 1928, they taught that the revolution had not yet succeeded but must continue to be pursued. This stance reflected the conclusion Sun Yat-sen had reached before his death in 1925 and legitimated what the Guomindang called its revolutionary program: first, the "National Revolution" of the military unification of China over the course of 1927 and 1928, and second, the developmental policies that the new Nanjing government attempted to pursue in the 1930s. The 1911 Revolution in this sort of historical narrative was not a failure but a first step on a longer revolutionary path.

What did various accounts of the 1911 Revolution have in common? All textbooks identified it as a progressive step. However, descriptions of the revolution focused on leaders, not the "nation." Nor did textbooks offer much analysis of the events, offering instead bare-bones accounts of major persons and events. I have found no history textbook that defined "revolution" (*geming*), or for that matter republic (*gonghe*) or restoration (*guangfu*). Definitions seem to have been left for civics textbooks, while histories focused on events. History textbooks did sometimes emphasize the uniqueness of the Republic in terms of its negative qualities: it was not an imperial system or autocratic government. But attempts to inscribe meaning to history in such direct terms were rare. We can contrast Chinese textbooks in this regard with American textbooks, which, though full of names and dates, also attempted to convey a macro-picture or narrative. A 1920 primary school textbook by the prominent Columbia University scholars Charles Beard and William Bagley was "designed to include the richest possible equipment for American citizenship."[38] It promised to emphasize the themes of the growth of American nationality; the constant struggle to improve the standards of American life; the role of individual opportunity in America; the "growth of humane and democratic ideals"; and the possibility of rise from poverty; as well as the new roles open to women, the rise of industry, and so forth. Beard and Bagley strove to reflect this "age of democracy" by writing a kind of biography of the American people rather than presenting biographies of a few so-called great men. In the preface to the 1925 edition of their work, Beard and Bagley announced that "One great motive has dominated

---

[38] Charles A. Beard and William C. Bagley, *A First Book in American History*, "Note to teachers."

the content and arrangement of this volume: the preparation of children for citizenship through an understanding of the ideals, institutions, achievement, and problems of our country."[39] They would not emphasize a bunch of facts, dates, and names, for, "It can only be done by teaching boys and girls to think of events and issues of the living present in the light of their historical past, by giving them, above all, a sense of historical continuity." American textbook authors were quick to inform students of their own judgments. Willis Mason West of the University of Minnesota concluded his *The Story of World Progress* on a nervous but ultimately optimistic note: that although "the World War [of 1914–1918] struck civilization a staggering blow, there are hopeful signs that the warning has not been in vain."[40] Some authors were less tempered in their optimism, one textbook concluding with a chapter on "Democracy's Victory and Its Meaning."[41]

One of the few Chinese textbooks to frankly note the sacrifice required by revolution was the *Contemporary Chinese History* of the First Girls' Normal School of Zhili.

> Revolution is the result of bloodshed, and bloodshed is the cost of revolution. To change the political structure to fulfill our hopes of peace could only come about through bloody revolution. This was also an unavoidable historical movement of the day. The imperial regime that had lasted in China for some four thousand years was wiped out by universal acclaim within a few months after the revolution started.[42]

This passage is also interesting for its invocation of a kind of revolutionary zeitgeist in which China could not but participate. But above all, it reflected a faith in republicanism as the path of the future. It naturally assumed that people would shape their behavior in accord with historical trends.

The last chapters of late Qing history textbooks, as we have seen, made for grim reading. Republican textbooks naturally followed this pattern. Zhao Yusen, a Commercial Press editor, wrote that already by the eighteenth century, Qing corruption had provoked the White Lotus Rebellion and other rebellions; although the Qing survived, it was already weakened by the time of the Opium War. Here, Zhao charged that opium was a poison destroying the country, though he took some satisfaction in Qing resistance against the British.[43] The Anglo-French expedition, territorial losses to Russia – all were matters of national humiliation, shaming both the rulers and the people.[44] At the same time, Zhao essentially blamed Qing misrule for the Taipings, the Nian, the Hui, and other rebellions, though the lesson he drew was not that rebellion was justified but rather that unity was necessary. Further foreign disasters such as the loss

---

[39] Ibid. (1925), p. v.   [40] Willis Mason West, *The Story of World Progress*, p. 667.
[41] William Backus Guitteau, *Our United States: A History*.
[42] Zhili diyi nüzi shifan xuexiao, *Benguo xiandaishi*, 1a.
[43] Zhao Yusen, *Xin lishi jiaoshoufa*, 4: 27a–b.   [44] Ibid., 4: 30b.

of the suzerain states of Vietnam and Burma culminated in the Sino-Japanese War and the loss of the Liuqiu (Ryukyu) Islands, Taiwan, influence in Korea, and numerous concession zones.

The shame continued as the Qing leaders remained unable to pursue fundamental solutions that had become obvious to many: institutional reform and self-strengthening (*bianfa ziqiang*) – self-strengthening not just for the government but all citizens; not just military reform, but reforms in scholarship, agriculture, industry, and commerce. For Chinese to erase their shame, they needed to learn self-strengthening from Japan.[45] Zhao's account of the last years of the Qing went something like this. The lesson of the Boxer disaster, aside from revealing the faults of Cixi, was that self-strengthening depended on human capacities, not divine intervention.[46] Finally, then, the Russo-Japanese War, fought over Chinese lands that the Qing was too weak to defend, led to calls for revolution.[47] The Qing court responded with gestures to turn itself into a constitutional monarchy. However, at least after Cixi's death, it became apparent that such gestures were doomed to failure. In the penultimate chapter, Zhao described the 1911 Revolution, beginning with the petition for a national parliament and railroad rights recovery movement, and finally turning to the armed revolt. It was the widespread response to the Wuchang Uprising in southern and central provinces that forced the Qing into negotiations and finally the agreement to abdicate in exchange for "favorable treatment." In the final chapter, Zhao spoke of "unifying" rather than founding the Republic, emphasizing the north-south agreement and the unity of the five races in the Republic. Zhao compared the relationship of the races to brothers in a family, and whereas previously under autocracy the races were unequal and each out for itself, today they share the burden of state, cooperating with one another as equals and indeed all one people (*wo minzu*).[48] For Zhao, the 1911 Revolution had nothing to do with race or Han-Manchu antagonisms but was purely about political change.

Zhao's denial of ethnic tensions perhaps reflected a fear that China was going to be dismembered or fall apart. As he noted, while the Han dominated the heartland, the peripheral areas were dominated by non-Han. On the one hand, he followed the standard line in insisting that racial mixing was a long-standing historical feature. On the other hand, he claimed that amalgamation and cooperation only really came to fruition with the Republic. Indeed, the virtues of republicanism were a repeating motif: Zhao repeatedly condemned despotic injustice and exploitation. He found many reflections of the superiority of republicanism in the mirror of history, often on the grounds that kings were prone to abuse their powers, as we have seen. Zhao also stressed the involvement of citizens in the state made for a stronger state. Imperial China

---

[45] Ibid., 4: 42b.　[46] Ibid., 4: 45b.　[47] Ibid., 4: 49a–51b.　[48] Ibid., 4: 56a–57a.

had depended on heroes, but a Republic is based on the whole people, which is ultimately more reliable – as long as the people do their duty.[49] In a democratic republic, the people elect good and competent officials, all matters are decided by the masses and carried out by popular will, and the people benefit.[50]

But Zhao's *New History* stressed one lesson even more important than the beauties of republicanism: the sacredness of Chinese territory and unity, and the responsibility of all Chinese to defend the nation. Territorial integrity, strong governance, good government, and unity were all linked. Just as a body becomes strong through exercise, so a country becomes strong through the wealth and power that stem from unity.[51] Disunity has always led to disaster, whereas unity leads to order (*geju ze luan, tongyi ze zhi*). Republicanism, with its emphasis on equality, encourages unity.[52] Like many textbooks of the day, *New History* presented essentially heroic images of such standard conquerors as Han Wudi, Sui Wendi, Tang Taizong, and Song Taizu, even if they were also responsible for some crimes. Zhao also praised those who pushed the borders outward like Ban Chao and Zhang Jian, and the standard loyal ministers such as Yue Fei and Fan Zhongyan. Men like these provide models for modern republican citizens. "Loyalty refers not only to loyalty to a particular emperor, but you should know that what is precious are the people who are loyal to their country."[53] Likewise, both the Ming loyalist Zheng Chenggong in Taiwan and the Qing conqueror Kangxi were virtuous. Zhao also claimed some of Chinggis Khan's glory on the grounds that as a kind of representative of one of the peoples of today's China, he was an Asian threat to the West.[54] So too Yuan Shizu (Kubilai Khan), who broke down boundaries among races and religions, prefiguring today's Republic.[55] By this standard, Ming Taizu's restoration of order was good, but his autocratic ways were bad. Rebels such as Hang Chao of the Tang and also Li Zicheng and Zhang Xianzhong of the Ming are undoubtedly evil figures, though Zhao is fairly consistent in making the point that it is misgovernment that gives rise to rebellion. Zhao marked two great moments in revolutionary history – the overthrow of the Xia by the Shang founder Tangwu and the overthrow of the Qing by the republicans.

Like many, Hu Chaoyang spoke of the popular roots of the 1911 Revolution and the process of provincial secession as "restoration" (*guangfu*). But he did not explicitly mention race – neither glorifying the Han nor extolling the "unity of the five races" – but rather focused on political events. For Zhao Yusen and Jiang Weiqiao, in the more magisterial Commercial Press approach, the question was precisely one of matching political form and the trends of the time: autocracy was not suitable for the twentieth century.[56] Essentially,

---

[49] Ibid., 2: 36a, 4: 4b. [50] Ibid., 4: 51b. [51] Ibid., 2: 35b, 2: 17b.
[52] Ibid., 4: 7b, 2: 15a–b. [53] Ibid., 2: 25a. [54] Ibid., 3: 1b. [55] Ibid., 3: 4b.
[56] Zhao Yusen and Jiang Weiqiao, *Benguoshi*, 2: 79.

for both these sets of textbooks, ideas about political reform had spread more quickly than the Qing was able or willing to react to them, as we will see in the next section.

In discussing the decline of the Qing, textbooks faced two narrative strategies, emphasizing either domestic rot or barbarian aggression. These could be seen as two sides of the same coin, but textbooks tended to emphasize one over the other. In telling the story of the Qing's decline, textbook authors sometimes began with the Opium War, which implied that the Qing was threatened from the outside, and sometimes with the White Lotus revolt, which implied domestic rot. Fu Yunsen, for example, moved from the White Lotus revolt to continue the story of domestic rebellion through the Taipings (1850–1865), before turning to the Opium War (1840–1842). This break with chronology perhaps made events easier to follow than if he had shifted back and forth between domestic and foreign affairs in strictly chronological fashion.[57] At any rate, Fu's account was consistent in its discussion of the basic causes of the 1911 Revolution: not fundamentally a response to imperialism but a reaction against the ever-heavier autocracy of the Ming-Qing emperors.[58] The revolution, for Fu, represented popular demands for a republic that the court was finally unable to resist. The 1920 China Bookstore textbook by Zhuang Qichuan and Lü Simian told the story of Qing decline largely in domestic terms right up to the 1911 Revolution, and only then turned to a more detailed examination of foreign affairs.[59] Indeed, many textbooks followed this strategy through the 1920s, but the trend was increasingly to emphasize the perfidy of the British, putting the main focus on opium and the series of lost battles that followed.

For example, a teacher's manual written by Jiang Jianqiu for the China Bookstore's "common knowledge" series in the 1930s, emphasized the annual calendar of "humiliation days." Students were to commemorate events ranging from the Nanjing Treaty, which marked China's loss of the Opium War in 1842 (August 29), to the Mukden Incident, which marked Japan's invasion of Manchuria in 1931 (September 18). Jiang treated the Boxer Uprising of 1900 as a reaction against imperialist oppression that the Qing government attempted to use to expel the foreigners.[60] The Eight-Army allied Invasion that followed led to the sacking of Beijing and the permanent stationing of foreign troops there. Thus the treaty that followed is commemorated as a national humiliation day on September 7. Jiang suggested that students could compare the humiliations of September with those of other months. At the same time, Jiang's manual encouraged objective historical analysis, using the Boxers to get students to think about the context of their actions, their own motives, the attitudes of

[57] Fu Yunsen, *Xin lishi*, 6: 13b–14a.   [58] Ibid., 6: 15b–16a.
[59] Zhuang Qichuan and Lü Simian, *Xinshi lishi jiaoshoufa*, vol. 6.
[60] Jiang Jianqiu, *Chuxiao changshi keben jiaoxuefa*, 7: 59–64.

Qing officials, and the views of the foreigners, and generally to examine causes and effects of events. Jiang's lesson on the Boxers was followed by one on the "unequal treaties" and then a general lesson on Chinese nationalism. These were in turn followed, in the spirit of the "common knowledge" textbooks, by a lesson on the water chestnut.

Jiang defined unequal treaties as those through which the power took territory, demanded payments, or established concessions to build railways, mines, and shipping lines, and station soldiers. The inequality lay in the lack of rights of Chinese to conduct any of these activities in foreign countries.[61]

Textbooks could use calendars to highlight memories of humiliation; maps to highlight sites of imperialist aggression; and charts to clarify chronology and details.

The list in Figure 33 begins with the loss of Hong Kong to Britain in the Opium War in 1842; includes the loss of Annan to the French in the Sino-French War in 1885; and ends with the loss of Korea, which gained independence in the Sino-Japan War of 1895 and was colonized by Japan in 1910; and the loss of border areas in the south to France and Britain in 1895 and 1905.[62] Maps were important in showing where China has lost sovereignty, and linking history and geography. But Jiang Jianqiu's emphasis was historical at least insofar as he described a process determined by statesmen and armies, not natural physical features. Teachers were to lead discussions on how China could recover its concessions. As the political and economic analysis of imperialism grew more sophisticated over the course of the twentieth century, the modern history of anti-Chinese aggression took on moral significance. National education demanded that students be taught the history of what became known as unequal treaties – not one, not two, but dozens forced on the Chinese by foreign powers over the decades.[63] Learning "national humiliation" was part of learning national pride, which was to be reasserted. Ritual observations of national humiliation days were first instituted in schools in the 1920s.[64] Then under the Nationalists, national humiliation days formed something like a political theology along with the ritual obeisance to Sun Yat-sen and the Three People's Principles.

The 1937 textbook of Fan Zuoguai and Han Feimu marched students through the Opium War, the Taiping Rebellion, the Second Opium War, the Sino-French

---

[61] Ibid., pp. 65–78.
[62] Zhao Tizhen and Ma Pengnian, *Xiaoxue shehui keben jiaoxuefa*, 7: 56; for more such charts, see inter alia Shen Liangqi, *Guochi yanshuo*, pp. 75–78; Fan Zuoguai and Han Feimu, *Gaoxiao lishi keben jiaoxuefa*, 4: 151–154.
[63] The concept of "unequal treaties" developed during the republican period. See Dong Wang, *China's Unequal Treaties*.
[64] See Robert Culp, *Articulating Citizenship*, pp. 216–220, 80–84; for the theme of "national humiliation" in modern China, see Paul A. Cohen, *Speaking to History*, esp. chapter 2; and William A. Callahan, "History, Identity, and Security."

9. 我國割讓地一覽表

年代	地方	割佔國	事由
一八四二年	香港	英	鴉片戰爭之役割去
一八五八年	黑龍江北岸	俄	璦琿條約訂約後割去現為俄阿穆爾省
一八六〇年	九龍司	英	英法聯軍之役割去
一八六〇年	烏蘇里江東岸	俄	北京條約訂約後割去現為俄東海濱省
一八七四年	琉球藩屬局	日	因臺灣生番事件被佔去
一八八一年	新疆霍爾果斯河以西地	俄	因伊犁還伊犁事件被換去
一八八五年	安南	法	中法戰爭之役被佔去
一八八七年	緬甸	英	中英協約後被佔去
一八八五年	澳門	葡	一八八九年英以兵取之葡統監明年遂有其地
一八九〇年	錫金	英	中日戰爭之役割去
一八九五年	臺灣	日	中日戰爭之役割去
一八九五年	澎湖羣島	日	中日戰爭之役割去
一八九五年	朝鮮	日	中日戰爭後脫離我國獨立一九一〇年併於日本
一八九五年	雲南湄公河上流東岸江洪岬地	法	俄口助我國索回遼東半島有功割去
一九〇五年	雲南滇灘界鐵壁關踏地	英	兩國勘界誤以姊妹山及大盈河為界遂失此地

Figure 33 Chart of territories lost to imperialist powers.

War, the Meiji Restoration and the Sino-Japanese War, the spread of foreign concessions, the failed Reform Movement of 1898, and the Boxer disaster in fairly straightforward fashion. In their teacher's notes, they called the Opium War the "first act" of foreign aggression against China.[65] Foreign imperialism combined with the government's decadence and incompetence led to utter

---

[65] Fan Zuoguai and Han Feimu, *Gaoxiao lishi keben jiaoxuefa*, 3: 156

disaster. The Fan-Han account of the Taipings was sympathetic.[66] This contrasts with earlier textbooks that saw the Taipings as a disaster. Teachers were to present its leader as a "revolutionary thinker; he was inspired to revolt by seeing the autocracy and oppression of the Manchu Qing. However, as a commoner he had little authority and so founded a religion with the goal of using its believers to make a political revolution." The Fan-Han textbook pictured the Taipings as something like modern progressives, and downplayed the Taiping religion and its imperial forms. In this view, the Taipings were significant for their support of equality between the sexes, use of the Western calendar, and prohibitions of footbinding, slavery, prostitution, gambling, drinking, and opium. Although their movement failed, they weakened the Qing. However, the story that followed the Taipings in this textbook was mainly one of ever-growing foreign imperialism. Teachers were to bring a "national humiliation chart" to every lesson. It is worth noting, however, that unlike some radical intellectuals and elements in the Guomindang, Fan and Han had no use for the Boxers, which they regarded not as patriotic anti-imperialist stalwarts but representative of the reactionary politics of the Qing court.[67] Another view was displayed by the World Bookstore's "masses history textbook," which treated the Boxers as a "national movement" in the same sense as the Taipings.[68] It criticized the Boxers as immature but applauded their resistance to foreign imperialism.

At least as blunt was the adult general education textbook by Yang Shuming. Yang summarized the Qing period in these terms: "China suffered the autocratic oppression of the Manchu-Qing for three hundred years, and suffered military invasions from numerous countries, and the pain felt by the people has been enormous."[69] Yang praised the "national movements" of both the Taipings and the Boxers. But whereas the Taipings, he said, advocated liberty, equality, and universal love, the Boxers were backward in their thinking. Rapidly moving on to the Republic, Yang claimed that China had been at least partly under Han rule at all times, except for the Yuan and the Qing, but "Han" was too narrow a definition of the Chinese today. Ringing the familiar bell of unity, Yang was glad that today, the peoples of China have come together as one family, but they still need to strengthen their unity to resist foreign imperialism.

Narratives of revolution and beyond

History was a mirror. In the wake of the revolution, the main Commercial Press teachers' manual offered a Q and A. Question: Are not the Western powers now at the height of power and prestige? Answer: Yes, so you need to know that the

---

[66] Ibid., 3: 165–174.   [67] Ibid., 3: 216–221.
[68] Zhou Chuangui, *Minzhong lishi keben jiaoxuefa*, p. 94.
[69] Yang Shuming, *Minzhong changshi keben jiaoshoufa*, pp. 130–133.

Western powers themselves arose out of turmoil; and in fact real danger lies in the complacency or decadence of eras like the Qing.[70] This brief example demonstrates both that the mirror of history was now focused on the West as much as on China, and that, at least in one view, the fundamental weakness of the Qing lay as much in its success in bringing about peace as in its oppression (though oppressive institutions were certainly part of a story of corruption and indolence). Europe's inter-state struggles and wars encouraged progress and, in the case of France, revolution. Destruction facilitated construction; both depended on the popular will. This all occurred while Qing China vegetated. Therefore, Zhao Yusen said, under those historical conditions, revolution (as in France) was necessary. Teachers were to tell their students that today China needed racial unity, political unity, and the support of the people. Another lesson to be derived from the Qing was that autocracies were inherently weak. They only know immediate advantage and lack a capacity for long-term strategic planning.[71] Finally, Zhao partially defined revolution, noting that it was not made by revolutionaries but required a majority of the people.[72] It took great stamina, and the role of revolutionaries lay in awakening the people.

As suggested earlier, in the *Chinese History* published by the Commercial Press, the revolution marked a turning point: on one side the Qing ("modern history"), on the other side the Republic ("contemporary history").[73] Obviously, however, the story of the revolution began in the late Qing and carried into the Republic. The textbook's narrative strategy was to tell the story twice. In other words, the revolution was both an end and a beginning, in narrative terms. On the one hand was a story of Qing failure and even treachery (false promises); on the other, a story of persistence and determination against apparently great odds. Focusing on the activities of revolutionaries, the Commercial Press's history tended to make the events of 1911 themselves sound like more of a coup than a popular revolution. Granted, the text referred to "the people" in various contexts and highlighted the fundamental change in political system. Still, its focus on the succession of failed plots led by Sun Yat-sen and others tended to convey a conspiratorial flavor.[74] Nor did the text say much about the ideas and goals of the revolutionaries. It described the Wuchang Uprising matter-of-factly. Once the uprising started to spread, the textbook explained, the popular feeling of the entire country was opposed to the imperial system. People were made joyful by word of the revolutionary army's success and depressed by news of setbacks.[75] All voices were raised in favor of reform (*gaige*). And so the Qing court itself suddenly understood that the autocracy could never be restored.

---

[70] Zhao Yusen, *Xinlishi jiaoshoufa*, 6: 57a–b.
[71] Ibid., 6: 60b–61a. This observation is interesting since the opposite view is widely held today.
[72] Ibid., 6: 63a–b. [73] Zhao Yusen and Jiang Weiqiao, eds., *Benguoshi*, vol. 2.
[74] Ibid., 2: 99–100. [75] Ibid., 2: 102.

A usable past   205

In effect, then, the revolution consisted in the response to the Wuchang Uprising, as much as the uprising itself. Zhao and Jiang's *Chinese History* then went on to describe the establishment of the Nanjing provisional government and the North-South negotiations. After all the fighting (mentioned but not described) and negotiations (described in greater detail), the Republic was actually born with the abdication of the Qing.[76] The *Chinese History*'s focus on events with little evaluation or explanation offered something less than a gripping narrative. It highlighted the deeds of a few figures whose personalities nonetheless remained blank: Yuan Shikai, Li Yuanhong, Sun Yat-sen, and others. Still, a basic narrative framework confirmed the fundamental move from beginning (backwardness: autocracy) via a process (uprising: revolution) to a conclusion (progress: republicanism).

No less important to this conclusion was national (specifically, racial) unity.[77] Here, the tone of the textbook was perhaps heightened. Its analytical description of political conditions shaped the narrative: in an age of competition among the various peoples of the world, China had been disadvantaged by the Qing's deliberate divisions of the people according to racial categories; as well, the imperial system itself divided the realm into ruler and ruled. The revolutionary narrative, then, was as much a story of overcoming division as of constructing a new state structure. Furthermore, the *Chinese History* suggested that the revolution was ultimately harmonious, as seen in the Qing's own agreement to abdicate for the sake of unity. It thus logically concluded that the Republican state was at least equally based on "the unity of the five races" as upon institutions as laid out in the new constitution.[78] Finally, it restored a "from-to" narrative format by a series of analytical comparisons of pre-revolutionary and republican "customs": the liberation of minorities, outcastes, prostitutes, slaves, and the like – "All persons, no matter what kind, possess all rights equally in regard to the national society."[79] The solar calendar has been adopted, the kowtow abolished, and queues and bound feet are disappearing.

The narrative structure of the 1911 Revolution was a doubled structure insofar as it centered around a pull toward revolution (Qing problems, also the end of a story) and a push (revolutionary energies, also the beginning). The push could be seen largely as intellectual or even cultural change: the rise of democratic and nationalist energies.[80] Coupled with the decadence and corruption of the late Qing autocratic government (pull), the result was to raise revolutionary consciousness, which in turn produced uprisings, assassinations, and propaganda that became self-perpetuating until the Qing was destroyed. This

---

[76] Ibid., 2: 106–108.   [77] Ibid., 2: 123–124.
[78] Ibid., 2: 114–116. In addition, the *Chinese History* presented a non-narrative outline or description of the Republican political system (president, parliament, premier, cabinet, judiciary, military, etc., etc.).
[79] Ibid., 2: 121.   [80] Zhili diyi nüzi shifan xuexiao, *Benguo xiandaishi*, 1a–2a.

story really revolved around the Qing's failure to reform until the point where "popular anger" could not be restrained. Again, the key to making the Wuchang Uprising a revolution lay in the response to it in other provinces.

The push-pull story was maintained in the new curriculum of the 1920s. A Commercial Press "society" textbook emphasized the revolutionary push and prefigured the cult of Sun Yat-sen that the Nationalists were to build.

> In the last years of the Qing dynasty, the Chinese saw that the state was languishing and governance corrupt, and as well Western democratic ideas were becoming more popular. So people who were resolved to pursue reform decided to overthrow the Qing and build a new political system. Sun Yat-sen was the first to pursue actual revolution.[81]

The Wuchang Uprising in this kind of account becomes part of the plan, rather than the accidental spark of revolution that it actually was. What emerges is a story of revolutionary triumph.

Revolutionary hopes did not last long. By the 1920s, many intellectuals were calling the revolution a failure. For the Nationalists this was not so. It was not that the 1911 Revolution failed, exactly; rather, it was still incomplete. Thus Nationalist-period textbooks emphasized Sun Yat-sen's indefatigable efforts right through his death on a trip to negotiate with the northern warlords in Beijing in 1925.[82] This suggested the continuity that ran through the revolutionary organizations from the late Qing right through the contemporary Guomindang. Imperialism, in 1930s histories, was the most fundamental problem facing the Chinese and hence the most important target of the revolution.[83] From the Opium War on, imperialist powers have exploited China for its resources and wealth; in this light, the Boxers' anti-imperialism was admirable. More to the point at the present time, the stage of "finance capitalism" has accentuated foreign monopoly control of the Chinese economy.

A slightly different view was offered in a China Bookstore "society" textbook from the early 1930s. It too condemned imperialism and celebrated popular resistance – from Guangdong villages in the Opium War to the Boxers and on to the May Fourth (1919) and May Thirtieth (1925) movements.[84] Modern imperialism in this view was a product of the industrial revolution, which led to the evolution from traditional military imperialism to economic imperialism.[85] But what made China vulnerable to imperialism in the first place. Here the answer was less the specific policies of the Qing than the nature of autocracy. The 1911 Revolution was not (merely) anti-Qing; it was about constructing a new national polity. This textbook saw the Versailles Treaty of 1919 as an

---

[81] Ding Xiaoxian and Chang Daozhi, *Shehui jiaokeshu*, 8: 1–2.
[82] Zhao Tizhen and Ma Pengnian, *Xiaoxue shehui keben jiaoxuefa*, 8: 28–35.
[83] Ibid., 8: 56–65.
[84] Wang Yunwen and Lou Sanli, *Xiaoxue shehui keben jiaoxuefa*, 1: 232–236.
[85] Ibid., 1: 241–258.

awakening for the Chinese, showing that there was no justice in international affairs but only force. It also highlighted the ties between the imperialist powers and China's own warlords.

Similarly, Jiang Jianqiu's "common knowledge" teacher's manual of 1937 emphasized that the point of revolution lay in the contrast between monarchy and democracy.[86] For Jiang, the question was not China's weaknesses but the people's strength. Historically, as the monarch's powers became greater, the political system became more oppressive, but the people gradually realized that it was they, and not the monarch, who constituted the state. This was to say that democratic revolution was historically inevitable. It first occurred in America and France, and eventually in China. Jiang further argued that constitutional monarchies such as Britain were also essentially democratic because of their parliamentary institutions. This was also to say that the people (renmin) were historical agents in their own right. Students were to discuss why the people were the basis of the state.

Even with a grand narrative that culminated in revolution, in the long history of China, especially as narrated in a single volume or two, the 1911 Revolution could be dwarfed by the sheer volume of events. It could be seen as a chapter in the larger opening to the West, for example, or simply one aspect of "modernity." In short order, it seemed that the significance of the revolution was best found in its negation. In other words, it was the failure of the revolution to create functioning republican institutions that showed how revolutionary it was. The standards of the revolutionaries determined whether the revolution should be regarded as a success, and conversely the perceived failure of the revolution defined what was meant by revolution. To speak of Yuan Shikai as "betraying" the revolution rested on the premise that only republicanism was a legitimate form of government. In his lower primary school history text, first written in the late Qing but updated, Hu Chaoyang spoke of how history should help people to appraise the current situation. Hu called for material reforms to enrich China and spiritual reforms through Wang Yangming Learning to rectify its people.[87] By the 1920s, the historical – and moral – significance of the revolution was clear: the Yuan monarchy was not only a betrayal (daoguo), but itself a failure, showing the futility of attempts to turn the clock back. Yuan was defeated by "unstoppable" opposition.[88] In other words, in some sense, republicanism was a historical force in its own right. This was further confirmed by the failure of the 1917 restoration of the monarchy – which in the end was nothing more than a "bubble dream."

The textbooks of Jiang and Hu demonstrate that history written in the late Qing and the early Republic could tell much the same story of the last years of

---

[86] Jiang Jianqiu, *Chuxiao changshi keben jiaoxuefa*, 7: 155–166.
[87] Hu Chaoyang, *Diyi jianmin lishi qimeng*, pp. 59a–b.   [88] Ibid., p. 57a.

the Qing. They emphasized the twinned nature of domestic disturbances and foreign incursions, including the Boxers, the invasion of Beijing, and the government's failure to pursue constitutionalism. Only this last issue was treated with more celebration in histories written before the 1911 Revolution. In those histories, as we have noted, a narrative climax came with the constitutional movement, whereas in Republican histories, that climax came instead with the revolution.

Once the Qing was history, it was possible for victors to dismiss it rather than fulminate against its evils. There were new evils to fulminate against. In the 1930s textbook by Fan Zuoquai and Han Feimu, volume 3 ended with the Qing battered, defeated, and hopeless, whereas volume 4 began bright-eyed and eager with Sun Yat-sen. Consistent with their earlier volumes, the authors displayed no anti-Manchu bias but spoke only of the Qing government's flaws, and Sun's desire "to restore the glory of the Chinese people."[89] The real problem, then and now, was how to deal with imperialism. In describing Sun's invention of the Three People's Principles, Fan and Han did not refer to the anti-Manchuism of the 1911 revolutionaries but rather the journey of liberation of the Chinese people in throwing off imperialism, as well as the freely chosen unity in equality of the various ethnic groups within China and even how the Chinese would help foreign victims of imperialism to achieve equality in the international sphere.

Teachers were to ask, what were the "past glories" of the Chinese people? The answer lay in their 4000 years of history as a civilized country, and the military achievements and territorial extents of the Qin, Han, Sui, Tang, Yuan, and Ming dynasties, and also that of the Qing through the eighteenth century. Under Sun's leadership, insurrection and assassinations over some 15 years led to the revolution in 1911 and the founding of the Republic.[90] As to why the revolution succeeded in 1911 after so many failures, teachers could explain two theories. One emphasized that revolutionaries had never become discouraged and, when the situation ripened, they were ready. The other emphasized the inspiration and the lessons learned from earlier experience.

Alas, Fan and Han had to go on to recount, Yuan Shikai turned out to be a murderous tyrant.[91] He suppressed the new parliament and tried to make himself emperor, a plan that republican opponents were able to defeat. Above all, in the Fan-Han account, Yuan's career represented both the failure of the revolution and its success, insofar as republican forces were ultimately able to defeat Yuan. Concentrating on contemporary history, students studied World War I, the Russian Revolution, the Versailles Treaty and the Washington system, and the League of Nations. Fan and Han told of the May Fourth

---

[89] Fan Zuoguai and Han Feimu, *Gaoxiao lishi keben jiaoxuefa*, 4: 1–14.
[90] Ibid., 4: 14–21.   [91] Ibid., 4: 27–38.

movement's resistance to the provisions of the Versailles Treaty that turned Germany's concessions in Shandong over to Japan, in spite of China's participation in the war on the side of the Allies. Beginning with a demonstration of students in Beijing on 4 May 1919, a national movement emerged that was based on anti-imperialism – but particularly focused on the actions of the Beijing government. With support from merchants and workers as well as educational circles around the country, this marked "the beginning of the modern mass movement in China."[92] But the real story, as it were, of the creation of the Republic belonged to Sun Yat-sen, the Nationalist Party, and Chiang Kai-shek (so not the masses after all).[93] Seeing the corruption of the officials and warlords of the 1910s and 1920s, Sun prepared for the Northern Expedition. After his death in 1925, Chiang continued the task Sun had laid down, and the army of the "National Revolution" (*guomin geming*) proceeded to conquer central China in 1927 and the north in 1928. China was again unified, to the acclaim of the people. Since then, in this account, the government had entered the stage of tutelage (explained in civics and society textbooks), struggled to raise China's international position, begun to construct necessary infrastructure, and in sum was laying the basis for a strong future.

Fan and Han did not discuss the radical cultural changes associated with the New Culture and May Fourth movements: anti-Confucianism, free marriage, individualism, vernacular writing, and the like. Nor did they mention the Communist Party. They did, however, reframe the long narrative of Chinese history to culminate in the revolutionary moment. Now, this was an extended revolution not focused entirely on 1911 but on the period from the late Qing through the 1920s. Today's government, teachers were to emphasize, was called the "national government" because it belonged to the whole people. Also, the authors implied, this distinguished it from the "republic" that it superseded. On the one hand, the National Revolution had been necessary because the so-called republic was in fact an undemocratic plaything of corrupt officials, warlords, and imperialists. By implication, little better than the Qing. Writing on the brink of the Japanese invasion of China and with an eye on Europe as well, Fan and Han warned students: it was a dangerous world, "the arrow is fitted to the bowstring," and a second world war could erupt at any moment.[94] China's position was thus precarious in spite of the success of the National Revolution.[95] The domestic political situation had been normalized, in this account, but facing increased danger from abroad, the Chinese people needed not only to strengthen the military but to improve their knowledge and morality and – taking domestic crises into account as well – to increase their productivity and improve the economy as well. It was in this light that Fan and Han explained the New Life movement. Indeed, although they did not quite put it this way, Fan and Han

[92] Ibid., 4: 74.   [93] Ibid., 4: 127–145.   [94] Ibid., 4: 251–253.   [95] Ibid., 4: 264–265.

might be read as saying that the New Life movement was the logical culmination of the National Revolution, and both were part of a larger revolutionary project to turn the Chinese people into full citizens. China, teachers were to exhort, "was like a ship sailing through parlous seas and massive waves" but with careful steering the ship could be righted and kept on course.

For the China Bookstore writers Wang Zhicheng and Fei Xiewei, the ongoing revolution of the 1920s and 1930s might be seen as simultaneously a top-down and bottom-up movement.[96] Understandably, they did not quite say so in the political climate of the 1930s, for the Nanjing government was wary of bottom-up movements. Wang and Fei emphasized that the Nationalists' plan of "tutelage" was now necessary because the 1911 Revolution had failed. They said republicanism had met with initial failure because the political knowledge and ability of the people left them too weak, prey to strongmen: the old officials and the new warlords. They also implied that at another level, the distance from a monarchy with all power in the hands of one man to a republic with sovereignty vested in the people was simply too great to be traversed in a single step. China made a mistake in trying to simply copy the constitutions of existing republics. Now, fortunately, the Guomindang has seen the light and is building the new five-power constitution. This is what tutelage is training the people for. In the words of another history textbook, the people were to learn how to "use" democracy, and once they understood the Three People's Principles and the five-power constitution, they would be ready to practice it.[97] Tutelage should last five years (this was said in 1930).

Wang and Fei, in a later volume of their history textbook series, for more advanced students, explained the roots of warlordism in the rise of regional armies designed to fight the Taipings in the mid-nineteenth century.[98] Seeing their mutual advantage, in the twentieth-century warlords learned to cooperate with the imperialist powers, which gave them cash and arms, thus creating a two-headed enemy for the revolution to defeat. Where the early Republic could claim success – as this and so many textbooks insisted – was in merging the five races into one Chinese people.[99] This did not mean that everyone had become alike but that all were equal as citizens. Actually, if Wang and Fei had remembered an earlier chapter in their book, they might have reminded students that this process had begun under the Qing.

At the same time, Wang and Fei suggested a bottom-up view of the continuing revolution in their discussion of the May Fourth and May Thirtieth movements.[100] Their calls to oppose imperialism and overthrow the warlords

---

[96] Wang Zhicheng and Fei Xiewei, *Lishi jiaoxuefa*, 2: 142–154.
[97] Zhou Chuangui, *Minzhong lishi keben jiaoxuefa*, p. 123.
[98] Wang Zhicheng and Fei Xiewei, *Lishi jiaoxuefa*, 3: 125–127.
[99] Ibid., 2: 153–154.   [100] Ibid., 2: 125–133.

had entered the consciousness of the masses. Wang and Fei not only implied that the revolution was ongoing from 1911, but also that in many ways it had begun by the mid-1800s. In the wake of the Opium War – which China lost but again which displayed popular resistance Chinese could take pride in – there arose the Taiping Heavenly Kingdom.[101] This was nothing less than an attempt to "arouse the national consciousness of the masses, go on to overthrow the Manchus, and carry out the national revolution." Wang and Fei cited progressive aspects of the Taiping program, such as the solar calendar, prohibitions on slavery and concubinage, and promotion of women officials. This was a fairly extreme view. Although, as we have seen, Nationalist historians were more sympathetic to the Taipings than the previous generation, more typical was the evaluation of Jin Zhaozi.[102] For Jin the Taiping leaders did demonstrate a spirit of nationalism, but they were misled by their monarchical views, and their Christian-influenced religion did not appeal to most Han. It was thus possible for the Qing to "attack Han with Han" – something to be regretted to be sure, but also a turning point. For Jin pointed out that this marked the beginning of a shift in the balance of power between Han and Manchus and would eventually lead to the overthrow of the Qing.[103]

For Wang and Fei, it was a tragedy that the Taipings lost, for this allowed the forces of imperialism to increase their grip. Echoing left-wing themes of the day, they argued that imperialism was essentially economic (that is, in addition to its obvious military aspects): Western powers first unloaded their overproduction of manufactured goods, which harmed Chinese handicrafts, and then set up sweatshops to take advantage of cheap Chinese labor.[104] The failure of the Qing to respond to these pressures gave rise to two movements: one for constitutional reform and one for revolution.[105] The problem with constitutionalism, in this analysis, was the Qing's own unwillingness to give up any of its power. That left revolution as the only alternative, as Sun Yat-sen clearly saw. "Why did Sun Yat-sen promote revolution? He saw that imperialist oppression of China was increasing all the time, so he determined that to save China, we had to overthrow the corrupt Manchu-Qing government and establish a republic." This was the heart of "national revolution" that continued beyond 1911 through the 1920s and into the 1930s.

By the 1930s, history textbooks taught that the 1911 Revolution was "nationalist" in a double sense. World-historical currents were showing that no people could oppress and rule over another people: "every people has the right of self-determination."[106] To overthrow the Qing was thus to carry out the principles of equality and liberty, and the means by which the five peoples of Han, Manchu,

---

[101] Ibid., 2: 66–67, 75–78. [102] Jin Zhaozi, *Xin Zhonghua benguoshi jiaokeshu*, 2: 80–85.
[103] Ibid., 2: 85. [104] Wang Zhicheng and Fei Xiewei, *Lishi jiaoxuefa*, 2: 93–94.
[105] Ibid., 2: 109–117. [106] Jin Zhaozi, *Xin Zhonghua benguoshi jiaokeshu*, 2: 123.

Mongol, Hui, and Tibetan would be unified. In broad historical perspective, nationalist revolution combined the goals of ridding China of the Qing monarchy and of all imperialist oppression. In this sense, the failure of 1911 was but a lesson in how to create the new China under the Nanjing government.[107]

The history of China is a most glorious history. Since the Yellow Emperor, our material life and our cultural life have consistently progressed. And since the Qin and Han, we have created a majestic unity that stabilized the foundations of the state and made China the leader of East Asia. Although there were periods of fighting and disunion, and even invasions by outside forces, the country always soon returned to its original state. And moreover, this is how what were originally distant regions were incorporated into "one family," leading to the assimilation of foreign groups. Isn't it true that China's constant progress is a wonderful bequest of our ancestors and our historical glory? Unfortunately, in the past decades foreign incursions have been unceasing, and when we examine the records, we find much "national humiliation." But if we remember the past, it can serve as our teacher. If only all the people living in China love and respect their history and endeavor to maintain its glory, then China will emerge even stronger – as we have seen in numerous historical cases. Those who know history, know how to deal with the present.[108]

These concluding words to a 1920 upper primary school history textbook stated a kind of creed. Or even more succinctly: love for country entails love for its history.

Chinese elites in the late Qing period regarded history textbooks as one important tool in the socialization of youth – a socialization process that involved the acquisition of the memory of the Chinese people. The construction of a common past would define the "Chinese" mnemonic community.[109] The goal of nation building through identification with the Chinese past only intensified in the republican period. Identification is less about memorizing historical details than remembering moments of glory and humiliation that somehow define the present day. History textbooks also aid forgetting, by leaving out stories that do not contribute to the larger goal. History textbooks repackaged stories that had long circulated in popular as well as elite forms. These stories now showed where "the Chinese" came from and how their civilization developed.

If we grant that two of the characteristics of modern historiography include treating the nation as the main historical subject and narrating a story in the form of more or less linear, progressive time, then history textbooks were the chief means of disseminating modern historical approaches. This is not to say that only the nation served as historical agents or subjects: individuals, dynasties,

---

[107] Zhu Yixin, *Lishi jiaoben jiaoxuefa*, 3: 56–57.
[108] Zhuang Qichuan and Lü Simian, *Xinshi lishi jiaoshoufa*, 6: 36b.
[109] For "mnemonic communities," see Eviatar Zerubavel, *Social Mindscapes*, pp. 97–99.

regions (the "West"), localities, civilizations, religions, and institutions could all be treated as historical subjects, but the majority of historical work focused on the nation. Nor is it to say that time was uniformly linear: there could also be stagnation, reversals, cycles, and so forth, but the basic story was presented in a linear framework. Thus traditional historical forms such as chronicles, moral fables, "mirrors for kings," and myths were replaced by careful narrativization.[110] Textbooks invariably abandoned the traditional annals-biography form of history writing and divided up their contents in roughly chronological sections and chapters. Thus did historical narrative become the primary mode of the discipline.[111]

History textbooks in the late Qing and early Republic tended to sound very objective. They recounted events – flatly – and they did not pass explicit judgments. Lü Simian, for one, explicitly announced his intention to objectively report on the "facts" as recorded in texts whose reliability could be evaluated and to avoid judgments, except when they were generally held by consensus of historians.[112] That was all very well, but in fact history textbooks rested on a hidden normative structure. True, they abandoned the traditional conflation of history with the cosmic, moral Dao, but they implicitly or explicitly praised that which contributed to China's development.[113] History was no longer seen as the field where moral forces played out their fates, but it could not be divorced from the question of what was good for China. From the creation of the Han or Chinese people 4000 or more years ago to the anti-imperialist movements of today: this was the very story of China. Scholars and educators saw modern schools as the key to creating an enlightened citizenry that was both progressive and equipped with a sense of its great cultural traditions. In this educational project, the discipline of history was designed to foster identity and values.

---

[110] Hayden White, "The Value of Narrativity in the Representation of Reality"; and "The Politics of Historical Interpretation," p. 60.

[111] See Prasenjit Duara, *Rescuing History from the Nation*; Q. Edward Wang on "Narrating the Nation," pp. 103–133.

[112] Lü Simian, *Benguoshi*, p. 106.

[113] For the centrality of ethics to traditional Chinese historiography, see Shi Naide (Axel Schneider), "Minzu, lishi yu lilun"; On-cho Ng and Q. Edward Wang, *Mirroring the Past*, pp. x–xii.

7 The importance of space

The Chinese territory is large. The Chinese people are numerous. China's soils are fertile and her resources abundant. The Chinese climate is moderate. China is the largest country in Asia, and Asia is the largest continent in a world that is full of different countries found in several continents. Also, China had developed its resources, agriculture, and manufacturing from a very ancient period. If they learned nothing else from geography classes, children would have learned these lessons.[1]

Much geographical knowledge was conveyed through maps. Twentieth-century textbooks used birds-eye maps like that in Figure 34 that emphasized administrative regions and borders as well as physical features such as mountains and rivers. The earth's surface is defined by imaginary lines of latitude and longitude. But geography was a broad discipline that included everything that went into understanding how space was constituted: hence geography textbooks spoke of numerous issues that other subjects also covered: history, race, religion, languages, customs, and political systems.[2] Geography textbooks of course also covered "physical geography": climate, resources, geology, but this chapter focuses on their treatment of "human geography."

For example, a normal school geography textbook's section on "customs" described the development of Chinese civilization in admittedly rough terms: simplicity during the Shang dynasty; civilized pursuits during the Zhou; military pursuits during the Qin, making the people tough; classical studies during the Han, making scholars righteous; then, since the Jin dynasty (third century CE), the north has been occupied by Manchus and Mongols and other more martial races, while the Han have cowered in the south.[3] This metahistorical narrative of early triumph and long stagnation was in accord with the diagnosis of late Qing political reformers. The normal school textbook then offered

---

[1] The most complete overview is Yang Yao, *Zhongguo jinxiandai zhongxiaoxue dili jiaoyushi*, vol. 1.
[2] Geography textbooks noted their close relationship to history; see for example, Cai Hejian, *Zhejiang xiangtu dili jiaokeshu*, "Fanli" 凡例, 1: 2a.
[3] Xu Nianci, *Zhongguo dili*, pp. 30b–31a.

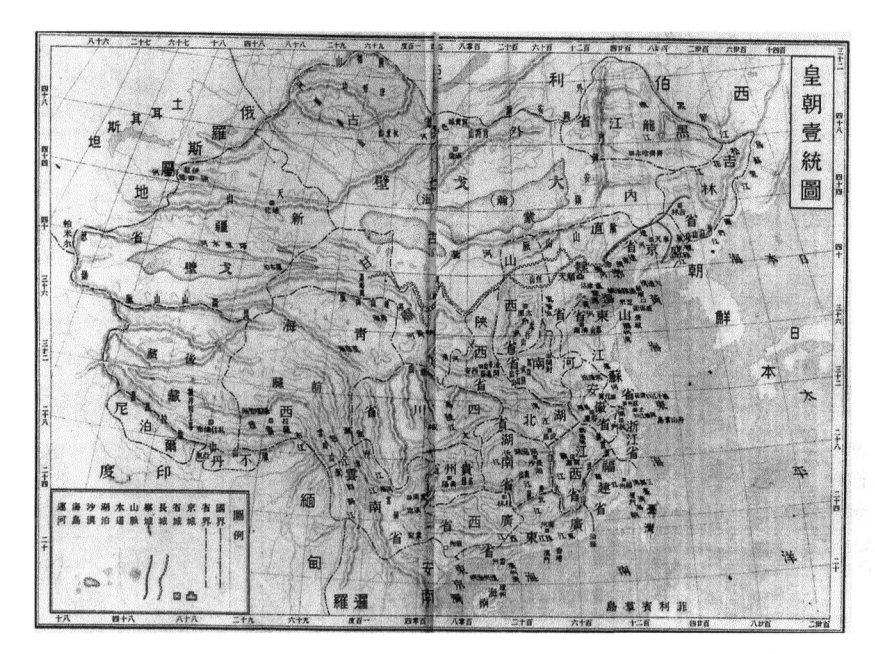

Figure 34 "General Map of the Dynasty."

a standard critique of contemporary Chinese culture, though with an unusual emphasis on gender inequality. The Chinese, it said, slighted women and valued men and practiced polygamy, which gave rise to quarrels in the family; and also, the economic opportunities open to women were very restricted. Science had failed to develop, leaving people to become superstitious idiots. People have become lazy, and the number of opium addicts increases while roads fall apart and are filled with filth. The textbook did praise the Chinese people as fundamentally frugal and diligent, idealistic, and even efficient, but blamed current "customs" for holding them back. A new morality was needed.

If readers and morality textbooks told students how to behave, and history textbooks told them who they were, then geography textbooks told them what they might become. Geography was not destiny: it was potential. A teacher's manual from 1906 proclaimed that the first goal of geography lessons was to teach patriotism, while other goals included fostering students' imaginations.[4] Thus geography would ultimately help students to enrich and strengthen China. Geography would encourage enterprise and help the state in raising revenues. It would enable students to protect "the old state" while opening up "new lands."

---

[4] Guan Qi, *Zhongguo dili xin jiaoke jiaoshoufa*, "zonglun" 總論, pp. 1a–b.

The study of the terrains, climates, resources, manufactures, transportation and communication systems, and like questions was hardly new to late Qing China. Elites had long written about local and regional geography; traveler's reports were a major literary subgenre; and the imperial court was always interested in keeping track of the space of the empire – none more than the Qing court with its ever-expanding frontiers and tributary states.[5] Western techniques in cartography were adapted for court use by sojourning Jesuits in the sixteenth and seventeenth centuries. But only in the last years of the Qing did geography emerge as a distinct discipline that was yoked to patriotic goals.[6]

The premises of social Darwinism and progress were built into geography textbooks as much – or more – than history textbooks. Geography textbooks reflected new knowledge of the Western conception of international order based on sovereign nation-states. As Huang Donglan has noted, the notion of a clearly demarcated national territory was at odds with the traditional view of "imperial lands," some of which were frontier areas whose leaders were regarded as vassals of the Qing.[7] On the one hand, textbooks never spoke of supposedly traditional notions that "all lands under Heaven belong to the emperor." On the other, the modern Western notion of "sovereign territory" under the complete legal control of one authority was utterly foreign to the Chinese conception of rulership, and late Qing textbooks struggled to distinguish between lands governed (and taxed) by the bureaucracy directed by the imperial court, lands (tribes or kingdoms) that acknowledged the Qing emperor as their overlord and supported a small Qing military presence, and lands that occasionally sent tribute to the Qing emperor.

Borrowing notion of racial traits and national character from the Western sociobiology of the day, geography textbooks offered students simplistic equations: Chinese = diligent; mountain folk = stubborn; temperate climates = intelligent people. At the least, such generalizations gave children a handle on the world. As early as 1902, the Commercial Press published a translation of Shōei Yazu's world geography teaching that humans banded together in "societies" because the individual's survival depended on the group.[8] Whether society progressed beyond a primitive stage depended on two factors: geography (climate and natural resources) and race (physical strength and nature, including its ability to unify).[9] "If geographers can comprehend this, then they have grasped most of the reasons for the rise and fall of nations."

---

[5] Laura Hostetler, *Qing Colonial Enterprise*.
[6] Zou Zhenhuan, *Wan-Qing xifang dilixue zai Zhongguo*; Guo Shuanglin, *Xichao jidangxia de wan-Qing dilixue*; Kō Tōran [Huang Donglan], "Shinmatsu-Minkokuki chiri kyōkasho no kūkan hyōshō"; Ni Wenjun, "Jindai xueke xingcheng guochengzhong de wan-Qing dili jiaokeshu."
[7] Kō Tōran, "Shinmatsu-Minkokuki chiri kyōkasho no kūkan hyōshō," pp. 233–236.
[8] Shōei Yazu, *Wanguo dizhi*.   [9] Ibid., 1: 7b.

The geography curriculum

During the late Qing, before the birth of civics classes, it was geography textbooks that detailed the organs and functions of the government, listing the major bureaus and describing their functions, and offering a description of society. As we have seen, history had long held a major place in the textual traditions of China. What is today classified as geographic knowledge was largely subsumed under the category of history. Scholars were concerned with what happened where in their efforts to recapture the past. And emperors and generals were concerned with questions of terrain and conquest.[10] World geographies began to be published in the early nineteenth century as the threat from the West became visible. By the 1850s, missionary teaching texts included sections on races, political systems, and trade, as well as concepts of physical geography such as watersheds, climates, and geology.[11] This was knowledge both as abstract as the definition of the continents and as concrete as mining and agriculture.

Many Chinese scholars found missionary accounts limited. And many wanted to use social Darwinism, which missionaries disdained, to understand historical geography. A Darwinian approach to geography offered knowledge about China's place amid a world of different races and nation-states. New European and American ideas about the relationship between geography and politics filtered into China largely through Japan, which was equally interested in understanding imperialism. The critical issue for Chinese intellectuals was how to define "China" in territorial terms. Revolutionaries, by emphasizing Han ethnicity, risked splitting the Qing Empire apart by giving legitimacy to the national aspirations of non-Han peoples, including the despised Manchus as well as Mongols, Tibetans, and Uighurs. (Though revolutionaries could, as we have seen, make historical claims to Han overlordship of the territories of such peoples.) Reformers like Liang Qichao, in contrast, argued that China could be conceived as a heartland that politically included dependent regions which shared enough of a common culture to be considered a single nation.

As with the other modern disciplines, Chinese educators learned much from Japan. Geography textbooks in Japan in the 1870s were based both on traditional geographies and on translations of Western textbooks.[12] They became more systematic in the 1880s, and students were also expected to explore their local geographies.[13] In the 1890s, more cultural geography was introduced to textbooks – a model the Chinese were to follow – and they exhibited a more explicitly patriotic flavor. Textbooks gave full accounts of areas associated with

---

[10] Laura Hostetler, *Qing Colonial Enterprise*.
[11] Zou Zhenhuan, "Shilun wan-Qing jindai dilixue jiaokeshu de biancuan," pp. 273–278.
[12] Kaigo Tokiomi and Naka Arata, *Kindai Nihon kyōkasho sōsetsu*, pp. 381–396.
[13] Ibid., pp. 402–421.

218 Educating China

Japan, especially Korea and Manchuria and also Taiwan. A 1903 Ministry of Education geography textbook proclaimed: "Our great Japanese Empire is composed out of many islands. Of these, the five biggest are Honshu, Shikoku, Kyushu, Hokkaido, and Taiwan."[14] A decade later the Korean peninsula was added. In terms of world geography, by the 1890s Japanese textbooks taught the theory of the five races, which were ranked according to their supposed degree of civilization, with the White and Yellow races at the top.[15] But it was not that simple, as textbooks also stated that "most" of the Yellow or Mongolian race were only semi-civilized, living under absolutist monarchies, displaying arrogance, and believing in myths. Simple racial theory did not fit Japanese needs very well, and after 1902 textbooks focused directly on civilization rather than race. Chinese textbooks never really followed this final turn, however. They continued to emphasize the importance of race – yet they did not confuse race with destiny. Geography offered ways of understanding topology, climate, and resources that promised to open roads to civilization.

Like history classes, late Qing geography classes were designed to reinforce pupils' patriotic spirit.[16] In the 1902 proposed curriculum, students were to begin with the earth and the solar system and gradually narrow their focus to continents, countries, and finally the geography of China.[17] In the 1904 and 1906 curriculums, however, lower primary school students started with the local, in parallel fashion to the history curriculum. In the first two grades of primary school, students learned of nearby roads, villages, mountains, rivers, and temples to worthies, whereas in year 3 students went on to their county and prefecture and began their study of China.[18] In year 4 students concentrated on Chinese territory and its famous mountains and rivers, and in year 5 looked at China and its neighboring countries.[19] Students were thus to understand China's place in the world. It is as if the Ministry of Education assumed modern patriotism rested on the extension of a concrete sense of locality to the more abstract sense of a territory defined historically and represented by lines on a map.

Although the geographic concepts grew more complex at higher grade levels, the patriotic orientation of geography classes did not change.[20] Upper

---

[14] Monbushō, comp., *Shōgaku chiri*, vol. 16, p. 351.
[15] See the thorough discussion in Jiang Sun, "Blumenbach in East Asia," pp. 107–153.
[16] Shangwu yinshuguan, "Seventh category," in *Da Qing xin faling*, 1: 81b.
[17] Kecheng jiaocai yanjiusuo, ed., *20 shiji Zhongguo zhongxiaoxue kecheng biaozhun*, vol. 13, pp. 3–4.
[18] See Cheng Meibao [May-bo Ching], "You aixiang er aiguo." Temples to worthies were sites of sacrifices performed to Confucian sages of the past. Again, the theme of emulation of the good and wise is seen in the schools, which also ignored the much larger number of non-Confucian temples.
[19] Shangwu yinshuguan, "Seventh category," in *Da Qing xin faling*, 2: 5a–6a; Kecheng jiaocai yanjiusuo, ed., *20 shiji Zhongguo zhongxiaoxue kecheng biaozhun*, vol. 13, pp. 5–6.
[20] Shangwu yinshuguan, "Seventh category," in *Da Qing xin faling*, 1: 81b; 1: 74a.

primary school students concentrated solely on Chinese geography, whereas middle school students studied both Chinese and foreign geography, including such global phenomena as climate and races.[21] By the first years of the twentieth century, geography textbooks were playing a large role in disseminating the new view of national territory as definite and of concern to every citizen. Thirty-odd geography textbooks compiled by Chinese authors were in print by 1906 and well over 100 by the end of the dynasty.[22] Publishers were quick to understand the importance of maps and illustrations.

The pictures in Figure 35 are from a primary school textbook that featured descriptions of Chinese cities and physical features. Most geography textbooks listed the new railway and telegraph lines that were reshaping China and emphasized the general importance of transportation and communication links. Long reliant on rivers and canals, China looked to railroads to develop the interior and bring crops and natural resources to markets.

Unlike the disciplines of self-cultivation and history, geography was little changed by the 1911 Revolution. In November 1912 the Ministry of Education defined the goals of primary school geography classes as basic knowledge of the surface of the globe and the living conditions of human groups, and the terrain and conditions of China – again, "in order to foster a patriotic spirit."[23] Gradually, however, Republican-era textbooks began to emphasize the theme of "lost territory" due to the imperialist incursions faced by the late Qing.[24] It is not that late Qing textbooks had ignored the facts: the loss of Taiwan; the loss of supposedly suzerain lands such as Korea, Burma, and Vietnam and other territories; the leaseholds and concessions given foreign powers on the Mainland. But they were not the focus of concern that they became later, when they became the prime symbol of China's "national humiliation." As we have seen, late Qing textbooks still reflected something of a worldview not accustomed to the notion of national sovereignty. Painful as the loss of, say, Taiwan was, it did not give rise to any kind of irredentism; likewise, no matter how annoying was, for example, the foreign-governed International Settlement in Shanghai, it was but a pinprick in a China that was not yet defined as inviolable.

In 1912, proclaiming China to be the state of the "five races" – Han, Manchu, Mongol, Hui, and Tibetan – the Republic laid claim to be the successor state of the Qing Empire, and the notion of national territory was clarified. This was also to let go of territorial claims to the peripheral states, at least in terms of international law, although textbooks still sometimes continued to refer to the

---

[21] Kecheng jiaocai yanjiusuo, ed., *20 shiji Zhongguo zhongxiaoxue kecheng biaozhun*, vol. 13, pp. 48–49.
[22] Zou Zhenhuan, "Shilun wan-Qing jindai dilixue jiaokeshu," pp. 281, 289.
[23] Kecheng jiaocai yanjiusuo, ed., *20 shiji Zhongguo zhongxiaoxue kecheng biaozhun*, vol. 1, p. 64; vol. 13, pp. 7, 50–51.
[24] Kō Tōran, "Shinmatsu-Minkokuki chiri kyōkasho no kūkan hyōshō," pp. 242–258.

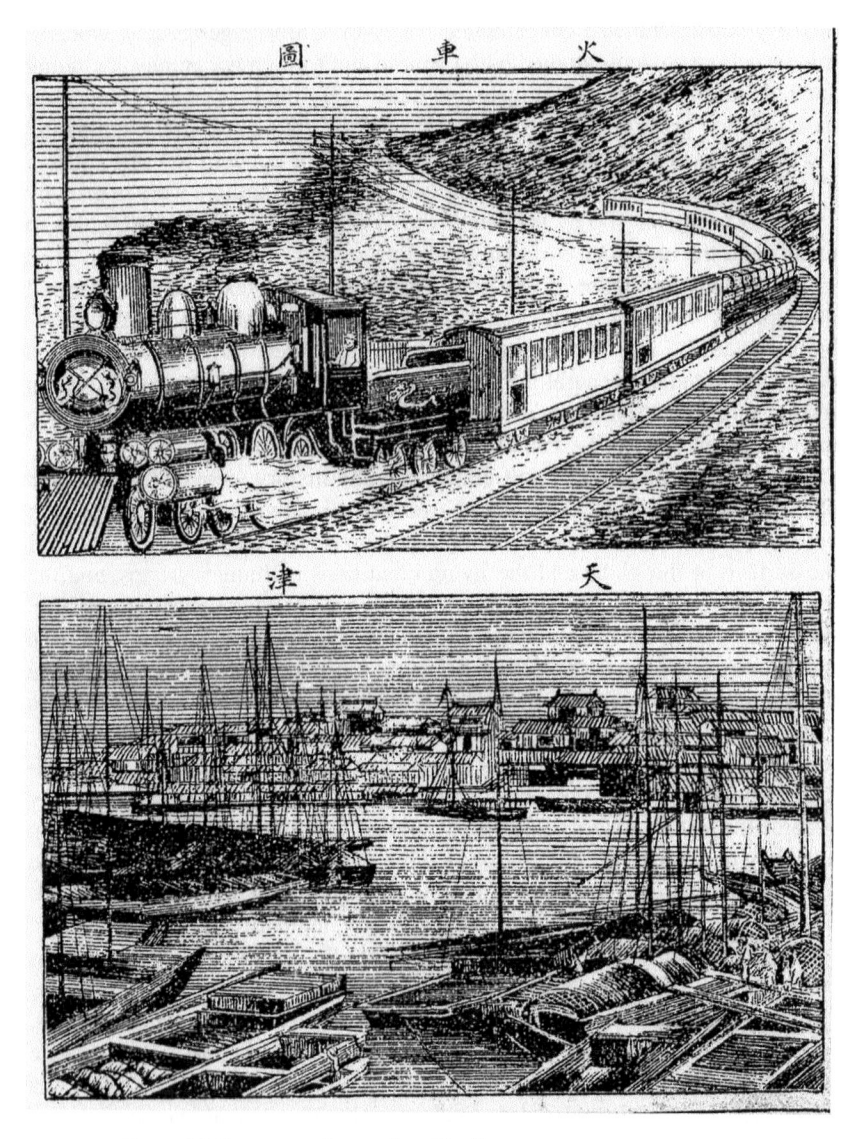

Figure 35 Transportation: trains, Tianjin.

"loss" of Korea or Burma. And it was to reassert claims to ultimate sovereignty over the foreign concessions and leaseholds.

The cosmopolitan approach of the 1923 curriculum proposals was reflected in geography course outlines, though naturally emphasis was still placed on learning about China.[25] One of the aims of lower middle school geography classes was to expand students' sense of connection with the entire world, while another aim was to nourish students' spirit of self-help and autonomy. "This subject should emphasize the lives of the whole of humanity, and so we should first break down the division between Chinese and foreign geographies, while we must only note the relationship of China to the rest of the world to enable us to determine its place in the world." The point was not to neglect China but to highlight its similarities, where appropriate, with other parts of the world, and especially how it fit into a global geography. Students should not begin their studies with their home province or with China but first gain a sense of the basic geographic features of the world as a whole. This would include the major continents, oceans, mountain ranges, rivers, climates, natural resources, and economic production, and then the world's races and nations, and transportation and communication networks.

This approach to geography changed again with the triumph of the Nationalists. By 1929, the Three People's Principles had redefined the subject of geography.[26] "Nationalism" required the study of the range of local customs in the various regions of China "in order to foster national spirit," even while study of international conditions should foster a world perspective. "Democracy" required knowledge of the geographical context of government policies and foreign relations, in order to turn students into "complete citizens." And "people's livelihood" could foster a positive and optimistic spirit by teaching how the needs of the people for food, clothing, shelter, and transportation could be met through the development of natural resources. Upper and lower middle school graduates alike were expected to be able to apply Sun Yat-sen's theories of modernization and to seek equality for China in the international sphere. The 1932 curriculum was similarly patriotic, emphasizing the need to protect China's territorial integrity.[27] Geography was a very practical discipline.

Commercial Press, Civilization Press, and modern Chinese geography

Probably the best-selling geography textbook of the late Qing and early Republic was that by Tu Ji for the Commercial Press, which went through many editions starting in 1905. But it was not alone.[28] Geography textbooks came in

---

[25] Kecheng jiaocai yanjiusuo, ed., *20 shiji Zhongguo zhongxiaoxue kecheng biaozhun*, vol. 13, pp. 9–10, 52–54.
[26] Ibid., vol. 13, pp. 55–61.   [27] Ibid., vol. 13, pp. 62–72.
[28] The first modern geography textbooks written by Chinese are usually attributed to Zhang Wenxiang (1866–1933), a teacher at the Nanyang Academy in Shanghai at the turn of the century who was close to the revolutionaries there. Zhang published his *Introductory Geography Textbook* (*Chudeng dili jiaokeshu* 初等地理教科書) and his *Middle-level Chinese Geography*

many forms, some beginning with the solar system and the earth, some emphasizing the physical terrain of regions of China, some dealing more with human geography: the distribution of races, political systems, and religions in China and the world. Tu Ji (1856–1921) was educated in the Confucian classics. He became a *jinshi* and joined the Hanlin Academy in 1892, and later joined the military staff in Heilongjiang to take charge of map-making while also working on a gazetteer for the province. He taught at the Imperial University (predecessor to Peking University), and in 1911 he was quick to support the revolution.

In his preface to the first edition of his *Chinese Geography*, Tu Ji began with the standard definition of the state that had become widely used in the previous few years: a state consisted of a certain territory, people, and sovereignty.[29] Tu then added that this was why Mencius referred to the three treasures of the lords as land, people, and governance. And this is why the science of geography today studies the nature and relationships of the land, people, and sovereignty of every country. Tu Ji compared the Chinese to the owner of a vast manor filled with all sorts of objects randomly piled up everywhere: was an owner who did not even know what he possessed truly their owner? Chinese scholars have not paid sufficient attention to what China consisted of, and so left a vacuum where geographic knowledge should be. Tu granted that his own knowledge of geography was deficient, but he claimed to have traveled across most of China (excepting the far west and southwest), and so began teaching the subject.

Tu Ji described China in terms of its physical geography of mountains and rivers; its political geography of provinces and cities; and its human geography. Patriotically, Tu described China's natural resources and fertile soils as the best in the world.[30] But because production techniques remained backward, manufacturing and commerce had failed to develop. Farmers lacked knowledge of the best practices and equipment. Tu then described the agricultural products of various parts of China – wheat in the north, rice in the south, tea in central China, the different fruits, and so forth, as well as commercial crops such as cotton, silk, and opium. Coal and iron and other minerals were abundant, and Western geologists had calculated that Shanxi alone could supply all the world's coal needs for 5000 years.[31] Manufacturing in China had begun well, in Tu's view, culminating early in fine porcelain, lacquer, ivory, and other luxury products, but had not progressed in 2000 years.[32] Tu seems to have regarded foreign trade as healthy, welcoming China's opening to the world.

Human geography, the *Chinese Geography* discussed both in terms of population statistics and in terms of the fundamental ways of living of various

(*Benguo zhongdeng dili jiaokeshu* 本國地理教科書) in 1901, and several more textbooks over the next few years. Zou Zhenhua, "Shilun wan-Qing jindai dilixue jiaokeshu de biancuan," pp. 280–281.
[29] Tu Ji, *Zhongguo dili jiaokeshu*, 1: "*Zixu*" 自序.
[30] Ibid., 2: 70. [31] Ibid., 2: 71. [32] Ibid., 2: 73.

groups. Tu divided the people of China into four main groups by language: Chinese speakers; Mongolian and Manchu speakers; Tibetan speakers; and various highland tribal speakers (of the far west and southwest).[33] In terms of racial analysis, Tu commented, most of these peoples possessed yellow skins and black hair and eyes and tended to be smaller than Europeans but larger than Japanese. Tu subdivided his four language groups into a total of seven distinct peoples. Chinese speakers were simply the Han race (*zu*), who had long dominated China proper and now Manchuria and Xinjiang as well. Moving into the realm of historical geography, Tu traced the Han people back 5000 years to nomadic tribes of the Kunlun Mountains who moved east, defeating native peoples, and occupied what are the northwestern districts of China today. The other peoples of China, Tu traced to other origins.

Tu described the "character" of the Chinese in what he admitted were very general terms: frugality; conservatism but coupled with a willingness to change when the advantage of doing so was clear; endurance; excessive idealism; talented in business; and lacking national spirit.[34] The lack of a unifying religion and constitutional government, coupled with strong local links and different customs, explained the lack of national spirit for Tu. Frugality he attributed to Confucianism. National spirit was prevalent in the ancient Zhou period, he claimed, but then degenerated. Though Tu cited a Japanese source for these remarks, he was in fact echoing the general attitudes of late Qing reformers. As we have seen in the previous chapters, in adopting the view that linear progress was the natural course of history, reformers were led to the conclusion that China, in spite of brilliant beginnings, had made a wrong turn somewhere.

There was a good deal of history in Tu's work, and also a good deal of what would now be called politics. The *Chinese Geography* included lengthy descriptions of the structure of government, beginning with the royal house and including the central and local bureaucracies, the military, the traditional and modern educational systems, the punishment system (Tu noted China did not have a legal system distinct from regular administration), and foreign relations. As for "religion," Tu began to exempting Confucianism from this category, on the grounds it was an upper-class ethical system without superstitious elements.[35] Tu began his account of religions with Buddhism, which he noted spread across China in the Han dynasty. Unfortunately, in the past few centuries Buddhist monks had become ignorant mendicants, despised by all except women and lower-class men. Tu then offered brief descriptions of Lamaism, Daoism, White Lotus (which he considered a branch of Daoism), Islam, Christianity, Nestorianism (a branch of Christianity), and primitive animism. Although he discussed religion as a political issue, Tu also noted that the government was not overly concerned with religious affairs.[36]

[33] Ibid., 2: 7–13.   [34] Ibid., 2: 15–17.   [35] Ibid., 2: 63   [36] Ibid., 2: 64.

Hou Hongjian's *Geography Textbook* was published by Civilization Press in 1905.[37] Hou (1872–1961) was to become a prominent educational official in the late Qing and Republic. Hou had studied in Japan, and his textbook was based on Japanese models. In discussing physical geography, Hou introduced the Darwinian notion of the evolution of the human species from animals over vast eons of time.[38] Numerous characteristics distinguished humans from their nearest animal relatives the apes, such as the location and size of the brain, upright posture, language, tools, and more developed consciousness. Humans spread throughout the world, human societies proving themselves capable actors in the universal struggle for survival. This was due both to national selection and to artificial selection.[39]

More systematically than Tu, Hou applied Darwinian principles to the development of the races, which he said were shaped by national struggle and competition.[40] And the very survival of humankind depended on such struggle. Though never defining "race" exactly, Hou insisted it did not merely amount to skin color; rather, numerous factors worked to distinguish the races and ethnic groups from one another – height, hair, and head shape, for example. Skin color also changed in response to different environments. Detailed consideration of racial differences brought Hou to the importance of environment, the differences between civilized and primitive countries, and the ultimate survival of the race. "Each environment leads to a different set of experiences, which are enough to change [a race's] nature. The outcome of the struggle for survival of the fittest among races leads to new mutations. This is the cause of the elimination [of some races]; it is also in accord with the universal principle of evolution."[41]

When he turned to human geography, Hou began his discussion with a description of the evolution of the state out of small communities and tribes.[42] The state emerged as stronger tribes conquered and swallowed weaker tribes. Implicitly, at least, Hou used social Darwinism to explain the structure of the state and the variety of strong and weak, civilized and barbarian states. The nature of the state, however, depends on its people. If the people are productive and understand the law and the political system, then the state will be rich and strong. The emperor or ruler, Hou said, was the representative (*daibiao*) of the people, chosen by them to carry out the affairs of state. Hou was not

---

[37] Hou Hongjian, *Zhongdeng dili jiaokeshu*. The copyright page is dated Guangxu 21 (1895), but this was evidently a typographical error for Guangxu 31 (1905); references to data from 1902 and the lack of references to the Qing court's plan for constitutional reform suggest the book was written about 1903–1904.
[38] Ibid., p. 51a. [39] Ibid., p. 52b. [40] Ibid., pp. 52b–56b.
[41] Ibid., p. 56b. In his later discussions of race, Hou was taxonomic. For example, there were three subgroups of the White race: Latins, Teutons, and Slavs. Customs were determined by the physical terrain and livelihood, climate, and race. Ibid., pp. 68a–69a, 70a–71a.
[42] Ibid., pp. 57a–b.

referring to institutions such as elections but rather to the moral nature of the rulership as absolutely disinterested commitment to the welfare of the whole people. Without this kind of ruler, the state would perish.

Hou implied that all countries – at least all countries destined to survive in the struggle for existence – were on a path of development from primitive through various stages of development and finally to the civilized.[43] At the same time, the actual fact was of simultaneous difference. Hou listed Britain, Germany, and the United States as "first-class" civilized countries; other European countries, some South American countries, and Japan as "second-class" civilized countries; and so forth. The primitive basically refers to nomadic tribes. Hou listed Egypt, Greece, and India as countries that were once civilized but today cannot be considered civilized. Perhaps China, he suggested, fit in this category. Most people regarded China as semi-developed, according to Hou. The question was how to become a civilized country.

In the usual political taxonomy of the day, Hou distinguished among forms of government (*zhengti*) as basically monarchical and democratic.[44] Monarchies are further divided between absolute and constitutional forms. At the present, the world's most absolutist states were Russia and China. In constitutional monarchies, the king's power is balanced by the parliament, and the constitution guarantees their subjects' rights to political participation. The result, Hou said, was a system suited to advanced societies. His praise was even more fulsome for the capacity of republics to elect the best leaders, who would be committed to the public weal. The rest of the volume discussed the military, national economy, and infrastructure – those elements associated with advanced societies and productivity such as good shipping, railroads, telegraphs, schools, and, not least, hygiene.

As for character and customs, Hou offered measured praise of the Chinese people as hard-working and determined, their enterprises successful, and the learning of their middle and upper classes as excellent, but he thought they lacked independence and creativity.[45] As Hou himself pointed out, this was the diagnosis of Westerners. Japanese, he thought, had the diligence of the Chinese plus the independence Chinese lacked. Manchus, he criticized for their arrogance and unreliability. In discussing Westerners, he reflected disdain for "Latins," while praising the Teutonic Britons, Germans, and Americans for their diligence, simplicity, and frugality, intelligence, and spirit of enterprise.

Other late Qing geographies: race, religion, and government

Most geography textbooks classified people by race, not language. "Race," however, was seldom defined but rather assumed to be obvious. Race was

[43] Ibid., pp. 57b–59a.   [44] Ibid., pp. 59a–60b.   [45] Ibid., p. 69a.

essentially skin color, which also corresponded to territory. Geography textbooks often began with a description of the world's major races, and then defined the sub-races of China. Usually, textbooks stated that the world consisted of five major races, though note was made of other theories, such as three races or six races. Yellow, White, Brown, Red, and Black. Textbooks in the early 1900s did not generally suggest that any other meaningful differences existed among the races but simply listed major "skin colors" and their geographical distribution in a section on race (*renzhong*).[46] (In more sophisticated accounts, bone structure, skull shape, body size were also part of the definition of race, but this mattered little to textbooks). Racial taxonomy had as much to do with place as ancestry. East Asia: Yellows (Mongols); Europe: Whites (or Caucasians when Southwest Asia, i.e., today's "Middle East" and India are added); Southeast Asia and Oceania: Browns (Malays); the Americas: Reds (Indians); Africa: Blacks (Negroes). One more slightly scientific approach used climate to explain skin color: temperate climates produced the Yellows, cold climates the Whites, and hot climates the Blacks.[47]

Some geography textbooks did stress the fear of extinction that much of the reformist press emphasized. One discussion of the world's races limited them to three: Mongols, Caucasians, and Malays.[48] Mongols, also called the Yellow race, are Asians, subdivided among Han, Tibetans, Southerners (Cochin, *jiaozhi*), and Siberians. The Siberians are further divided among Tungusics (Manchus and northern Koreans), Mongols, Turks, and Japanese. This taxonomic approach was then carried through to Caucasians and Malays. Then race was associated with national character: Japanese are warlike and capable of surviving in a competitive world; southern Asians are stupid and face the prospect of slavery; Chinese are diligent and frugal, developed since ancient times but prone to an individualism that weakens the state in the international sphere. "Scholars of racial science say that the Yellow race will survive but the Black, Red, and Brown races will become extinct." Thus the Chinese people should rally themselves. That said, geography textbooks did not tend to claim that essential qualities of races led to success or failure, but rather emphasized the different degrees of civilization achieved by different peoples (not exactly the same thing as races). Whether societies or peoples or nations or races, a threefold or fourfold division applied. That is, there were the civilized, the semi-civilized, the uncivilized, and the downright primitive.[49]

---

[46] For example, Wang Bangshu, *Zhongguo dili jiaokeshu* (n.p.: Nanyang guanshuju, 1907); Xu Nianci, *Zhongguo dili*, 28a–30a; Zhou Yunlin, *Mingde xuetang dili kecheng* (no publishing information), pp. 33b–34b.

[47] Tan Lian, *Dili jiaokeshu xiangjie*, 3: 3b.

[48] I.e., Yellow, White, and Brown. Hu Shitan, *Dili jiangyi*, pp. 11a–12a.

[49] Wang Bangshu, *Zhongguo dili jiaokeshu*, 1: 7a.

Whereas some textbooks began by listing the world's races, others began with Asia or Chinese. One upper primary school text described the Yellow race as consisting of two branches: the Kunlun and the Altaic.[50] In passing, the textbook noted that Westerners also called the Yellow race the Mongoloid Race, which it said should be taken as a compliment, marking respect for the race's courage and ferocity on the basis of the Mongol invasion of Europe. The Han, Hui, and Tibetans belonged to the Kunlun branch, whereas the Tungusics and Tartars belonged to the Altaic branch. In this account – following the Western origins theory discussed in Chapter 5 – the Miao people were the original inhabitants of China, occupying the shores of the Yellow and Yangzi Rivers, but they were driven south by the more intelligent Han people. Han strength grew from ancient times through the Tang dynasty, but their martial vigor has declined since then. Other groups include the Tungusics, Mongols, Turks, and Tibetans.

Racial distinctions were fundamental to textbooks. In a geography textbook published by a government school in the late Qing (Figure 36), the five races of the world were given more scientific-sounding names instead of being color-coded: Negroid, Malay, Mongolian (center), [Amer-]Indian, and Caucasian. In fact, all geography textbooks noted that the major races could be subdivided into numerous sub-races. This was a necessary move for talking about the Han and other Chinese peoples. A Commercial Press normal school textbook stated:

It was the Han race that developed China. They first emerged from the Pamir plateau, moving east along the [Yellow and Wei] rivers to expel the Miao. They gradually developed culture along the rivers, multiplied, and spread to the Huai and Yangzi river plains and then to the southern coast. The Han thus held all of China proper. They generally held the emperorship, and they were the earliest race to become civilized, always following morality and political principles. No other race can match their pure natures or their intelligence. It is only because they over-valued civilized affairs [neglecting the practical and the military] that they developed vulgar and decadent ways and ceased to progress.[51]

This normal school textbook then went on to describe the other races of China in terms of skin color, eye color, head shape, and main places of origin and settlement.

Most late Qing geography textbooks thus told the same story of the origins and development of the Han race as did history textbooks. Not all geography textbooks followed the Western origins theory of the Han, but they all tended to regard the Han as conquerors of the original inhabitants and to present China as a multi-ethnic place.[52]

---

[50] Tan Lian, *Dili jiaokeshu xiangjie*, 2: 17b.   [51] Xu Nianci, *Zhongguo dili*, p. 28b.
[52] For example, Wang Bangshu, *Zhongguo dili jiaokeshu*, 1: 11b–12a.

Figure 36 The world's major races.

In all, geography textbooks treated races essentially like nations: groups of peoples each with their own continuous history. Genealogies were frequently provided as groups moved around and their names changed. The Mongols, for example, had originated in Siberia but moved to Mongolia; previously they had been the Xiongnu. Manchus were previously known as the Xianbei. Geography textbooks understandably tended to include different races, or sub-races, or ethnic groups under the broad national label of "Chinese" – understandably, because it was court policy to equate the Qing empire with the Chinese nation.[53]

But not all textbooks took this position. Revolutionaries insisted the Manchus were a foreign race and, as such, the Qing dynasty represented illegitimate

---

[53] Gang Zhao, "Reinventing China."

imperial conquest of the real China, that is, the Han nation. One group of revolutionaries equated the Han race with the "national essence" of China – that is, the immense range of cultural productions, especially from the ancient period. The *Chinese Geography Textbook* of Liu Shipei is representative of this school of thought. As was his wont, Liu began with a series of citations from ancient texts to demonstrate the sophistication of ancient Chinese views of the earth.[54] Ancient Chinese geographical knowledge encompassed astronomy, topography, and human geography. For Liu, human geography referred to natural resources, census-taking, and maps, which ancient officials had managed, as well as popular customs and economic commodities, which officials had understood. In some ways, Liu's geography was a traditional-looking description of government administration. Typically for Liu, however, he did not think much of Chinese geographical practice of the last 2000 years. The ancients had practical knowledge, but with few exceptions later scholars simply commented on texts instead of studying the conditions of their own times.

Unlike some authors, Liu did not worry about the name of China, which he simply said was in ancient times "Zhongxia."[55] This, he said, was the land where the first state was established by the Han people, moving out of the west and eventually following the Yellow River, as they chased the Miao people south. Liu's emphasis on ethnicity was in accord with his concern to trace the borders and administrative districts of China as they changed over time. Liu's analysis of the races of China basically followed a common approach that he himself had helped to establish. He listed six groups: the Han of China proper, the descendants of the Miao in the south, the Tibetans of the west, the Turks of the far northwest, the "Tungusics" (Manchus) of the northeast, and the Mongols of the north.[56] The latter two groups were found in military bases throughout China, Liu noted. He distributed these six groups into two main categories: "Chinese" including Miao, Han, and Tibetans, and "Siberians" including Tungusics, Turks, and Mongols. There are also Arabs, Jews, Westerners, and Japanese in China. In his *Records of the Chinese Nation* written in 1903, Liu had emphasized that although races mixed, it was the historical case that since the time of the Yellow Emperor, foreign races assimilated into Han civilization, leaving the Han race dominant.[57] Liu recognized that it was not "blood" alone, but a range of factors, that determined a people's identity. Nonetheless, he generally equated the notion of a "people" (*renmin*) with that of a "race" (*zhongzu*) or "bloodline" (*xiezu*). He recognized that in historical fact many states were composed of several distinct peoples, but he thought such states were unstable. More successful were states formed out of a single

---

[54] Liu Shipei, *Zhongguo dili jiaokeshu*, in *Liu Shipei quanji*, 4: 371 (1a–b).
[55] Ibid., 4: 372–373 (1a–2a). [56] Ibid., 4: 389–390 (33b–36a).
[57] Liu Shipei, *Zhongguo minzu zhi*, in *Liu Shipei quanji*, 1: 598 (2a).

race.[58] Liu thus read much of the history of China in terms of a twinned set of territorial advances and retreats of the Han and their foreign enemies. The latest such enemy was the "Whites," Liu said, and he listed the recent "loss of coastal territories" to Russia, Britain, Germany, Portugal, and France in his geography textbook.[59] Still, he remained focused on the need to expel the Manchus forthwith. Although not the most consistent of social Darwinists, Liu postulated that the struggle between nations was a natural outgrowth of each society seeking its own benefit – and hence the impulse to "expel foreigners" was entirely natural as well.[60]

From one point of view, the racial taxonomies of reformers (who comprised most textbook writers and publishers) and revolutionaries were quite similar. Late Qing intellectuals saw that big groups – even perhaps assuming a single big group, that is, the monogenesis of humanity – gradually segmented into smaller and smaller subgroups, while subgroups mixed together, producing a constant change. In this view, of today's major races, none was entirely "pure" in the sense favored by Western race theorists. Nonetheless, no one doubted that races had formed; the question was how today's races could and should relate to one another. The Han nation was an ancient nation, but it needed the prod of nationalism to wake it up to its modern destiny. The Han nation was composed of various groups, but it was still a bloodline in its own right. So did the flow of blood matter, or did the progress of civilization matter? Liu Shipei's students would have learned that at any rate Manchus were Manchus, Han were Han, and Whites were Whites. However, even these basic taxonomies depended on context to make sense or be useful – for in the context of imperialist aggression against China, Liu grouped Japanese with the Whites.[61]

Religion was another key element of human geography, but textbooks were generally content to list and briefly describe the world's major religions, or at least those that could be found in China. Generally, the religions that students should know about were Confucianism, Buddhism, Daoism, Lamaism (i.e., Tibetan Buddhism), White Lotus (said to be an offshoot of Buddhism or Daoism), Islam, Catholicism, Protestantism, and Orthodox Christianity.[62] This account suggested that more local religions like China's Daoism and Japan's Shintoism were gradually diminishing. In another account, the chief Asian religions were listed as Hinduism, Buddhism, Islam, and also Judaism and Christianity, each associated with its geographical origins: India, Arabia, Israel.[63] Geography textbooks also listed Hinduism animism. Such primitive superstitions as animism could be assigned to backward races: the Chinese Miao, Africans, South Pacific islanders.

---

[58] Ibid., 1: 620 (43a). [59] Liu Shipei, *Zhongguo dili jiaokeshu* 4: 378 (12a).
[60] Liu Shipei, *Zhongguo minzu zhi*, 1: 597 (1a).   [61] Ibid., 1: 625 (53b).
[62] Tan Lian, *Dili jiaokeshu xiangjie*, 2: 22b–23a, 3: 4a–5a; Xu Nianci, *Zhongguo dili*, pp. 31a–b.
[63] Hu Shitan, *Dili jiangyi*, pp. 12b–13a.

The importance of space   231

It was not that textbook writers considered Confucianism to be a "religion" in the same sense as, say, Buddhism or Christianity, but that they lacked any other category in which to put it. Textbooks found the core of Confucianism in self-cultivation and governance. Confucianism thus could be considered a morality, a philosophy, and a theory of politics, but not a religion as such.[64] In the tension over how to classify Confucianism, textbooks reflected the difficulties late Qing intellectuals found in adopting the new category of "religion" (zongjiao). Confucianism – and other major traditions such as Buddhist and Daoist sects – had traditionally been considered Teachings (jiao), so if the latter were "religions," it seemed natural to consider Confucianism a religion as well, even if reservations had to be made.[65] But what was religion? Few textbooks bothered with a definition, but Zhou Zhenlin, for one, told his students that religion was a universal phenomenon referring to that which lay beyond human strength.[66] All people, he said, believed in a power that transcends humanity and controls human affairs. This describes both monotheistic and polytheistic belief systems.

As for government, geography textbooks again took a taxonomic approach that was in accord with the reformist literature of the day. There were autocracy, constitutional monarchism, and republicanism, as well as colonies. Existing nations could be matched to each category.[67] China, Persia, Russia, and Turkey were all examples of autocratic monarchies, although they were pursuing constitutionalism, and autocracy was disappearing from the globe. Constitutional monarchies included Japan, Britain, Germany, Austria, and other European countries. Republics included the United States, France, and Switzerland. "China is an independent empire, governed as an autocracy," explained an elementary Commercial Press textbook.[68] However, today China has begun to build constitutional government. Geography textbooks thus coordinated their materials with those of history and self-cultivation textbooks.

Another approach geography textbooks took was historical – to describe the evolution of the Chinese state from ancient tribal chiefs to imperial government – but often in a more theoretical way than history textbooks. Geographies might attribute the first real state-building to the Yellow Emperor.[69] The basic form of empire further evolved into aristocracy and then, with the Xia dynasty, the hereditary monarchy with the throne passed down from father to son. Thenceforth, evil rulers sometimes provoked rebellion and dynastic change, but the imperial form of government never changed. Today, however, under the influence of Western ideas, constitutionalism has become popular and the court is pursuing it. Again, the really key – if implicit – issue was how

[64] Wang Bangshu, Zhongguo dili jiaokeshu, 1: 12a.
[65] The issue was contentious. See Hsi-yuan Chen, "Confucianism Encounters Religion."
[66] Zhou Yunlin, Mingde xuetang dili kecheng, p. 36b.
[67] Tan Lian, Dili jiaokeshu xiangjie, 3: 4b–5a.   [68] Tong Zhencao, Jianyi dili keben, p. 14b.
[69] Xu Nianci, Zhongguo dili, p. 32a.

"civilized" China was. An account of governments in Asia distinguished among the nomadic tribes of the frontiers who lacked statehood; relatively primitive states based on village and tribal organization (such as Afghanistan or India); and the two types of monarchism: the constitutional monarchy of Japan and the absolutist monarchies of China, Korea, Persia, and Siam.[70] The point here seems to have been that the absolutist monarchies were all weak, although they had retained their formal independence.

Early Republican geographies

Chinese geography did not change with the 1911 Revolution, and yet it did change: administrative borders were redrawn, the relative importance of cities shifted, in time railroads were built, and even the name of the country changed. A 1912 Commerce Press "Republican Series" geography textbook by Zhuang Yu began by explaining that the name of China had for thousands of years followed the name of the particular ruling dynasty, and hence changed from era to era.[71] But the Chinese had generally called their country Zhongguo or Huaxia, and so since the revolution China has been called Zhonghua. "In the imperial era, the government was autocratic and so used the name of whatever dynasty was in power. Today, we have become a republic (*minguo*), and so we are called the Zhonghua minguo (Republic of China)." The 1926 Commercial Press "new geography" textbook by Tan Lian and Tan Yunhua began with the same point.[72] In a note to teachers, they explained that "Republic" referred to the fact that since the revolution China had no longer belonged to the emperor but to the people.[73] China was the largest country on the Asian continent, including Hainan and the Paracels in the oceans to the southeast. The island of Taiwan had been taken by Japan, they noted. Yet the Tans' emphasis was not on the iniquities of imperialism but rather the responsibilities of citizens. Teachers were to explain that the Chinese were "to take on national affairs as if they were family affairs, to endeavor to benefit the country and the people, to work to rid the county and the people of harm, and to avoid selfishness and accept hardships and dangers."

Children were to acquire a sense of the territory of China by using the begonia leaf – or sometimes a flattened mulberry leaf – as a mnemonic (Figure 37). But they were also to realize that China's territory was threatened. Zhuang Yu defined the concessions or foreign-controlled territories in China as "territories occupied by foreigners through force."[74] In return for payment, these territories are euphemistically called "concessions." Zhuang then described strategically

---

[70] Hu Shitan, *Dili jiangyi*, pp. 13b–14b.   [71] Zhuang Yu, *Xin dili*, 1: 1a.
[72] Tan Lian and Tan Yunhua, *Xinzhuan dili jiaoshoushu*, 1: 1–2.
[73] Ibid., 1: 5.   [74] Zhuang Yu, *Xin dili*, 3: 12a.

The importance of space   233

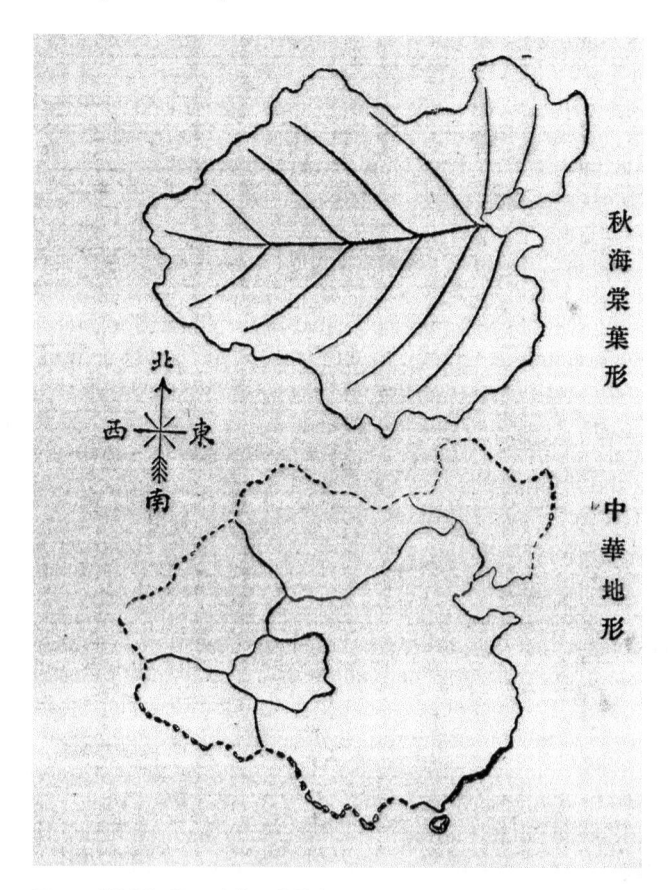

Figure 37 The Republic of China as a begonia leaf, a common mnemonic.

critical sites from Lüshun (Port Arthur) in the hands of the Japanese in the north, through to Hong Kong and Macao in the hands of the British and the Portuguese in the south.[75] Similarly, the *Practical Geography Textbook* of 1915 explained that it would include the concessions because, even though China no longer possessed "sovereignty" over them, they are traditionally Chinese territories.[76] This was a curious way to put it, because in international law China did retain sovereignty over the concessions, though China had lost sovereignty over permanently alienated territories such as Hong Kong and Taiwan. The *Practical Geography* did note the distinction between the two types of territories, but considered that China had conceded both types only under duress and had

---

[75] Ibid. 3: 12a–14b.
[76] Beijing jiaoyu tushushe, comp., *Shiyong dili jiaokeshu*, 1: "Bianji dayi" 編輯大意, 1b.

lost effective control over both types: both were therefore defined as "national humiliation."[77]

Possibly race, though still a geographic fact of life, became less central to textbooks in the early Republic because the revolution seemed to solve the Manchu issue that had fueled late Qing fascination with the subject. The nationalities (or races) of China being as "close as brothers," the remaining issue was one of unifying China's various languages, a matter for the educational system.[78] Language, religion, politics, and business were all progressing, and the Chinese were becoming "civilized" according to modern standards.

In his middle school geography published by the China Bookstore, Li Tinghan began by defining geography as the study of the earth's terrain, climate, resources, and human living conditions.[79] Li followed the theory of the single origins of the species, which then divided into five major races in response to environmental conditions.[80] In his later discussion of the natural environment, Li said that the tropics, which were rich in natural products, produced lazy peoples.[81] The arctic, so difficult to survive, produces people who are too independent and lacking a cooperative spirit. Temperate climates, however, encourage people to develop civilization. Proof of this, Li said, lay in the fact that all political and economic power was concentrated in temperate regions. Of the world's five major races, according to Li, Mongols (Yellows) and Caucasians (Whites) were historically dominant, although recently the Whites had edged out the Yellows.[82] This had of course been a common view since the late Qing reformers began to talk about the future of world racial struggle. Although the Yellows were the dominant race in Asia, had conquered eastern Europe in the past, and now the Chinese were immigrating to America, Li said, the Whites had begun to spread out of Europe to the Americas, southern Africa, and Oceania, as well as Siberia, beginning in the fifteenth century. Li said that the subgroup of the Whites with the highest level of civilization were the Aryans of Europe and America. Blacks, Browns, and Reds did not entirely lack civilization, according to Li, but were less advanced. When he discussed the political conditions of the contemporary world, Li suggested that only about 20 states were truly independent – the rest were dependencies and colonies – and most of the independent states were those of Whites, who controlled most of the globe.[83] Only the Yellow race could offer some resistance. Both China and Japan can be considered independent, but Japan in Li's eyes was a kind of race traitor: invading and occupying fellow members of the Yellow race such as the Ryukyu Islands, Taiwan, and Korea, and allying with Britain in hopes of taking Mongolia and Manchuria.

---

[77] Ibid., 4: 6b–7a., 8b–9a.
[78] Zhuang Yu, *Xin dili*, 4: 15a, 13b; Beijing jiaoyu tushushe, *Shiyong dili jiaokeshu*, 4: 15a–b.
[79] Li Tinghan, *Zhongxue dili jiaokeshu*, 1: 1–2.   [80] Ibid., 1: 55–50.
[81] Ibid., 4: 122–123.   [82] Ibid., 4: 135–139.   [83] Ibid., 4: 147–148.

For Li, as for others in the late Qing and the first years of the Republic, imperialism and colonialism did not raise moral issues. There were merely forces to be resisted. They were a natural phenomenon that social Darwinism and geographical knowledge helped to explain, just as such knowledge would help China strengthen itself. This morally neutral view was to change within a few years, and indeed there was something of a tradition from the late Qing of Chinese linking themselves with other victims of imperialism. The entire discourse of patriotism and state building, with its consideration of world racial structures and conflicts, was based on the need for resistance. But as Li put it matter-of-factly, "As their power grows, states manifest their authority and annex weaker states or seek undeveloped territories to occupy by releasing their excess power. The number of what they call their dependent territories increases, and the state itself becomes stronger."[84] Li sought to analyze the different types of dependent territories and the range of policies that colonial powers used to maintain and augment their power. Geography had much to say about how colonial powers could utilize native people's talents and resources – and how knowledge of the world enables people to improve their lives.

As for China, "The Republic was formed out of the Han, Manchu, Mongol, Hui, and Tibetans peoples, and from now on should merge in a united form and never again be divided into governing districts based on race." In other words, Chinese society after the revolution had no racial divisions.[85] "Society" was the result of the natural tendency of people to group together for mutual protection.[86] Once formed, different societies then progressed on the basis of local conditions. Having matured to a certain point to fit their environment, societies then progressed on the basis of what the people or race could do based on its intelligence, strength, morality, and education. The result was a world composed of societies that were relatively primitive or advanced on a kind of ladder of civilization. Li said that there were five main steps of social development or types of society: gathering, hunting, nomadic, agricultural, and industrial. The "state" was simply a type of society that was independent and sovereign. States were composed of people cooperating for mutual benefit, but – unlike other social forms – states were also marked by their sovereign capacity to make laws. Li followed the usual definition of the state in terms of sovereignty, land, and people, but emphasized sovereignty, leaving aside the question of whether nomadic societies could ever be considered states.

Much of Li's discussion could have come from a civics textbook. But he emphasized that his views were actually based on "bio-geography" and that geography spoke to the issues of the relationship between people and land.[87] Li's handling of the concepts of national polity and forms of government differed slightly from the mainstream approach. First, rather than distinguishing between monarchies and republics, he based his taxonomy whether states

[84] Ibid., 4: 150–151. [85] Ibid., 1: 144–149. [86] Ibid., 1: 59–60. [87] Ibid., 4: 141–143.

possessed sovereignty in the international sphere; thus, he divided polities between independent countries and dependencies.[88] He subdivided the former into the familiar forms of monarchies and republics, and the latter into vassal states, which possessed no self-determination, and protectorates, which retained some powers of their own. Yet another category was "colonies" (*zhimindi*), referring to settler colonies where the lands of nomads (presumed to be stateless) were settled by outsiders. Li did not say where China would fall in this taxonomy.

Li dismissed religion as the result of primitive ignorance of natural causes.[89] The major religions today include Buddhism, Hinduism, Islam, and Christianity. In line with mainstream intellectual opinion, Li distinguished Confucianism, which was a form of humanism, from religion. In a later section, Li pointed out that all the world's religions originated in Asia and first flourished in Asia, while Christianity and Islam spread beyond its borders.[90] Again, he insisted that Confucianism cannot be considered a religion, and so when foreigners regard Confucius as a religious founder, they are simply mistaken. However, Li also insisted on Confucianism's universal value. Any attempt to raise the moral stature of humanity and move the world toward the Great Commonwealth utopia (*Datong*) depends on Confucianism.

The claims of geography to nearly universal knowledge in the human sciences were also demonstrated in the reference work by Ding Cha'an for the China Bookstore publishing company.[91] Ding's first volume focused on places, but his second volume touched on demography, race, customs, religion, society, government, and the effects of climate on populations. Ding offered an intelligent if inconclusive discussion of the origins of the Han people.[92] He cited different theories as to their origins in Central Asia, western Asia or Babylonia, and China itself. None had been proved, he rightly noted. What was clear was that civilization developed around the Yellow River and spread out from there. Ding also noted competing theories of the origins of the human species – single versus plural – and of Chinese views of themselves as descended from the Yellow Emperor. This last view Ding disputed on the grounds that groups (in China) have been merging and assimilating for eons. This implied that the Chinese people were fundamentally unified, and if they might be subdivided into different groups or nations, there was no such thing as racial purity in the first place.

Ding's interpretation of the state was in accord with mainstream views. The state, Ding said, consisted of three elements: territory, people, and government

---

[88] Ibid., 1: 60–62. But Li returned to the standard approach in a later volume, 4: 145–146.
[89] Ibid., 1: 62–64.   [90] Ibid., 1: 96.
[91] Ding Cha'an, *Xin benguo dili cankaoshu*; although published in 1929, the book reflected views from before the Nanjing government was established – such as that Beijing was still the capital.
[92] Ibid., 2: 105.

(rather than "sovereignty").[93] Ding thought China was well off in terms of its territory: it benefited from the natural advantages of unity and good climate. He was nonetheless sharply aware of the threats facing China from the foreign powers, concluding with a discussion of their "invasion" of China.[94] They "opened" China for its markets: to sell to its consumers and to buy (cheaply) its resources. The imperialists protect their own markets while denying China the right to set tariffs and protect domestic industry. Now, however, Chinese are aware of the unequal nature of the treaties and of the threat of economic invasion. So movements have arisen to buy domestic products and to agitate for the abolition of the unequal treaties. Ding's discussion reflected the more critical views of imperialism that had become mainstream by the late 1920s. By his tone, Ding condemned the Western and Japanese imperialists. Yet he did not call for revolution but rather for Chinese unity. That tone and those calls were to change in the next decade.

The Nationalists' geographies

By the 1930s, geography textbooks were emphasizing two of Sun Yat-sen's Three People's Principles. First, nationalism. But now China was territorialized more clearly than ever – and nationalism referred to the need for unity within the space of the Republic of China. In an implicit but key sense, land trumped race as the key determinant of nationhood. Textbooks emphasized that nationality or national identity was a single, unitary concept, even if the Chinese nation could also be subdivided into smaller groups. The various groups of China, however, were ultimately Chinese because of their spatial location, not because of descent. The geography textbooks of the 1930s (like other textbooks) particularly targeted Japan, which had seized Manchuria and attacked Shanghai's Zhabei district. Geographical analysis also put Japanese imperialism in the context of the world capitalist system. That is, imperialism was the natural outgrowth of capitalism in the international sphere, whereas in the case of Japan, its capitalists felt a special need to catch up with the West.[95] China's nearby resources and labor power were especially attractive to the Japanese.

Geography textbooks had little to say about the second of the Three People's Principles, democracy. But the third of the Three People's Principles, the people's livelihood, led to geographical analysis of how China could develop economically. China's natural resources and diligent workers should make the country wealthy. All that was needed was proper organization – railroads, roads, mines, ports, factories, and more railroads. For textbook writers, nationalism and economic development were related issues, both necessary to make China a

---

[93] Ibid., 2: 3.   [94] Ibid., 2: 211–212.
[95] Zhonghua shuju, comp., *Gaoji xiaoxueyong geke jiaokeshu jiaoxuefa yangben*, 4: 160–166.

stronger country. Likewise, Nationalist textbooks analyzed the threat of imperialism in terms of both the political and the economic. Therefore, Chinese resistance to imperialism required both political and economic policies. A World Bookstore geography textbook even stated that these two themes would run through its four volumes.[96] First, the nation: through geographic knowledge students learn of the invasion of China by foreigners. And second, livelihood: through knowledge of local products and transportation routes and the like, as well as of Sun Yat-sen's development plans, the economy can be managed.

One common pattern in 1930s geography textbooks was to begin with a discussion of the capital, Nanjing, move on to other important places and regions, and then in later volumes turn to races, customs, religions, languages, and the solar system and world geography. A World Bookstore geography also described the "revolutionary sites" of Guangdong Province, offering a history lesson of the revolution and the special role played by Guangdong.[97] Local students could visit various sites, including the martyrs' shrine at Huanghuagang (site of a failed uprising in Guangzhou), while other students could investigate the revolutionary histories of their own localities. Many textbooks emphasized China's size – largest territory in Asia, third largest in the world – natural resources, and large and industrious population. Given these advantages, economic development should be possible. Often specifically citing Sun Yat-sen, textbooks emphasized big investment projects in infrastructure as well as basic industries such as iron and cement.[98] A Commercial Press textbook wanted students to consider Sun Yat-sen's development plans in geographic terms.[99] Where exactly should railroads be placed? How can agriculture be developed? What kinds of places are suitable for forestation? Why are primary industries like iron, shipbuilding, and cement important? Many geography textbooks claimed to focus on the relationship between people and the environment, and there were calls for victory over Nature.[100]

A Commercial Press geography defined the concept of national territory as "the place under the rule of a state, and which other states cannot invade."[101] This was similar to the standard civics definition of a "state" as people plus territory plus sovereignty, yet the emphasis differed – here, sovereignty was no legal abstraction but simply freedom from outside control. Geography textbooks no less than history textbooks insisted on the historical continuity of China, even though they too noted that the name of the state had undergone many changes.

---

[96] Dong Wen, *Xinzhuyi dili keben*, 1: "Bianji dagang," 1–2.
[97] Dong Wen, *Dili keben jiaoxuefa*, 1: 115.
[98] Feng Dafu, *Fuxing dili jiaokeshu*, 3: 43–46; Feng Dafu, Chen Gaoji, and Fu Weiping, *Fuxing dili jiaokeshu*, 3: 41–44; Dong Wen, *Xinzhuyi dili keben*, 3: 7–10.
[99] Yu Shumin, *Fuxing gaoxiao dili jiaoxuefa*, 3: 142–152.
[100] Ge Suicheng, *Chuzhong benguo dili*, 1: 1–2.
[101] Yu Shumin, *Fuxing gaoxiao dili jiaoxuefa*, 1: 1.

They stressed that dynasties historically had different names, and in ancient times the people and territory were called Hua or Xia, or Huaxia, but the key lay in the people – the Han.[102] A World Bookstore geography textbook supported the old Western origins theory of the Han.[103] Most textbooks of the 1930s no longer discussed the Western origins theory, however.

Nationalist geography textbooks included sections on the customs of different peoples, which could merge into discussions of national character. Textbooks tended to agree that Han were industrious and frugal, and also known for their endurance, truthfulness, and loyalty to family and clan. A primary school textbook, however, also blamed long years of monarchical oppression for turning the Chinese into – in the phrase of the day – a sheet of loose sand, lacking national spirit.[104] Following Sun Yat-sen, the textbook urged that national spirit be built up from clan loyalties and the restoration of traditional morality: loyalty, filiality, trust, peace, and so forth. This geography book made its way back to the *Great Learning* to point to the process leading from making one's will sincere to rectifying one's mind to cultivating oneself to harmonizing one's clan and finally to governing one's country (but stopping short of bringing peace to the world as the ancient text promised).

Once the Han people were characterized, other nationalities needed to be described. A China Bookstore textbook said Mongols are tough and conservative. Manchus easily accept other cultures (this was a reference to assimilation). Hui believe in their religion (Islam) and stick together. And the Tibetans are also religious and their women strong.[105] At the same time, Han are not all the same. According to this textbook, northerners and southerners differ due to environmental factors. Northern Han are more industrious and straightforward while southern Han are cleverer and risk-taking by nature. This textbook emphasized that on the one hand all nationalities are, as Sun Yat-sen said, equal; all belong to the same Chinese people; and all should be unified into the Chinese nation.[106] On the other hand, this seemed to imply that the Chinese nation was not in fact unified. A key role for geography was to link the different peoples to their home areas. Not accidently, this defined the territory of China.

Considering China's population, another question was, how many was ideal? Geography textbooks invariably followed Sun Yat-sen's dictum that China was losing the demographic race.[107] True, Chinese constituted a quarter of the world's population at 440 million, but their numbers had not increased for two centuries. This while Britain, America, Germany, France, Japan, and Russia were experiencing demographic explosions. Textbooks maintained that China

---

[102] Ge Suicheng and Yu Pu, *Xin Zhonghua yuti benguo dili xiangjie*, 1: 1–2.
[103] Dong Wen, *Dili keben jiaoxuefa*, 3: 75.   [104] Feng Dafu, *Fuxing dili jiaokeshu*, 3: 47–48.
[105] Ge Suicheng, *Chuzhong benguo dili*, 4: 7–9.
[106] See also Dong Wen, *Dili keben jiaoxuefa*, 3: 16–17.
[107] Ibid., 3: 10–15; Dong Wen, *Xinzhuyi jiaokeshu jiaoyuan yongshu*, 3: 72–73.

faced the threat of larger populations crushing smaller populations; they echoed an old trope that Westerners not only threatened the Chinese state but even threatened the extinction of the race. A Commercial Press textbook maintained that, "In terms of power in the world today, only the Yellow and White races can survive in the competition for survival; the other races of Black, Brown, and Red have already been severely weakened by the White race and will soon disintegrate."[108]

As a World Bookstore textbook put it, "Imperialism is the ultimate stage of the development of capitalism, seeking to monopolize the entire world in order to increase political and economic power."[109] Again we see that the imperialist threat was as much economic as political or military. What, then, was to be done? Another World Bookstore textbook linked the liberation of the Chinese nation in international terms to the equality of all the Chinese nationalities.[110] Adopting a historical mode, the textbook claimed that the 1911 Revolution made unity possible by destroying the old Manchu divide-and-rule policies. However, the warlords who had followed the revolution actually kept imperialism alive. They had oppressed minority nationalities, who naturally came to doubt all Chinese leaders, even the Guomindang. To defeat imperialism now, it was necessary that every nationality have the right of self-determination (*zijuequan*). A Republic of China composed of freely united nations could achieve victory in the battles against imperialism and warlordism.

As we have seen, the threat of Japan loomed large. A China Bookstore geography as early as 1933 described the extent of the Japanese Empire.[111] Students were told that Japan was a constitutional monarchy and that Japan proper consisted only of four large islands, together amounting to about one-thirtieth of China, mountainous lands with few plains but many earthquakes. However, the Japanese annexed Korea, which had previously been a Chinese vassal state, giving China and Japan a common border. Then in 1931, the Japanese attacked Manchuria, now their puppet. "All the people of our country should be determined to take back our lost territories." Teachers were to draw maps illustrating the threat from Japan. Nonetheless, the textbook also conveyed a sense of admiration for Japan's accomplishments in the Meiji Restoration. It had defeated China, Russia, and Germany to become a major power: the implication was that China could still learn from Japan, including from the vaunted Japanese sense of national unity.

The textbook had highlighted the importance of Manchurian resources such as coal, iron, forests, and soybeans.[112] And it concluded with a discussion

---

[108] Feng Dafu et al., *Fuxing dili jiaokeshu*, 3: 53–55.
[109] Tan Lianxun, *Chuzhong benguo dili*, 4: 59   [110] Dong Wen, *Dili keben jiaoxuefa*, 3: 75.
[111] Yu Pu, Han Feimu, and Lou Yunlin, *Xiaoxue dili keben jiaoxuefa*, 4: 27–29.
[112] Ibid., 1: 14.

of "China's position in the world."[113] With 5000 years of history, China was the first Asian civilization to develop. It possessed vast territories and numerous people, as well as a temperate climate with every geographic advantage. However, the textbook told students, over the past century it had become a victim of political and economic imperialism, which destabilized its politics. The Japanese occupation of Manchuria not only destroyed China's territorial integrity but threatened the world's balance of power. The Chinese people must resolve to recover Manchuria, and if this led to a second world war, there should be no regrets. Teachers were instructed to highlight strengths of China even while emphasizing the tasks that lay before it. These include the need to reform politics to make China a less attractive target for imperialists, and to aid the small and weak nations around the world; to provide schooling for all Chinese, taking best of Western civilization and traditional Chinese scholarship and morality; to abolish the unequal treaties; and to develop industry, which should also make China a less attractive target for economic imperialism.

National humiliation maps were widely used in textbooks throughout the 1930s. They listed territories "lost" to foreign imperialists since the late Qing. The map in Figure 38 distinguishes among three sorts of lost territory: directly governed lands, vassal states, and tribute states (though these had never been under Qing control), and shows which territories had been lost to which foreign powers when.

Textbooks on social studies, common knowledge, and practical knowledge naturally included sections on geography. In their teachers' manual for primary school social studies, Zhao Tizhen and Ma Pengnian tied the lesson on the capital Nanjing into the unit on the commemoration of the founding of the Republic. This linked geography and history. Teachers were thus to introduce not only the geography of the city but the history of the Guomindang party-state as well.[114] Students were to consider the relationship between Nanjing and Sun Yat-sen, why the capital was moved away from Beijing, and similar questions, and to take the opportunity to organize their own class assembly, with the implication that it could be organized somewhat along the lines of the national government. The next lesson in the unit introduced the northern cities of Beiping (the renamed traditional capital of Beijing), with its tasteful air of antiquity, and Tianjin, modern industrial powerhouse. The unit on the Chinese Revolution began with a consideration of races before turning to nationalism and the experiences of 1911 and the May Fourth movement.[115] Students were offered a fairly extensive list of Chinese peoples: Han, Manchu, Mongol, Hui,

---

[113] Ibid., 4: 230–233.
[114] Zhao Tizhen and Ma Pengnian, *Xiaoxue shehui keben jiaoxuefa*, 5: 138–145.
[115] Ibid., 6: 101–110.

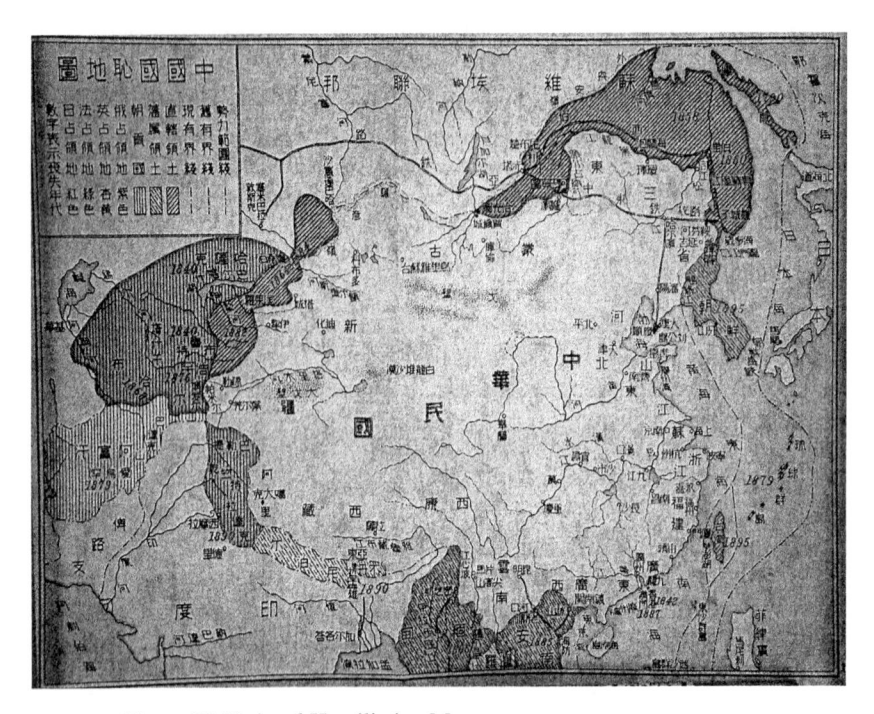

Figure 38 National Humiliation Map.

Tibetan, Miao, Yao, and Li, "and so forth." They were instructed that Manchus had completely assimilated with the Han, as was mostly but not entirely true for the Hui, Miao, Yao, and Li as well, whereas Mongols and Tibetans had retained more of their own language and customs. Teachers' reference materials, citing Sun Yat-sen, emphasized that whatever their differences, all these people comprised a single "Chinese nation" that had existed for 2000 years, united by natural forces of blood, lifestyle, language, religion, and customs. How this unity could be reconciled with the differences just discussed was not entirely clear, but the textbook claimed that unity stemmed both from common descent and from assimilation. Again citing Sun, reference materials stipulated that the Han constituted 90 percent of China's population, with the implication that other groups were relatively insignificant peoples of the frontiers. While attempting to provide an anthropologically informed analysis of the lifestyles of the various groups – Mongolian pastoralism, for example – Zhao and Ma did not avoid generalizations such as "The uncleanliness of the Mongols: Mongols really pay no attention to hygiene. When they have eaten, they clean their bowls by licking them, and these bowls are never washed with water. They also never use water to wash their faces or hands..."

The next lesson dealt with the imperialists' invasion of China, and the "position of the Chinese nation" as a "weak and small nation."[116] This was of course a common phrase of the day that masked no little tension with the well-trumpeted facts of China's territorial and demographic size. What the phrase captured was China's subordination to the Western powers and Japan. Teachers' materials suggested that the goal of the class was to create a sense of humiliation and anger, and then harness this to the task of China's economic development. This task would be possible given China's natural resources if people properly understood their responsibilities. Geography was central to understanding how China might develop and to understanding the specific elements of the imperialist presence. This could be a matter of historical geography: how the British got to Hong Kong via their command of the sea or the Japanese to Manchuria via Korea. Or it could be a matter of strategic geography: in particular the Japanese threat to northern China, or foreign ownership of railway lines.

All persons must understand the world; otherwise, they will behave irrationally. In today's struggles among the Great Powers, the strong survive and the weak perish. To understand the principles of evolution, we must study the world; otherwise, the spirit of loyalty will fail to rise and there will be no way to understand historical and political change. Yet we cannot understand the world through empty theorizing but rather must begin by studying the geography of the globe. It is because foreign schools all teach world geography that foreign peoples are patriotic and the progress of their culture and governance is immeasurable.[117]

So wrote Zhou Zhenlin (1875–1960), who taught geography at the Bright Virtue Academy (Mingde xuetang) in Changsha from its founding in 1903. Zhou was a radical political thinker, and he supported the 1911 Revolution. He was one of many who regarded geographical knowledge as key to the major issues facing the Chinese.

Zhou's expansive view of geography encompassed the flora, fauna, and climates of the physical terrain; race and demography; society; languages; religions; the state; and transportation and communications. The social Darwinism that formed the foundation of his views applied equally to revolutionary and to reformist programs. "Society" Zhou defined as any group of persons uniting together in a group for a common purpose.[118] Society is necessary for human life, because individuals cannot survive on their own. Societies fail when their organization is inadequate. Much depends on the conditions of the land and the people. This, Zhou said, is what geographers study. Generally speaking, societies prosper when the climate is temperate, transportation convenient, and natural resources abundant; and also, when the people are strong, industrious,

---

[116] Ibid., 6: 111–118.
[117] Zhou Zhenlin, *Mingde xuetang dili kecheng*, p. 2a.   [118] Ibid., pp. 35a–36a.

and united. Like other intellectuals of the late Qing, Zhou was concerned with the question of how to make the Chinese people feel more united. In tracing the scale from primitive to civilized societies, Zhou stressed five characteristics of civilized societies: excellent organization, governance rooted in popular opinion, security of life and property, universal education, widespread knowledge, and high moral standards.

In the late Qing, many geography textbooks began with descriptions of the "imperial capital" (*jingshi*) of Beijing. Chinese people who are ignorant of their capital are like children ignorant of their parents' hometown: they have forgotten their roots.[119] Thus a lesson on the location of the capital was also a lesson on reverence for the emperor designed to raise students' patriotism. Students were to perceive the absolute centrality of the emperor through understanding how the capital was sited, fortified, and made magnificent. Or take the otherwise insignificant prefecture of Weihui, north of Kaifeng City in Henan.[120] There was Bi Gan (c. eleventh century BCE), whose emperor ordered his heart torn from his body for his excessively frank advice. Jing Ke (d. 227 BCE), who failed to assassinate the man who would found the Qin dynasty. And Confucius's disciple Zigong. Other heroes and villains from popular legends and long-told stories populated so many sites that the entire myth-history of China could be captured by geography. The loyal hero Yue Fei (twelfth century), the traitor Cao Cao (second century). The battle of Fancheng (third century). Countless sites of ancient kingdoms and dynastic capitals, but also places where more modern history had happened, such as treaties signed with the Western powers. Even imaginary geography, such as local claims to host the Peach Blossom Spring (based on a poem by Tao Yuanming, 365–427).

Place was never exempt from ideological significance. In the wake of the 1911 Revolution, geography textbooks proclaimed that China was the only republic in East Asia.[121] Republican geography textbooks confirmed that, however unique, China was one country in a big world. In the first years of the Republic, they continued the Qing practice of noting a hierarchy of nations determined by race and level of civilization, but suggested that independent nations were the same kind of entity whether rich or poor, strong or weak. The existence of borders, armies, flags, and so forth confirmed this. Even that all independent states possessed capitals was a sign of a kind of equal status. However, by the end of the 1920s, a sharper sense of the threat of imperialism reshaped textbooks' views of the world: if it had always been a dangerous place, now it was a deeply and immorally unequal one. Imperialism was not diminishing but rather expanding, and threats to China were becoming more dire. As always, this led to renewed calls for national unity, and by the 1930s the

---

[119] Guan Qi, *Zhongguo dili xin jiaokeshu jiaoshoufa*, 1: 1a–3a.
[120] Ibid., 3: 5b–6b. [121] For example, Zhuang Yu, *Xin dili*, 4: 14a.

Nanjing government was able to implement many school programs devoted to the cause. At the same time, political and economic imperialism were increasingly understood to be dysfunctional aspects of a globalizing capitalist system that needed thorough reform. Nationalist geography textbooks did not promote world revolution, but they sought to convey a sense of the ongoing Chinese revolution that would have world effects. Geography contributed to the image of China as a natural as well as historical Great Power. Given its size, its population, its resources, and its ancient civilization, "we should stand equal to the West, but in fact we do not do so" – at least so far.[122]

[122] Zhonghua shuju, comp., *Gaoji xiaoxueyong geke jiaokeshu jiaoxuefa yangben*, 8: 15.

Conclusion

What is a textbook, and what does it do? More specifically, what did Chinese textbooks do in the first decades of the twentieth century? Textbooks convey knowledge and in a sense construct it – along with curriculum committees, school heads, teachers, and many others. Informally, more knowledge is probably conveyed to children by parents, siblings, other kin, neighbors, and employers, as well as the popular media (novels, newspapers, operas, and today TV, films, and the Internet) than through formal systems. Nonetheless, textbooks are one key source of knowledge, and in modern school systems they specifically convey knowledge that the state wishes to have conveyed.[1] Textbooks are authoritative, or at any rate they pose as authoritative.

In the critical period during which the modern Chinese state was formed, Chinese textbooks conveyed abstract knowledge, concrete knowledge and skills, behavioral norms, and political values. Unlike traditional educational materials, or at least to a much greater degree, they introduced specific areas of learning in systematic ways, from simple to complex, with much repetition. By following curricular standards, they represented an ideal in which every student of a particular age on a particular day would be reading the same materials. This was of course an ideal never reached. Textbooks spoke in many voices; teachers, we know in rough terms, spoke in many more voices yet.

Still, as the state school system grew, more and more students were drawn into it, subject to textbooks for years on end. And it is worth remembering, as Paul Bailey points out, that not only did the new official schools coexist with more or less traditional private schools throughout this entire period, but also official concerns were not limited to the new schools.[2] Officials as well as local gentry were interested in providing part-time education, vocational training, and, in the cities, night schools to teach basic literacy to workers. Such schools

---

[1] Of course, the state does not necessarily speak with one voice – in fact, it never does. A concise overview is Michael W. Apple and Linda K. Christian-Smith, "The Politics of the Textbook," pp. 1–21.
[2] Paul Bailey, *Reform the People*, esp. chapter 3.

might use the simpler textbooks written for the official schools; by the 1920s, some textbooks were written specifically for nonofficial schools even while they followed official curricular standards.

Even after two decades of growth of the school system, at the end of the 1920s relatively few children attended school regularly. Town children might attend a few years of primary school. In the countryside, village children might at best pick up a few lessons in basic literacy. Children attending secondary school were preparing to join commercial, educational, official, and military elites. Yet textbooks, sometimes sold by traveling peddlers, reached many places far from urban centers.

Textbooks in early twentieth-century China taught children about the growth of the state and officialdom even in an era of great political instability. They did this in part by their very existence, and they did it through lessons on the nation. No doubt, textbooks reflected, ratified, and constructed modern Chinese nationalism and civic consciousness. They spoke to the myriad processes of socialization that students needed to undergo – or, as a recent Chinese work puts it, enlightenment and modernity.[3] On the one hand, textbooks fostered an image of a world that did not exist – say, a world of orderly relations, selfless behavior, and loving families. On the other, the gap between reality and ideal was precisely the point: students were being equipped to build such a world.

Textbooks constituted a major part of epistemological change in modern Chinese consciousness. Textbooks gradually redefined knowledge of the natural world and of much of the social world in terms of "Western learning." Textbooks defined the disciplines, and the disciplines of, say, geography and physics represented not the transfer of packets of knowledge, but new systems of knowledge: ways of categorizing knowledge by discipline and within each discipline. Correspondingly, textbooks gradually reduced Confucianism or "traditional morality" to the sphere of the family and individual self-cultivation. Yet the result was not so much separate spheres for distinct types of learning but rather a kind of hybridization of knowledge, at least in study of the social world. Textbooks used social Darwinism – the struggle for survival and selection of the fittest – to explain much about the world, but no such doctrine could explain what was right and what was wrong.

Textbooks taught students about their relation to family, community, nation, and world – that is, their identities. And they did so largely though stories. The narrative structure of the vast majority of the materials presented in language readers, morality and civics textbooks, histories, and even geographies was a powerful means to convey knowledge, because it worked indirectly and

---

[3] Wu Xiaoou, *Zhongguo jindai jiaokeshu de qimeng jiazhi.*

so could not be argued with. Narrative was a way to construct subjectivities, and students learned to conceive of themselves as members of particular families, genders, schools, neighborhoods, the nation, and the world community.[4] In other words, officials, educators, and textbook writers regarded their task to be shaping students into "selves" who belonged to many groups, but took family and nation as the main goals of "technologies of the self" that schooling provided.

The narrative packaging that textbooks tend to give their materials seems so natural that we may neglect the effects it produces. One of the powers of narrative, for our purposes at least, lies in the ways it implies cause and effect. Simply by creating a timeline, it suggests that event "A" leads to event "B." This may be due to the will of the gods, objective historical conditions, or the actions of Great Men, but generally human will of even ordinary people plays some role. Human will is not merely willful but based on moral direction. As well, narratives are a relatively effective way to convey information. That is, readers remember more information from a narrative account than they remember from other ways of presenting information. It may be that narrative has a neurological basis; at the very least, it is universal to all cultures. In other words, people in all cultures tell stories about their experiences, the experiences of others, and the collective experience. Memory is preserved only through narrative. In turn, the individual self and the collective self are constructed through memory. And it is worth remembering that the self is constructed through encounters with the other, so there are always "shared scripts."

The relationship between knowledge and narrative is ambiguous. Much narrative is fictional or even fantasy. Fiction may convey knowledge (albeit through metaphor). Conversely, knowledge is often conveyed in non-narrative forms. So-called facts are expressed in tables, maps, and graphs. "Facts" in this sense are non-narrative.[5] Yet even when dealing with "facts," people tend to situate them in time – in other words, there are always a sequence of facts. Once facts are presented in a sequence, they are already close to narrative. "Narrative knowledge" goes beyond merely conveying facts. Narrative operates indirectly, by suggestion.

Narrative can never prove that certain conditions directly cause certain results, but it is all the more powerful for being implicit: it is impossible to deny the logic of narrative with the tools of logic. Telling stories is a particularly effective way of reaching young children; descriptive analysis can be added later and for students in the higher grades. Educators sought to socialize their students. This goal, in the language of the day, revolved around

---

[4] There is an extensive theoretical literature to which these points are indirectly indebted; see esp. Paul Ricoeur, *Time and Narrative*.

[5] Mary Poovey, *A History of the Modern Fact*.

citizenship – that is, embedding oneself in the national narrative; understanding the proper ways to treat family members, classmates, teachers, and members of the wider world that stretched out to countrymen and ultimately all human beings; and accepting responsibility as an active participant in society.

An examination of textbooks outside the natural sciences reveals that knowledge of the past and of the relationship between the individual and society in the present (and future) was built through stories. The simple stories of Chinese readers and the complex stories of history textbooks constitute their major means of conveying a sense of identity and knowledge about how society worked. (By calling the narrative strategies of history textbooks complex, in contrast to the stories of Chinese readers, I mean simply to highlight that while readers consisted mostly of individual, unconnected stories briefly told, history textbooks consisted of stories within stories, with shifting narrative subjects that ranged from nations to emperors to philosophers.)

Language readers, history textbooks, and especially self-cultivation and civics textbooks made use of other rhetorical modes, including declaratory and analytical description, but they were dominated by narratives. Stories of children and of kings, of Chinese philosophers and of Western inventors, of wars and of elections: these offered maps of the world. More memorable and yet more complex than mere facts, narrative representations transmit knowledge without seeming to do so. Through shared stories, the student was made a member of the community. Through knowledge of the past, the student was placed in relationship to both small (local) and great (national) traditions, and learned something of the "others" of the world as well. Through knowledge of society, the student was placed in relationship to family, school, neighborhood, region, nation, and world.

Primary schooling in the late Qing and republican periods emphasized specific skills such as reading and bodies of knowledge such as history, geography, arithmetic, and general science; secondary schooling further developed the specific scientific fields chemistry, physics, and biology, as well as providing professional training in commerce, agronomy, and teaching. But in addition to such testable bodies of knowledge, great emphasis was also placed on moral training, body discipline and hygiene, and civics, the last of which included both testable knowledge about government theory and behavioral norms. Loosely speaking, this might be called "social knowledge" – not in the sense of sociology but as a set of *internalized* skills allowing the student to both understand and operate successfully in society.[6] Discrete and testable bodies of knowledge are efficiently conveyed in declarative sentences ("Japanese forces defeated Qing

---

[6] There is an extensive theoretical literature to which these points are indirectly indebted; see esp. Michel Foucault, *Discipline and Punish*.

forces in 1895"; "Water is composed of two parts hydrogen and one part oxygen"). Knowledge of identity and social knowledge, however, are more effectively conveyed in less direct modes. Exhortation ("wash your face"; "respect your parents") was unavoidable in primary school morality textbooks.

The preceding chapters give several examples of the speed with which textbooks were quick to propagate discoveries of new knowledge. It should be further noted that textbooks "modeled" modern knowledge as well as transmitting it. There were two aspects to this. First, textbooks classified knowledge into discrete categories or fields, which in turn related to one another and to the entire field of knowledge in particular ways. Physics and chemistry, for example, shared basic features and techniques and required some shared knowledge (mathematics, for example); and both along with mathematics, biology, geology, and so forth were sub-branches of "science." Similarly, art classes were simultaneously devoted to developing aesthetic appreciation, hand and eye coordination that promised useful skills, and moral training as well, thus sharing some features with morality and civics classes. Second, textbooks presented knowledge as cumulative. Learning was a step-by-step process followed by groups of age-specific (or at least grade-specific) students. That this was conceived as a process that could be made ever more efficient through the science of pedagogy is of less importance here than the way this concept was expressed in textbooks themselves. Textbooks in a given field marched progressively from simple to complex, from sketchy outline to host of details, and from the immediate to the distant. Week after week, semester after semester, year after year (for those students who continued), knowledge was piled up; it did not depend on leaps of enlightenment. General science and arithmetic evolved into biology, physics, chemistry, and geology; history and geography moved from the native place to China to the world (and back again), accumulating more detail at every level; behavioral norms shaded into ever more complex knowledge of the social and political orders. Textbooks thus helped to construct taxonomies of knowledge that formed the common cultural capital of educated classes. Textbooks were also critical to the very creation of the modern Chinese language: the "vernacular" Mandarin (*guoyu, putonghua*) used today.

The initial school planning of the late Qing reveals the nationalist and modernizing goals of elites. Late Qing officials shared a basic vision of the purpose of education: to produce good and useful subjects of the emperor. That said, however, the official vision of "subjects" was not of abject servants but essentially citizens of a modernizing state. The purpose of schooling was simultaneously to socialize boys into their local and national communities and mobilize them for state service, and to produce men who would be knowledgeable, active, and even entrepreneurial. The victory of Japan over Russia in 1905 was often attributed to the superiority of constitutional monarchism, but it was

Conclusion 251

also attributed to Japan's primary schools.[7] Specifically, Chinese elites woke up to the power of schools to convey new knowledge *and* create a patriotic community.

In fits and starts, too, educators attempted to institute more "child-centered" approaches. Ideally, students should do more than memorize and regurgitate. Teacher's manuals sometimes emphasized the importance of class discussion and encouraged students to think for themselves, but textbooks only sparsely reflected liberal pedagogy. It was only with the "partification" of schools under the Guomindang after 1928 that course content was really affected, with new controls imposed over students and teachers. The Nanjing government had the power and the will to shape educational policy in ways unavailable to previous regimes.[8] The "Three People's Principles" were to be integrated into the curriculum at all possible opportunities. As Robert Culp has pointed out, a key theme of party educational materials was to reconstitute society as a modernizing but stable organic whole.[9] Yet the vision of society as an organism was much older than the Guomindang. Conversely, the Guomindang's vision of a society in lockstep faced considerable resistance. Partification in curriculum announcements did not necessarily translate into radical reforms in the classroom. Teachers and students did not openly challenge the Three People's Principles, but those principles could be understood in different ways.

Over the first decades of the twentieth century, China's schools certainly produced patriotic citizens. These young citizens, however, had been trained to be capable of criticism and resistance, as well as support for any given government. As noted at the beginning of this book, the late Qing and Republican school systems produced young radicals as well as stolid burghers. History textbooks created a historical subject with which the student was to identify, and language readers constructed social subjectivity through empathy and self-recognition. Textbooks dealing with morality and civics fostered both identity and political subjectivity. At the same time, language readers also conveyed moral lessons, and it may be that their influence was greater than that of morality and civics textbooks because of the sheer number of hours devoted to language work (as well as the practice of recitation). Thus did textbooks mold modern Chinese subjectivity through an onslaught of knowledge.

Yet there is no simple answer to the question, Whose knowledge? The Chinese content of non-science textbooks can scarcely be doubted. Although Western missionary and Japanese school materials at the turn of the century shaped

---

[7] Indeed, the importance of universal primary education in the balance of military power had become a cosmopolitan commonplace since the Franco-Prussian War. Alexander Woodside, "Real and Imagined Continuities," p. 39.
[8] For a careful analysis of the formation of Nationalist educational policy, see Chiu-chun Lee, "Liberalism and Nationalism at a Crossroads."
[9] Robert Culp, "Setting the Sheet of Loose Sand."

the new educational system, the moment of direct borrowing was brief. More general Chinese participation in a global system of knowledge and pedagogy is another matter. "Global" here does not mean homogenous, nor does it imply equal conditions of production and transmission. But it does suggest that we need to pay attention to a process of continuous if uneven interactions across state borders, as well as to the decisions made by Chinese textbook authors and publishers and the relevant officials.

Glossary

ai tonglei 愛同類
ai guojia 愛國家
aiguo 愛國
Aixinjueluo 愛新覺羅

ba 霸
bansei itsukei (J) 萬世一系
baobian 褒貶
baojia 保甲
baoshen 保身
Benguoshi 本國史
bianfa ziqiang 變法自強
boai 博愛

Cai Yuanpei 蔡元培
Chaoshi 巢氏
Chen Dong 陳東
Chen Duxiu 陳獨秀
Chen Hongmou 陳宏謀
Cheng Yi 程頤
chuanshuo 傳說
chushi 處世
ci zhimindi 次殖民地

Dai Jitao 戴季陶
daibiao 代表
dairen 待人
danghua 黨化
Dangyi 黨義
daoguo 盜國
Datong 大同
di 帝

dihuang 地皇
diwang 帝王
Donghu 東胡
Donghuzu 東胡族

Erya 爾雅

Fan Zhongyan 范仲淹
fanshu 藩屬
Feng Zikai 豐子愷
fengjian 封建
fucong 服從
Fuxi 伏羲

gaige 改革
Ge Hong 葛洪
geju ze luan, tongyi ze zhi 割據則亂, 統一則治
geming 革命
gong 公
gongde 公德
gonggongxin 公共心
gonghe 共和
gongli 公理
gongmin 公民
gongmin daode 公民道德
gongmin jiaokeshu 公民教科書
gongmin xunlian 公民訓練
gongmin zhishi 公民智識
gongtong shenghuo 共同生活
gu 古
Gu Jiegang 顧頡剛
guangfu 光復
guanhua 官話
gongdu 工讀
gongzhi 共治
guochi 國恥
Guocui xuebao 國粹學報
guojia 國家
guomin 國民
guomin geming 國民革命
guomin jiaoyu 國民教育
guomin xuexiao 國民學校

Glossary

guomin zhi zhiqi 國民之志氣
guomin zhongai 國民忠愛
guoti 國體
guowen 國文
guoxue 國學
guoyu 國語
guozhu 國主
guwen 古文
guyou daode 固有道德

Han Wudi 漢武帝
Hanren 漢人
Hanzu 漢族
Hanzu fuxing 漢族復興
Hanzu qunxiong 漢族群雄
He Bingsong 何炳松
heping 和平
hequn 合群
Hua 華
Hua Tuo 華佗
Huang Di 黃帝
Huang Xiang 黃香
Huang Zongxi 黃宗羲
Huaqiao 華僑
Huaren 華人
Huaxia 華夏
Huazhong 華種

Jiang Weiqiao 蔣維喬
Jianguo dagang 建國大綱
Jianguo fanglue 建國方略
jiaozhi 交趾
jiazu 家族
Jie 桀
Jimmu (J) 神武
jingshi 京師
jingtian 井田
jingushi 近古史
jinian 紀年
jinshi (modern) 近世
jinshi (civil service examination degree) 進士
jinshishi 近世史

jiuzhou 九州
junguomin 軍國民
junguomin zhuyi 軍國民主義
junmin yiti 君民一體
junzhu 君主
junzhu shixi zhi zhi 君主世襲之制
junzhu zhengzhi 君主政治

Kaiming shuju 開明書局
Kang Youwei 康有為
Kangxi 康熙
keji 克己
kokki (J) 克己
kokutai (J) 國體
Kong Rong 孔融

Li Hongzhang 李鴻章
Li Zicheng 李自成
Liang Qichao 梁啟超
Lidai shilue 歷代史略
Liji 禮記
Lin Shu 林紓
Liu Shipei 劉師培
Liu Yizheng 柳詒徵
Liu Zongzhou 劉宗周 (Zhongjie 忠介)
lizhi 立志
Lu Jiushao 陸九韶
lunchang 倫常
lunli 倫理

Manzhouzhong 滿洲種
Mengxue duben 蒙學讀本
mengxuetang 蒙學堂
Miao 苗
Ming (dynasty) 明
Mingde xuetang 明德學堂
minguo 民國
minquan 民權
minzhong xuexiao 民眾學校
minzhu 民主
minzu 民族
minzu geming 民族革命

Glossary

minzu jingshen, guojia jingshen 民族精神、國家精神
Miyama Toratarō 深山虎太郎

Nanyang gongxue 南洋公學
neiluan waihuan 內亂外患

Pangu 盤古
Peng Xiu 彭修
pingmin xuexiao 平民學校
pingmin zhuyi 平民主義
pingminhua 平民化
putonghua 普通話

qiangbao de ren 強暴的人
Qianlong 乾隆
Qianziwen 千字文
Qin Shihuang 秦始皇
qin'ai 親愛
Qing (dynasty) 清
Qu Li 曲禮

ren 仁
ren'ai 仁愛
rende 仁德
renhuang 人皇
renmin 人民
renren junzi 仁人君子
Renpu 人譜
rensheng guannian 人生觀念
renzhong 人種

sanhuang wudi 三皇五帝
Sanmin zhuyi 三民主義
Sanzijing 三字經
Shang 商
shanggong 尚公
shanggushi 上古史
shangshi (ancient) 上世
shangshi (esteem for the practical arts) 尚實
shangwu 尚武
shanshu 善書
shehui 社會

Sheng Langxi 盛朗西
shengdezheng 聖德政
shenghuo yanjin 生活演進
shengwang 聖王
Shennong 神農
Shi Kefa 史可法
shijie qushi 世界趨勢
Shijie shuju 世界書局
shijie zhuyi 世界主義
shijieguan 世界觀
shu 恕
Shun 舜
si 私
side 私德
Sima Guang 司馬光
Sima Qian 司馬遷
sonnō aikoku (J) 尊王愛國
Suiren 燧人
Sun Yat-sen 孫逸仙 [Zhongshan 中山]

Taihao 太皞
Tang (dynasty) 唐
Tang (King) 湯
Tang Gaozong 唐高宗
Tang Zhansheng 唐湛聲
Tao Menghe 陶孟和
Tian 天
tianhuang 天皇
tianzi 天子
tonghua 同化
tongyi Zhongguo 統一中國
tongyi wo Zhongguo 統一我中國
tuantihua 團體化
tuhao 土豪

waizu 外族
wang 王
Wang Rongbao 汪榮寶
Wang Yangming 王陽明
Wang Zhongqi 王鍾麒
wanquan zhi guomin 完全之國民
wanquan zhi ren 完全之人

Glossary

wanquan zhi shehui 完全之社會
wen 文
Wen Tianxiang 文天祥
Wenming shuju 文明書局
woguo 我國
women de Zhongguoren de touyige zuzong 我們的中國人的頭一個祖宗
wo minzu 我民族
wuchan jieji 無產階級
wuyishi 無意識
Wuzhong yigui 五種遺規

Xia 夏
Xia Zengyou 夏曾佑
Xianbei 鮮卑
xiandaishi 現代史
xiezu 血族
xin guomin 新國民
xinyi 信義
xinzheng 新政
Xiongnu 匈奴
xiuji 修己
xiushen 修身
xiushen jiaokeshu 修身教科書
Xue Fucheng 薛福成

Yandi 炎帝
Yao 堯
Ye Shengtao 葉聖陶
yi (righteousness) 義
yizu 異族
Yongzheng 雍正
youyishi 有意識
Yu (King, Sage-Emperor) 禹
Yu Lingyi 于令儀
Yuan (dynasty) 元
Yuan Shikai 袁世凱
Yue Fei 岳飛
yuefu 樂府

Zeng Guofan 曾國藩
Zhang Binglin 章炳麟
Zhang Xiangwen 張相文

Zhao Yusen 趙玉森
Zheng Chenggong 鄭成功
Zheng Guanying 鄭觀應
zhengjiao 政教
zhengti 政體
zhengtong 正統
zhi (ordering) 治
zhimindi 殖民地
Zhina renzhong 支那人種
Zhongguo 中國
Zhongguoren 中國人
Zhongguo renzhong 中國人種
zhonggushi 中古史
Zhonghua 中華
Zhonghua minguo 中華民國
Zhonghua minzu 中華民族
Zhonghua renmin 中華人民
Zhonghua shuju 中華書局
zhongjun 忠君
Zhongshan zhuyi 中山主義
Zhongxia 中夏
zhongxiao 忠孝
zhongzu 種族
Zhou 周
Zhu Yuanzhang 朱元璋
zhuquan 主權
zijuequan 自決權
zili 自立
zixing 自省
ziyou 自由
ziyouquan 自由權
zizhi (self-control) 自制
zizhi (self-rule) 自治
zongli 總理
zu 族
Zuixin zhongxue Zhongguo lishi jiaokeshu 最新中學中國歷史教科書
zun Kong 尊孔
Zuozhuan 左傳

Bibliography

Abe, Hiroshi, "Borrowing from Japan: China's First Modern Educational System," in Ruth Hayhoe and Marianne Bastid, eds., *China's Education and the Industrialized World*, New York: M. E. Sharpe, 1987, pp. 57–80.
Akiyama Shirō 秋山四郎, *Lunli jiaoke fanben* 倫理教科範本, trans. Dong Ruichun 董瑞椿, Shanghai: Wenming shuju, 1905.
Ames, Edgar W., and Arvie Eldred, *Community Civics*, New York: MacMillan, 1921.
Angle, Stephen, "Did Someone Say 'Rights?' Liu Shipei's Concept of Quanli," *Philosophy East & West* 48.4 (October 1998), pp. 623–651.
Apple, Michael W., and Linda K. Christian-Smith, "The Politics of the Textbook," in idem., eds. *The Politics of the Textbook*, New York: Routledge, 1991, pp. 1–21.
Bai Zuolin 白作林, trans., *Xiaoxue geke jiaoshoufa* 小學各科教授法 (orig. authors Terauchi Ei 寺内穎 and Kosaki Biitsuchi 兒崎為槌?), Shanghai? Wenming shuju? 1902.
Bai, Limin, *Shaping the Ideal Child: Children and Their Primers in Late Imperial China*, Hong Kong: Chinese University Press, 2005.
Bailey, Paul, "'Modernising Conservatism' in Early Twentieth-Century China: The Discourse and Practice of Women's Education," *European Journal of East Asian Studies* 3.2 (2004), pp. 217–241.
Bailey, Paul, *Reform the People: Changing Attitudes towards Popular Education in Early 20th Century China*, Vancouver: University of British Columbia Press, 1990.
Bastid, Marianne, *Educational Reform in Early 20th-Century China*, trans. Paul J. Bailey, Ann Arbor: Center for Chinese Studies, University of Michigan, 1988.
Bastid, Marianne "Servitude or Liberation: The Introduction of Foreign Educational Practices and Systems to China from 1840 to the Present," in Ruth Hayhoe and Marianne Bastid, eds., *China's Education and the Industrialized World*, New York: M. E. Sharpe, 1987, pp. 3–20.
Beard, Charles A., and William C. Bagley, *A First Book in American History*, New York: Macmillan, 1920.
Beijing jiaoyu tushushe 北京教育圖書社, comp., *(Gaodeng xiaoxuexiao) Shiyong dili jiaokeshu* (高等小學社) 實用地理教科書, Shanghai: Shangwu, 1918 [1915].
Bergère, Marie-Claire, *Sun Yat-sen*, trans. Janet Lloyd, Stanford, CA: Stanford University Press, 1998.
Berghahn, Volker R. and Hanna Schissler, eds., *Perceptions of History: International Textbook Research on Britain, Germany, and the United States*, New York: Berg, 1987.

Bernal, Martin, "Liu Shih-p'ei and National Essence," in Charlotte Furth, ed., *The Limits of Change: Essays on Conservative Alternatives in Republican China*, Cambridge, MA: Harvard University Press, 1976, pp. 90–112.

Bi Yuan 毕苑, "Cong 'xiushen' dao 'gongmin': jindai jiaokeshuzhong de guomin suxing" 从'修身'到'公民': 近代教科书中的国民塑性, *Jiaoyu xuebao* 教育学报 (2005.01), pp. 90–95.

Bi Yuan 毕苑, *Jianzao changshi: jiaokeshu yu jindai Zhongguo wenhua zhuanxing* 建造常识: 教科书与近代中国文化转型, Fuzhou: Fujian jiaoyu chubanshe, 2010.

Bi Yuan 毕苑, "'Minguo' de dansheng: jiaokeshu zhong de guojia xushu (1900–1915)" "民国"的诞生: 教科书中的国家叙述 (1900–1915), *Ershiyi shiji* 二十一世紀 (2012.04), pp. 42–52.

Biggerstaff, Knight, *The Earliest Modern Government Schools in China*, Ithaca, NY: Cornell University Press, 1961.

Borthwick, Sally, *Education and Social Change: The Beginnings of the Modern Era*, Stanford, CA: Hoover Institution Press, 1983.

Bourdillon, Hilary, ed., *History and Social Studies: Methodologies of Textbook Analysis*, Amsterdam: Swets & Zeitlinger, 1992.

Cai Hejian 蔡和鏗, *Zhejiang xiangtu dili jiaokeshu* 浙江鄉土地理教科書, Ningbo: Ningbo jibianzhai, 1908.

Cai Yuanpei 蔡元培, "Duiyu jiaoyu fangzhen zhi yijian," 對於教育方針之意見, in Sun Dezhong 孫德中, ed., *Cai Yuanpei xiansheng yiwen leichao* 蔡元培先生遺類鈔, Taibei: Fuxing shuju, 1966, pp. 77–84.

Cai Zhen 蔡振 [Cai Yuanpei], *Zhongxue xiushen jiaokeshu* 中學修身教科, Shanghai: Shangwu, 1912 [1907–8].

Callahan, William A., *China: The Pessoptimist Nation*, New York: Oxford University Press, 2010.

Callahan, William A., "History, Identity, and Security: Producing and Consuming Nationalism in China," *Critical Asian Studies* 38.2 (2006), pp. 179–208.

Chang, Hao, *Chinese Intellectuals in Crisis: Search for Order and Meaning, 1890–1911*, Berkeley: University of California Press, 1987.

Chen Duxiu 陳獨秀, *Duxiu wencun* 獨秀文存, 4 vols., Shanghai: Yadong tushuguan, 1927.

Chen Guanghui 陳光輝, "Qingmo Minchu zhongxuetang (xiao) xiushen jiaokeshu de fazhan (1902–1922 nian)" 清末民初中學堂 (校) 修身教科書的發展 (1902–1922年), *Guoli Taiwan Shifan daxue gongmin xunyu xuebao* 國立臺灣師範大學公民訓育學報 3 (June 1993), pp. 1–10.

Chen Qingnian 陳慶年, *Zhongguo lishi jiaokeshu* 中國歷史教科書, Shanghai: Shangwu, 1913 [1910].

Chen, Hsi-yuan, "Confucianism Encounters Religion: The Formation of Religious Discourse and the Confucian Movement in Modern China," Ph.D. dissertation, Harvard University, 1999.

Cheng Meibao 程美寶 [May-bo Ching], "You aixiang er aiguo: Qingmo Guangdongsheng xiangtu jiaocai de guojia huayu" 由爱乡而爱国: 清末广东省乡土教材的国家话语, *Lishi yanjiu* 历史研究 (2003.4), pp. 68–84.

Cheng, Weikun, "Going Public through Education: Female Reformers and Girls' Schools in Late Qing Beijing," *Late Imperial China* 21.1 (June 2000), pp. 107–144.

Chiang, Yung-chen, *Social Engineering and the Social Sciences in China, 1919–1949*, Cambridge, UK: Cambridge University Press, 2001.

Chow, Tse-tsung, *The May Fourth Movement: Intellectual Revolution in Modern China*, Cambridge, MA: Harvard University Press, 1960.

Clopton, Robert W., and Tsuin-chen Ou, eds. and trans., *John Dewey: Lectures in China, 1919–1920*, Honolulu: East-West Center, University Press of Hawaii, 1973.

Cohen, Paul, "Christian Missions and Their Impact to 1900," in Denis Twitchett and John K. Fairbank, eds., *The Cambridge History of China*, vol. 10, Cambridge, UK: Cambridge University Press, 1978, pp. 543–590.

Cohen, Paul A., "Remembering and Forgetting National Humiliation in Twentieth-Century China," *Twentieth-Century China* 27.2 (April 2002), pp. 1–39.

Cohen, Paul A., *Speaking to History: The Story of King Goujian in Twentieth-Century China*, Berkeley: University of California Press, 2009.

Cong, Xiaoping, *Teachers' Schools and the Making of the Modern Chinese Nation-State, 1897–1937*, Vancouver: University of British Columbia Press, 2007.

Cremin, Lawrence A., *The Transformation of the School: Progressivism in American Education, 1876–1957*, New York: Vintage Books, 1967.

Culp, Robert, *Articulating Citizenship: Civic Education and Student Politics in Southeastern China, 1912–1940*, Cambridge, MA: HUAC, Harvard University Press, 2007.

Culp, Robert, "'China – The Land and Its People': Fashioning Identity in Secondary School History Textbooks, 1911–37," *Twentieth-Century China* 26.2 (April 2001), pp. 20–21.

Culp, Robert, "Cultivating Cultural Citizenship: Shanghai's Commercial Publishers and the Southeast Asian Textbook Market," paper delivered to the International Conference on Historical Knowledge and Textbook Production, Shueyan University, Hong Kong, 28–29 June 2013.

Culp, Robert, "Mass Production of Knowledge and the Industrialization of Mental Labor: The Rise of the Petty Intellectual," in Eddy U, Robert Culp, and Wen-hsin Yeh, eds., *Knowledge Acts in Modern China: Ideas, Institutions, and Identities* (Berkeley: Institute for East Asian Studies Publications, forthcoming).

Culp, Robert, "Setting the Sheet of Loose Sand: Conceptions of Society and Citizenship in Nanjing Decade Party Doctrine and Civics Textbooks," in Terry Bodenhorn, ed., *Defining Modernity: Guomindang Rhetorics of a New China, 1920–1970*, Ann Arbor: Center for Chinese Studies, University of Michigan, 2002, pp. 45–90.

Culp, Robert, "Teaching *Baihua*: Textbook Publishing and the Production of Vernacular Language and a New Literary Canon in Early Twentieth Century China," *Twentieth-Century China* 34.1 (November 2008), pp. 4–41.

Culp, Robert, "'Weak and Small Peoples' in a 'Europeanizing World': World History Textbooks and Chinese Intellectuals' Perspectives on Global Modernity," in Tze-ki Hon and Robert J. Culp, eds., *The Politics of Historical Production in Late Qing and Republican China*, Leiden: Brill, 2007, pp. 211–245.

Curran, Thomas D., *Educational Reform in Republican China: The Failure of Educators to Create a Modern Nation*, Lewiston, NY: Edwin Mellen Press, 2005.

Dai Jiyu 戴季虞, ed., *(Zhongshan zhuyi) Xin'guomin duben* (中山主義) 新國民讀本, Guangzhou: Guangzhou gonghe shuju, 1926.

DeFrancis, John, *Nationalism and Language Reform in China*, Princeton: Princeton University Press, 1950.
Deng Yuhao 鄧毓浩, "Sun Zhongshan sixiang yu guomin zhengfu shiqi de gongmin jiaokeshu" 孫中山思想與國民政府時期的公民教科書, *Sunxue yanjiu* 100.11 (2011), pp. 103–140.
Des Forges, Alexander, "The Uses of Fiction: Liang Qichao and His Contemporaries," in Joshua S. Mostow, *The Columbia Companion to Chinese Literature*, New York: Columbia University Press, 2003, pp. 341–347.
Ding Baoshu 丁寶書, *Mengxue Zhongguo lishi jiaokeshu* 蒙學中國歷史教科書, Shanghai: Wenming shuju, n.d.
Ding Cha'an 丁察盦, *(Chuji zhongxueyong) Xin benguo dili cankaoshu* (初級中學用) 新本國地理參考書, Shanghai: Zhonghua shuju, 1929.
Ding Xiaoxian 丁曉先 and Chang Daozhi 常道直, *Shehui jiaokeshu (Xinxuezhi/xiaoxuexiao chujiyong)* 社會教科書 (新學制/小學校初級用), Shanghai: Shangwu yinshuguan, 1926 [1924].
Ding Zhongxuan 丁重宣, "Zeyang kaocha ertong de coaxing yu gongmin xunlian" 怎樣考查兒童的操行與公民訓練, *Jiaoyu zazhi* 教育雜誌 27.3 (1937), pp. 47–54.
Ding, Gang, "Nationalization and Internationalization: Two Turning Points in China's Education in the Twentieth Century," in Glen Peterson, Ruth Hayhoe, and Yongling Lu, eds., *Education, Culture, and Identity in Twentieth-Century China*, Ann Arbor: University of Michigan Press, 2001, pp. 161–186.
Dirlik, Arif, "The Ideological Foundations of the New Life Movement: A Study in Counterrevolution," *Journal of Asian Studies* 34.4 (August 1975), pp. 945–980.
Dirlik, Arif, *Revolution and History: The Origins of Marxist Historiography in China, 1917–1937*, Berkeley: University of California, 1978.
Dirlik, Arif, Guannan Li, and Hsiao-pei Yen, eds., *Sociology and Anthropology in Twentieth-Century China: Between Universalism and Indigenism*, Hong Kong: Chinese University Press, 2012.
Dong Wen 董文 *(Xinzhuyi jiaokeshu jiaoyuan yongshu/gaoji xiaoxue) Dili keben jiaoxuefa* (新主義教科書教員用書/高級小學) 地理課本教學法, Shanghai: Shijie, 1932.
Dong Wen 董文, *Gongmin keben* 公民課本, Shanghai: Zhonghua shuju, 1923.
Dong Wen 董文, *(Xiaoxue gaoji xuesheng yong) Xinzhuyi dili keben* (小學高級學生用) 新主義地理課本, Shanghai: Shijie, 1932.
Duara, Prasenjit, *Rescuing History from the Nation: Questioning Narratives of Modern China*, Chicago: University of Chicago Press, 1995.
Dunn, Arthur W., *Community Civics and Rural Life*, Boston: D. C. Heath & Co., 1929 rev. ed. [1920].
Elman, Benjamin A., *A Cultural History of Civil Examinations in Late Imperial China*, Berkeley: University of California Press, 2000.
Fan Zuoguai 范作乖, *Xiaoxue lishi keben jiaoxuefa* 歷史課本教學法, Shanghai: Zhonghua, 1934.
Fan Zuoguai 范作乖 and Han Feimu 韓非木, *(Xiuzheng kecheng biaozhun shiyong) Gaoxiao lishi keben jiaoxuefa* (修正課程標準適用) 高小歷史課本教學法, Shanghai: Zhonghua, 1937.
Fang Qinzhao 芳欽照, Zhu Wenshu 朱文叔, and Yu Shouzhen 喻守真, *Xin Zhonghua guoyu duben jiaoshoufa* 新中華國語讀本教授法, Beiping and Shanghai: Xin'guomin tushushe 新國民圖書社 and Zhonghua shuju, 1931–32 [1928].

Farquhar, Mary Anne, *Children's Literature in China*, Armonk, NY: M. E. Sharpe, 1999.
Feng Dafu 馮達夫, *(Xiaoxuexiao gaojiyong) Fuxing dili jiaokeshu* (小學校高級用) 復興地理教科書, Shanghai: Shangwu, 1933.
Feng Dafu 馮達夫, Chen Gaoji 陳鎬基, and Fu Weiping 傅緯平, *(Xiaoxuexiao gaojiyong) Fuxing dili jiaokeshu* (小學校高級用) 復興地理教科書, Shanghai: Shangwu, 1937.
Ferlanti, Federica, "The New Life Movement in Jiangxi Province, 1934–1938," *Modern Asian Studies* 44.5 (September 2010), pp. 961–1000.
Finch, Charles Edgar, *Everyday Civics: Community, State, and Nation*, New York: American Book Co., 1921.
Fitzgerald, John, *Awakening China: Politics, Culture, and Class in the Nationalist Revolution*, Stanford: Stanford University Press, 1996.
Foucault, Michel, *Discipline and Punish: The Birth of the Prison*, trans. Alan Sheridan, New York: Vintage Books, 1995.
Fridell, Wilbur M., "Government Ethics Textbooks in Late Meiji Japan," *Journal of Asian Studies* 29.4 (August 1970), pp. 823–833.
Fu Guangnian 富光年, *Jianyi lishi keben* 簡易歷史課本, Shanghai: Shangwu yinshuguan, 1906.
Fu Yunsen 傅運森, *Xin lishi (gongheguo jiaokeshu/gaodeng xiaoxue yong)* 新歷史 (共和國教科書/高等小學用), Shanghai: Shangwu, 1920 [1912]).
Gao Buying 高步瀛 and Chen Baoquan 陳寶泉, *(Tongsu) Guomin bidu* (通俗) 國民必讀, Shanghai: Nanyangguan shuju, 1905.
Gao Fengqian 高鳳謙, Cai Yuanpei 蔡元培, and Zhang Yuanji 張源濟, *Zuixin xiushen jiaokeshu jiaoshoufa* 最新修身教科書教採法, Shanghai: Shangwu, 1906.
Gao Fengqian 高鳳謙, Zhang Yuanji 張元濟, and Jiang Weiqiao 蔣維喬, *(Zhonghua minguo gaodeng xiaoxueyong) Zuixin guowen jiaokeshu* (中華民國高等小學用) 最新國文教科書, Shanghai: Shangwu, 1913 [1907].
Ge Suicheng 葛綏成, *(Xinkecheng biaozhun shiyong) Chuzhong benguo dili* (新課程標準使用) 初中本國地理, Shanghai: Zhonghua, 1933.
Ge Suicheng 葛綏成 and Yu Pu 喻璞, *(Chuji zhongxueyong) Xin Zhonghua yuti benguo dili xiangjie* (初級中學用) 新中華語體本國地理詳解, Shanghai: Zhonghua, 1933.
Gluck, Carol, *Japan's Modern Myths: Ideology in the Late Meiji Period*, Princeton, NJ: Princeton University Press, 1985.
Gu Jiegang 顧頡剛 and Wang Zhongqi 王鍾麒, *(Xiandai chuzhong jiaokeshu) Benguoshi* (現代初中教科書) 本國史, Shanghai: Shangwu, 1926–1927.
Gu Zhuo 顧倬, *(Gaodeng xiaoxue) Guowen duben* (高等小學) 國文讀本, Shanghai: Wenming, 1906.
Guan Qi 管圻, *Zhongguo dili xin jiaokeshu jiaoshoufa* 中國地理新教科書教授法, Shanghai: Shanghai lequn tushu bianyiju, 1906.
Guan Xiaohong 关晓红, *Wan-Qing xuebu yanjiu* 晚清学部研究, Guangzhou: Guangdong jiaoyu chubanshe, 2000.
Guitteau, William Backus, *Our United States: A History*, New York: Silver, Burdett and Co., 1919.
Guo Shuanglin 郭双林, *Xichao jidangxia de wan-Qing dilixue* 西潮激荡下的晚清地理学, Beijing: Beijing daxue chubanshe, 2000.
Han Hua 韩华, *Minchu Kongjiaohui yu guojiao yundong yanjiu*, 民初孔教会与国教运动研究, Beijing: Beijing tushuguan chubanshe, 2007.

Harrison, Henrietta, *The Making of the Republican Citizen: Political Ceremonies and Symbols in China, 1911–1929*, Oxford University Press, 2000.
Hayford, Charles W., *To the People: James Yen and Village China*, New York: Columbia University Press, 1990.
Hayhoe, Ruth, "Cultural Tradition and Educational Modernization: Lessons from the Republican Era," in Ruth Hayhoe, ed., *Education and Modernization: The Chinese Experience*, Oxford: Pergamon Press, 1996, pp. 47–72.
He Bingsong 何炳松, "Lishi jiaoshoufa (shang)" 歷史教授法 (上), *Jiaoyu zazhi* 教育雜誌 17.2 (1925), n.p.
He Bingsong 何炳松, "Lishi jiaoshoufa (xia)" 歷史教授法 (下), *Jiaoyu zazhi* 教育雜誌 17.3 (1925), n.p.
Hill, Michael Gibbs, "National Classicism: Lin Shu as Textbook Writer and Anthologist, 1908–1924," *Twentieth-Century China* 33.1 (November 2007), pp. 17–51.
Hon, Tze-ki, "Educating the Citizens: Visions of China in Late Qing History Textbooks," in Tze-ki Hon and Robert J. Culp, eds., *The Politics of Historical Production in Late Qing and Republican China*, Leiden: Brill, 2007, pp. 79–105.
Hon, Tze-ki, and Robert J. Culp, eds., *The Politics of Historical Production in Late Qing and Republican China*, Leiden: Brill, 2007.
Hon, Tze-ki, *Revolution as Restoration: Guocui xuebao and China's Path to Modernity, 1905–1911*, Leiden: Brill, 2013.
Horio, Teruhisa, *Educational Thought and Ideology in Modern Japan: State Authority and Intellectual Freedom*, ed. and trans. Steven Platzer, Tokyo: University of Tokyo Press, 1989.
Hostetler, Laura, *Qing Colonial Enterprise: Ethnography and Cartography in Early Modern China*, Chicago: University of Chicago Press, 2005.
Hou Hongjian 侯鴻鑒, "Guoxue, guochi, laoku sanda zhuyi biaolie" 國學國恥勞苦三大主義表例, *Jiaoyu zazhi* 教育雜誌 7.7 (1915), pp. 21–24.
Hou Hongjian 侯鴻鑒, "Xiaoxuexiao feiqu xiushen kaoshi ji kaocha xingxing zhi taolun" 小學校廢去修身考試及考察性行之討論, *Jiaoyu zazhi* 教育雜誌 7.10 (1915), pp. 184–188.
Hou Hongjian 侯鴻鑒, *Zhongdeng dili jiaokeshu* 中等地理教科書, Shanghai: Wenming, "1895" [1905].
Hu Chaoyang 胡朝陽, *Diyi jianming lishi qimeng* 第一簡明歷史啟蒙, Shanghai: Xinxue huishe, 1923 [1908].
Hu Shitan 胡師澹, *(Lujiang gongli zhongxuetang) Dili jiangyi* (淥江公立中學堂) 地理講義, n.p., 1908.
Huang Jinlin 黃金麟, *Lishi, shenti, guojia: jindai Zhongguo de shenti xingcheng, 1895–1937* 歷史、身體、國家: 近代中國的身體形成, 1895–1937, Taibei: Lianjing, 2000.
Huang Jinxing 黃進興, "Zhongguo jindai shixue de shuangchong weiji: shi lun 'Xin shixue' de dansheng jiqi suo mianlin de kunjing" 中國近代史學的雙重危機: 式論「新史學」的誕生及其所面臨的困境, *Zhongguo wenhua yanjiu xuebao* 中國文化研究學報 6 (1997), pp. 263–284.
Huang Kewu 黃克武 and Zhang Zhejia 張哲嘉, eds., *Gong yu si: jindai Zhongguo geti yu qunti zhi chongjian* 公與私: 近代中國個體與群體之重建, Taibei: Zhongyang yanjiuyuan jindaishi yanjiusuo, 2000.

Huang Shuguang 黄书光, "Jiazhi chonggu yu Minguo chunian zhongxiaoxue deyu kecheng jiaoxue de shenceng biange" 价值重估与民国初年中小学德育课程教学的深层变革, *Jiaoyu xuebao* 教育学报 4 (2008), pp. 73–79.

Huang Xingtao 黄兴涛 and Zeng Jianli 曾建立, "Qingmo xinshi xuetang de lunli jiaoyu yu lunli jiaokeshu tanlun: jian lun xiandai lunlixue xueke zai Zhongguo de xingqi" 清末新式学堂的伦理教育与伦理教科书探论 – – 兼论现代伦理学学科在中国的兴起, *Qingshi yanjiu* 清史研究 (2008.01), pp. 51–72.

Huang Jianli, *The Politics of Depoliticization in Republican China: Guomindang Policy towards Student Political Activism, 1927–1949*, Bern: Peter Lang, 1996.

Hughes, R. O., *Community Civics*, Boston: Allyn and Bacon, 1921 [1917].

Hughes,, R. O., *A Text-Book in Citizenship*, Boston: Allyn and Bacon, 1928 [1923].

Ijichi Sadaka 伊地知真馨, *Kogaku Nihon shiryaku zennisatsu* 小學日本史略全二冊 (publisher? 1880), in Kaigo Tokiomi 海後宗臣 and Naka Arata 仲新, eds., *Nihon kyōkasho taikei: kindai hen* 日本教科書大系: 近代編, Tokyo: Kodansha, 1975, vol. 18, pp. 259–318.

Ishikawa Yoshihiro 石川禎浩, "20 seiki shotō no Chūgoku ni okeru 'Kōtei' netsu" 20世紀初頭のおける '黃帝' 熱, *Nijū seiki kenkyū*; 二十世紀研究 3 (December 2002), pp. 1–22.

Jia Fengzhen 賈豐臻, "Xiushen jiaoshou ji caoxing diaocha shuo" 修身教授及操行調查說, *Jiaoyu zazhi* 5.6 教育雜誌 (1913), pp. 55–62.

Jiang Jianqiu 蔣鑒秋, *(Xiuzheng kecheng biaozhun shiyong) Chuxiao changshi keben jiaoxuefa* (修正課程標準適用) 初小常識課本教學法, Shanghai: Zhonghua shuju, 1937.

Jiang Weiqiao 蔣維喬, "Bianyi xiaoxue jiaokeshu zhi huiyi" 編輯小學教科書之回憶, in Zhang Jinglu 張靜廬, ed., *Zhongguo jindai chuban shiliao: bubian* 中國近代出版史料: 補編, Shanghai: Shanghai shudian, 2003, vol. 6, pp. 138–145.

Jiang Weiqiao 蔣維橋 and Zhuang Yu 莊俞, *Zuixin guowen jiaokeshu (chudeng xiaoxuetang yong)* 最新國文教科書 (初等小學堂用), Shanghai: Shangwu, 1904–1911.

Jiaoyubu 教育部, comp., *Sanmin zhuyi qianzike (zhuanxingben jiazhong)* 三民主義千字課 (暫行本甲種), Shanghai: Dadong shuju, 1932.

Jin Guantao 金觀濤 and Liu Qingfeng 劉青峰, "Cong 'qun' dao 'shehui', 'shehui zhuyi' – Zhongguo jindai gonggong lingyu bianqian de sixiangshi yanjiu" 從「群」到「社會」、「社會主義」——中國近代公共領域變遷的思想史研究, *Zhongyang yanjiuyuan jindaishi yanjiusuo jikan* 中央研究院近代史研究所季刊 35 (June 2001), pp. 1–66.

Jin Zhaozi 金兆梓, *(Chuji zhongxueyong) Xin Zhonghua benguoshi jiaokeshu* (初級中學用) 新中華本國史教科書, n.p.: Xin guomin tushushe, 1934 [1929].

Jones, Andrew F., *Developmental Fairy Tales: Evolutionary Thinking and Modern Chinese Culture*, Cambridge, MA: Harvard University Press, 2011.

Judge, Joan, "Between Nei and Wai: Chinese Women Students in Japan in the Early Twentieth Century," in Bryna Goodman and Wendy Larson, eds., *Gender in Motion: Divisions of Labor and Cultural Change in Late Imperial and Modern China*, Lanham, MD: Rowman & Littlefield, 2005, pp. 121–143.

Judge, Joan, "The Culturally Contested Student Body: Nü xuesheng at the Turn of the Twentieth Century," in Doris Croissant, Catherine Vance Yeh, and Joshua S. Mostow, eds., *Performing "Nation": Gender Politics in Literature, Theater, and the Visual Arts of China and Japan, 1880–1940*, Leiden: Brill, 2008, pp. 103–142.

Judge, Joan, "Gaizao guojia: wan-Qing de jiaokeshu yu guomin duben" 改造國家: 晚清的教科書與國民讀本, trans. Sun Huimin, *Xinshixue* 新史學 12.2 (June 2001), pp. 1–40.

Judge, Joan, "Meng Mu Meets the Modern: Female Exemplars in Early-Twentieth-Century Textbooks for Girls and Women," *Jindai Zhongguo funüshi yanjiu* 近代中國婦女史研究 8 (2000), pp. 129–177.

Kaigo Tokiomi 海後宗臣 and Naka Arata 仲新, *Kindai Nihon kyōkasho sōsetsu* 近代日本教科書総說, Tokyo: Kodansha, 1969.

Kametani Seiken 龜谷省軒, *Shūshin jikun* 修身兒訓 (orig. Tokyo: Kōfūsha, 1880), in Kaigo Tokiomi 海後宗臣 and Naka Arata 仲新, eds., *Nihon kyōkasho taikei: kindai hen* 日本教科書大系: 近代編, Tokyo: Kodansha, 1975, vol. 2, pp. 39–80.

Kang Youwei, *Ta t'ung shu: The One-World Philosophy of K'ang Yu-wei*, trans. Laurence G. Thompson, London: Routledge, 2005.

Karl, Rebecca E., "On Comparability and Continuity: China, circa 1930s and 1990s," *Boundary 2* 32.2 (summer 2005), pp. 169–200.

Kaske, Elisabeth, *The Politics of Language in Chinese Education, 1895–1919*, Leiden: Brill, 2008.

Kecheng jiaocai yanjiusuo 课程教材研究所, ed., *20 shiji Zhongguo zhongxiaoxue kecheng biaozhun: jiaoxue dagang huibian* 20 世纪中国中小学课程标准: 教学大纲汇编, 15 vols., Beijing: Renmin jiaoyu chubanshe, 2001.

Keenan, Barry, *The Dewey Experiment in China: Educational Reform and Political Power in the Early Republic*, Cambridge, MA: CEAS, Harvard University Press, 1977.

Keenan, Barry C., *Imperial China's Last Classical Academies: Social Change in the Lower Yangzi, 1864–1911*, Berkeley: Institute of East Asian Studies, University of California Press, 1994.

Kiely, Jan, "Shanghai Public Moralist Nie Qijie and Morality Book Publication Projects in Republican China," *Twentieth-Century China* 36.1 (January 2011), pp. 4–22.

Kō Tōran 黃東蘭 [Huang Donglan], "Shinmatsu-Minkokuki chiri kyōkasho no kūkan hyōshō: ryōdo, kyōiki, kokuchi" 清末民国期地理教科書の空間表象－－領土、疆域、國恥, in Namiki Yorihisa 並木賴壽, Ōsato Hiroaki 大里浩秋, and Sunayama Yukio 砂山幸雄, eds., *Kindai Chūgoku – kyōkasho to Nihon* 近代中国・教科書と日本, Tokyo: Kenbun shuppan, 2010, pp. 233–285.

Lam, Tong, *A Passion for Facts: Social Surveys and the Construction of the Chinese Nation State, 1900–1949*, Berkeley: University of California Press, 2011.

Lee, Chiu-chun, "Liberalism and Nationalism at a Crossroads: The Guomindang's Educational Policies, 1927–1930," trans. Tze-ki Hon, in Tze-ki Hon and Robert J. Culp, eds., *The Politics of Historical Production in Late Qing and Republican China*, Leiden: Brill, 2007, pp. 295–315.

Lee, Ger-bei, "Values, Tradition, and Social Change: A Study of School Textbooks in Taiwan and in China," Ph.D. dissertation, University of California, Los Angeles, 1987, pp. 10–13.

Leung, Angela, and Charlotte Furth, eds., *Health and Hygiene in Chinese East Asia: Politics and Publics in the Long Twentieth Century*, Durham, NC: Duke University Press, 2010.

Li Guojun 李國鈞 and Wang Bingzhao 王炳照, eds., *Zhongguo jiaoyu zhidu tongshi* 中国教育制度通史, 8 vols., Jinan: Shandong jiaoyu chubanshe, 2000.

Li Jiagu 李嘉穀, *Mengxue xiushen jiaokeshu* 蒙學修身教科書, Shanghai: Wenming shuju, 1905.

Li Jinhui 黎錦暉 and Lufei Kui 陸費逵, *(Xinxuezhi shiyong) Guoyu duben* (新學制適用) 國語讀本, Shanghai: Zhonghua, 1927 [1923].

Li Tinghan 李廷翰, *Zhongxue dili jiaokeshu* 中學地理教科書, Shanghai: Zhonghua shuju, 1914.

Li Xiaoqian 李孝迁, "Qingji Zhinashi, Dongyangshi jiaokeshu jieyi chutan" 清季之那史、东洋史教科书介译初探, *Shixue yuekan* 史学月刊 2003.9, pp. 101–110.

Li Xiaoqian 李孝迁, *Xifang shixue zai Zhongguo de chuanbo, 1882–1949* 西方史学在中国的传播 (1882–1949), Shanghai: Huadong shifan daxue chubanshe, 2007.

Li Zheng 李征, "Xiaoxuesheng yuwen shiti da'an yin gefan zhenglun" 小学生语文试题答案引各方争论, *Dongfangwang* 东方网 (18 April 2012), http://sh.eastday.com/m/20120418/ula6497074.html, accessed 27 September 2012.

Liang Qichao 梁啟超, "Xin shixue" 新史學, *Yinbingshi heji* 飲冰室合集, Beijing: Zhonghua shuju, 1996, wenji 9: 1–32.

Liang Xin 梁心, *Guochi shiyao* 國恥史要, Taibei: Wenhai, 1973 [1931]).

Liu Jianbai 劉劍白, *Xiaoxue xiushen jiaokeshu* 小學修身教科書, Shanghai: Wenming shuju, 1903.

Liu Shipei 劉師培, *Lunli jiaokeshu* 倫理教科書, in *Liu Shipei quanji* 劉師培全集, Beijing: Zhonggong zhongyang dangxiao chubanshe, 1997, vol. 4, pp. 123–169.

Liu Shipei, *Zhongguo dili jiaokeshu* 中國地理教科書, in *Liu Shipei quanji* 劉師培全集, Beijing: Zhonggong zhongyang dangxiao chubanshe, 1997, vol. 4, pp. 371–461.

Liu Shipei 劉師培, *Zhongguo lishi jiaokeshu* 中國歷史教刻書 in *Liu Shipei quanji* 劉師培全集, Beijing: Zhonggong zhongyang dangxiao chubanshe, 1997, vol. 4, pp. 275–370.

Liu Shipei, *Zhongguo minzu zhi* 中國民族志, in *Liu Shipei quanji* 劉師培全集, Beijing: Zhonggong zhongyang dangxiao chubanshe, 1997, vol. 1, pp. 579–626.

Liu Yizheng 柳詒徵, *Lidai shilue* 歷代史略, Taizhong: Wenyinge tushu, 2010 [1902].

Liu Zhemin 刘哲民, comp., *Jinxiandai chuban xinwen fagui huibian* 近现代出版新闻法规汇编, Beijing: Xuelin chubanshe, 1992.

Lü Boyou 呂伯攸, *Xin Zhonghua dangyi keben jiaoshoufa (xiaoxuexiao chujiyong)* 新中華黨議課本教授法 (小學校初級用), Shanghai: Zhonghua, 1932 [1929].

Lü Jinlu 呂金錄 et al., eds., *Fuxing gongmin jiaokeshu (gaoxiao)* 復興公民教科書 (高小), Shanghai: Shangwu, 1941 [1939].

Lu Shaochang 陸紹昌, *Xin Zhonghua sanmin zhuyi keben (xiaoxuexiao gaojiyong)* 新中華三民主義課本 (小學校高級用, Shanghai: Xin'guomin tushushe/Zhonghua, 1932 [1927].

Lü Simian 呂思勉, *Baihua benguoshi* 白話本國史, Shanghai: Shanghai shudian, 1990 [Shangwu, 1923].

Lü Simian 呂思勉 *Minguo guowen keben: baihua zhenzangban* 民國國文課本: 白话珍藏版, Chen Zhiyang 陈志扬 and Ye Xianyun 叶仙云, eds., Beijing: Jiuzhou chubanshe, 2011 [1916]).

Luo Xianglin 羅香林, *Gaozhong benguoshi* 高中本國史, Nanjing: Zhengzhong shuju, 1935.

Luo Zhitian 羅志田, "Baorong ruxue, zhuzi yu Huangdi de guoxue: Qingji shiren xunqiu minzu rentong xiangzheng de nuli" 包容儒學、諸子與黃帝的國學:

清季士人尋求民族認同象徵的努力, *Taida lishi xuebao* 臺大歷史學報 29 (June 2002), pp. 87–105.
Ma Jingwu 馬精武 and Wang Zhicheng 王志成, *(Chuxiao) Fuxing shehui jiaokeshu* (初小) 復興社會教科書, Shanghai: Shangwu, 1934.
Mao Lirei 毛禮銳 and Shen Guanqun 沈灌群, eds., *Zhongguo jiaoyu tongshi* 中國教育通史, 6 vols., Jinan, Shandong jiaoyu chubanshe, 1988.
Mao Zedong, *Selected Works of Mao Tse-tung*, 5 vols., Peking: Foreign Languages Press, 1966–1977.
Mazur, Mary, "Discontinuous Continuity: The Beginnings of a New Synthesis of 'General History' in 20th-Century China," in Tze-ki Hon and Robert J. Culp, eds., *The Politics of Historical Production in Late Qing and Republican China*, Leiden: Brill, 2007, pp. 131–136.
Meng, Yue, *Shanghai and the Edges of Empires*, Minneapolis: University of Minnesota Press, 2006.
Mengxue duben quanshu sanbian 蒙學讀本全書三編 (no publishing information; in possession of the Shanghai Library), 3 vols.
Moloughney, Brian, and Peter Zarrow, "Making History Modern: The Transformation of Chinese Historiography, 1895–1937," in idem., eds., *Transforming History: The Making of a Modern Academic Discipline in Twentieth-Century China*, Hong Kong: Chinese University Press, 2011, pp. 1–45.
Monbushō 文部省, comp., *Jinjō shōgaku Nihon kokushi* 尋常小學日本國史, Tokyo: Monbusho, 1908.
Monbushō 文部省, comp., *Jinjō shōgaku shūshinsho* 尋常小學修身書 (1910), in Kaigo Tokiomi 海後宗臣 and Naka Arata 仲新, eds., *Nihon kyōkasho taikei: kindai hen* 日本教科書大系: 近代編, Tokyo: Kodansha, 1975, vol. 3, pp. 61–123.
Monbushō 文部省, comp., *Jinjō shōgaku shūshinsho: jidōyō*; 尋常小學修身書: 兒童用 Tokyo: Monbushō, 1910–1911.
Monbushō 文部省, comp., *Shōgaku chiri* 小學地理 (1903), in Kaigo Tokiomi 海後宗臣 and Naka Arata 仲新, eds., *Nihon kyōkasho taikei: Kindai hen* 日本教科書大系: 近代編 (Tokyo: Kodansha, 1975), vol. 16, pp. 349–390.
Monbushō 文部省, comp., *Shōgaku sakuhōsho* 小學作法書 (1883), in Kaigo Tokiomi 海後宗臣 and Naka Arata 仲新, eds., *Nihon kyōkasho taikei: kindai hen* 日本教科書大系: 近代編, Tokyo: Kodansha, 1975, vol. 2, pp. 179–193.
Morgan, Carol, ed., *Inter- and Intracultural Differences in European History Textbooks*, Bern: Peter Lang, 2005.
Mullaney, Thomas S., ed., *Critical Han Studies: The History, Representation, and Identity of China's Majority*, Berkeley: University of California Press, 2012.
Nagai, Michio, "Westernization and Japanization: The Early Meiji Transformation of Education," in Donald H. Shively, ed., *Tradition and Modernization in Japanese Culture*, Princeton, NJ: Princeton University Press, 1971, pp. 35–76.
Nakamura Kikuji 中村紀久二, *Fukkoku kokutei rekishi kyōkasho kaisetsu* 複刻國定歷史教科書解說, Tokyo: Ōzorasha, 1987.
Namiki Yorihisa 並木賴壽, "Shinmatsu minkoku kokubun – kokugo kyōkasho no kōsō 清末民国国文、国号教科書の構想, in Namiki Yorihisa 並木賴壽, Ōsato Hiroaki 大里浩秋, and Sunayama Yukio 砂山幸雄, eds., *Kindai Chūgoku – kyōkasho to Nihon* 近代中国・教科書と日本, Tokyo: Kenbun shuppan, 2010, pp. 91–136.

Namiki Yorihisa 並木賴寿, Ōsato Hiroaki 大里浩秋, and Sunayama Yukio 砂山幸雄, eds., *Kindai Chūgoku – kyōkasho to Nihon* 近代中国・教科書と日本, Tokyo: Kenbun shuppan, 2010.

Nedostup, Rebecca, *Superstitious Regimes: Religion and the Politics of Chinese Modernity*, Cambridge, MA: HUAC, Harvard University Press, 2009.

Ng, On-cho, and Q. Edward Wang, *Mirroring the Past: The Writing and Use of History in Imperial China*, Honolulu: University of Hawaii Press, 2005.

Ni Wenjun 倪文君, "Jindai xueke xingcheng guochengzhong de wan-Qing dili jiaokeshu shulun" 近代学科形成过程中的晚清地理教科书述论, *Huadong shifan daxue xeubao (zhexue shehui kexue ban)* 38.5 (September 2006), pp. 107–112.

Passin, Herbert, *Society and Education in Japan*, New York: Teachers College Press, Columbia University, 1965.

Peake, Cyrus H., *Nationalism and Education in Modern China*, New York: Howard Fertig, 1970 [1932].

Peake, Cyrus H., "The Reminiscences of Cyrus H. Peake," Oral History Research Office, Columbia University, 1961.

Poovey, Mary, *A History of the Modern Fact: Problems of Knowledge in the Sciences of Wealth and Society*, Chicago: University of Chicago Press, 1998.

Qian Zhonghan 錢宗翰, *Huitu Zhongguo baihua shi* 繪圖中國白話史, n.p., 1906.

Qin Tongpei 秦同培, *Xin xiushen (gongheguo jiaokeshu)* 新修身教科書 (共和國教科書), Shanghai: Shangwu, 1912–1918.

Qin Tongpei 秦同培, *Xin xiushen jiaoshoufa (Guomin xuexiao/gongheguo jiaokeshu)* 新修身教授法 (國民學校/共和國教科書), Shanghai: Shangwu, 1912–18.

Qiu Xiuxiang 邱秀香, *Qingmo xinshi jiaoyu de lixiang yu xianshi: yi xinshi xiaoxuetang xingban wei zhongxin de tantao* 清末新式教育的理想與現實: 以新式小學堂興辦為中心的探討, Taibei: Zhengzhi daxue lishixi, 2000.

Qu Xingui 璩鑫圭 and Tang Liangyan 唐良炎, eds., *Zhongguo jindai jiaoyushi ziliao huibian* 中国近代教育史资料汇编, 10 vols., Shanghai: Shanghai jiaoyu chubanshe, 1991.

Ramirez, Francisco O. and John Boli, "The Political Construction of Mass Schooling: European Origins and Worldwide Institutionalization," *Sociology of Education* 60 (January 1987), pp. 2–17.

Rawski, Evelyn Sakakida, *Education and Popular Literacy in Ch'ing China*, Ann Arbor: University of Michigan Press, 1979.

Reed, Christopher A., *Gutenberg in Shanghai: Chinese Print Capitalism, 1876–1937*, Vancouver: University of British Columbia Press, 2004.

Reed, Thomas Harrison, *Loyal Citizenship*, Yonkers-on-Hudson, NY: World Book Company, 1922.

Reynolds, Douglas R., *China, 1898–1912: The Xinzheng Revolution and Japan*, Cambridge, MA: CEAS, Harvard University Press, 1993.

Ricoeur, Paul, *Time and Narrative*, trans. Kathleen Blamey and David Pellauer, 3 vols., Chicago: University of Chicago Press, 1984–1988.

Rigby, Richard W., *The May 30 Movement: Events and Themes*, Canberra: Australian National University Press, 1980.

Rogawski, Ruth, *Hygienic Modernity: Meanings of Health and Disease in Treaty-Port China*, Berkeley: University of California Press, 2004.

Sang Bing 桑兵, *Wan-Qing xuetang xuesheng yu shehui bianqian* 晚清學堂學生與社會變遷, Xinzhuang, Taiwan: Daohe chuban, 1991.
Schneider, Laurence A., *Ku Chieh-kang and China's New History: Nationalism and the Quest for Alternative Traditions*, Berkeley: University of California Press, 1971.
"Shanghai tushu gongsi cheng chudeng xiaoxue xiushen jiaoshouben ji keben qing shending pi" 上海圖書公司呈出等小學修身教授本及科本請審定批, *Jiaoyu zazhi* 教育雜誌 2.2 (1910), fulu p. 7.
Shangwu yinshuguan 商務印書館, comp., *Da Qing xin faling* 大清新法令, 3 vols., Beijing: Shangwu, 1909.
Shangwu yinshugan bianyisuo 商務印書館編譯所, comp. *(Gaodeng xiaoxue tang yong) Zhongguo ditu* (高等小學堂用) 中國地圖, Shanghai: Shangwu, 1908.
Shen Guowei 沈国威, "Guanyu Qing xuebu bian *Jianyi shizi keben* (1909)" 关于清学部编《简易识字课本》(1909), *Wakumon* 或問 17 (2009), pp. 83–100.
Shen Liangqi 沈亮棨, *Guochi yanshuo* 國恥演說 (Taibei: Wenhai chubanshe, 1987 [1921].
Shen Songqiao 沈松僑, "Wo yi woxie jian Xuanyuan: Huangdi shenhua yu wan Qing de guozu jiangou" 我以我血建軒轅－黃帝神話與晚清的國族建構, *Taiwan shehui yanjiu jikan* 台灣社會研究季刊 28 (December 1997), pp. 1–77.
Shen Yi 沈頤, Dai Kedun 戴克敦, Lufei Kui 陸費逵, and Hua Hongnian 華鴻年, *(Xinzhi) Zhonghua (guomin xiaoxue) guowen jiaokeshu* (新制) 中華 (國民小學) 國文教科書, Shanghai: Zhonghua shuju, 1920 [1913].
Sheng Langxi 盛郎西, "Cong xiushenke shuo dao gongmin xunlianke" 從修身科說到公民訓練科 in *Xiaoxue kecheng yange* 小學課程沿革, Shanghai: Zhonghua shuju, 1934), pp. 5–58.
Shi Naide 施耐德 [Axel Schneider], "Minzu, lishi yu lilun: Zhongguo houdizhi shiqi (post-imperial) shixue zhi jueze" 民族、歷史與論理——中國後帝制時期 (post-imperial) 史學之抉擇, *Xinshixue* 新史學 19.2 (June 2008), pp. 47–83.
Shin Kokui [Shen Guowei] 沈国威 and Son Sei [Sun Qing] 孫青, "Gen Fuku to Shinmatsu gakubu hen *Kokumin hitsudoku kahon shokō*; (1910)" 厳復と清末学部編『国民必読課本初稿』(1910), in Akira Matsuura 松浦章, ed., *Higashi Ajia ni okeru bunka jōhō no hasshin to juyō*; 東アジアにおける文化情報の発信と受容, Tokyo: Yūshōdō Shuppan: 2010, pp. 31–54.
Shin Kokui [Shen Guowei] 沈国威, "Shinmatsu no kokumin hitsudoku ni tsuite: keishiki to naiyō no aide 清末の国民必読について：形式と内容の間で, in Shin Kokui and Uchida Keiichi 内田慶市, eds., *Kindai higashi Ajia ni okeru buntai no hensen: keishiki to naijitsu no sōkoku o koete* 近代東アジアにおける文体の変遷：形式と内実の相克を超えて, Tokyo: Hakuteisha, 2010, pp. 233–275.
Shōei Yazu 矢津昌永, *(Zhongxue) Wanguo dizhi* (中學) 萬國地誌, trans. Chuyang xuesheng bianyisuo 出洋學生編譯所, Shanghai: Shangwu, 1902.
Shu Xincheng 舒新城, ed., *Jindai Zhongguo jiaoyu sixiangshi* 近代中國教育思想史, Shanghai, Shanghai shuju, 1992.
Son Ansoku 孫安石, "Nankin kokumin seifu to kyōkasho shintei: kyōikubu henshincho to kokuritsu henyakukan no kaigi kiroku o chūshin ni" 南京国民政府と教科書審定：教育部編審処と国立編訳館の会議記録お中心に, in Namiki Yorihisa 並木頼寿, Ōsato Hiroaki 大里浩秋, and Sunayama Yukio 砂山幸雄,

eds., *Kindai Chūgoku – kyōkasho to Nihon* 近代中国・教科書と日本, Tokyo: Kenbun shuppan, 2010, pp. 137–160.

Son Kō [Sun Jiang] 孫江, "Renzoku to danzetsu: nijū seiki shoki Chūgoku no rekishi kyōkasho ni okeru Kōtei jojutsu 連続と断絶 -- 二十世紀初期中国の歴史教科書における黃帝叙述, in Namiki Yorihisa 並木賴寿, Ōsato Hiroaki 大里浩秋, and Sunayama Yukio 砂山幸雄, eds., *Kindai Chūgoku – kyōkasho to Nihon* 近代中国・教科書と日本, Tokyo: Kenbun shuppan, 2010, pp. 163–195.

Strand, David, *An Unfinished Republic: Leading by Word and Deed in Modern China*, Berkeley: University of California Press, 2011.

Sun, Jiang [孫江], "Blumenbach in East Asia: The Dissemination of the 'Five-Race Theory' in East Asia and a Textual Comparison," *Oriens Extremus* 51 (2012), pp. 107–153.

Sun, Jiang [孫江], "Continuity and Discontinuity: Narratives of the Yellow Emperor in Early Twentieth-Century History Textbooks," *Frontiers of History in China* 8.2 (June 1913), pp. 176–201.

Taixuan 太玄, "Gongmin de xunlianfa" 公民的訓練法, *Jiaoyu zazhi* 教育雜誌 10.4 (1918), pp. 93–100.

Takada Yukio 高田幸男, "Minkokuki kyōiku ni okeru pragumateizumu to minshu shugi" 民國期教育におけるプラグマテイズムと民主主義, in Kubo Tōru 久保亨 and Saga Takashi 嵯峨隆, eds., *Chūka Minkoku no kensei to dokusai 1912–1949* 中華民国の憲政と独裁 1912–1949, Tokyo: Keiō gijuku daigaku shuppankai, 2011, pp. 147–175.

Tan Lian 譚廉, *(Zuixin gaodeng xiaoxue) Dili jiaokeshu xiangjie* (最新搞等小學) 地理教科書詳解, Shanghai: Shangwu, 1909–10.

Tan Lian 譚廉 and Tan Yunhua 譚蘊華, *(Xin xuezhi xiaoxuexiao gaoji yong) Xinzhuan dili jiaoshoushu* (新學制小學校高級用) 心撰地理教授書, Shanghai: Shangwu, 1926.

Tan Lianxun 譚廉遜, *(Chuji zhongxue xuesheng yong Tan shi) Chuzhong benguo dili* (初級中學學生用譚氏) 初中本國地理, Shanghai: Shijie, 1933.

Tanaka Hiroshi 田中比呂志, "Tsukurareru dentō: Shinmatsu minsho no kokumin keisei to rekishi kyōkasho" 創るられる伝統: 清末民初の国民形成と歴史教科書, *Rekishi hyōron* 歷史評論 659 (March 2005), pp. 42–56.

Tang Zhansheng 唐湛聲, *Xiaoxue gongmin jiaoxuefa* 小學公民科教學, Shanghai: Zhonghua shuju, 1925 [1924].

Tao Baochuan 陶百川, *Dangyi (gaoji zhongxuexiao ben)* 黨議 (高級中學校本), Shanghai: Dadong shuju, 1932.

Tao Menghe 陶孟和, *Shehui wenti (xinxuezhi gaoji zhongxue jiaokeshu)* 社會問題 (新學制高級中學教科書), Shanghai: Shangwu, 1924.

Tarumoto Teruo 樽本照雄, "Xinhai geming qian de Shangwu yinshuguan he Jingangtang zhi hezi jingying" 辛亥革命时期的商务印书馆和金港堂之合资经营, trans. Chen Wei 陈薇, in Tarumoto Teruo 樽本照雄 ed., *Qingmo xiaoshuo jigao* 清末小说研究集稿, Jinan: Qilu shushe, 2006, pp. 218–236.

Tianmin 天民, "Gongmin jiaoyu wenti" 公民教育問題, *Jiaoyu zazhi* 教育雜誌 5.10 (1914), pp. 115–122.

Tillman, Margaret, "The Authority of Age: Institutions for Childhood Development in China, 1895–1910," *Frontiers of History in China* 7.1 (March 2012), pp. 32–60.

Tong Zhencao 童振藻, *Jianyi dili keben* 簡易地理課本, Shanghai: Shangwu, 1906.
Tsin, Michael, "Imagining 'Society' in Early Twentieth-Century China," in Joshua A. Fogel and Peter Zarrow, eds., *Imagining the People: Chinese Intellectuals and the Concept of Citizenship, 1890–1920*, Armonk, NY: M. E. Sharpe, 1997, pp. 212–231.
Tsuchiya Hiroshi 土屋洋, "Shinmatsu no shūshin kyōkasho to Nihon" 清末の修身教科書と日本, in Namiki Yorihisa 並木賴寿, Ōsato Hiroaki 大里浩秋, and Sunayama Yukio 砂山幸雄, eds., *Kindai Chūgoku – kyōkasho to Nihon* 近代中国・教科書と日本, Tokyo: Kenbun shuppan, 2010, pp. 286–328.
Tu Ji 屠寄, *Zhongguo dili jiaokeshu* 中國地理教科書, Shanghai: Shangwu, 1905.
Tu, Wei-ming, "Selfhood and Otherness in Confucian Thought," in Anthony J. Marsella, George DeVos, and Francis L.K. Hsu, eds., *Culture and Self: Asian and Western Perspectives* (New York: Tavistock Publications, 1985), pp. 231–251.
van de Ven, Hans J., *War and Nationalism in China, 1925–1945*, London: Routledge-Curzon, 2003.
VanderVen, Elizabeth, "Village-State Cooperation: Modern Community Schools and Their Funding, Haicheng County, Fengtian, 1905-1931," *Modern China* 31.2 (April 2005), pp. 204–235.
Vogelsang, Kai, "Chinese 'Society': History of a Troublesome Concept," *Oriens Extremus* 51 (2012), pp. 155–192.
Vollmer, Klaus, "The Construction of 'Self' and Western and Asian 'Others' in Contemporary Japanese Civics and Ethics Textbooks," in Gotelind Müller, ed., *Designing History in East Asian Textbooks; Identity Politics and Transnational Aspirations*, London: Routledge, 2011, pp. 60–84.
Wan Liangjun 萬良濬, *Xinxuan gongmin jiaoshoushu (xinxuezhi xiaoxuexiao gaojiyong)* 新選公民教授書 (新學制小學校高級用), Shanghai: Shangwu, 1926 [1925].
Wang Bangshu 王邦樞, *(Chudeng) Zhongguo dili jiaokeshu* (初等) 中國地理教科書, n.p.: Nanyangguan shuju, 1907.
Wang Fansen 王汎森, "Wan-Qing de zhengzhi gainian yu 'Xin shixue'" 晚清的政治概念與 '新史學' in Luo Zhitian 罗志田, ed., *20 shiji de Zhonggon: xueshu yu shehui – shixue zhuan* 20 世纪的中国: 学术与社会. 史学卷, Jinan: Shandong renmen chubanshe, 2001, vol. 1, pp. 1–30.
Wang Jianjun 王建军, *Zhongguo jindai jiaokeshu fazhan yanjiu* 中国近代教科书发展研究, Guangdong: Guangdong jiaoyu chubanshe, 1996.
Wang Jianxing 王劍星 and Zhu Liangji 朱亮基, *Sanmin zhuyi keben jiaoshoufa (qianqi xiaoxue)* 三民主義課本教授法 (前期小學), Shanghai: shijie, 1932 [1931]).
Wang Jiarong 汪家熔, *Minzuhun: jiaokeshu bianqian* 民族魂: 教科书变迁, Beijing: Shangwu, 2008.
Wang Rongbao 汪榮寶, *Qingshi jiangyi* 清史講義 (reprt. Taibei: Wenhai chubanshe, 1982 [preface dated 1908]).
Wang Xiaojing 王小静, *Qingmo minchu xiushen sixiang yanjiu: yi xiushen jiaokeshu wei zhongxin de kaocha* 清末民初修身思想研究: 以修身教科书为中心的考察, Beijing: Renmin, 2012.
Wang Yunwen 王允文 and Lou Sanli 樓三立, *Xiaoxue shehui keben jiaoxuefa (Xin kecheng biaozhun shiyong/gaoji)* 小學社會課本教學法 (新課程標準實用/高級), Shanghai: Zhonghua shuju, 1933.

Wang Zhicheng 王志成 and Fei Xiewei 費燮威, *Lishi jiaoxuefa (fuxing jiaokeshu)* 歷史教學法 (復興教科書), Shanghai: Shangwu 1938–39 [1937].

Wang Zhijiu 王芝九, "Xiaoxue lishi jiaoxue shangque" 小學歷史商榷, *Jiaoyu zazhi* 教育雜誌 16.2 (1924), n.p.

Wang, Dong, *China's Unequal Treaties: Narrating National History*, Lanham, MD: Lexington Books, 2005.

Wang, Q. Edward, *Inventing China through History: The May Fourth Approach to Historiography*, Albany: State University of New York Press, 2001.

Wang, Q. Edward, "Narrating the Nation: Meiji Historiography, New History Textbooks, and the Disciplinarization of History in China," in Brian Moloughney and Peter Zarrow, eds., *Transforming History: The Making of a Modern Academic Discipline in Twentieth-Century China*, Hong Kong: Chinese University Press, 2011, pp. 103–133.

Wei Bingxin 魏冰心, *Chuzhong dangyi zhidaoshu (chuji zhongxue jiaoshi xueshengyong)* 初中黨議指導書 (初級中學教師學生用), Shanghai: Shijie, 1930–31.

Wei Bingxin 魏冰心, *Guoyu duben* 國語讀本, Shanghai: Shanghai kexue jishu wenxian chubanshe, 2005 [1930?].

Wei Bingxin 魏冰心, *Sanmin zhuyi keben (xiaoxue gaoji xuesheng yong)* 三民主義課本 (小學高級學生用), Shanghai: Shijie, 1932 [1931].

Wei Bingxin 魏冰心 and Dai Weiqing 戴渭清, *(Pingmin jiaoyu yongshu) Qianzi keben* (平民教育用書) 千字課本, Shanghai: Shijie, 1925.

Wei Bingxin 魏冰心 and Yin Shuping 殷叔平, "Qianqi xiaoxue guoyu duben jiaoxuefa gaiyao" 前期小學國語讀本教學法概要, in *(Xin zhuyi jiaokeshu jiaoyuan yongshu, qianqi xiaoxue) Guoyu duben jiaoxuefa* (新主義教科書教員用書,前期小學) 國語讀本教學法, Shanghai: Shijie shuju, 1932.

Wertsch, James, *Voices of Collective Memory*, Cambridge, Cambridge University Press, 2002.

West, Willis Mason, *The Story of World Progress*, Boston, Allyn and Bacon, 1922.

White, Hayden, "The Politics of Historical Interpretation: Discipline and De-Sublimation" in idem., *The Content of the Form: Narrative Discourse and Historical Representation*, Baltimore: Johns Hopkins University Press, 1987, pp. 58–82.

White, Hayden, "The Value of Narrativity in the Representation of Reality," in idem., *The Content of the Form: Narrative Discourse and Historical Representation*, Baltimore: Johns Hopkins University Press, 1987, pp. 1–25.

Woodside, Alexander, "Real and Imagined Continuities in the Chinese Struggle for Literacy," in Ruth Hayhoe, ed., *Education and Modernization: The Chinese Experience*, Oxford: Pergamon Press, 1992, pp. 23–45.

Wu Binggui 吳永貴, *Minguo chuban shi* 民國出版史, Fuzhou: Fujian renmin chubanshe, 2011.

Wu Jiazhen 吳家鎮 and Gao Shiliang 高時良, "Xianjieduan Zhongguo gongmin xunlian zhi niaokan ji qi gaijin" 現階段中國公民訓練之鳥瞰及其改進, *Jiaoyu zazhi* 教育雜誌 26.3 (1936), pp. 43–56.

Wu Xiaoou 吳小鸥, *Zhongguo jindai jiaokeshu de qimeng jiazhi* 中国近代教科书的启蒙价值, Fuzhou: Fujian jiaoyu chubanshe, 2011.

Xia Zengyou 夏曾佑, *Zuixin zhongxue Zhongguo lishi jiaokeshu* 最新中學中國歷史教科書 [Shanghai: Shangwu, 1904–06], republished as *Zhongguo gudaishi* 中國古代史, Shanghai: Shanghai shudian: 1990.

Xia Zengyou 夏曾佑, *Xiaoxue duben shi* 小學讀本史 (no publishing information; in possession of the Shanghai Library).

Xie Xingyao 謝興堯, *Chuzhong benguoshi* 初中本國史, Shanghai: Shijie shuju, 1933.

Xiong Xianjun 熊賢君, *Qianqiu jiye: Zhongguo jindai yiwu jiaoyu yanjiu* 千秋基業: 中國近代義務教育研究, Wuchang: Huazhong shifan daxue chubanshe, 1998.

Xiong Yuezhi 熊月之, *Zhongguo jindai minzhu sixiangshi* 中國近代民主思想史, Shanghai: Shanghai shehui kexueyuan chubanshe, 2002.

Xu Nianci 徐念慈, *(Chuji shifan xuexiao jiaokeshu) Zhongguo dili* (初級師範學校教科書) 中國地理, Shanghai: Shangwu, 1907.

Yang Shuming 楊叔明, *(Minzhong xuexiao jiaoyuan yongshu) Minzhong changshi keben jiaoshoufa* (民眾學校教員用書) 民眾常識課本教授法, Shanghai: Shijie shuju, 1932.

Yang Yao 杨尧, *Zhongguo jinxiandai zhongxiaoxue dili jiaoyushi* 中国近现代中小学地理教育史, 2 vols., Xi'an: Shaanxi renmin jiaoyu chubanshe, 1991.

Yang, C. K., *A Chinese Village in Early Communist Transition*, Cambridge, MA: MIT Press, 1965.

Yao Zuyi 姚祖義, *Zuixin gaodeng xiaoxue Zhongguo lishi jiaokeshu* 最新高等小學中國歷史教科書, Shanghai: Shangwu yinshuguan, 1904.

Yasuda Motohisa 安田元久, *Rekishi kyōiku to rekishigaku* 歴史教育と歴史学, Tokyo: Yamakawa shuppansha, 1991.

Ye Shengtao, *Guoyu duben* 國語讀本, Shanghai: Shanghai kexue jishu wenxian chubanshe, 2005 [Kaiming, 1932].

Yi Zhengyi 易正義, "Minguo chunian zhongxue 'gongmin' kecheng de jianli" 民國初年中學「公民」課程的建立, *Yadong xuebao* 亞東學報 29 (June 2009), pp. 329–340.

Yu Pu 玉璞, Han Feimu 幹非木, and Lou Yunlin 樓雲林, *(Xinkecheng biazhun shiyong) Xiaoxue dili keben jiaoxuefa*, Shanghai: Zhonghua, 1936 [1934].

Yu Shumin 郁樹敏, *(Gaoji xiaoxue shiyong) Fuxing gaoxiao dili jiaoxuefa* (高級小學適用) 復興高小地理教學法, Shanghai: Shangwu, 1938 [1937].

Yü, Ying-shih, "The Radicalization of China in the Twentieth Century," *Daedalus* 122.2 (Spring 1993), 125–150.

Yuan Yingguang 袁英光 and Zhong Weimin 仲伟民, "Liu Shipei yu 'Zhongguo lishi jiaokeshu' yanjiu" 刘师培与〈中国历史教科书〉研究, *Huadong shifan daxue xuebao (zhexue shehui kexueban)* 华东师范大学学报 (哲学社会科学版) (1988.4), pp. 67–75.

Zarrow, Peter, *After Empire: The Conceptual Transformation of the Chinese State, 1895–1924*, Stanford, CA: Stanford University Press, 2012.

Zarrow, Peter, *China in War and Revolution*, London: Routledge, 2005.

Zarrow, Peter, "Old Myth into New History: The Building Blocks of Liang Qichao's 'New History'," *Historiography East and West* 1.2 (December 2003), pp. 204–241.

Zarrow, Peter, "The Origins of Modern Chinese Concepts of Privacy: Notes on Social Structure and Moral Discourse," in Bonnie S. McDougall and Anders Hansson, eds., *Chinese Concepts of Privacy*, Leiden: Brill, 2002, pp. 121–146.

Zerubavel, Eviatar, *Social Mindscapes: An Invitation to Cognitive Sociology*, Cambridge, MA: Harvard University Press, 1997.

Zhang Gengxi 張耿西 et al., eds., *(Xiaoxuexiao chuji yong) Zhongguo gongmin* (小學校初級用) 中國公民, Shanghai: Shangwu, 1939 [1934].

Zhang Kuang 張匡, *Gaoxiao gongmin keben jiaoxuefa (Xiuzheng kecheng biaozhun shiyong/xinbian)* 高小公民課本教學法 (修正課程標準適用/新編), Shanghai: Zhonghua, 1937.

Zhang Yunjun 張运君, *Wan-Qing shubao jiancha zhidu yanjiu* 晚清书报检查制度研究, Beijing: Shehui kexue wenxian chubanshe, 2011.

Zhang Zheying 张哲英, *Qingmo minguo shiqi yuwen jiaoyu guannian kaocha: yi Li Jinxi, Hu Shi, Ye Shengtao wei zhongxin* 清末民国时期语文教育观念考察: 以黎锦熙、胡适、叶圣陶为中心, Fuzhou: Fujian jiaoyu chubanshe, 2011.

Zhao Lüqing 趙侶青 et al., eds., *Gongmin keben (Xiaoxue)* 公民課本 (小學), Shanghai: Zhonghua shuju, 1934.

Zhao Tizhen 趙體真 and Ma Pengnian 馬彭年, *Xiaoxue shehui keben jiaoxuefa (xin kecheng biaojun shiyong)* 小學社會課本教授法 (新課程標準適用), Shanghai: Zhonghua, 1933–34.

Zhao Yusen 趙玉森, *Xinlishi jiaoshoufa (gongheguo jiaokeshu/gaodeng xiaoxuexiao)* 新歷史教授法 (共和國教科書/高等小學校), Shanghai: Shangwu, 1913–14.

Zhao Yusen 趙玉森 and Jiang Weiqiao, 蔣維喬, *Benguoshi (zhongxuexiao yong/gongheguo jiaokeshu)* 本國史 (中學校用/共和國教科書), Shanghai: Shangwu, 1926 [1913].

Zhao Zhengduo 趙鉦鐸, *Gaodeng xiaoxue lishi keben* 高等小學歷史課本, n.p.: Zhongguo tushu gongsi, 1907–10.

Zhao, Gang, "Reinventing China: Imperial Qing Ideology and the Rise of Modern National Identity in the Early Twentieth Century," *Modern China* 32.1 (January 2006), pp. 3–30.

Zheng Hang 鄭航, *Zhongguo jindai deyu kechengshi* 中国近代德育课程史, Beijing: Renmin jiaoyu chubanshe, 2004.

Zheng Yuan, "The Status of Confucianism in Modern Chinese Education, 1901–1949," in Glen Peterson, Ruth Hayhoe, and Yongling Lu, eds., *Education, Culture, and Identity in Twentieth-Century China*, Ann Arbor: University of Michigan Press, 2001, pp. 193–216

Zhili diyi nüzi shifan xuexiao 直隸第一女子師範學校, *Benguo xiandaishi* 本國現代史, n.p., 1924.

Zhonghua shuju, comp., *(Xiuzheng kecheng biaozhun shiyong) Gaoji xiaoxueyong geke jiaokeshu jiaoxuefa yangben* (修正課程標準適用) 高級小學用各科教科書教學法樣本, Shanghai: Zhonghua, 1937.

Zhou Bangdao 周邦道, ed., *Diyici Zongguo jiaoyu nianjian* 第一次中國教育年鑑, 5 vols., reprt. Wu Xiangxiang 吳相湘 and Liu Shaotang 劉紹唐 eds., Taibei: Chuanji wenxue chubanshe, 1971.

Zhou Chuangui 周傳珪, *Minzhong lishi jiaoben jiaoxuefa* 民眾歷史科本教學法, Shanghai: Shijie shuju, 1930.

Zhou Jinglian 周景濂, *Benguoshi jiaoyuan zhunbeishu* 本國史教員準備書, Shanghai: Shangwu, 1935.

Zhou Qihou 周其厚, *Zhonghua shuju yu jindai wenhua* 中华书局与近代文化, Beijing: Zhonghua shuju, 2007.

Zhou Zhenlin 周震鱗, *Mingde xuetang dili kecheng* 明德學堂地理課程 (no publishing information; in possession of the Shanghai Library).

Zhu Bingu 朱賓谷, *Dangyi keben (fuxi xuexiao, minzhong xuexiao)* 黨議課本 (複習學校, 民眾學校), Shanghai: Dadong shuju, 1929.

Zhu Shizhai 鑄史齋, *Gailiang huitu sizishu* 改良繪圖四字書, Guangzhou: n.p., 1903.

Zhu Wenshu 朱文叔, *Xin Zhonghua guoyu yu guowen jiaokeshu* 新中華國語與國文教科書, n.p.: Xin guomin tushushe 新國民圖書社 and Zhonghua shuju, 1932 [1928].

Zhu Yixin 朱翊新, *Lishi jiaoben jiaoxuefa* 歷史科本, Shanghai: Shijie shuju, 1932 [1928].

Zhu Yixin 朱翊新, Huang Renji 黃人濟, and Lu Bingqian 陸並謙, *Chuzhong benguoshi* 初中本國史, Shanghai: Shijie shuju, 1930.

Zhuang Qichuan 莊啟傳 and Lü Simian 呂思勉, *Xinshi lishi jiaokeshu* 新式歷史教科書, Shanghai: Zhonghua shuju, 1920 [1917].

Zhuang Qichuan 莊啟傳 and Lü Simian 呂思勉, *Xinshi lishi jiaoshoufa (gaodeng xiaoxue)* 新式歷史教授法 (高等小學), Shanghai: Zhonghua, 1920 [1917].

Zhuang Yu 莊俞, "Bianji dayi" 編輯大意, *Chuji mengxue xiushen jiaokeshu* 初級蒙學修身教科書, Shanghai: Wenming shuju, 1906 [1904].

Zhuang Yu 莊俞, *Guoyu jiaokeshu* 國語教科書, Shanghai: Shangwu, 1917.

Zhuang Yu 莊愈, *(Chongding gaodeng xiaoxuexiao gongheguo jiaokeshu) Xin dili* (重訂高等小學校共和國教科書) 新地理, Shanghai: Shangwu, 1918 [1912].

Zhuang Yu 莊俞 and Shen Yi 沈頤, eds., *Xin guowen (gongheguo jiaokeshu/minguo xuexiao chunji shiye xueshengyong)* 新國文 (共和國教科書/民國學校 春季始業學生用), Shanghai: Shangwu, 1921 [1912].

Zinda, Yvonne Schulz, "Propagating New 'Virtues' – 'Patriotism' in Late Qing Textbooks for the Moral Education of Primary Students," in Michael Lackner and Natascha Vittinghoff, eds., *Mapping Meanings: The Field of New Learning in Late Qing China*, Leiden: Brill, 2004, pp. 685–710.

Zou Zhenhuan 邹振环, "Shilun wan-Qing jindai dilixue jiaokeshu de biancuan" 试论晚清近代地理学教科书的编纂, *Lishi wenxian* 历史文献 5, Shanghai: Shanghai kexue jishu wenxian chubanshe, 2001, pp. 273–278.

Zou Zhenhuan 邹振环, *Wan-Qing xifang dilixue zai Zhongguo: yi 1815 zhi 1911 nian xifang dilixue yizhu de quanbo yu yingxiang wei zhongxin* 晚清西方地理学在中国: 以 1815 至 1911 年西方地理学译著的传播与影响为中心, Shanghai: Shanghai guji chubanshe, 2000.

Index

1911 Revolution, 219, 243
   as turning point, 18, 27, 45, 77, 84, 96, 232, 244
   Nationalists' views of, 36, 130, 155, 188, 206
   textbook treatments of, 2, 111, 126, 142, 167, 175, 182, 186, 188, 195–200, 205–212, 240

Akiyama Shirō, 81
anti-communism, 3, 39, 113
anti-imperialism, 3, 6, 28, 35, 67, 121, 123, 126, 127, 140, 206, 209. *See also* imperialism
anti-Manchuism, 26, 28, 35, 54, 186, 208. *See also* Manchu
anti-superstition campaign. *See* superstition
Asia, 57, 60, 94, 150, 151, 175, 187, 232, 234, 236, 241, 274
   geographic concept of, 50, 54, 214, 230, 232, 238

Bagley, William, 196
Bailey, Paul, 246
Beard, Charles, 196
Boxer Uprising, 178–179, 198, 200, 202–203, 206, 208
Burma, 179, 194, 198, 219, 220

Cai Yuanpei, 28, 33–36, 84, 89, 93, 153
capitalism, 48, 61, 117, 125, 126, 134, 135, 206, 237, 240
censorship, 18, 25, 39, 83, 182
Central Asia, 179, 187, 194, 236. *See also* Inner Asia
Chaoshi, 167, 169, 253
Chen Baoquan, 92
Chen Duxiu, 31
Chen Hongmou, 83
Chiang Kai-shek, 28, 35, 113, 141, 209
China Bookstore, 27
   teacher's manual, 122, 125
   textbooks of, 59, 136
Chinese Communist Party, 3, 28, 143. *See also* communism
citizenship, 67, 123, 210, 249
   American, 108–109, 196
   as educational goal, 10, 11, 29, 31, 36, 213
   in civics textbooks, 77–79, 83–95, 98, 101, 111, 113–115, 119–123, 132, 137–138, 141–145
   in geography textbooks, 221, 232
   in history textbooks, 153, 166, 186, 198, 199
   in language primers, 41, 43, 57, 60
civic virtue, 94, 104, 121, 139
civics. *See* citizenship, civic virtue
civil service examination system, 9, 12, 16, 44, 133
Civilization Press, 17, 25, 57, 81, 151
clan, 52, 68, 152, 169, 170, 239. *See also* family
Classic of Filial Piety, 25, 82
classical Chinese, 2, 24, 25, 34, 44–48. *See also* vernacular Chinese
Commercial Press, 17, 25, 27, 69, 81, 206
   Chinese language primers of, 42, 44, 45, 59
   Nanjing Decade textbooks of, 132
   Republican textbooks of, 96
communism, 3, 39, 118. *See also* Chinese Communist Party; anti-communism
Confucian classics, 8–9, 12, 22, 25, 27, 42–48, 81–86, 129, 147
   in Japan, 80
Confucianism, 66, 79, 90, 94, 96, 144, 159, 223, 236, 247
   as educational goal, 19, 21, 24, 84, 86
   criticism of, 31, 47, 111
   in Japanese schools, 14
   Nationalists' views of, 113, 145
Confucius, 19, 20, 21, 49, 82, 84, 85, 129, 181, 230–231, 236, 244

279

constitutional government, 16, 26, 36, 49, 87, 123, 130, 188, 198, 211, 223
  description of, 57, 91, 107, 145, 225, 231–232, 250
  movement for, 1, 83, 163, 179, 182
Culp, Robert, 36, 43, 45, 47, 145, 251
curriculum, 10, 12, 146, 148
  1920s, 32–35, 47, 86–88, 113
  early Republic, 27, 29, 30–31, 84–86, 105, 108, 111, 114, 153, 206, 220
  late Qing, 13, 20–23, 25, 42–45, 81–83, 95, 150–151, 218
  Meiji, 79–81
  Nanjing Decade, 35–39, 48, 67, 79, 113–115, 119–121, 142–144, 149, 153–156, 221, 251

Dai Jitao, 35, 36
democracy, 26, 35, 36, 45, 47, 48, 57, 67, 106–107, 112, 116–121, 129–135, 166, 172, 199, 207, 210, 221, 225. *See also* republicanism
  American, 196
Dewey, John, 32, 111
Ding Baoshu, 151, 158, 161, 163, 175, 178, 180
Ding Cha'an, 236

Enlightenment Bookstore, 27, 69
Extending Knowledge Bookstore, 17

family, 1, 20, 46, 48, 51–52, 63, 71, 76, 84–88, 89–95, 99, 111, 114, 138, 166, 215, 239, 247–249. *See also* clan
  relationship to state, 2, 77–81, 119, 129, 203, 232
Fan Zhongyan, 199
Fan Zuoguai, 170, 171, 191, 201, 208
Fei Xiewei, 190, 210
Feng Zikai, 69
filial piety, 1, 12, 20, 49, 51, 77, 78, 82, 83–86, 88, 89, 90, 91, 93, 96–98, 111, 119, 128, 143, 163, 239
  in Japan, 14, 80–81
five races
  peoples of China, 55, 68, 166, 186, 188, 190, 192, 198, 199, 205, 210, 219
  world races, 54, 218, 227
Fu Guangnian, 162, 170, 179
Fu Yunsen, 200
Fuxi, 162, 167, 169

Gao Buying, 92
Gao Shiliang, 143
gender, 58, 63, 81, 104, 142, 215

girls' education, 13, 15, 19, 29, 31, 46, 58, 86, 115, 134
Great Learning, 78, 82, 93, 129, 239
Gu Jiegang, 155, 167
Guomindang, 27, 35, 116, 121, 142, 203, 206, 240, 241. *See also* Nationalists
  education policies of, 35, 48, 121, 143, 154, 251
  ideology of, 67, 130, 140, 196, 210, 251

Han
  dynasty, 125, 155, 164, 166, 174, 175, 191, 208, 212, 223
  people, 148, 164, 172, 175, 177, 189–194, 199, 203, 211, 214, 223, 226–229, 230, 242
    as Chinese, 26, 35, 125, 157, 193, 198, 217, 239
    one of "five races," 55, 211, 219, 235
    origins of, 53, 157, 158, 161, 168, 227, 236
Han Feimu, 170, 171, 191, 201, 208
Han Wudi, 180, 199, 255
He Bingsong, 148–149
Hill, Michael Gibbs, 45
Hong Kong, 2, 178, 201, 233, 243
Hou Hongjian, 224
Hu Chaoyang, 173, 174, 199, 207
Hu Shi, 46, 48, 68
Huang Donglan, 216
Hui, 55, 124, 191, 192, 212, 219, 227, 235, 239, 241
  rebellion of, 197
hygiene, 99, 113, 114, 249
  as school subject, 7, 9, 33, 35, 37, 88, 114
  in civics textbooks, 87, 93, 96, 101, 103, 115, 130
  in geography textbooks, 225, 242
  in Japan, 81
  in language primers, 41, 64–65

Imperial Rescript on Education, 15, 80
imperialism, 38, 48, 50, 68, 111, 116–119, 123–127, 135, 136, 139, 143, 148, 149, 153–154, 196, 200–203, 206–212, 217, 219, 230, 232, 235, 237–238, 240–245. *See also* anti-imperialism
Inner Asia, 193, 195. *See also* Central Asia

Japan. *See also* Meiji
  as model, 92
  threat from, 3, 71, 169, 188, 192, 209, 233, 237, 240, 243
Jiang Jianqiu, 200, 207
Jiang Weiqiao, 167, 186, 199

Index

Jimmu, 81, 152, 181, 255
Jin Zhaozi, 194, 211

Kang Youwei, 179
Kaske, Elisabeth, 42, 44
Kong Rong, 73, 74
Korea, 56, 177, 187, 201, 219, 220, 232, 243
  colonized by Japan, 116, 125, 152, 178, 218, 234, 240
  traditional Chinese dependency, 178, 179, 193, 195, 198

Lacouperie, Terrien de, 157
Li Jiagu, 91
Li Tinghan, 234
Liang Qichao, 46, 48, 56, 59, 126, 147, 165, 217
Liezi, 68
Lin Shu, 45
literacy, 12, 25, 40, 41–46, 48, 138, 246
Liu Jianbair, 89–91
Liu Shipei, 26, 158
  ethics textbook of, 95–96
  geography textbook of, 229–230
  history textbook of, 172
Liu Yizheng, 24, 151
loyalty, 8, 14, 19, 20–21, 49, 56, 68, 77, 79–85, 88, 90, 119, 128, 142, 143, 144, 150, 152, 182, 192, 199, 239, 243
Lü Simian, 60, 61, 64, 65, 155, 165, 186, 200, 213

Ma Pengnian, 139, 241
Macao, 56, 233
Manchu, 214, 223, 234
  as race, 55, 124, 157, 166, 167, 177, 198, 211, 217, 219, 225, 226, 228–230, 235, 239, 241
  Qing rulers, 26, 39, 54, 127, 160, 176, 185, 190–194, 211, 240
Manchuria, 71, 166, 178, 200, 218, 223, 234, 237, 240, 241, 243
maps, 149, 214, 219, 222, 240, 248, 249
  geographical, 214, 218, 229
  highlighting China's losses, 56, 201, 241
  historical, 156, 175, 179, 181, 193, 194, 195
  of Sun Yat-sen, 135
Marxism, 110, 118–119, 170, 184
May Fourth movement, 2, 125, 206, 209, 210, 241
Meiji, 9, 15, 181
  educational influence of, 14, 80, 217–218
  school system, 9, 11, 12, 14–15, 20, 24, 250
  textbooks of, 23, 24, 42, 81, 85, 151–152, 217

Meiji Restoration, 14, 116, 152, 202, 240
Mencius, 51, 62, 68, 82, 84, 129, 166, 222
Meng, Yue, 40
Miao, 53, 124, 157, 158, 227, 229, 230, 242, 256
Ming dynasty, 11, 12, 42, 50, 53, 155, 166, 174–177, 179, 187, 189–194, 199, 200, 208
Ming Taizu, 190, 199. *See also* Zhu Yuanzhang
Ministry of Education, 13, 92
  early Republic, 27, 29, 32, 34, 39, 45, 153, 219
  late Qing, 14, 18, 25, 49, 82–84, 218
  Nanjing Decade, 36, 123, 150, 154, 155
  textbooks by, 25, 43, 68, 84
missionary schools, 11, 13, 14, 37, 125, 251
missionary textbooks, 217
Miyama Toratarō, 57
Mongol, 55, 124, 157, 160, 174–175, 187, 189–194, 212, 214, 217, 223, 226–229, 235, 239, 241
Mongolia, 106, 187, 193, 228, 234, 242
Montesquieu, 172
moral education. *See* self-cultivation

Nanjing government, 3, 5, 25, 27, 39, 49, 115, 123, 132, 188, 196, 210, 212
  educational policies of, 7, 39, 113, 130, 245, 251
Nankai Academy, 31
Nanyang gongxue, 18
narrativization, 8, 9, 41, 44, 71, 102, 108, 125, 148, 149, 151, 152, 171–172, 177, 181, 184, 194, 196, 200, 204–209, 213, 214, 247–249
nation, 18, 21, 22, 28, 34, 84, 89, 151, 154, 172, 196, 199
  as educational goal, 9, 10, 17, 20, 28, 35, 36, 121, 144, 147, 247
  historical roots of, 3, 24, 128, 150, 152, 154, 157, 159, 161, 168, 188, 242
  identity of, 52, 68, 77, 79, 80, 91, 125, 128, 137, 153, 171, 181, 193, 212, 228, 230, 237, 239, 247
national character, 150, 188, 226, 239. *See also* nation, race
National Essence Journal, 26, 95, 172
national humiliation, 21, 179, 197, 200, 201, 219, 234, 241
nationalism, 6, 194, 201, 211, 237, 241, 247. *See also* patriotism
  and the Three People's Principles, 67, 68, 120, 121, 126, 134, 221, 237
  early Republican, 29, 86, 116, 118, 153
  late Qing, 26, 95, 230, 250

Nationalists, 28, 39, 79, 112, 117, 123, 137, 143, 145, 153, 168, 188, 196, 201, 206, 210. *See also* Nanjing government; Guomindang
   educational policies of, 35, 66–68, 88, 113, 115, 142, 143, 154, 221, 237
nation-state. *See* state
Neo-Confucianism, 12, 21. *See also* Confucianism
New Culture movement, 31, 46, 68, 79, 86, 111, 112, 126, 127, 209
New Life movement, 3, 113, 139–142, 143, 209
New Policy reforms, 16, 18, 179
Nian Rebellion, 197

Opium War, 13, 57, 68, 178, 187, 197, 200, 201, 206, 211

partification, 35, 113, 143, 251. *See also* Nationalists
party-state. *See* state
patriotism, 21, 35, 45, 49–54, 56, 66, 79, 83, 89, 90, 105, 119, 122, 123, 127, 144, 235. *See also* nationalism
   educational goal, 1, 2, 10, 14, 15, 22, 38, 39, 46, 82, 85, 94, 150, 215, 218, 244
   Japanese, 80
Peake, Cyrus, 35
people's livelihood, 35, 36, 39, 48, 67, 118, 135, 136, 221, 237
periodization, 149, 151, 154, 184

Qian Zonghan, 161, 163
Qin dynasty, 53, 125, 155, 166, 171, 173, 208, 212, 244
Qin Shihuang, 53, 166, 172–174, 180, 181
Qing dynasty, 1, 9, 11, 12, 18, 19, 27, 42, 50, 54, 144, 155, 160, 166, 167, 171, 177, 182, 184, 185, 188, 190, 191, 198, 204, 205, 209, 210, 211, 216, 217, 219, 228
   crimes of, 123, 186, 191, 194
   decline of, 177–179, 187, 194, 197–198, 199, 201, 204, 208, 211, 219
   glory of, 56, 150, 179, 194
   rise of, 53, 150, 166, 175–177, 186, 190, 192–193

race, 1, 3, 8, 117, 157. *See also* Han (people); White race; Yellow race
   in civics textbooks, 93, 94
   in geography textbooks, 214, 216, 223, 224, 225–230, 234, 236, 238, 241, 243, 244

   in history textbooks, 10, 148, 155, 158, 159, 161, 164, 168, 175, 177, 180, 186, 189, 190, 192, 198, 204, 205
   in language primers, 54–56, 68
   Japanese views of, 81, 218
religion, 1, 13, 21, 29, 84, 107, 124, 138, 164, 172, 199, 203, 211, 213, 214, 222, 223, 230, 234, 236, 238, 239, 242, 243. *See also* superstition
republicanism, 2, 26, 33, 39, 57, 111, 128, 148, 181, 183, 197, 198–199, 205, 207, 210, 231. *See also* democracy
Revolution of 1911. *See* 1911 Revolution
Rousseau, 96, 129
Russo-Japanese War, 178, 198, 250
Ryukyus, 56, 179, 234

sage-king, 51, 53, 157, 167, 168, 170, 172, 189
Sandeng Public Academy, 49
schools
   number of, 13
self-cultivation, 22, 93, 247
   and Cai Yuanpei, 29, 93
   and Liu Shipei, 95
   in language primers, 45
   in late Qing schools, 19, 21, 22, 38, 81
   in Republican schools, 34, 84, 96–101, 108, 111, 113, 142, 219
   Japanese, 24, 79, 152
   textbooks, 1–3, 77–78, 82, 89–91, 101, 113, 129, 140, 144–145, 231, 249
Shang dynasty, 53, 165, 171, 173, 189, 199, 214
Shen Guowei, 43
Sheng Langxi, 113
Shennong, 162, 169, 258
Shōei Yazu, 216
Shun, 53, 150, 162, 163–164, 167, 170, 171
Sima Qian, 160, 258
Sino-Japanese War of 1894–5, 13, 23, 178, 198, 201, 202, 250
Sino-Japanese War of 1937–45, 5, 28, 36
social Darwinism, 7, 8, 10, 28, 126, 147, 149, 216, 217, 224, 230, 235, 243, 247
socialism, 34, 36, 88, 136
socialization, 7, 8, 78, 212, 247. *See also* society
society
   and goal of socialization, 9, 38, 40, 48, 58, 61, 66, 68, 86, 90, 93, 96, 108, 112, 120, 121, 132, 137, 154, 249–250
   curriculum in, 3, 34, 88, 108, 115, 121, 123, 142, 145, 206, 209

Index

teaching about, 43, 59, 76, 79, 84, 86–89, 101–105, 113, 114, 132, 134, 136, 149, 155, 217, 236, 243, 249
understanding of, 5, 11, 36, 79, 91, 94, 123, 130, 137, 138, 145, 148, 170, 216, 235, 251
Song dynasty, 39, 44, 54, 100, 132, 175, 190, 191
Song Taizu, 199
state, 19, 120, 146
  and education, 5, 6, 11, 16, 26, 28, 29, 40, 42, 83, 86, 101, 102, 215, 243, 246–247, 250
  concept of, 1, 5, 8, 10, 19, 34, 35, 50, 56, 57, 87, 89–95, 104, 105–106, 112, 114, 119, 121, 124–125, 132, 137, 144, 145, 180, 188, 190, 198, 205, 207, 212, 219, 222, 224, 235, 236, 238
  duties to, 43, 58, 77, 108, 128, 133, 137, 142, 226
  dynastic, 160, 163, 170, 171, 174, 177, 180, 181, 184, 186, 191
  Japanese, 15, 80, 81, 152
  origins of, 38, 152, 155, 158, 160, 162, 169–170, 189, 229, 231
  party-state, 67, 89, 142, 241
  relationship to family, 2, 52, 77–79, 119, 129, 166
  symbols of, 2, 48, 67, 89, 102, 103, 116, 121, 142, 144
state-building, 6, 36, 67, 121
student assemblies, 3, 102, 132–133
student associations, 33, 102
students
  number of, 13, 26
Sui dynasty, 166, 208
Sui Wendi, 199
Suiren, 167, 169
Sun Jiang, 158
Sun Yat-sen, 3, 28, 68, 117, 121, 123, 134, 135, 140, 142, 188, 201, 204–206, 208, 209, 241
  as exemplar, 48, 68, 88, 115, 140
  ideology of, 35, 36, 67, 68, 79, 115, 118, 123–128, 130, 133, 138, 144, 196, 211, 221, 238, 239, 242
Sunism, 115, 118, 121, 139. *See also* Three People's Principles
superstition, 48, 81, 83, 88, 102, 140, 215, 230. *See also* anti-superstition campaign

Taiping Rebellion, 12, 178, 185, 187, 197, 200, 201–203, 210–211
Taiwan, 56, 178, 179, 193, 198, 199, 218, 219, 232, 233, 234
Tan Lian, 232
Tan Yunhua, 232
Tang, 155, 179
Tang dynasty, 44, 166, 174, 181, 190, 191, 199, 208, 227
Tang Gaozong, 181, 258
Tang Taizong, 199
Tang Zhansheng, 111
Tangwu, 165, 171, 199
Tao Menghe, 109–111, 137
Three Bonds, 21, 96
Three People's Principles, 3, 35–37, 116, 126, 134, 201, 208, 210
  curriculum in, 39, 67, 79, 88, 113, 121, 123–124, 132, 138, 142, 154, 221, 237, 251
Tibet, 106, 179, 187, 193, 195
Tibetan, 55, 124, 157, 191, 192, 212, 217, 219, 223, 226, 227, 229, 235, 239, 242
Trimetrical Classic, 49, 73
Tsuchiya Hiroshi, 144
Tu Ji, 221–223
Tu, Wei-ming, 78
tutelage, 36, 67, 79, 123, 130–131, 209, 210
Twenty-four Exemplars of Filial Piety, 49, 74, 96, 139

United States, 234
  civics education in, 108
  educational system of, 32–35, 184
  history education in, 196
universal schooling, 9, 11–19, 21, 136, 244

vernacular Chinese, 2, 8, 25, 33, 46–47, 92, 126, 209, 250. *See also* classical Chinese
Vietnam, 116, 125, 178, 179, 194, 198, 219

Wang Jiarong, 24, 144
Wang Rongbao, 166, 258
Wang Zhicheng, 190, 210
Wang Zhongqi, 155
Wei Bingxin, 128, 133, 134, 138, 142
Wen Tianxiang, 190, 259
West, Willis Mason, 197
Western learning, 14, 19, 32, 247
Western origins theory, 157, 158, 165, 168, 172, 189, 227, 239
White Lotus Rebellion, 178, 179, 197, 200
White race, 54, 55, 68, 93, 218, 226, 230, 234, 240
World Bookstore, 27
Wu Jiazhen, 143

Xia dynasty, 53, 165, 170–171, 173, 189, 199, 231

Xia Zengyou, 151
Xie Xingyao, 188

Yang Shuming, 203
Yao, 150, 162, 163, 164, 167, 170, 171
Yao Zuyi, 160–161, 170, 179
Ye Shengtao, 69–73
Yellow Emperor, 50, 53, 150, 152, 157–163, 164–165, 167–170, 181, 189, 212, 229, 231, 236
Yellow race, 52, 54, 68, 157, 159, 162, 179, 218, 226–227, 234, 240
Yu the Great, 53, 163, 164, 165, 167, 170, 171, 181
Yuan dynasty, 160, 166, 167, 174–175, 186–187, 189, 190–193, 203, 208
Yuan Shikai, 27, 28, 29, 85, 86, 116, 135, 205, 207, 208
Yue Fei, 39, 53, 190, 191, 192, 199, 244

Zhang Baixi, 14
Zhang Binglin, 158, 259
Zhang Kuang, 124, 128–129
Zhang Shizhao, 48
Zhang Zhidong, 14, 16, 18–20, 24, 151
Zhao Tizhen, 139, 241
Zhao Yusen, 165, 167, 186, 197, 199, 204
Zhao Zhengduo, 161, 162, 163, 170, 171, 177, 178
Zhou dynasty, 53, 164, 166, 170, 171, 172, 180, 189, 214
Zhou Yunlin, 243
Zhou Zhenlin, 231
Zhou Zuoren, 68
Zhu Yuanzhang, 175. *See also* Ming Taizu
Zhuang Qichuan, 186, 200
Zhuang Yu, 81, 232